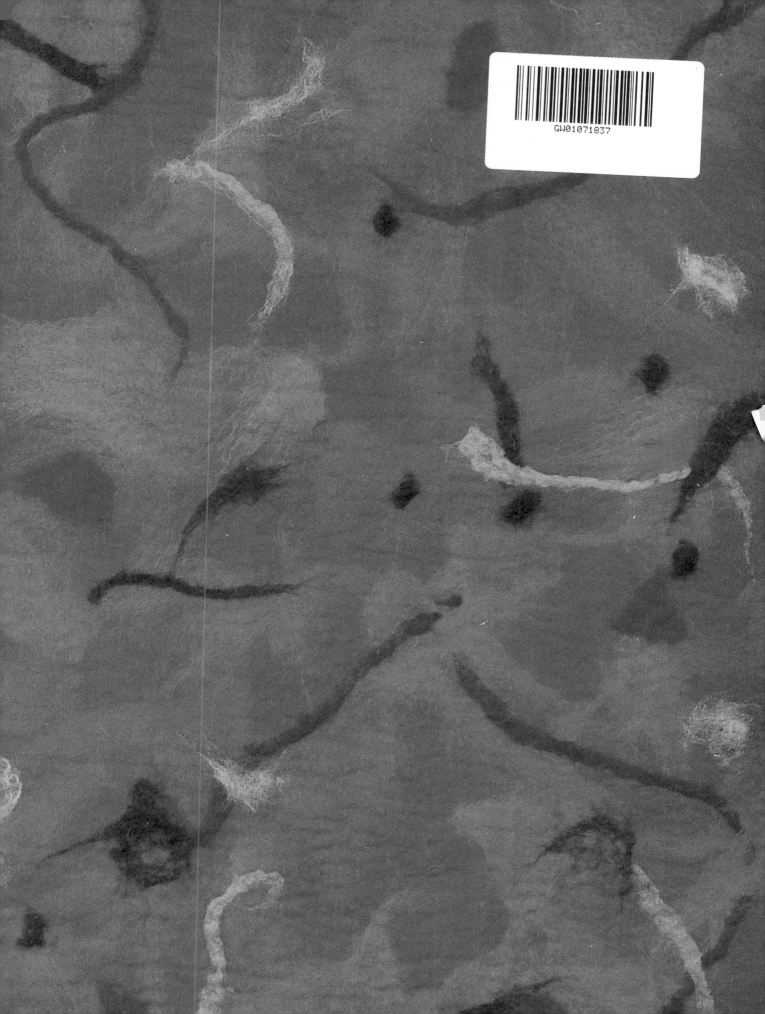

CRAFT
COLLECTION

SANDSTONE

CRAFT
COLLECTION

**Friendly step-by-step guidance and a wealth of craft
projects to inspire the absolute beginner and delight the expert**

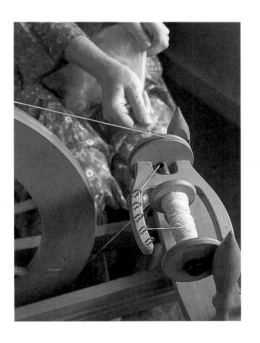

SANDSTONE BOOKS

ACKNOWLEDGEMENTS

The Publisher would like to thank the following for providing items or photographs to enhance the illustration of this book. The craftspeople of Avalon Craft Cottage; Coats Patons; Colourwall Curtains; Craft Australia; the Crafts Council of New South Wales; Elna Australia; Hoechst Australia; Brother Industries (Australia) Pty Ltd.

Published by Sandstone Books
56 John Street, Leichhardt, NSW 2040, Australia
Tel: (02) 552 2799 Fax: (02) 552 1538

First published by Lansdowne Press 1973
as *The Complete Book of Handcrafts*
Reprinted 1977, 1978 (limp)
Revised edition 1982
Reprinted 1986
Second revised edition published by Ure Smith Press 1991
This revised edition 1995

© Lansdowne Publishing Pty Ltd 1995
© Copyright design: Lansdowne Publishing Pty Ltd

Produced by Lansdowne Publishing Pty Ltd
Level 5, 70 George Street, Sydney 2000, Australia
Managing Director: Jane Curry
Production Manager: Sally Stokes
Publishing Manager: Cheryl Hingley
Designed by Avenir Design
Additional photographs by Kim Saunders
Printed in Singapore by Kyodo Printing Co Ltd

National Library Cataloguing-in-Publication data:

Craft collection.

Includes index.
ISBN 1 86302 413 1.

1. Handicraft. I. Title: Craft collection.

745.5

Photographs:
Front jacket background, handwoven silk stoles by Mary Williams, courtesy Craft Australia; front jacket inset, top left, Avalon Craft Cottage; inset bottom right, Coats Patons Ltd.

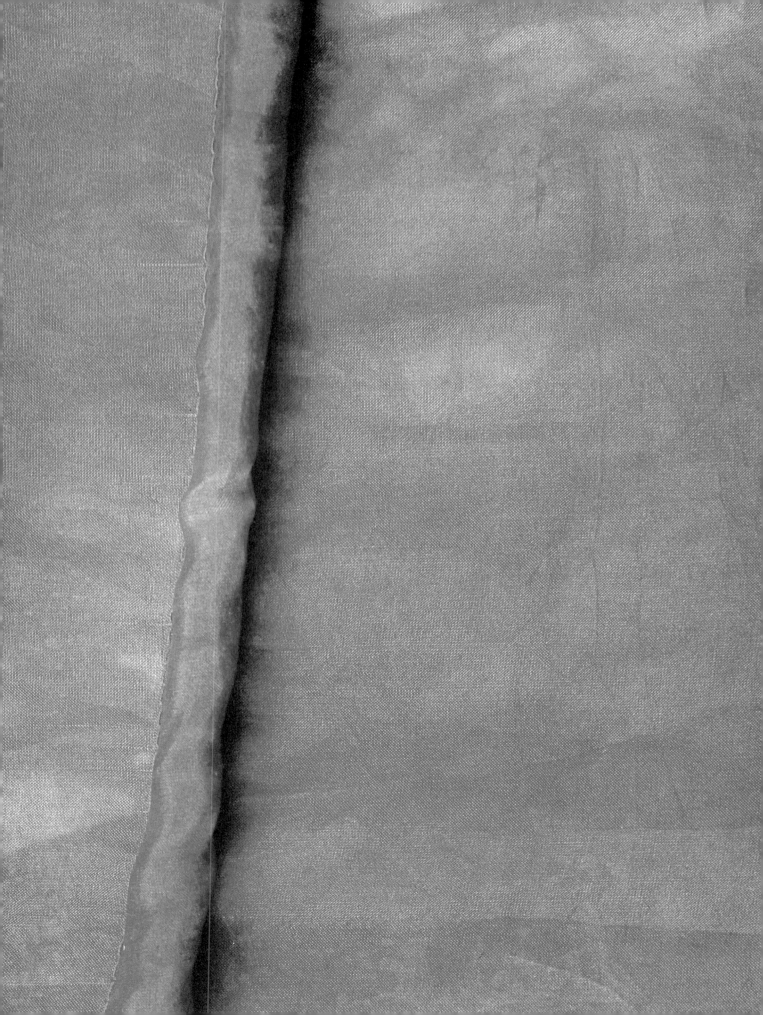

Contents

Handcraft Hints for Measurement

Where possible in this book, metric measures and imperial measures have been included together in instructions.

SYMBOLS

These are the units most commonly used for measuring length.

mm— millimeters
cm— centimeters
m— meters
km— kilometer

These are the units most commonly used for measuring the volumes of liquids.

l— liters
ml— milliliters

These are the units most commonly used for measuring mass (weight).

g— gram
kg— kilogram
t— tonne

CLOTHING AND TEXTILES

The following gives comparisons for metric and imperial measurement of fabrics and textiles.

Examples: As 1 in is 2.54 cm, a man's singlet sized as 40 in is 102 cm and a 36 in width dress material is 91 cm. In clothing sizes, numeric sizes are given such as Size 12 for a woman, and the body measurements are given in centimeters, viz. (87 cm x 65 cm x 91 cm).

Where piecegoods such as furnishing fabrics, dress, and curtain materials are sold by the meter, remember that a meter is 10 per cent more than a yard.

Bed and table linen is described in rounded metric units (centimeters).

METRIC UNITS FOR EVERYDAY USE

Conversion factors (approximate)

Quantity	Metric unit and symbol	Imperial to Metric Units	Metric to Imperial Units
Length	millimeter (mm)	1 in = 25.4 mm	1 mm = 0.0394 in
	centimeter (cm, 10 mm)	1 in = 2.54 cm	1 cm = 0.394 in
		1 ft = 30.5 cm	
	meter (m, 100 cm)	1 yd = 0.914 m	1 m = 3.28 ft
	kilometer (km, 1000 m)	1 mile = 1.61 km	1 km = 0.62 mile
Mass (commonly called "weight")	gram (g)	1 oz = 28.3 g	1 g = 0.0353 oz
	kilogram (kg, 1000 g)	1 lb = 454 g l	kg = 2.2 lb
		1 stone = 6.35 kg	1 kg = 0.157 stone
	tonne (t, 1000 kg)	1 ton = 1.02 t	1 t = 0.98 ton
Area	square centimeter (cm^2)	1 in^2 = 6.45 cm^2	1 cm^2 = 0.155 in^2
	square meter (m^2, 10 000 cm^2)	1 ft^2 = 929 cm^2	1 m^2 = 10.8 ft^2
		1 yd^2 = 0.836 m^2	1 m^2 = 1.2 yd^2
		1 perch = 25.3 m^2	1 ha = 9.88 roods
	hectare (ha, 10 000 m^2)	1 acre = 0.405 ha	1 ha = 2.47 acres
	square kilometer (km^2)	1 $mile^2$ = 2.59 km^2	1 km^2 = 0.386$mile^2$
	1 000 000 m^2, 100 ha)		= 247 acres
Volume	cubic centimeter (cm^3)	1 in^3 = 16.4 cm^3	1 cm^3 = 0.061 in^3
	cubic meter (m^3, 1 000 000 cm^3)	1 ft^3 = 28 300 cm^3	1 m^3 = 35.3 ft^3
		1 yd^3 = 0.765 m^3	1 m^3 = 1.31 yd^3
		1 bushel = 0.0364 m^3	1 m^3 = 27.5 bushels
Volume (liquids and gases)	milliliter (ml)	1 fl oz = 28.4 ml	1 ml = 0.0352 fl oz
	liter (L, 1000 ml)	1 pint = 568 ml	1 liter = 1.76 pints
	kiloliter (kl, 1000 L, 1 m^3)	1 gal = 4.55 liters	1 kl = 220 gal

Traditional patchwork.

CONVERSION TABLE: OUNCES TO GRAMS

(With the compliments of the Hand Knitting Yarn Manufacturers of Australia.)

1 oz = 28.3495 grams

1 oz Balls	25 gram Balls*	2 oz Balls	50 gram Balls*
1	1	1	1
2	3	2	3
3	4	3	4
4	5	4	5
5	6	5	6
6	7	6	7
7	8	7	8
8	9	8	9
9	10	9	10
10	12	10	12
11	13	11	13
12	14	12	14
13	15	13	15
14	16	14	16
15	17	15	17
16	18	161	8
17	20	17	20
18	21	18	21
19	22	19	22
20	23	20	23
21	24	21	24
22	25	22	25
23	26	23	26
24	27	24	27
25	29	25	29
26	30	26	30
27	31	27	31
28	32	28	32
29	33	29	33
30	34	30	34
31	35	31	35
32	37	32	37

*Suggested use.

CONVERSION TABLE: INCHES TO CENTIMETERS

Measurement in inches	Measurement in centimeters	Measurement in inches	Measurement in centimeters
10	25.4	29	73.7
11	27.9	30	76.2
12	30.5	31	78.7
13	33.0	32	81.3
14	35.6	33	83.8
15	38.1	34	86.4
16	40.6	35	89.0
17	43.2	36	91.4
18	45.7	37	93.9
19	48.3	38	96.5
20	50.8	39	99.1
21	53.3	40	101.6
22	55.9	41	104.1
23	58.4	42	106.7
24	61.0	43	109.2
25	63.5	44	111.8
26	66.0	45	114.3
27	68.6	46	116.8
28	71.1	47	119.4
		48	121.9

It is a good idea to compile a list of body and other useful measurements in centimeters and keep it for reference when you are checking a pattern. It is easy enough for you to check your metric measurements by using the next conversion table.

VOLUME

Because there is no exact conversion between metric and imperial units, it is suggested if you are converting, 1 ounce should be replaced with 30 grams and 1 fluid ounce with 30 milliliters. To preserve the correct ratio of ingredients in work such as tie dyeing, strict conversion to metric need not be applied and liquid proportions may need to be adjusted to maintain correct consistencies. Each imperial measure — whether pint, pound or cup — would be related to the base unit of the imperial system, the ounce or fluid ounce. The number of ounces and fluid ounces should be multiplied by the recommended metric equivalent — 30 g (ml) = 1 oz (fl oz) — and rounded to the closest convenient number, to give the metric quantities and thereby preserving the proportions.

Both metric and imperial knitting, crochet, and dress patterns are now in use. In most cases in this book, both imperial and metric sizes are given.

Balls and skeins of knitting yarn are sold in weights of 25 g (gram) or of 1 oz (ounce), which is about 12 per cent less than the 25 g ball, so that a pattern requiring fifteen 1 oz balls will need seventeen 25 g balls.

Detail of fine-ply traditional patterned sweater knitted by R.A. Gabbott.

Knitting

HOW TO KNIT

◆
Yarn

Always buy the brand of yarn specified in the instructions. Substituting brand names will only lead to difficulties and incorrect fit. Remember that a certain ply produced by one manufacturer may not necessarily correspond with a similar ply produced by another manufacturer.

◆
Needles

To ensure that your work is even, use good quality straight knitting needles.

The length of the needle is also important: eg 14" (35.6 cm) length needles are adequate for knitting an average size sweater or jacket. If, however, the number of stitches will not fit comfortably on your needles, try using a circular needle.

COMPARATIVE KNITTING NEEDLE SIZES			
British	Metric	Continental	American
14	2.00	2	00
13	2.25		0
		2½	1
12	2.75		
11	3.00	3	2
10	3.25	3	3½
9	3.75		4
8	4.00	4	5
7	4.50	4½	6
6	5.00	5	7
5	5.50	5½	8
4	6.00	6	9
3	6.50	6½	10
2	7.00	7	10½
1	7.50	7½	11
0	8.00	8	12
00	9.00	9	13
000	10.00	10	15

◆
Accessories

The following is a list of items you may need to complete your project.

1. Stitch holders. These are usually required to hold neck edge stitches until the neckband stage is reached.

2. Tape measure.

3. A row counter. This is used when working intricate patterns to keep a record of the rows being worked.

4. Tapestry needle. This is a large-eyed, blunt-pointed needle used for making up garments.

5. Pins.

6. Scissors.

7. Cable needle. This is a small, double-pointed needle made specifically for cabling.

8. A clean cloth or knitting bag to keep work in when not in use.

9. Zip, buttons, elastic etc.

◆
Knitting know-how

The following is a list of golden rules to help you obtain a professional look to your finished garments.

1. Never rush your work — relax and enjoy it.

2. Always have smooth, clean hands.

3. As dye-lots vary, always buy the full quantity of yarn required to complete the garment.

4. Check your tension from time to time during the making.

5. Keep your needles and yarn clean. Watch out for worn points on metal needles — these can discolor light shades of yarns.

6. Join in new yarn only at the end of a row.

7. Do not leave your knitting in the middle of a row.

Opposite: This delicate lady's top was knitted on an electronic chunky knitting machine, the Brother KH-270. © Courtesy Brother Industries.

8. Never push your needles through the ball of yarn.

9. Correct and neat making up is just as important as good knitting.

10. Wash knitted garments frequently and carefully.

11. Always use the yarn specified in the instructions.

12. Never alter the size of your needles in an attempt to produce a larger or smaller garment, only if necessary to achieve correct tension.

13. If knitting has been left unworked for a time, unpick a few rows before beginning again.

14. No two people knit alike — don't allow anyone to "help you with a few rows".

15. When instructions call for a marker to be attached to a stitch, use a contrasting yarn.

16. Always measure knitting on the flat.

17. Make sure you cast off at the same tension as you have worked your garment.

18. Don't be too ambitious in your choice of intricate patterns until you have perfected simple fabrics. Progress slowly.

19. When knitting in rounds, mark the beginning by tying a marker over the needles, then pass it from point to point as each round is finished.

20. If you have difficulty in understanding a pattern and have reached the point of exasperation, don't persevere. Lay the work aside and come back to it later on when you will no doubt see your error clearly.

◆

Metric guide

Both Imperial Standard and metric sizes, measurements, and weights are given in the knitting instructions. Imperial measurements are given first and the metric equivalent follows in brackets, e.g.

Work measures 10½ (12) ins [26.7 (30.5) cm].

A simple conversion chart is given on page 10 as a guide for converting to the appropriate metric equivalents.

◆

Understanding your instructions

* Asterisk. If an asterisk appears it indicates that:

(a) certain pattern rows have to be repeated, i.e. Front. Work as given for Back to *; or

(b) indicates that a section of work is to be repeated, i.e. repeat from * 3 times, or from ** to ** once.

( ) Brackets. These have two meanings:

(a) the instructions inside the brackets are repeated the number of times stated after the brackets, i.e. (k2, p2) twice; or

(b) the figures inside the brackets denote the instructions for the various sizes in which the instructions have been written, i.e. to fit 32 (34, 36, 38) in bust, or k12 (14, 16, 18) sts.

Work or continue straight means to work in the same stitch as before without shaping.

When you are instructed to turn in your work, continue on these first stitches only, leaving remaining stitches on a spare needle or stitch holder.

Slipping a stitch or stitches means to transfer stitch(es) from one needle to another without knitting or purling stitch(es).

Row means the number of stitches on one needle — the first row being knitted on the cast-on stitches. This is the first of odd-numbered rows and is usually the right side of work, unless otherwise instructed.

A stitch pattern is the manner in which rows or groups of stitches are worked so as to form a pattern that can be repeated regularly throughout the instructions.

A repeat of a pattern denotes the number of stitches that form the complete design and are repeated across the work. The repeat is therefore where one pattern ends and another begins.

Abbreviations

K/k	— knit	yfwd	— yarn forward
P/p	— purl	yrn	— yarn round needle
st(s)	— stitch(es)	rep	— repeat
in(s)	— inch(es)	patt	— pattern
cm	— centimeters	dc	— double crochet
st st	— stocking stitch	tbl	— through back of loops
approx	— approximately	no(s)	— number(s)
beg	— beginning	ch	— chain
rem	— remain(ing)	sl st	— slip stitch
cont	— continue	mb	— make a bobble: (k1, p1, k1, p1, k1) into next stitch, pass 1st, 2nd, 3rd, and 4th stitches over last stitch
inc	— increase		
dec	— decrease		
foll	— following	c 4f	— slip next 2 stitches onto cable needle and keep at front, knit 2, then knit 2 stitches from cable needle
rsf	— right side facing		
tog	— together		
m	— main yarn shade	cr 2 over 1 b	— slip next stitch onto cable needle and keep at back, knit 2 stitches, then purl 1 from cable needle
c	— contrasting yarn shade		
alt	— alternate		
g st	— garter stitch	cr 2 over 1 f	— slip next 2 stitches onto cable needle and keep at front, purl next stitch, then knit 2 from cable needle
m st	— moss stitch		
sl	— slip		
psso	— pass slip stitch over	k1 b	— knit into back of stitch
yon	— yarn over needle	k1 d	— knit into row below

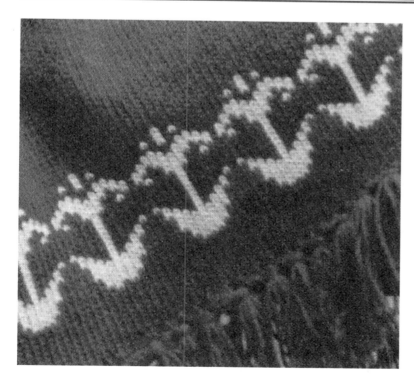

*Fair Isle knitting on a child's poncho.
See pages 73-5.*

LEARNING TO KNIT

◆

Casting on

Casting on is the first step in knitting, as it provides the first row of stitches on the needle. There are various methods of casting on, but the following two methods are the most popular:

1. THE THUMB METHOD
Using one needle (see diagrams 1 to 3).

(a) Make a slip loop (diagram 1) about one yard before the end of the yarn and place the loop on the right-hand needle. Draw the knot firmly round the needle.

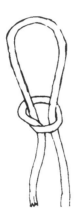

diagram 1

(b) Working with the short length of yarn in the left hand, pass this round the left-hand thumb (diagram 2).

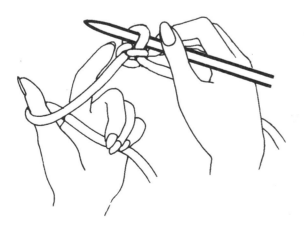

diagram 2

(c) Insert the point of the needle beneath the loop on the thumb and draw the loop up firmly (diagram 3).

(d) Holding the yarn from the ball in the right hand, pass it round the point of the needle and draw it through the loop on the thumb.

(e) Draw the stitch up firmly on the needle. Repeat the last four operations for the required length.

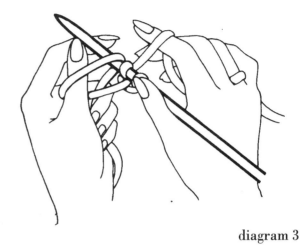

diagram 3

2. THROUGH THE STITCH METHOD
Using two needles (see diagrams 4 to 7).

(a) Make a slip loop (diagram 1) about 3 in (7.6 cm) before the end of the yarn and place it on the left-hand needle.

(b) Holding the yarn from the ball in your right hand, place the right-hand needle through the loop and pass the yarn round the point of the right-hand needle (diagram 4).

diagram 4

(c) Draw the yarn through the loop on the left-hand needle (diagram 5 on page 18).

Examples of skip stitch, a fabric pattern which can be created on electronic knitting machines. © Courtesy Brother Industries.

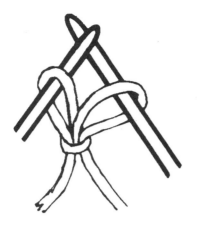

diagram 5

(d) Place the new loop formed on the right-hand needle onto the left-hand needle (diagram 6). There are now two stitches on the left-hand needle.

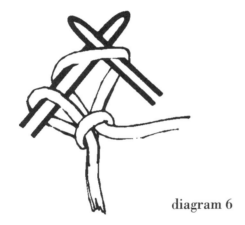

diagram 6

(e) Insert the point of the right-hand needle between these two stitches and wrap the yarn round the end of the right-hand needle (diagram 7).

(f) Draw this new loop between the last two stitches and place it on the left-hand needle. Repeat the last two operations for the required length.

diagram 7

◆

Basic stitches

There are only two stitches used in knitting and these are called knit and purl (sometimes referred to as plain and purl). Every knitted fabric, no matter how complicated, is a combination or variation on these two stitches.

THE KNIT STITCH (see diagrams 8 to 11)

(a) Insert the point of the right-hand needle in through the first stitch on the left-hand needle from front to back (diagram 8).

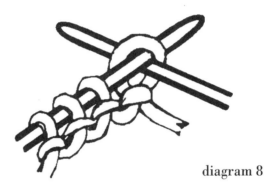

diagram 8

(b) While holding the yarn in the right hand, pass the yarn over the point of the right-hand needle (diagram 9).

diagram 9

(c) Draw the loop through the stitch on the left-hand needle with the point of the right-hand needle (diagram 10).

diagram 10

(d) Slip the stitch off the left-hand needle (diagram 11).

diagram 11

THE PURL STITCH (see diagrams 12 to 15)
(a) Insert the point of the right-hand needle in through the first stitch on the left-hand needle from back to front (diagram 12).

diagram 12

(b) Pass the yarn over the point of the right-hand needle (diagram 13).

diagram 13

(c) Draw the loop through the stitch on the left-hand needle (diagram 14).

diagram 14

(d) Slip the stitch off the left-hand needle (diagram 15).

diagram 15

CASTING OFF (see diagrams 16 and 17)
(a) Knit the two stitches on the left-hand needle in the usual way.

(b) Place the point of the left-hand needle under the first stitch on the right-hand needle and lift it over the second stitch (diagram 16).

(c) Drop this stitch off the needle and then continue in the same way (diagram 17).

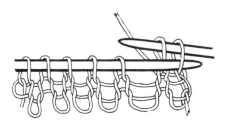

diagram 16

(d) When the required number of stitches have been cast off, cut yarn and draw the end through the last stitch.

diagram 17

IF A PATTERN SAYS ...
Cast off ribwise
Either knit or purl the stitch to be cast off, keeping continuity of the ribbing as set.

Cast off in pattern
Either knit or purl the stitch to be cast off, as it would have been worked in the corresponding row of the pattern.

◆
Tension

(See diagram 18)

Before beginning any garment, work a small stitch sample about 4 ins by 4 ins (10.2 cm) in the main pattern and on the needles stated. Place the knitted sample on a flat surface and mark out 1 in (2.54 cm) (or 2 ins [5.1 cm] if stated) with pins (diagram 18). Count the number of stitches between the pins carefully and if your tension is correct then you may proceed with the garment. If you have fewer stitches to the inch than stated, your tension is too loose and you should work another sample, using a size smaller needle. If you have more stitches to the inch, then your tension is too tight and you should work another sample, using a size larger needle. Continue in this way, altering the size of your needles until you obtain the correct tension given.

Do not proceed with your garment until you are satisfied that your tension is correct.

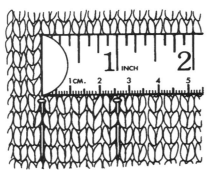

diagram 18

◆
Basic fabrics

GARTER STITCH (see diagram 19)
This fabric is formed by knitting every row.

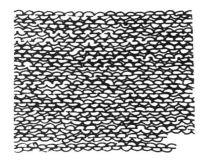

diagram 19

STOCKING STITCH (see diagram 20)
This fabric is formed by knitting one row and then purling one row alternately. The knit row is the right side of work.

diagram 20

REVERSED STOCKING STITCH
Worked exactly the same as stocking stitch. The purl row is the right side of work.

MOSS STITCH (see diagram 21)
Moss stitch is normally worked over an uneven number of stitches, thus:

Moss stitch row: K1, (p1, k1) to end. This row is repeated throughout

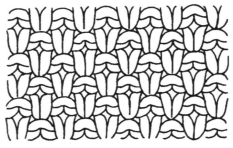

diagram 21

RIBBING (see diagram 22)
The closest form of ribbing is k1, p1 rib, normally worked over an even number of stitches, thus:

Rib row: (K1, p1) to end. This row is repeated throughout.

There are many variations in ribbing built up from the basic k1, p1 rib, such as:

K2, p2 rib

Cast on a multiple of 4 stitches.

Opposite: An attractive pattern using the machine stitch called plated tuck. © Courtesy Brother Industries.

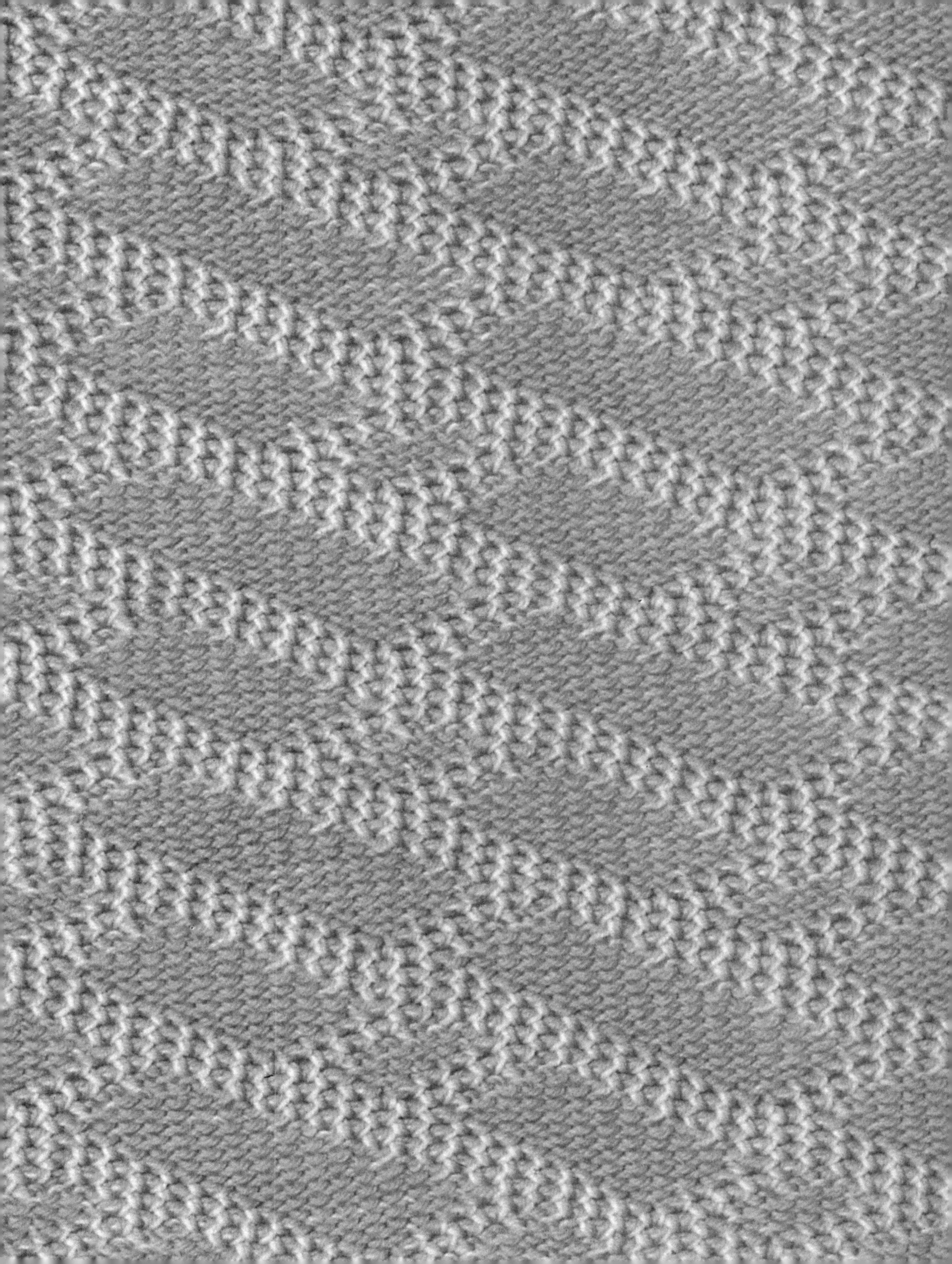

Rib row: (K2, p2) to end. This row is repeated throughout.

K3, p3 rib

Cast on a multiple of 6 stitches.

Rib row. (K3, p3) to end. This row is repeated throughout.

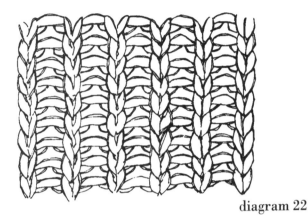

diagram 22

◆

Shaping

DECREASING ON A KNIT ROW
(see diagrams 23 to 26)

1. To decrease one stitch put right-hand needle knitwise through the next 2 stitches and knit them together in the usual way. The abbreviation for this is "k2 tog" (diagram 23).

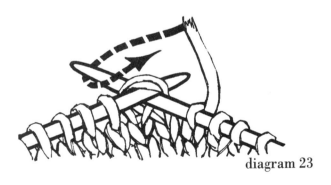

diagram 23

2. To decrease one stitch, slip the next stitch purlwise onto the right-hand needle, knit the next stitch, put the point of the left-hand needle purlwise into the slipped stitch and lift this over the knitted stitch and off the right-hand needle. The abbreviation for this is "sl1, k1, psso" (diagram 24).

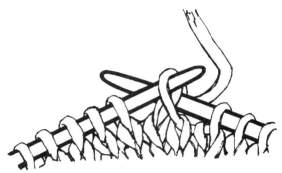

diagram 24

3. To decrease 2 stitches, put the right-hand needle knitwise through the next 3 stitches and knit them together in the usual way. The abbreviation for this is "k3 tog" (diagram 25).

diagram 25

4. To decrease 2 stitches, slip next stitch purlwise onto the right-hand needle, knit the next 2 stitches together, put the point of the left-hand needle purlwise into the slipped stitch and lift this over the 2 stitches knitted together and off the right-hand needle. The abbreviation for this is "sl1, k2 tog, psso" (diagram 26).

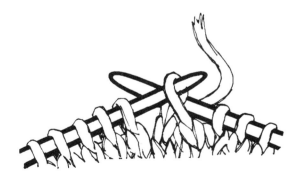

diagram 26

DECREASING ON A PURL ROW
(see diagram 27)

To decrease one stitch, put the right-hand needle purlwise through the next 2 stitches and purl them together in the usual way. The abbreviation for this is "p2 tog" (diagram 27).

diagram 27

DECREASING BY KNITTING THROUGH BACK OF LOOPS
(See diagram 28)

Knitting 2 stitches together through back of loops is a form of decreasing by "twisting" the stitch:

On a knit row
Knit 2 stitches together in the usual way to form one stitch, but work through the BACK loops instead of the front loops. The abbreviation for this is "k2 tog tbl".

On a purl row
Purl 2 stitches together in the usual way to form one stitch, but work through the BACK loops instead of the front loops. The abbreviation for this is "p2 tog tbl".

diagram 28

INCREASING BY MEANS OF A STITCH
(see diagrams 29 and 30)

1. To increase one stitch, put the point of the right-

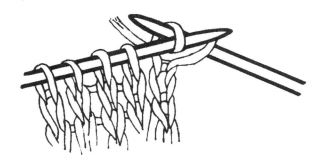

diagram 29

hand needle into the back of the stitch and knit or purl into the stitch again. Slip both these stitches onto the right-hand needle, thus making two stitches out of one. The abbreviation for this is "inc" (diagram 29).

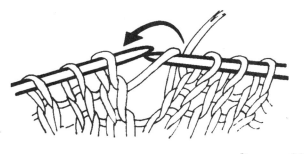

diagram 30

2. To increase one stitch, pick up the horizontal loop lying between the two needles, place it on the left-hand needle and knit into the back of it. The abbreviation for this is "m1" (diagram 30).

INCREASING BY MEANS OF A LOOP
(see diagrams 31 to 33)

These operations are used in fancy patterns:

1. Make a stitch on a knit row by bringing the yarn forward between the needles, then knit the next stitch in the usual way, carrying the yarn over the right-hand needle. The abbreviation for this is "yfwd" (diagram 31).

diagram 31

2. Make a stitch on a purl row by bringing the yarn over and round the right-hand needle to the front, then purl the next stitch in the usual way. The abbreviation for this is "yrn" (diagram 32).

diagram 32

3. Make a stitch between a purl and a knit stitch by purling the stitch in the usual way, then take the yarn over the right-hand needle and knit the next stitch in the usual way. The abbreviation for this is "yon" (diagram 33).

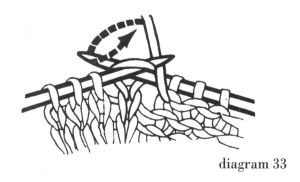

diagram 33

JOINING IN NEW YARN

Always join in a new ball of yarn at the beginning of a row, leaving about 3 ins (7.6 cm) hanging at the end to darn into the work when you are making-up.

PICKING UP DROPPED STITCHES
(see diagram 34)

Use a crochet hook to pick up the dropped stitch, drawing the released strands through the stitch row by row, replacing the stitch on the needle.

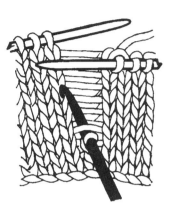

diagram 34

KNITTING INTO ROW BELOW
(see diagram 35)

The abbreviation for this is k1 d. Knit through the loop below the next stitch, dropping the stitch above off the left-hand needle.

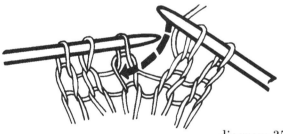

diagram 35

KNITTING INTO BACK OF STITCH
The abbreviation for this is k1 b. Knit a stitch in the usual way, but through the BACK loop.

THE CABLE STITCH (see diagram 36)
The principle of cable knitting is to slip a given number of stitches onto a cable needle and leave them either at the front or back of work as directed. Work the given number of stitches from the left-hand needle, then work the stitches from the cable needle which completes the cable operation. Diagram 36 shows a simple form of the cable stitch: slip 2 stitches onto cable needle and hold at front of work, knit the next 2 stitches, then knit the 2 stitches from the cable needle.

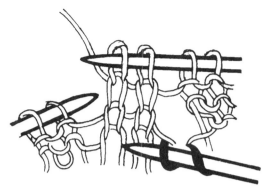

diagram 36

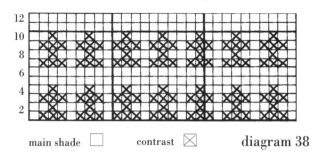

main shade ☐   contrast ⊠   diagram 38

TWO-COLOR KNITTING (see diagram 37)

If a large number of stitches are to be worked in different colors, either vertically or otherwise, use a separate ball of yarn for each color or shade and twist the yarn firmly on the wrong side of work when changing colors to avoid a hole.

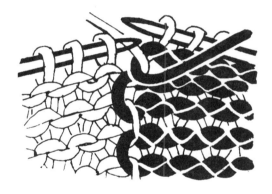

diagram 37

FAIR ISLE KNITTING (see diagrams 38 to 40)

These patterns are always worked in stocking stitch, with groups of stitches knitted in different colors to form a pattern. The Fair Isle design is usually given in the instructions in the form of a chart, with each square representing one stitch and a different symbol representing each color. When working from a chart the odd-numbered rows are the knit rows and the right side of work, and the purl rows are the even-numbered rows and the wrong side of work. The chart is read from right to left on the knit rows and from left to right on the purl rows (diagram 38)

When changing colors horizontally, the change can be made by either weaving or stranding:

WEAVING

This method gives a professional finish, especially if a color is out of use across a large number of stitches.

The principle is to weave the color not in use under that being used. This is done by taking the color in use under the out-of-work strand before working the next stitch (diagram 39).

STRANDING

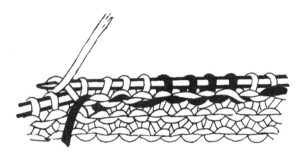

diagram 39

The color which is not in use is taken across the back of the work while the color in use is being worked. It is important not to pull the yarn too tight or the work will "pucker" (diagram 40).

diagram 40

MARKERS (see diagram 41 overleaf)

Sometimes it is necessary to mark a particular point in the work as a visual guide later. A short length of contrasting yarn is threaded through the stitch and tied in place so that it does not accidentally come out. Once it has served its purpose, simply pull it out.

diagram 41

CIRCULAR KNITTING (see diagram 42)
Working with four double-pointed needles or a circular needle creates a tubular type of seamless fabric suitable for neckbands, skirts, etc — one round equals one row in flat knitting — with the right side of work facing all the time.

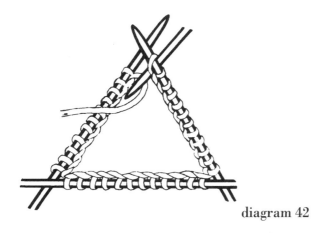

diagram 42

Casting on with four needles
Cast on 45 sts evenly divided on three of the needles (15 x 15 x 15); forming a triangle. Using the fourth needle, knit across the stitches on the first needle, then work across the second and third needles, thus ending one round.

Using a circular needle
These are used on the same principle as above, except that you have only one needle. Aero circular needles are made in varying sizes and lengths ... the minimum number of stitches to be knitted decides the maximum needle length required.

Circular Fair Isle knitting
If you are working Fair Isle on four needles, or on a

circular needle, then every row on your chart will be a knit row and each row will read from right to left.

◆

Yarn embroidery
Any knitted garment will be enhanced by embroidery (see diagrams 43a, b, c, d):

KNITTING STITCH (see diagram 43)
This type of embroidery is always worked over stocking stitch fabric. Using a tapestry needle and a contrasting yarn of the same thickness as the fabric, embroider over each individual stitch so that the finished pattern or motif has the appearance of being knitted in. This type of embroidery is often used in Fair Isle designs, in which case a graph is given in the instructions. Read the graph exactly as you would for a normal Fair Isle chart.

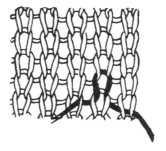

diagram 43

LAZY DAISY STITCH (see diagram 43a)
Bring tapestry needle through the fabric at the base of the stitch; insert the needle in the same place again, then run it up behind the fabric at the point, outlining the size of the required stitch. The point of the needle must come out through the loop formed by the yarn on the front of the fabric. Insert the needle over the top of the yarn again, thus catching the formed loop.

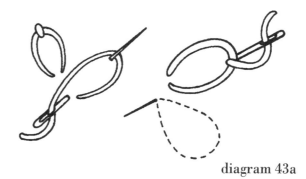

diagram 43a

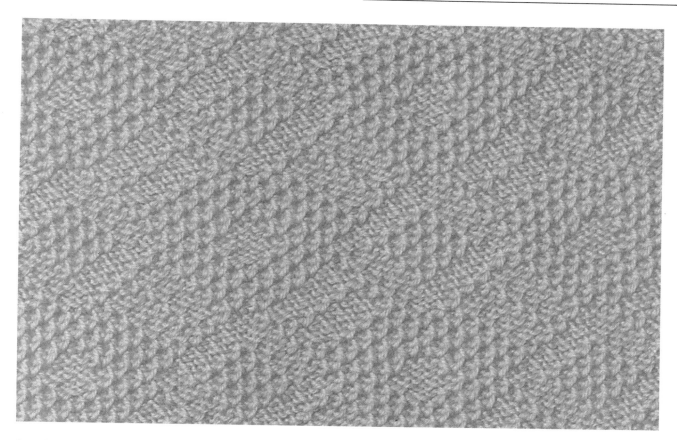

Samples of tuck stitch, knitted on a machine. © *Courtesy Brother Industries.*

SATIN STITCH (see diagram 43b)

Simply a series of flat stitches made parallel with each other, forming solid masses of color on the surface of the work. Bring tapestry needle through the fabric at the point where the stitch is to begin then re-insert it at the second point, outlining the length of the stitch, at the same time, bringing the point of the needle out through the fabric again where the next stitch is to begin. Continue in this way.

diagram 43b

STEM STITCH (see diagram 43c)

An outline stitch — bring tapestry needle through the fabric, make a short diagonal stitch in the direction of the required outline, bringing the needle out again half-way down the first stitch; make a second stitch the same length as the first stitch.

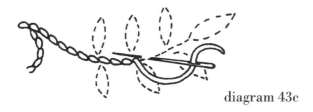

diagram 43c

BLANKET STITCH (see diagram 43d)

Bring tapestry needle through at the point where the stitch is to begin, hold the yarn down in a loop with the thumb and insert the needle through while holding the yarn in position.

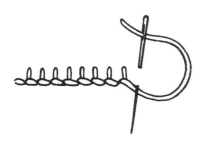

diagram 43d

GRAFTING (see diagram 44)

This means the joining of two sets of stitches, horizontally and invisibly. First, you must have the same number of stitches on each of the needles facing each other (wrong sides of work together) then, with a tapestry needle and the same yarn as you have been working with, proceed as follows: * Insert sewing needle knitwise through the first stitch on the front needle, draw yarn through and slip stitch off knitting needle; insert sewing needle purlwise through next stitch on front needle, draw yarn through and leave stitch on knitting needle; insert sewing needle purlwise through first stitch on back needle; insert sewing needle knitwise through next stitch on back needle, draw yarn through and leave on knitting needle; repeat from * until all stitches are worked off both needles.

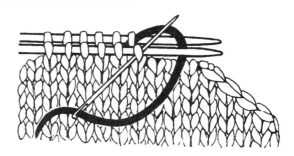

diagram 44

PICKING UP STITCHES (see diagram 45)

When you are instructed to pick up stitches around a neckline, armhole, etc, have yarn at back of work * put knitting needle through from front to back, pick up a loop of yarn and bring loop through to right side and leave on needle; repeat from * for required number of stitches, being careful to knit up in a smooth curve.

diagram 45

LEFT-HAND KNITTING

Follow the instructions but change your copy to read left hand where it says "right hand" and vice versa. Use a mirror to study diagrams and charts, as this will reverse the image for you.

MEASURING (see diagram 46)

Always lay knitting on a flat surface then, with a ruler or clearly marked tape, measure on the straight of the fabric. Never measure round curves or along a shaped edge.

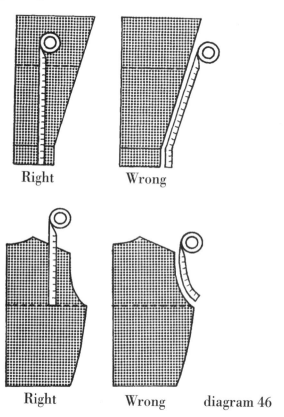

Right   Wrong

Right   Wrong   diagram 46

PULLING A THREAD

This is done to alter the length of knitteds.

To lengthen

Cut the thread at each edge of the work. Draw the cut thread out to the side and cut it to release the stitches on each side of the thread ... a few stitches at a time. Use a smaller needle to pick up the released stitches, then with the right size needles work the required number of rows. Finally, graft the stitches together as shown in diagram 44.

To shorten

Unravel the required number of rows, then graft the stitches together as shown in diagram 44.

◆
Making up

First, using a tapestry needle, darn in all ends.

PRESSING

Yarn

Press lightly on the wrong side with a steam iron, or with a warm iron over a damp cloth.

Synthetics

Do not press unless instructed.

Mixtures of yarn and synthetics

Press LIGHTLY on the wrong side, using a warm iron.

Embossed patterns

Heavy cables, Aran stitches, etc, should be steamed rather than pressed, using a very damp cloth and holding the iron over the surface, so as not to use any pressure which would "flatten" the knitting.

BLOCKING (see diagram 47)

When pressing is directed, place each piece on a padded surface with wrong side of work facing you. Without stretching any of the fabric, pin pieces to the padded surface as shown in diagram 47, then press. Wait until the fabric has cooled before taking out the pins.

Note: Do not press ribbing.

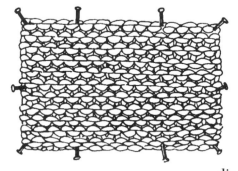

diagram 47

◆
Seaming

Only two seams are used for joining knitted garments — a backstitch seam for the body of garment, and a flat seam for ribbed sections (unless otherwise instructed). Use a tapestry needle threaded with the same yarn you have used in making the original garment. If a chunky yarn has been used, strand the plys and use two of these strands together for seaming.

If the yarn is not suitable for sewing, use a 3-ply yarn in the same shade.

THE BACKSTITCH SEAM (see diagram 48)
Place the two pieces of fabric with right sides facing each other, so that the rows of knitting in each piece correspond.

Pin the pieces together about ½ in (1.3 cm) from the edge. Now sew the pieces together one stitch in from the edge, using a backstitch seam. Finally, remove pins and, using the point of an iron at the correct temperature for the fabric, press the seam open.

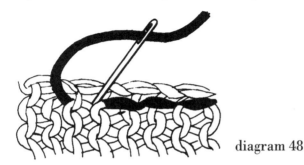

diagram 48

THE FLAT SEAM (see diagram 49)
Place the two pieces together edge to edge with right sides facing each other. With the forefinger of the left hand placed under the line of the seam, draw the two edges together with an overstitch so that they lie flat against each other, moving the finger along as the seaming proceeds.

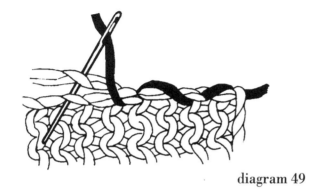

diagram 49

THE SLIP STITCH (see diagram 50)
Use a fine slip stitch for sewing hems, matching stitch for stitch.

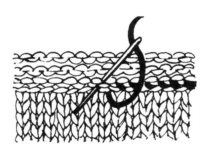

diagram 50

SHOULDER SEAMS
Backstitch firmly, taking the stitching across the shaped steps in a straight line.

SET-IN SLEEVES
Mark middle top of sleeve and pin in position to shoulder seam, then pin cast-off stitches of sleeve to cast off stitches at underarm of body of garment. Backstitch firmly around the curves as near to the edge as possible.

SIDE AND SLEEVE SEAMS
Join with a backstitch in one complete seam as near to the edge as possible.

SEWING ON COLLARS
Place right side of collar to wrong side of neck, matching middle backs and taking care not to stretch the neckline. Join with a flat seam.

SEWN-ON BANDS
Ribbed bands, whether worked in one piece or two pieces, are joined to the body of garment by a flat seam.

SEWN-ON POCKETS
Using matching yarn, slip stitch pocket in position, taking care to keep the line absolutely straight.

HERRINGBONE STITCH (see diagram 51)
For encasing waist elastic use a herringbone stitch. Cut elastic to the size required and join into a circle. Pin elastic into position on the wrong side of work. Hold the knitting over the fingers of the left hand and with the elastic slightly stretched, work a herringbone stitch, catching the elastic above and below as you work.

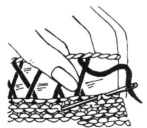

diagram 51

POCKET LININGS

Pin linings in place along each side and lower edge in a straight line, then slip stitch linings into position.

INSERTING A ZIPPER (see diagram 52)

Pin the zipper into position, taking care not to stretch the knitting. Using a backstitch and working as near as possible to the zipper edge, sew zipper into position.

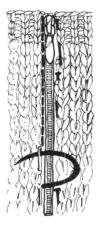

diagram 52

◆

Washing

Some yarns are machine washable. However, if you intend to hand wash your garment, the following points should be of interest to you.

1. Never allow the garment to get too dirty. Gentle washing does not damage any fabric, but when a knitted garment is very soiled normal use of washing powders will not remove all the dirt without rubbing, and it is this rubbing action which causes damage to the fibers.

2. Choose a washing powder suitable for handknits.

3. Make sure the washing powder is thoroughly dissolved before putting the garment in the solution. Make sure also that there is enough water to completely cover the garment.

4. Never boil your garment. The water temperature should be hand hot.

5. Do not bleach handknits.

6. Do not stretch the garment by lifting it in and out of the water.

7. Remove the garment from the water and gently squeeze out as much water as you can.

8. Rinse the garment several times until the rinsing water is absolutely clear.

9. Remove the garment from the water and gently squeeze (never wring), then roll garment in a clean, dry towel, thus absorbing the moisture.

10. Spread the garment out flat on the towel and ease it into the correct shape and size. Allow it to dry free from any direct sunlight or artificial heat. Never hang your garment to dry.

◆

Looking after your handknits

Keep your handknits folded in individual polythene bags when not in use, with tissue paper in the folds to prevent creases forming, then lay them in a drawer or on a shelf.

NEVER leave your handknits on a hanger or hook, as the weight will cause them to drop.

PATTERNED FABRICS

CABLE
(figure 1)

Cast on a multiple of 9 sts plus 5.

1st row: Sl 1, * p3, k6; rep from * to last 4 sts, p3, k1.

2nd row: Sl 1, * k3, p6; rep from * to last 4 sts, k4.

Rep above 2 rows once more.

5th row: Sl 1, * p3, sl next 3 sts on a cable needle and hold at back of work, k3, then k 3 sts from cable needle; rep from * to last 4 sts, p3, k1.

6th row: As 2nd row.

Rep 1st and 2nd rows 3 times.

13th row: Sl 1, * p3, sl next 3 sts on a cable needle and hold at front of work, k3, then k 3 sts from cable needle; rep from * to last 4 sts, p3, k1.

14th row: As 2nd row.

Rep 1st and 2nd rows once more.

Rep above 16 rows for length required.

Figure 1

FISHERMAN RIB
(figure 2)

Cast on an even number of sts.

1st row: K.

2nd row: K1, (k1 d, p1) to last st, k1.

Rep 2nd row for length required.

Note: see diagram 35 on page 24 for k1 d.

Figure 2

BASKET STITCH
(figure 3)

Cast on a multiple of 6 sts.

1st row: (K3, p3) to end.

Rep 1st row twice.

4th row: (P3, k3) to end.

Rep 4th row twice.

Rep above 6 rows for length required.

Figure 3

EASY LACE PATTERN
(figure 4)

Cast on a multiple of 6 sts plus 2.

1st row: K1, * k3, yfwd, sl1, k2 tog, psso, yfwd; rep from * to last st, k1.

2nd row: P.

3rd row: K1, * yfwd, sl1, k2 tog, psso, yfwd, k3; rep from * to last st, k1.

4th row: P.

Rep above 4 rows for length required.

Opposite: Fair Isle pattern worked by a machine knitter.
© Courtesy Brother Industries.

figure 4

BLACKBERRY STITCH
(figure 5)

Cast on a multiple of 4 sts plus 2.

1st row: K1, * (k1, p1, k1) all into next st, p3 tog; rep from * to last st, k1.

2nd row: P.

3rd row: K1, * p3 tog, (k1, p1, k1) all into next st; rep from * to last st, k1.

4th row: P.

Rep above 4 rows for length required.

figure 5

DOUBLE MOSS STITCH
(figure 6)

Cast on a multiple of 4 sts.

1st row: (K2, p2) to end.

2nd row: As 1st row.

3rd row: (P2, k2) to end.

4th row: As 3rd row.

Rep above 4 rows for length required.

figure 6

VANDYKE PATTERN (figure 7)

Cast on a multiple of 12 sts plus 2.

1st row: K1, * k3, yfwd, sl1, k1, psso, k2, k2 tog, yfwd, k1, yfwd, sl1, k1, psso; rep from * to last st, k1.

2nd row: P.

3rd row: K1, * k1, k2 tog, yfwd, k1, yfwd, sl1, k1, psso, k1, k2 tog, yfwd, k1, yfwd, sl1, k1, psso; rep from * to last st, k1.

4th row: P.

5th row: K1, * k2 tog, yfwd, k3, yfwd, sl1, k1, psso, k2 tog, yfwd, k1, yfwd, sl1, k1, psso; rep from * to last st, k1.

6th row: P.

Rep above 6 rows for length required.

figure 7

RIB VARIATION (figure 8)

Cast on a multiple of 5 sts plus 3.

1st row: (P3, k2) to last 3 sts, p3.

2nd row: (K3, p2) to last 3 sts, k3.

3rd row: As 1st row.

4th row: As 2nd row.

Fair Isle pullover by Mrs S.E. Millington.

5th row: (P3, k second st on left-hand needle then first st) to last 3 sts, p3.

6th row: As 2nd row.

Rep above 6 rows for length required.

figure 8

ARAN KNITTING
(figure 9)
Of all the hundreds of stitches available to the home knitter today, the most interesting and rewarding of all must be Aran patterning. Of course, Aran knitting is not for the beginner knitter to tackle, as true Aran designs are made up of at least four different designs in the one garment, and it takes an experienced knitter to cope with the longer-than-usual instructions.

Traditional Aran garments are made in thick, cream-hued, partly scoured, pure yarn — partly scoured in order to retain much of the natural oil which makes the yarn wind resistant. It has never been discovered exactly where the people of Aran derived their intricate form of knitting, but we know that for hundreds of years Irish women have knitted Aran fishing jerseys for their menfolk. At one time every village on the western seaboard had its own individual patterns to enable any fisherman, who may be washed ashore far from home, to be easily identified.

Not all Aran patterns, however, have such a tragic meaning. For example, "the tree of life", off-shooting branches from a central trunk, expresses the fisherman's wish for his sons to follow him to the sea; "the diamond" is symbolic of wealth; "honeycomb" represents hard work such as "the busy bee produces golden honey", etc.

Modern basic Aran patterns usually consist of a middle panel with an equal number of side panels, the division between these panels being emphasized by cable (sometimes bobble) patterns. The following sample is a typical example:

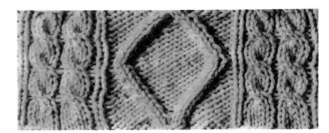

figure 9

Cast on 114 sts.

1st row: K1, p1, * k1, (p1, c 4f) twice, p1, k1 **, p6, sl next st on cable needle and keep at back, sl next 2 sts on another cable needle and keep at front, k 2 sts, p1 from first cable needle, p 1 st, then k2 from second cable needle, p6; rep from * to ** once ***, p22, rep from * to *** once, p1, k1.

2nd row: P1, k1, * p1, k1, p4, k1, p4, k1, p1 **, k6, p2, k2, p2, k6; rep from * to ** once *** k1, [p3 tog, (k1, p1, k1) into next st] 5 times, k1; rep from * to *** once, k1, p1.

3rd row: K1, p1, * k1, p1, k4, p1, k4, p1, k1 **, p5, cr 2 over 1 b, p2, cr 2 over 1 f, p5; rep from * to ** once, ***, p22; rep from * to *** once, p1, k1.

4th row: P1, k1, * p1, k1, p4, k1, p4, k1, p1 **, k5, p2, k4, p2, k5; rep from * to ** once ***, k1, [(k1, p1, k1) into next st, p3 tog] 5 times, k1; rep from * to *** once, k1, p1.

5th row: K1, p1, * k1, p1, k4, p1, k4, p1, k1 **, p4, cr 2 over 1 b, p4, cr 2 over 1 f, p4; rep from * to ** once ***, p22; rep from * to *** once, p1, k1.

6th row: P1, k1, * p1, k1, p4, k1, p4, k1, p1 **, k4, p2, k6, p2, k4; rep from * to ** once ***, k1, [p3 tog, (k1, p1, k1) into next st] 5 times, k1; rep from * to *** once, k1, p1.

7th row: K1, p1, * k1, (p1, c 4f) twice, p1, k1 **, p3, cr 2 over 1 b, p6, cr 2 over 1 f, p3; rep from * to ** once ***, p22; rep from * to *** once, p1, k1.

8th row: P1, k1, * p1, k1, p4, k1, p4, k1, p1 **, k3, p2, k8, p2, k3; rep from * to ** once ***, k1, [(k1, p1, k1) into next st, p3 tog] 5 times, k1; rep from * to *** once, k1, p1.

Opposite: An attractive example of a weaving pattern produced on a machine. © Courtesy Brother Industries.

9th row: K1, p1, * k1, p1, k4, p1, k4, p1, k1 **, p2, cr 2 over 1 b, p8, cr 2 over 1 f, p2; rep from * to ** once ***, p22; rep from * to ***, p1, k1.

10th row: P1, k1, * p1, k1, p4, k1, p4, k1, p1 **, k2, p2, k10, p2, k2; rep from * to ** once ***, k1, [p3 tog, (k1, p1, k1) into next st] 5 times, k1; rep from * to *** once, k1, p1.

11th row: K1, p1, * k1, p1, k4, p1, k4, p1, k1 **, p1, cr 2 over 1 b, p10, cr 2 over 1 f, p1; rep from * to ** once ***, p22; rep from * to *** once, p1, k1.

12th row: P1, k1, * p1, k1, p4, k1, p4, k1, p1 **, k1, p2, k12, p2, k1; rep from * to ** once ***, k1, [(k1, p1, k1) into next st, p3 tog] 5 times, k1; rep from * to *** once, k1, p1.

13th row: K1, p1, * k1, (p1, c 4f) twice, p1, k1 **, p1, cr 2 over 1 f, p10, cr 2 over 1 b, p1; rep from * to ** once ***, p22; rep from * to *** once, p1, k1.

14th row: As 10th row.

15th row: K1, p1, * k1, p1, k4, p1, k4, p1, k1 **, p2, cr 2 over 1 f, p8, cr 2 over 1 b, p2; rep from * to ** once ***, p22; rep from * to *** once, p1, k1.

16th row: As 8th row.

17th row: K1, p1, * k1, p1, k4, p1, k4, p1, k1 **, p3, cr 2 over 1 f, p6, cr 2 over 1 b, p3; rep from * to ** once **, p22; rep from * to *** once, p1, k1.

18th row: As 6th row.

19th row: K1, p1, * k1, (p1, c 4f) twice, p1, k1 **, p4, cr 2 over 1 f, p4, cr 2 over 1 b p4; rep from * to ** once ***, p22; rep from * to *** once, p1, k1.

20th row: As 4th row.

21st row: K1, p1, * k1, p1, k4 p1, k4, p1, k1 **, p5, cr 2 over 1 f, p2, cr 2 over 1 b, p5; rep from * to ** once ***, p22; rep from * to *** once, p1, k1.

22nd row: As 2nd row.

23rd row: K1, p1, * k1, p1, k4, p1, k4, p1, k1 **, p6, cr 2 over 1 f, cr 2 over 1 b, p6; rep from * to ** once ***, p22; rep from * to *** once, p1, k1.

24th row: P1, k1, * p1, k1, p4, k1, p4, k1, p1 **, k7, p4, k7; rep from * to ** once ***, k1, [(k1, p1, k1) into next st, p3 tog] 5 times, k1; rep from * to *** once, k1, p1. These 24 rows form the Aran pattern.

MIX AND MATCH BABY'S CLOTHING

◆

Materials

CARRYING CAPE
8 balls of Patons Feathersoft 3 ply; a pair of long No. 11 needles; required length of ribbon.

DRESS
4 balls of Patons Feathersoft 3 ply; a pair of No. 11 needles and a No. 2.50 crochet hook; 3 buttons; required length of ribbon.

ANGEL TOP
5 balls of Patons Feathersoft 3 ply; a pair of long No. 11 needles and a No. 2.50 crochet hook; 6 press studs; required length of ribbon.

JACKET
3 balls of Patons Feathersoft 3 ply; a pair of Nos. 11 and 12 needles; 4 buttons.

VEST
2 balls of Patons Feathersoft 3 ply; a pair of No. 11 needles and a No. 2.50 crochet hook.

PANTS
2 balls of Patons Feathersoft 3 ply; a pair of No. 11 needles; 2 buttons; ribbon.

BONNET
1 ball of Patons Feathersoft 3 ply; a pair of No. 11 needles; ribbon.

BOOTEES AND MITTS
1 ball of Patons Feathersoft 3 ply; a pair of No. 11 needles; ribbon.

SHAWL
14 balls of Patons Feathersoft 3 ply; a pair of long No. 10 needles.

◆

Measurements

CARRYING CAPE
To fit from birth to 18 in (45.7 cm) chest. Length, 22 ¼ ins (56.5 cm).

DRESS
To fit 18 in (45.7 cm) chest. Length, 14 ins (35.6 cm).

ANGEL TOP

To fit 18 in (45.7 cm) chest. Length, 11 ins (28 cm). Sleeve, 5 ins (12.7 cm).

JACKET

To fit 18 in (45.7 cm) chest. Length, 8¼ ins (21 cm). Sleeve, 5 ins (12.7 cm).

VEST

To fit 18 in (45.7 cm) chest. Length, 10¼ ins (26 cm).

PANTS

Around widest part, 19¾ ins (50.16 cm).

BONNET

Around face edge, 12½ ins (31.8 cm).

BOOTEES

Leg seam, 3 ins (7.6 cm). Foot, 3½ ins (8.9 cm).

MITTS

3¾ ins (9.5 cm).

SHAWL

Approx 41 ins square (104.4 cm).

◆

Tension

8 sts to 1 in (2.54 cm) over patt on No. 11 needles. 7 sts to 1 in (2.54 cm) over patt on No. 10 needles.

◆

Abbreviations

See page 15.

◆

Carrying cape

MAIN PART *(worked in one piece)*
With No. 11 needles cast on 251 sts and work in g st for 6 rows, then cont in patt:

1st row: K5, (yfwd, k2 tog, k4) to end.

2nd to 8th rows: K.

9th row: K8, (yfwd, k2 tog, k4) to last 3 sts, k3.

10th to 16th rows: K.

Rep above 16 rows until work measures 8 ins (20.3 cm), ending so that a k row will follow on next row.

Next (dec) row: K11, (k2 tog, k18) to end (239 sts). Cont in patt until work measures 10 ins (25.4 cm).

Next (dec) row: K11, (k2 tog, k17) to end (227 sts).

Cont in patt until work measures 12 ins (30.5 cm).

Next (dec) row: K11, (k2 tog, k16) to end (215 sts). Cont in patt until work measures 14 ins (35.6 cm).

Next (dec) row: K11, (k2 tog, k15) to end (203 sts). Cont in patt until work measures 16 ins (40.6 cm).

Next (dec) row: K11, (k2 tog, k14) to end (191 sts). Cont in patt until work measures 18 ins (45.7 cm).

Next (dec) row: K11, (k2 tog, k13) to end (179 sts). Cont in patt until work measures 20 ins (50.8 cm).

Next (dec) row: K11, (k2 tog, k12) to end (167 sts). Cont in patt until work measures 22 ins (55.9 cm).

Next (dec) row: K14, (k2 tog, k1) 46 times, k to end (121 sts).

Next (ribbonhole) row: K1, (yfwd, k2 tog, k1) to end. K 2 rows, then cast off.

HOOD

With No. 11 needles cast on 53 sts and work in 16-row patt, as given for main part, until work measures 13¼ ins (34.3 cm). Cast off.

TO MAKE UP

Using a small backstitch join side of piece tog to form "hood". Using a flat seam attach hood to main part, placing hood seam at middle of main part and leaving approx 1 in (2.54 cm) free at each outer edge. Thread ribbon through ribbonholes and tie at front.

◆

Dress

BACK

With No. 11 needles cast on 119 sts and work in g st for 6 rows, then cont in 16-row patt as given for main part of carrying cape, until work measures 10½ ins (26.7 cm).

Next (dec) row: K22, (k2 tog) 37 times, k to end (82 sts).

Next (ribbonhole) row: K2, (yfwd, k2 tog, k2) to end. Work 3 rows in g st.

Shape armholes: Cont in g st and cast off 4 sts at beg of next 2 rows, then dec 1 st each end of next row and every foll alt row until 66 sts rem. Cont straight until armholes measure 1 1/4 ins (3.2 cm). **

Divide for back opening. Next row: K35, turn and cont on these sts only.

Next row: K.

Next (buttonhole) row: K to last 3 sts, yfwd, k2 tog, k1. Cont in g st, making another buttonhole in same way as before when armhole measures 2¼ ins (5.7 cm). Cont straight until armhole measures 3¼ ins (8.25 cm), ending at side edge.

Shape shoulder. Cast off 7 sts at beg of next row and foll alt row, then 6 sts on foll alt row. Work 1 row, then cast off rem sts.

Return to sts on needle. Rejoin yarn to inner end of rem sts and cast on 4 sts, then work to correspond in g st with other side, reversing shapings and omitting buttonholes.

FRONT

Work as given for Back to **. Cont in g st until armholes measure 2 ins (5.1 cm).

Shape neck. Next row: K27, turn and cont on these sts only.

Dec 1 st at neck edge on foll 7 rows, then cont straight until armhole measures same as back armhole, ending at side edge.

Shape shoulder. Cast off 7 sts at beg of next row and foll alt row, work 1 row, then cast off rem sts.

Return to sts on needle. Rejoin yarn to inner end of rem sts and cast off middle 12 sts, then cont on rem sts in g st to correspond with other side, reversing shapings.

TO MAKE UP

Using a small backstitch join shoulder, side seams.

CROCHET EDGING

Rsf and with No. 2.50 hook, work 1 row of dc around each armhole edge and 2 rows of dc around neck edge, making final buttonhole in first row.

TO FINISH OFF

Sew on buttons. Thread ribbon through ribbonholes and tie at front.

◆

Angel top

MAIN PART (worked in one piece)

With No. 11 needles cast on 215 sts and k 2 rows, then cont in patt:

1st row: K5, (yfwd, k2 tog, k4) to end.

2nd to 8th rows: K.

9th row: K8, (yfwd, k2 tog, k4) to last 3 sts, k3.

10th to 16th rows: K.

Rep above 16 rows until work measures 7 ins (17.8 cm), ending on a k row.

Divide for armholes. Keeping patt as established, work as follows:

Next row: Patt 53 sts, turn and cont on these sts for left back. * Work 19 rows, break yarn and leave sts on a holder *. Join yarn to inner end of rem sts and patt 109 sts, turn and work as given for left back from * to *. Join yarn to inner end of rem sts and work 20 rows. Break yarn and leave sts on a holder.

SLEEVES

With No. 11 needles cast on 45 sts and work 5 rows in g st.

Next (inc) row: (Inc k4) to end (54 sts).

Now cont in patt:

1st row: K3, (yfwd, k2 tog, k4) to last 3 sts, yfwd, k2 tog, k1.

2nd to 8th rows: K.

9th row: K6, (yfwd, k2 tog, k4) to end.

10th to 16th rows: K.

Cont in 16-row patt until work measures 5 ins (12.7 cm). Mark each end of last row with a brightly colored thread, then patt another 18 rows. Break yarn and leave sts on holder.

YOKE

Rsf and with No. 11 needles join pieces tog as follows:

Left back: K5, * k2 tog, k1; rep from * 15 times.

First sleeve: K3, * k2, k2 tog, k2; rep from * 7 times, k3.

Front: K2, * k2 tog, k1; rep from * 34 times, k2.

Second sleeve: Work as given for first sleeve.

Right back: * K1, k2 tog; rep from * 15 times, k5.

Cont on these 240 sts and work 7 rows in g st.

Next (dec) row: K6, (k1, k2 tog, k6) to end (214 sts). K 5 rows.

Next (dec) row: (K4, k2 tog, k2) to last 6 sts, k6 (188 sts). K 5 rows.

Next (dec) row: K6, (k1, k2 tog, k4) to end (162 sts). K 5 rows.

Next (dec) row: (K3, k2 tog, k1) to last 6 sts, k6 (136 sts). K 5 rows.

Next (dec) row: K6, (k2 tog, k3) to end (110 sts). K 5 rows.

Next (dec) row: K3, (k1, k2 tog, k1) to last 3 sts, k3 (84 sts). K 3 rows.

Next (ribbonhole) row: (K1, yfwd, k2 tog) to end. K 3 rows, then cast off.

TO MAKE UP

Using a small backstitch join sleeves to colored threads, then join underarm seams. Rsf and with No. 2.50 hook work 3 rows of dc down each raw edge at back to neaten. Attach first press stud to neck edge, then sew others down opening at 2 in (5.1 cm) intervals. Finally, thread ribbon through ribbonholes at neck and tie at back.

◆

Jacket

BACK

With No. 12 needles cast on 77 sts and work in k1, p1 rib for 10 rows. Change to No. 11 needles and patt:

1st row: K5, (yfwd, k2 tog, k4) to end.

2nd to 8th rows: K.

9th row: K8, (yfwd, k2 tog, k4) to last 3 sts, k3.

10th to 16th rows: K.

Rep above 16 rows until work measures 5 ins (12.7 cm).

Shape raglan armholes. Cont in patt and cast off 3 sts at beg of next 2 rows, then dec 1 st each end of next row and every foll alt row until 25 sts rem. Work 1 row, then cast off.

RIGHT FRONT

With No. 12 needles cast on 41 sts and work in k1, p1 rib for 10 rows. Change to No. 11 needles and cont in 16-row patt as given for back until work measures same as back to beg of armhole shaping, ending at side edge.

Shape raglan armhole and "V" front. Next row: Cast off 3 sts, patt to last 2 sts, k2 tog. Cont to dec at armhole edge on every foll alt row to correspond with back, at the same time, dec at front slope on every foll 4th row until 13 sts rem, then on every foll 3rd row until 3 sts rem. Dec once more at armhole edge

only, then cont on rem 2 sts until front measures same as back. K2 tog and fasten off.

LEFT FRONT

Work as given for Right Front, reversing shapings.

SLEEVES

With No. 12 needles cast on 47 sts and work in k1, p1 rib for 10 rows. Change to No. 11 needles and cont in patt as given for Back, inc 1 st each end of 3rd row and every foll 6th row to 59 sts, including the extra sts into the patt as they occur. Cont straight until work measures 5 ins (12.7 cm)

Shape raglan top: Cont in patt and cast off 3 sts at beg of next 2 rows, then dec 1 st each end of next row and every foll alt row until 5 sts rem. Work 1 row, then cast off.

TO MAKE UP

Using a small backstitch join raglan, side, and sleeve seams.

FRONT BAND (*worked in one piece*)

With No. 12 needles cast on 8 sts and work 4 rows in k1, p1 rib.

* 1st (buttonhole) row: Rib 3, yfwd, k2 tog, rib to end. Rib 14 rows. *

Rep from * to * 3 times, then cont straight in rib until band is long enough to fit around entire front edge, slightly stretched.

Cast off ribwise.

TO FINISH OFF

Using a flat seam attach band to garment. Sew on buttons.

◆

Vest

BACK AND FRONT ALIKE

With No. 11 needles cast on 77 sts and k 2 rows, then cont in patt as given for back of jacket until work measures 7½ ins (19.1 cm).

Shape armholes. Cont in g st and cast off 5 sts at beg of next 2 rows (67 sts).

Cont in g st until work measures 9 ins (22.9 cm).

Shape neck. Next row: K18, turn and cont on these sts only until work measures 10½ ins (26.7 cm). Cast off.

Return to sts on needle. Rejoin yarn to inner end of rem sts and cast off middle 31 sts, then cont on rem sts to correspond with other side.

TO MAKE UP

Using a small backstitch join shoulder and side seams. Rsf and with No. 2.50 hook, work 1 row of dc around neck edge to neaten.

◆
Pants

FRONT

With No. 11 needles cast on 83 sts and work in k1, p1 rib for 6 rows.

Next (ribbonhole) row: K1, (yfwd, k2 tog, rib 2) to end. Work 7 more rows in k1, p1 rib, then cont in patt as given for back of jacket until work measures 6¼ ins (15.9 cm).

Keeping patt as established, dec 1 st each end of every foll row until 25 sts rem K 3 rows then fasten off.

BACK

With No. 11 needles cast on 83 sts and work in k1, p1 rib for 6 rows.

Next (ribbonhole) row: K1, (yfwd, k2 tog, rib 2) to end. Work 7 more rows in k1, p1 rib.

Shape back. 1st row: K to last 10 sts, turn.

2nd row: As 1st row.

3rd row: K to last 20 sts, turn.

4th row: As 3rd row.

5th row: K to last 30 sts, turn.

6th row: As 5th row.

7th row: K to end.

Cont in patt as given for back of jacket until work measures 6¼ ins (15.9 cm).

Keeping patt as established, dec 1 st each end of every foll row until 25 sts rem. Cont straight in g st for 7 rows.

Next (buttonhole) row: K6, cast off 3 sts, k7, cast off 3 sts, k6.

Next row: K and cast on 3 sts over those sts cast off in previous row.

K 3 rows, then cast off.

TO MAKE UP

Using a flat seam for ribbing and a small backstitch for remainder, join side seams. Sew buttons on front to correspond with back buttonholes. Thread ribbon through ribbonholes at waist and tie at front.

◆
Bonnet

With No. 11 needles cast on 101 sts and work in g st for 14 rows. Change to No. 10 needles and cont in patt as follows:

1st row: K5, (yfwd, k2 tog, k4) to end.

2nd to 8th rows: K.

9th row: K8, (yfwd, k2 tog, k4) to last 3 sts, k3.

10th to 16th rows: K.

Rep above 16 rows until work measures 4¾ ins (12.1 cm).

Shape crown: 1st row: K1, * k2 tog, k10; rep from 6 times, k2 tog, k14.

2nd row: K.

3rd row: K1, * k2 tog, k9 rep from * 6 times, k2 tog, k13.

Cont to dec in this way, working 1 st less between decs on every alt row until 21 sts rem. K 1 row.

Next row: K1, (k2 tog) to end.

Break yarn; thread through rem sts; draw up and fasten off.

TO MAKE UP

Using a small backstitch join seam, leaving 2 ins (5.1 cm) open at outer edge. Thread ribbon through first row of holes of patt.

◆
Bootees

With No. 11 needles cast on 40 sts and k 2 rows then work in patt as follows:

1st row: K4, (yfwd, k2 tog, k4) to end.

2nd to 6th rows: K.

7th row: K1, (yfwd, k2 tog, k4) to last 3 sts, yfwd, k2 tog, k1.

A little poncho made in two pieces, joined and adorned with a fringe. For instructions, see page 44.
Photograph by Ian Morgan.

8th to 12th rows: K.

Rep above 12 rows once.

Next (ribbonhole) row: K1, (yfwd, k2 tog, k1) to end. K 1 row.

Next row: K26, turn.

Next row: K12, turn and work 20 rows in g st on these sts for instep. Break yarn.

Rsf, pick up and k 13 sts on side of instep, k across 12 instep sts, pick up and k 13 sts on other side of instep, then k rem sts (66 sts). Work 9 rows in g st.

Shape toe. Next row: K1, k2 tog, k29, (k2 tog) twice, k29, k2 tog, k1.

Next row: K30, (k2 tog) twice, k30.

Next row: K1, k2 tog, k26, (k2 tog) twice, k26, k2 tog, k1.

Next row: K27, (k2 tog) twice, k27.

Next row: K26, (k2 tog) twice, k26. Cast off.

TO MAKE UP
Using a small backstitch join leg and foot seams. Thread ribbon through ribbonholes and tie at front.

◆

Mitts

With No. 11 needles cast on 34 sts and k 2 rows, then work in patt as follows:

1st row: K4, (yfwd, k2 tog, k4) to end.

2nd to 6th rows: K.

7th row: K1, (yfwd, k2 tog, k4) to last 3 sts, yfwd, k2 tog, k1.

8th to 12th rows: K.

Rep 1st row of patt again, then work 10 rows in g st.

Next (ribbonhole) row: K2, (k2 tog, yfwd, k2) to end. K 2 rows.

Next (inc) row: K2, (k4, inc, k5) to last 2 sts, k2 (37 sts).

Work in g st for 2 ins (5.1 cm).

Shape top. Next row: K1, (k2 tog, k4) to end.

Next row: K.

Next row: K1, (k2 tog, k3) to end.

Cont to dec in this way, working 1 st less between decs until 7 sts rem.

Next row: K1, (k2 tog) 3 times.

Break yarn; thread through rem sts; draw up and fasten off.

To make up
Using a small backstitch join seam. Thread ribbon through ribbonholes and tie at front.

◆

Shawl

With No. 10 needles cast on 287 sts and work in g st for 10 rows, then cont in patt as follows:

1st row: K5, (yfwd, k2 tog, k4) to end.

2nd to 8th rows: K.

9th row: K8, (yfwd, k2 tog, k4) to last 3 sts, k3.

10th to 16th rows: K.

Rep above 16 rows until work measures approx 40 ¼ ins (102.2 cm), ending with 1st or 9th patt row.

K 10 rows to correspond with other edge, then cast off loosely.

◆

Yellow poncho

MATERIALS
6 balls of Patons Feathersoft 4 ply; a pair of No. 9 needles, crochet hook.

MEASUREMENTS
To fit 19 - 22 ins (48.3 - 55.9 cm) chest. Approx length from V of neck to front point, 12 ins (30.5 cm).

TENSION
6¼ sts to 1 in (2.54 cm).

ABBREVIATIONS
See page 15.

METHOD
Make two pieces.

With No. 9 needles cast on 58 sts and work in patt as follows:

1st row: (wrong side of work) K2, (p5, k2) to end.

2nd row: K2, (k2 tog, yfwd, k1, yfwd, k2 tog tbl, k2) to last 7 sts, k2 tog, yfwd, k1, yfwd. k2 tog tbl, k2.

Rep above 2 rows until work measures 16 ins (40.6 cm) ending on 2nd row.

Cast off in pattern.

TO MAKE UP
Using a flat seam join one narrow end of each strip to the long side of other strip.

FRINGE
Cut four 8 in (20.3 cm) lengths of yarn for each tassel and proceed as follows: with the wrong side of the edge to be fringed facing you, insert a crochet hook as near as possible to the edge, fold strands in half to form a loop, put loop on hook, pull through edge of work, place hook behind all strands of yarn and draw through loop. Cont along outer edge of poncho in this way at regular intervals. Finally, trim ends of fringing with scissors to neaten.

◆

Blue stocking and garter stitch bootees

MATERIALS
1 ball of Patons Feathersoft 4 ply; a pair of No. 10 needles; ¾ yd (0.70 m) ribbon.

MEASUREMENTS
Leg seam: 2½ ins (6.6 cm). Foot: 3 ins (7.6 cm).

Tension
7½ sts to 1 in (2.54 cm).

ABBREVIATIONS
See page 15.

METHOD
With No. 10 needles cast on 44 sts.

1st row: K.

2nd row: K3, inc, k14, inc, k6, inc, k14, inc, k3.

3rd row: K.

4th row: K4, inc, k14, inc, k8, inc, k14, inc, k4.

5th row: K.

A selection of baby's bootees worked in a variety of stitches. See the following pages for instructions. Photograph by Ian Morgan.

6th row: K5, inc, k14, inc, k10, inc, k14, inc, k5, (56 sts).

Work in g st for 18 rows.

Shape toe. Next row: K20, k2 tog tbl, k12, k2 tog, k20.

Next row: P20, p2 tog, p10, p2 tog tbl, p20.

Next row: K20, k2 tog tbl, k8, k2 tog, k20.

Next row: P20, p2 tog, p6, p2 tog tbl, p20.

Next row: K20, k2 tog tbl, k4, k2 tog, k20.

Next row: P20, p2 tog, p2, p2 tog tbl, p20.

Next row: K20, k2 tog tbl, k2 tog, k20 (42 sts). P1 row.

Next (ribbonhole) row: K2, (yfwd, k2 tog) to last 2 sts, k2. Work in g st for 16 rows, then cast off.

TO MAKE UP

Using a small backstitch join leg and foot seams. Thread ribbon through ribbonholes and tie at front.

◆
Blue garter stitch bootees

MATERIALS
1 ball Patons Feathersoft 4 ply; a pair of No. 11 needles; 3/4 yd (0.70 m) ribbon.

MEASUREMENTS
Leg seam: 3 ins (7.6 cm). Foot: 3½ ins (8.9 cm).

TENSION
8 sts to 1 in (2.54 cm).

ABBREVIATIONS
See page 15.

METHOD
With No. 11 needles cast on 45 sts.

1st row: K.

2nd row: (Inc, k20, inc) twice, k1.

3rd row: K.

4th row: (Inc, k22, inc) twice, k1.

5th row: K.

6th row: (Inc, k24, inc) twice, k1.

Cont in g st and inc as above on every alt row to 69 sts, then work straight in g st for 11 rows.

Shape toe. Next row: K40, k2 tog, turn.

Next row: K12, k2 tog, turn.

Rep above row until 45 sts rem.

K 2 rows.

Next (ribbonhole) row: (K1, yfwd, k2 tog) to end.

Cont in g st for 30 rows, then cast off.

TO MAKE UP
Using a small backstitch join leg and foot seams. Thread ribbon through ribbonholes and tie at front.

◆

Yellow stocking stitch bootees with reversed stocking stitch cuff

MATERIALS
1 ball of Patons Feathersoft 4 ply; a pair of No. 11 needles; ¾ yd (0.70 m) ribbon.

MEASUREMENTS
Leg seam: 3 ins (7.6 cm) (with cuff). Foot: 3½ ins (8.9 cm).

TENSION
8 sts to 1 in (2.54 cm).

ABBREVIATIONS
See page 15.

METHOD
With No. 11 needles cast on 43 sts.

1st row: (Inc, k19, inc) twice, k1.

2nd row: P.

3rd row: (Inc, k21, inc) twice, k1.

4th row: P.

5th row: (Inc, k23, inc) twice, k1.

6th row: P.

7th row: (Inc, k25, inc) twice, k1.

8th row: P.

9th row: K.

Rep 9th and 10th rows twice, then begin shaping:

Next row: K34, sl1, k1, psso, turn.

Next row: P10, p2 tog, turn.

Next row: K10, sl1, k1, psso, turn.

Rep above 2 rows 8 times.

Next row: P10, p2 tog turn.

Next row: K.

Next row: P.

Next (ribbonhole) row: K2, (yfwd, k2 tog) to last st, k1.

Beg p row, cont in st st for 3 ins (7.6 cm), then cast off.

TO MAKE UP
Using a small backstitch join leg and foot seams. Thread ribbon through ribbonholes. Turn st st over to wrong side and form cuff as pictured.

◆

Yellow patterned bootees

MATERIALS
1 ball of Sirdar Wonderland Courtelle 3 ply; a pair of No. 12 needles; ¾ yd (0.70 m) ribbon.

MEASUREMENTS
Leg seam: 3 ins (7.6 cm). Foot: 3½ ins (8.9 cm).

TENSION
8 sts to 1 in (2.54 cm) over st st.

ABBREVIATIONS
See page 15.

METHOD
With No. 12 needles cast on 42 sts and work in patt:

1st row: K1, (yfwd, k2, k3 tog, k2, yfwd, k1) to last st, k1.

2nd row: P.

3rd row: As 1st row.

4th row: K.

Rep above 4 rows until work measures 2 ins (5.1 cm), ending on 4th row.

Next (ribbonhole) row: K1, (yfwd, k2 tog) to last st, k1. P 1 row.

Next row: K27, turn.

Next row: P12, turn and work 20 rows in st st on these sts for instep. Break yarn.

Rsf, pick up and k 13 sts on side of instep, k across

12 instep sts, pick up and k 13 sts on other side of instep, then k rem sts (68 sts). Beg p row, work in st st for 9 rows.

Shape toe. Next row: K1, k2 tog, k29, (k2 tog) twice, k29, k2 tog, k1.

Next row: P30, (p2 tog) twice, p30.

Next row: K1, k2 tog, k26, (k2 tog) twice, k26, k2 tog, k1.

Next row: P27, (p2 tog) twice, p27.

Next row: K26, (k2 tog) twice, k26. Cast off.

TO MAKE UP

Using a flat seam, join leg and foot seams. Thread ribbon through ribbonholes and tie at front.

◆

White lacy bootees

MATERIALS

1 ball Patons Feathersoft 4 ply; a pair of No. 11 needles, ¾ yd (0.70 m) ribbon.

MEASUREMENTS

Leg seam: 3¾ ins (8.9 cm). Foot: 3½ ins (8.9 cm).

TENSION

8 sts to 1 in (2.54 cm) over st st.

ABBREVIATIONS

See page 15.

METHOD

With No. 11 needles cast on 45 sts and k2 rows, then cont in patt:

1st row: K2, * yfwd, k2 tog tbl, k1, k2 tog, yfwd, k1; rep from * ending last rep with k2.

2nd row: K1, p2, * yfwd, p3 tog, yfwd, p3; rep from * ending last rep with p2, k1, instead of p3.

3rd row: K.

4th row: K1, * p1, p2 tog tbl, yrn, p1, yrn, p2 tog; rep from * to last 2 sts, p1, k1.

5th row: K1, k2 tog, * yfwd, k3, yfwd, k3 tog; rep from * to last 6 sts, yfwd, k3, yfwd, k2 tog tbl, k1.

6th row: P.

Rep above 6 rows 3 times.

Next (dec) row: (K10, k2 tog) to last 9 sts, k9 (42

sts). K 1 row.

Next (ribbonhole) row: K1, (yfwd, k2 tog) to last st, k1.

K 1 row.

Next row: K28, turn.

Next row: P14, turn and work 20 rows in st st on these 14 sts for instep. Break yarn.

Next row: Rsf, pick up and k 11 sts on side of instep, k across 14 instep sts, then pick up and k 11 sts on other side of instep, k rem sts (64 sts).

Beg p row, work 8 rows in st st.

Shape toe. Next row: K1, k2 tog tbl, k21, k2 tog tbl, k12, k2 tog, k21, k2 tog, k1.

Next row: P.

Next row: K1, k2 tog tbl, k20, k2 tog tbl, k10, k2 tog, k20, k2 tog, k1.

Next row: P.

Next row: K1, k2 tog tbl, k19, k2 tog tbl, k8, k2 tog, k19, k2 tog, k1.

Next row: P.

Cast off.

TO MAKE UP

Using a flat seam join leg and foot seams. Thread ribbon through ribbonholes and tie at front.

◆

White bootees in bell stitch design

MATERIALS

1 ball of Sirdar Wonderland Courtelle 3 ply; a pair of No. 12 needles; ¾ yd (0.70 m) ribbon.

MEASUREMENTS

Leg seam: 3¾ ins (9.5 cm). Foot 3½ ins (8.9 cm).

TENSION

8 sts to 1 in (2.54 cm) over st st.

ABBREVIATIONS

See page 15.

METHOD

With No. 11 needles cast on 41 sts and k3 rows, then cont in patt:

1st row: K4, (p2, k1, p2, k3, yfwd, sl1, k2 tog, psso, yfwd, k3) to last 9 sts, p2, k1, p2, k4.

2nd row: P4, (k2, p1, k2, p9) to last 9 sts, k2, p1, k2, p4.

3rd row: As 1st row.

4th row: As 2nd row.

5th row: As 1st row.

6th row: As 2nd row.

7th row: K2 tog, k2, yrn, (p2, k1, p2, yon, k3, sl1, k2 tog, psso, k3, yrn) to last 9 sts, p2, k1, p2, yon, k2, k2 tog.

8th row: P2 tog, p1, yon, (k3, p1, k3, yrn, p2, p3 tog, p2, yon) to last 10 sts, k3, p1, k3, yrn, p1, p2 tog.

9th row: K2 tog, yrn, (p4, k1, p4, yon, k1, sl1, k2 tog, psso, k1, yrn) to last 11 sts, p4, k1, p4, yon, k2 tog.

10th row: K6, p1, k5, (yrn, p3 tog, yon, k5, p1, k5) to last st, k1.

11th row: P2, (k3, yfwd, sl1, k2 tog, psso, yfwd, k3, p2, k1, p2) to last 11 sts, k3, yfwd, sl1, k2 tog, psso, yfwd, k3, p2.

12th row: K2, (p9, k2, p1, k2) to last 11 sts, p9, k2.

13th row: As 11th row.

14th row: As 12th row.

15th row: As 11th row.

16th row: As 12th row.

17th row: P2, (yon, k3, sl1, k2 tog, psso, k3, yrn, p2, k1, p2) to last 11 sts, yon, k3, sl1, k2 tog, psso, k3, yrn, p2.

18th row: K3, (yrn, p2, p3 tog, p2, yon, k3, p1, k3) to last 10 sts, yrn, p2, p3 tog, p2, yon, k3.

19th row: (P4, yon, k1, sl1, k2 tog, psso, k1, yrn, p4, k1) to last 13 sts, p4, yon, k1, sl1, k2 tog, psso, k1, yrn, p4.

20th row: (K5, yrn, p3 tog, yon, k5, p1) to last 13 sts, k5, yrn, p3 tog, yon, k5, inc (42 sts).

Next (ribbonhole) row: K1, (yfwd, k2 tog) to last st, k1. P 1 row.

Next row: K27, turn.

Next row: P12, turn and work 20 rows in st st on these sts for instep. Break yarn.

Rsf, pick up and k 13 sts on side of instep, k across 12 instep sts, pick up and k 13 sts on other side of instep, then k rem sts (68 sts). Beg p row, work in st st for 9 rows.

Shape toe. Next row: K1, k2 tog, k29, (k2 tog) twice, k29, k2 tog, k1.

Next row: P30, (p2 tog) twice, p30.

Next row: K1, k2 tog, k26, (k2 tog) twice, k26, k2 tog, k1.

Next row: P27, (p2 tog) twice, p27.

Next row: K26, (k2 tog) twice, k26.

Cast off.

TO MAKE UP
Using a flat seam, join leg and foot seams. Thread ribbon through ribbonholes and tie at front.

◆

Rosebud loop stitch bootees

MATERIALS
1 ball of Sirdar Wonderland Courtelle 4 ply; a pair of No. 12 needles; ¾ yd (0.70 m) ribbon.

MEASUREMENTS
Leg seam: 2 ins (5.1 cm). Foot: 3½ ins (8.9 cm).

TENSION
7½ sts to 1 in (2.54 cm) over st st.

ABBREVIATIONS
See page 15.

METHOD
With No. 10 needles cast on 36 sts and work in loop patt as follows:

1st row: K.

2nd row: K1, (wind yarn over needle and first finger, then over needle only, draw through st, place loops back on left needle and k in usual way) to last st, k1.

Rep above 2 rows until work measures 1 in (2.54 cm), ending on 2nd row.

Next (ribbonhole) row: K1, (yfwd, k2 tog) to last st, k1. P 1 row.

Next row: K24, turn.

Next row: P12, turn. Rep 1st and 2nd rows of loop patt on these 12 sts until 18 rows have been worked. Break yarn.

Next row: Rsf, pick up and k 12 sts on side of instep, k across 12 instep sts, pick up and k 12 sts on other side of instep, then k rem sts (60 sts).

Beg p row, work 9 rows in st st.

Shape toe. Next row: K1, k2 tog, k25, (k2 tog) twice, k25, k2 tog, k1.

Next row: P2 tog, p to last 2 sts, p2 tog.

Next row: K1, k2 tog, k22, (k2 tog) twice, k22, k2 tog, k1.

Next row: P23, (p2 tog) twice, p23.

Next row: K1, k2 tog, k19, (k2 tog) twice, k19, k2 tog, k1.

Cast off.

TO MAKE UP
Using a flat seam, join leg and foot seams. Thread ribbon through ribbonholes and tie at front.

◆

Rosebud patterned bootees

MATERIALS
1 ball of Sirdar Wonderland Courtelle 3 ply; a pair of No. 12 needles; ¾ yd (0.70 m) ribbon.

MEASUREMENTS
Leg seam: 3 ins (7.6 cm). Foot: 3¼ ins (8.3 cm).

TENSION
8 sts to 1 in (2.54 cm) over st st.

ABBREVIATIONS
See page 15.

METHOD
With No. 12 needles cast on 35 sts and work in g st for 5 rows, then cont in patt:

1st row: K2, * yfwd, (k1, k2 tog) twice, k1, yfwd, k1; rep from * to last st, k1.

2nd and alt rows: P.

3rd row: As 1st row.

5th row: K2, * k2 tog, k1, (yfwd, k1) twice, k2 tog,

k1; rep from * to last st, k1.

7th row: As 5th row.

8th row: P.

Rep above 8 rows once more.

Next (ribbonhole) row: K3, (yfwd, k2 tog, k2) to end.

Next row: P and inc 1 st at beg of row (36 sts).

Next row: K24, turn.

Next row: P12, turn and work 15 rows in st st on these sts for instep. Break yarn.

Next row: Rsf, pick up and k12 sts on side of instep, k across 12 instep sts, pick up and k 12 sts on other side of instep, then k rem sts (60 sts).

Work in g st for 14 rows.

Shape toe. Next row: K1, k2 tog, k24, k2 tog, k2, k2 tog, k24, k2 tog, k1.

Next row: K.

Next row: K1, k2 tog, k22, k2 tog, k2, k2 tog, k22, k2 tog, k1.

Cont to dec as above on every foll alt row until 44 sts rem, then cast off.

TO MAKE UP
Using a flat seam join leg and foot seams. Thread ribbon through ribbonholes and tie at front.

◆

Crew neck sweater

MATERIALS
17 (18, 18, 19) balls of Villawool Derwent 8 ply; a pair of Nos. 7 and 9 needles.

MEASUREMENTS
To fit 34 (36, 38, 40) in [86.4 (91.4, 96.5, 101.5) cm] chest. Length, 24 (24 ½, 25, 25½) ins [61 (62, 63.5, 64) cm]. Sleeve, 17 (18, 18, 19) ins [43 (45.7, 45.7, 48.3) cm] (or length required).

TENSION
5 sts to 1 in (2.54 cm).

ABBREVIATIONS
See page 15.

BACK
With No. 9 needles cast on 94 (98, 102, 106) sts and

work in patt as follows:

1st row: (K2, p2) to last 2 sts, k2.

2nd row: P.

Rep above 2 rows until work measures 4 ins (10.2 cm). Change to No. 7 needles and cont in patt until work measures 16 (16, 16, 17) ms [40.6 (40.6, 40.6, 43) cm], ending on wrong side.

Shape armholes. Cast off 6 sts at beg of next 2 rows, then dec 1 st each end of every foll row until 70 (74, 78, 82) sts rem. Cont straight until armholes measure 8 (8½, 9, 9½) ins [20.3 (21.6, 22.9, 24.1) cm], ending on wrong side.

Shape shoulders. Cast off 6 sts at beg of next 6 rows, then 4 (5, 6, 7) sts at beg of foll 2 rows. Leave rem 26 (28, 30, 32) sts on a holder.

FRONT

Work as given for Back until armholes measure 6 (6½, 7, 7½) ins [15.2 (16.5, 17.8, 19.1) cm].

Shape neck. Next row: Patt 27 (28, 29, 30) sts, turn and cont on these sts only. Dec 1 st at neck edge of next row and every foll alt row until 22 (23, 24, 25) sts rem. Cont straight until armhole measures same as Back armhole, ending at side edge.

Shape shoulder. Cast off 6 sts at beg of next row and foll 2 alt rows. Work 1 row, then cast off rem sts.

Return to rem sts. Place middle 16 (18, 20, 22) sts on a holder. Rejoin yarn to inner end of rem sts and work to correspond with other side.

SLEEVES

With No. 9 needles cast on 42 (42, 46, 46) sts and work in patt as given for Back for 2 ins (5.1 cm). Change to No. 7 needles and cont in patt, inc 1 st each end of next row and every foll 8th row to 66 (70, 74, 78) sts. Cont straight until work measures 17 (18, 18, 19) ins [43 (45.7, 45.7, 48.3) cm] (or length required). Cast off 6 sts at beg of next 2 rows, then dec 1 st at beg of every foll row until 28 sts rem. Cast off 2 sts at beg of next 6 rows, then cast off rem sts.

NECKBAND

First, join right shoulder seam. Rsf, with No. 9 needles pick up and k 18 sts down left front neck, k across middle 16 (18, 20, 22) sts, pick up and k 18 sts

up right side of neck and, finally, k across sts at back neck (78, 82, 86, 90 sts). Work in k2, p2 rib for 3 ins (7.6 cm), then cast off ribwise.

TO MAKE UP

Join rem shoulder seam and neckband end. Join side and sleeve seams. Set in sleeves. Lightly press seams.

◆

Child's school sweater

MATERIALS

11 (11, 12, 12, 13, 13) balls of Villawool Machinewash 5 ply; a pair of Nos. 10 and 12 needles; a set of 4 double-pointed No. 12 needles.

MEASUREMENT

To fit 26 (28, 30, 32, 34, 36) in [66.4 (71.2, 76.2, 81.3, 86.4, 91.4) cm] chest. Length, 16½ (17, 18½, 19½, 20½, 21½) ins [42 (44.5, 47, 49.5, 52.1, 54.6) cm]. Sleeve, 12½ (13½, 14½, 15½, 16½, 17½) ins [31.2 (34.3, 36, 39.3, 41, 44) cm] (or length required).

TENSION

7 sts to 1 in (2.54 cm).

ABBREVIATIONS

See page 15.

BACK

With No. 12 needles cast on 94 (102, 110, 118, 126, 134) sts and work in k1 p1 rib for 2 (2, 2, 3, 3, 3) ins [5.1 (5.1, 5.1, 7.6, 7.6, 7.6) cm]. Change to No. 10 needles and cont in st st until work measures 10 (10½, 11, 11½, 12, 12½) ins [25.4 (26.7, 28, 29.2, 30.5, 31.8) cm], ending on p row.

Shape raglan. Cast off 3 (4, 5, 6, 7, 8) sts at beg of next 2 rows **.

Next row: K2, k2 tog, k to last 4 sts, k2 tog tbl, k2.

Next row: K2, p to last 2 sts, k2.

Rep above 2 rows until 28 (30, 32, 34, 36, 38) sts rem. Leave sts on a holder.

FRONT

Work as given for Back to **.

Opposite: For sweaters made by machine, a weaving pattern enhances an otherwise simple garment.
© Courtesy Brother Industries.

Shape neck. Next row: K2, k2 tog, k40 (43, 46, 49, 52, 55), turn and cont on these sts only. Work as follows:

1st row: P2 tog, p to last 2 sts, k2.

2nd row: K2, k2 tog, k to end.

3rd row: P to last 2 sts, k2.

4th row: K2, k2 tog, k to end.

Rep above 4 rows until 13 (14, 15, 16, 17, 18) decs at neck edge altogether have been worked, then cont to dec at raglan edge only as set until 2 sts rem. K2 tog and fasten off.

Return to sts on needle. Rejoin yarn to inner end of rem sts and work as follows:

1st row: K to last 4 sts, k2 tog tbl, k2.

2nd row: K2, p to last 2 sts, p2 tog.

3rd row: K to last 4 sts, k2 tog tbl, k2.

4th row: K2, p to end.

Now cont to correspond with other side.

SLEEVES

With No. 12 needles cast on 46 (48, 50, 52, 54, 56) sts and work in k1, p1 rib for 3 ins (7.6 cm).

Next (inc) row: Rib 5 (1, 2, 3, 4, 5), [inc, rib 3 (4, 4, 4, 4, 4)] 10 times, inc, rib to end (56, 58, 60, 62, 64, 66 sts).

Change to No. 10 needles and cont in st st, inc 1 st each end of 3rd row, then every foll 10th (9th, 8th, 7th, 7th, 7th) row to 72 (78, 84, 90, 96, 102) sts. Cont straight until work measures 12½ (13½, 14½, 15½, 16½, 17½) ins [31.8 (34.3, 36, 39, 41, 44) cm] (or length required), ending on p row.

Cast off 3 (4, 5, 6, 7, 8) sts at beg of next 2 rows.

Next row: K2, k2 tog, k to last 4 sts, k2 tog tbl, k2.

Next row: K2, p to last 2 sts, k2.

Rep above 2 rows until 6 sts rem. Leave sts on holder.

NECKBAND

First, join raglan seams. Rsf, with set of No. 12 needles, pick up and k 58 (60, 62, 64, 66, 68) sts down left side of neck, 1 middle st, pick up and k 58 (60, 62, 64, 66, 68) sts up right side of neck, k

across 6 sts on holder, then sts at back of neck and, finally, 6 sts of second sleeve (157, 163, 169, 175, 181, 187 sts). Work 6 (6, 8, 8, 10, 10) rounds in k1, p1 rib, dec 1 st either side of middle V st on every row, thus: k2 tog tbl, work middle st, k2 tog. Cast off ribwise.

TO MAKE UP

Press work on the wrong side. Join side and sleeve seams. Press seams

◆

Lady's sweater

(See opposite.)

MATERIALS

Patons Bluebell 5 ply yarn 50 g balls;

Long sleeves: 12 (12, 12, 13, 13, 13)

Short sleeves: 10 (10, 10, 11, 11, 11)

Needles: Millward 1 pair each 3.75 mm (No. 9) and 3.00 mm (No. 11) or sizes needed to give correct tension.

Accessories: 6 buttons, shoulder pads.

MEASUREMENTS

This garment is designed to be a generous fit, and should be worn with shoulder pads.

To fit 75 (80, 85, 90, 95, 100) cm bust.

Length 95 (99, 103, 107, 111, 115) cm.

Long sleeve 43 (43, 43, 43, 43, 43) cm or length desired.

Short sleeve 8 (8, 9, 9, 10, 10) cm or length desired.

TENSION

26.5 sts to 10 cm in width over stocking st.

FIRST — CHECK YOUR TENSION. Please check your tension carefully. If less sts use smaller needles, if more sts use bigger needles.

ABBREVIATIONS

"Dec 3B" = Slip next 3 sts onto cable needle and hold at back of work, (knit tog 1 st from needle and 1 st from cable needle) 3 times; "Dec 3F" = Slip next 3 sts

Opposite: A hand-knitted lady's sweater with a delicate lace pattern (see pages 52-60 for instructions). Photo courtesy Coats Patons.

onto cable needle and hold at front of work, (knit tog 1 st from cable needle and 1 st from needle) 3 times. "M1" = pick up loop which lies before next st, place on left-hand needle and knit into back of it.

BACK
Using 3.00 mm needles, cast on 117 (123, 129, 133, 139, 145) sts.

1st row: K2, * p1, k1, rep from * to last st, k1.

2nd row: K1, * p1, k1, rep from * to end.

Rep 1st and 2nd rows 15 times, inc 10 sts evenly across last row ...127 (133, 139, 143, 149, 155) sts (32 rows rib in all).

Change to 3.75 mm needles.

1st row: K5 (8, 11, 13, 16, 19), * k2 tog, yfwd, k1, yfwd, sl1, k1, psso, k11, rep from * ending last rep with k5 (8, 11, 13, 16, 19) instead of k11.

2nd and alt rows: Purl.

3rd row: K4 (7, 10, 12, 15, 18), * k2 tog, yfwd, k3, yfwd, sl1, k1, psso, k9, rep from * ending last rep with k4 (7, 10, 12, 15, 18) instead of k9.

5th row: K3 (6, 9, 11, 14, 17), * (k2 tog, yfwd) twice, k1, (yfwd, sl1, k1, psso) twice, k7, rep from * ending last rep with k3 (6, 9, 11, 14, 17) instead of k7.

7th row: K2 (5, 8, 10, 13, 16), *(k2 tog, yfwd) twice k3, (yfwd, sl1, k1, psso) twice k5, rep from * ending last rep with k2 (5, 8, 10, 13, 16) instead of k5.

9th row: K1 (4, 7, 9, 12, 15), * (k2 tog, yfwd) 3 times, k1, (yfwd, sl1, k1, psso) 3 times, k3, rep from ending last rep with k1 (4, 7, 9, 12, 15) instead of k3.

11th row: As 7th row.

13th row: As 5th row.

15th row: As 3rd row.

17th row: As 1st row.

19th row: K6 (9, 12, 14, 17, 20), * k2 tog, yfwd, k14, rep from * ending last rep with k7 (10, 13, 15, 18, 21) instead of k14.

21st row: K13 (16, 19, 5, 8, 11), * k2 tog, yfwd, k1, yfwd, sl1, k1, psso, k11, rep from * ending last rep with k13 (16, 19, 5, 8, 11) instead of k11.

23rd row: K12 (15, 18, 4, 7, 10), * k2 tog, yfwd, k3, yfwd, sl1, k1, psso, k9, rep from * ending last rep with k12 (15, 18, 4, 7, 10) instead of k9.

25th row: K11 (14, 17, 3, 6, 9), * (k2 tog, yfwd) twice, k1, (yfwd, sl1, k1, psso) twice, k7, rep from * ending last rep with k11 (14, 17, 3, 6, 9) instead of k7.

27th row: K10 (13, 16, 2, 5, 8), * (k2 tog, yfwd) twice, k3, (yfwd, sl1, k1, psso) twice, k5, rep from * ending last rep with k10 (13, 16, 2, 5, 8) instead of k5.

29th row: K9 (12, 15, 1, 4, 7), * (k2 tog, yfwd) 3 times, k1, (yfwd, sl1, k1, psso) 3 times, k3, rep from * ending last rep with k9 (12, 15, 1, 4, 7) instead of k3.

31st row: As 27th row.

33rd row: As 25th row.

35th row: As 23rd row.

37th row: As 21st row.

39th row: K14 (17, 20, 6, 9, 12), * k2 tog, yfwd, k14, rep from * ending last rep with k15 (18, 21, 7, 10, 13) instead of k14.

40th row: Purl.

Cont in st st until work measures 41 cm from beg, ending with a purl row.

Shape raglan armholes: Cast off 2 (2, 4, 2, 2, 4) sts at beg of next 2 rows. Work a further 6 (4, 4, 2, 2, 2) rows st st.

Next row: K1, Dec 3B, knit to last 7 sts, Dec 3F, k1.

Sizes 14, 16, and 18 only: Dec (as before) at each end of foll 4th rows until (127, 115, 129) sts rem.

All sizes: Dec (as before) at each end of foll 6th rows until 39 (39, 41, 43, 43, 45) sts rem. Work 1 row. Cast off.

LEFT FRONT
Using 3.00 mm needles, cast on 57 (61, 63, 65, 69, 71) sts.

Opposite: The delicate patterns used for some women's garments can also be produced in machine knitting. Here is a sample of lace stitch. © Courtesy Brother Industries.

Work 32 rows rib as for back, inc 6 (5, 6, 6, 5, 6) sts evenly across last row ... 63 (66, 69, 71, 74, 77) sts.

Change to 3.75 mm needles. **

1st row: K5 (8, 11, 13, 16, 19), * k2 tog, yfwd, k1, yfwd, sl1, k1, psso, k11, rep from * ending last rep with k5 instead of k11.

2nd and alt rows: Purl.

3rd row: K4 (7, 10, 12, 15, 18), * k2 tog, yfwd, k3, yfwd, sl1, k1, psso, k9, rep from * ending last rep with k4 instead of k9.

5th row: K3 (6, 9, 11, 14, 17), * (k2 tog, yfwd) twice, k1, (yfwd, sl1, k1, psso) twice, k7, rep from * ending last rep with k3 instead of k7.

7th row: K2 (5, 8, 10, 13, 16), * (k2 tog, yfwd) twice, k3, (yfwd, sl1, k1, psso) twice, k5, rep from * ending last rep with k2 instead of k5.

9th row: K1 (4, 7, 9, 12, 15), * (k2 tog, yfwd) 3 times, k1, (yfwd, sl1, k1, psso) 3 times, k3, rep from * ending last rep with k1 instead of k3.

11th row: As 7th row.

13th row: As 5th row.

15th row: As 3rd row.

17th row: As 1st row.

19th row: K6 (9, 12, 14, 17, 20), * k2 tog, yfwd, k14, rep from * ending last rep with k7 instead of k14.

21st row: K13 (16, 19, 5, 8, 11), * k2 tog, yfwd, k1, yfwd, sl1, k1, psso) k11, rep from * ending last rep with k13 instead of k11.

23rd row: K12 (15, 18, 4, 7, 10), * k2 tog, yfwd, k3, yfwd, sl1, k1, psso, k9, rep from * ending last rep with k12 instead of k9.

25th row: K11 (14, 17, 3, 6, 9), * (k2 tog, yfwd) twice, k1, (yfwd, sl1, k1, psso) twice, k7, rep from * ending last rep with k11 instead of k7.

27th row: K10 (13, 16, 2, 5, 8), * (k2 tog, yfwd) twice, k3, (yfwd, sl1, k1, psso) twice, k5, rep from * ending last rep with k10 instead of k5.

29th row: K9 (12, 15, 1, 4, 7), * (k2 tog, yfwd) 3 times, k1 (yfwd, sl1, k1, psso) 3 times, k3, rep from * ending last rep with k9 instead of k3.

31st row: As 27th row.

33rd row: As 25th row.

35th row: As 23rd row.

37th row: As 21st row.

39th row: K14 (17, 20, 6, 9, 12), * k2 tog, yfwd, k14, rep from * ending last rep with k15 instead of k14.

40th row: Purl.

Cont in st st until work measures same as Back to armholes, ending with a purl row.

Shape raglan armhole: Cast off 2 (2, 4, 2, 2, 4) sts at beg of next row. **

Work 1 row.

Shape front slope: Dec at end of next row.

Size 8 only: then in foll 4th row.

All sizes: Work 1 (3, 3, 1, 1, 1) row(s) st st.

Next row: K1, Dec 3B, knit to last 0 (2, 2, 0, 0, 0) sts, k0 (2, 2, 0, 0, 0) tog.

Sizes 14, 16, and 18 only: Dec (as before) at armhole edge in foll 4th row(s) (1, 4, 2) time(s),

AT SAME TIME Dec at front edge in foll 4th row from previous dec (1, 4, 2) time(s) ... (61, 52, 61) sts.

All sizes: Dec (as before) at armhole edge in foll 6th rows 5 (4, 6, 7, 5, 7) times, AT SAME TIME dec at front edge in foll 4th rows from previous dec 8 (6, 9, 11, 8, 11) times ... 33 (41, 33, 29, 29, 29) sts.

Dec (as before) at armhole edge in foll 6th rows 7 (9, 7, 6, 6, 6) times, AT SAME TIME dec at front edge in foll 6th rows 7 (9, 7, 6, 6, 6) times ... 5 sts.

Work 1 row.

Next row: K1, k2 tog, k2.

Next row: P4.

Next row: K1, k2 tog, k1.

Next row: P3.

Next row: K1, k2 tog.

Next row: P2, turn, k2 tog. Fasten off.

RIGHT FRONT
Work as for Left Front to **.

Detail of five ply sweater hand-knitted by Mrs E.A. Boschen.

1st row: K5, * k2 tog, yfwd, k1, yfwd, sl1, k1, psso, k11, rep from * ending last rep with k5 (8, 11, 13, 16, 19) instead of k11.

2nd and alt rows: Purl.

3rd row: K4, * k2 tog, yfwd, k3, yfwd, sl1, k1, psso, k9, rep from * ending last rep with k4 (7, 10, 12, 15, 18) instead of k9.

5th row: K3, * (k2 tog, yfwd) twice, k1, (yfwd, sl1, k1, psso) twice, k7, rep from * ending last rep with k3 (6, 9, 11, 14, 17) instead of k7.

7th row: K2, * (k2 tog, yfwd) twice, k3, (yfwd, sl1, k1, psso) twice, k5, rep from * ending last rep with k2 (5, 8, 10, 13, 16) instead of k5.

9th row: K1, * (k2 tog, yfwd) 3 times, k1, (yfwd, sl1 k1, psso) 3 times, k3, rep from * ending last rep with k1 (4, 7, 9, 12, 15) instead of k3.

11th row: As 7th row.

13th row: As 5th row.

15th row: As 3rd row.

17th row: As 1st row.

19th row: K6, * k2 tog, yfwd, k14, rep from * ending last rep with k7 (10, 13, 15, 18, 21) instead of k14.

21st row: K13, * k2 tog, yfwd, k1, yfwd, sl1, k1, psso, k11, rep from * ending last rep with k13 (16, 19, 5, 8, 11) instead of k11.

23rd row: K12, * k2 tog, yfwd, k3, yfwd, sl1, k1, psso, k9, rep from * ending last rep with k12 (15, 18, 4, 7, 10) instead of k9.

25th row: K11, * (k2 tog, yfwd) twice, k1, (yfwd, sl1, k1, psso) twice, k7, rep from * ending last rep with k11 (14, 17, 3, 6, 9) instead of k7.

27th row: K10, * (k2 tog, yfwd) twice, k3, (yfwd, sl1, k1, psso) twice, k5, rep from * ending last rep with k10 (13, 16, 2, 5, 8) instead of k5.

29th row: K9, * (k2 tog, yfwd) 3 times, k1, (yfwd, sl1, k1, psso) 3 times, k3, rep from * ending last rep with k9 (12, 15, 1, 4, 7) instead of k3.

31st row: As 27th row.

33rd row: As 25th row.

35th row: As 23rd row.

37th row: As 21st row.

39th row: K14, * k2 tog, yfwd, k14, rep from * ending last rep with k15 (18, 21, 7, 10, 13) instead of k14.

40th row: Purl.

Cont in st st until work measures same as Back to armholes, working 1 extra row.

Shape raglan armhole: Cast off 2 (2, 4, 2, 2, 4) sts at beg of next row. ***

Shape front slope: Dec at beg of next row.

Size 8 only: then in foll 4th row.

All sizes: Work 1(3, 3, 1, 1, 1) row(s) st st.

Next row: K0 (2, 2, 0, 0, 0) tog, knit to last 7 sts, Dec 3F, k1.

Sizes 14, 16, and 18 only: Dec (as before) at armhole edge in foll 4th row(s) (1, 4, 2) time(s) AT SAME TIME dec at front edge in foll 4th row(s) from previous dec (1, 4, 2) time(s) ... (61, 52, 61) sts.

All sizes: Dec (as before) at armhole edge in foll 6th rows 5(4, 6, 7, 5, 7) times, AT SAME TIME dec at front edge in foll 4th rows from previous dec 8 (6, 9, 11, 8, 11) times ... 33 (41, 33, 29, 29, 29) sts.

Dec (as before) at armhole edge in foll 6th rows 7 (9, 7, 6, 6, 6) times, AT SAME TIME dec at front edge in foll 6th rows 7 (9, 7, 6, 6, 6) times ... 5 sts.

Work 1 row.

Next row: K2, sl1, k1, psso, k1.

Next row: P4.

Next row: K1, sl1, k1, psso, k1.

Next row: P3.

Next row: Sl1, k1, psso, k1.

Next row: P2, turn, k2 tog. Fasten off.

LONG SLEEVES
Using 3.00 mm needles, cast on 57 (57, 57, 59, 59, 59) sts.

Work 23 rows rib as for Back.

Opposite: A fine lace pattern made by machine.
© Courtesy Brother Industries.

24th row: Rib 6 (6, 2, 10, 8, 8), * inc in next st, rib 2 (2, 2, 1, 1, 1), rep from * to last 6 (6, 4, 11, 9, 9) sts, inc in next st, rib 5 (5, 3, 10, 8, 8) ... 73 (73, 75, 79, 81, 81) sts.

Change to 3.75 mm needles.

1st row: K10 (10, 11, 13, 14, 14), * k2 tog, yfwd, k1, yfwd, sl1, k1, psso, k11, rep from * ending last rep with k10 (10, 11, 13, 14, 14) instead of k11.

2nd row: Purl.

3rd row: K9 (9, 10, 12, 13, 13), * k2 tog, yfwd, k3, yfwd, sl1, k1, psso, k9, rep from * ending last rep with k9 (9, 10, 12, 13, 13) instead of k9.

4th row: Purl.

5th row: K2, M1, k6 (6, 7, 9, 10, 10), * (k2 tog, yfwd) twice, k1, (yfwd, sl1, k1, psso) twice, k7, rep from * ending last rep with k6 (6, 7, 9, 10, 10), M1, k2 instead of k7.

Work a further 35 rows patt as for Back, AT SAME TIME, working extra sts into st st, inc (as before) at each end of foll 6th (6th, 6th, 6th, 4th, 4th) rows until there are 85 (85, 87, 91, 95, 99) sts.

Size 16 only: then in foll 6th row ... 97 sts.

All sizes: Cont in st st, inc (as before) at each end of next and foll 8th (6th, 6th, 6th, 6th, 4th) rows until there are 99 (99, 109, 113, 119, 107) sts.

Sizes 10 and 18 only: then in foll (8th, 6th) rows until there are (105, 123) sts.

All sizes: Cont in st st until work measures 40 cm (or 3 cm less than desired length to allow for deep armhole) from beg, ending with a purl row.

Shape raglan: Cast off 2 (2, 4, 2, 2, 4) sts at beg of next 2 rows.

Work a further 6 (4, 4, 2, 2, 2) rows st st.

Next row: K1, Dec 3B, knit to last 7 sts, Dec 3F, k1.

Sizes 14,16, and 18 only: Dec (as before) at each end of foll 4th row(s) until (97, 85, 97) sts rem.

All sizes: Dec (as before) at each end of foll 6th rows until 11(11, 11, 13, 13, 13) sts rem.

Work 1 row. Cast off.

SHORT SLEEVES

Using 3.00 mm needles, cast on 71 (73, 79, 85, 87, 93) sts.

Work 11 rows rib as for Back.

12th row: Rib 4 (8, 6, 4, 4, 8), * inc in next st, rib 3 (2, 4, 6, 5, 6), rep from * to last 7 (8, 8, 4, 5, 8) sts, inc in next st, rib 6 (7, 7, 3, 4, 7) ... 87 (93, 93, 97, 101, 105) sts.

Change to 3.75 mm needles.

Work 4 rows st st.

5th row: K2, M1, knit to last 2 sts, M1, k2. Cont in st st, inc (as before) at each end of alt rows until there are 99 (105, 109, 113, 119, 123) sts.

Work 3 rows st st.

Shape raglan: As for Long Sleeves.

FRONT BAND

Using backstitch, join raglan seams, noting that tops of sleeves form part of neckline.

Using 3.00 mm needles, cast on 9 sts.

Work 4 rows rib as for Back.

**** 5th row: Rib 4, cast off 2 sts, rib 3.

6th row: Rib 3, cast on 2 sts, rib 4 ... buttonhole.

Work a further 16 rows rib.

Rep 5th and 6th rows once.

Work a further 40 rows rib. ****

Rep from **** to **** once, then 5th and 6th rows once.

Work a further 16 rows rib.

Rep 5th and 6th rows once ...

6 buttonholes.

Cont without further buttonholes until band is length required to fit (slightly stretched) along fronts and across back neck.

Cast off in rib.

TO MAKE UP

With a slightly damp cloth and warm iron, press lightly, taking care not to flatten patt. Using backstitch, join side and sleeve seams. Sew front band in position. Sew on buttons. Press seams. Insert shoulder pads.

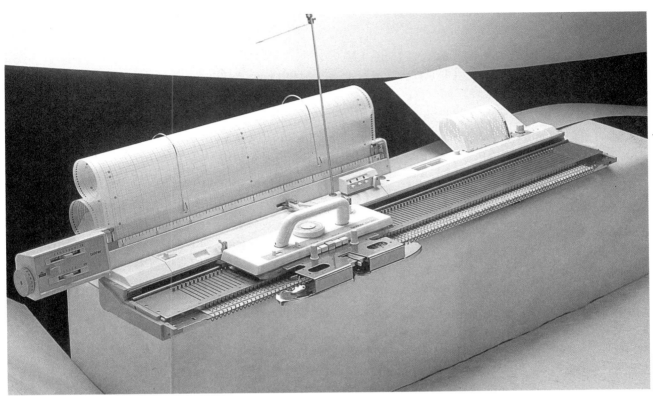

A modern knitting machine with a knit-leader attachment on top (the KL116). © Courtesy Brother Industries.

◆

His and hers Aran sweater

MATERIALS
16 (17, 18, 19, 20) balls of Villawool Machinewash 8 ply; a pair of Nos. 7 and 9 needles; 2 cable needles.

MEASUREMENTS
To fit 32 (34, 36, 38, 40) in [81.3 (86.4, 91.4, 96.5, 101.5) cm] bust/chest. Length, 22 (23, 24, 24½, 25 ½) ins [55.9 (58.5, 61, 62, 64) cm]. Sleeve, 17 (18, 18, 19, 19) ins [43 (45.7, 45.7, 48.3, 48.3) cm] (or length required).

TENSION
5½ to 1 in (2.54 cm) over st st.

ABBREVIATIONS
See page 15.

BACK
With No. 9 needles cast on 110 (114, 118, 122, 126) sts and work in k1 b, p1 rib for 2½ (2½, 2½, 3, 3) ins [6.4 (6.4, 6.4, 7.6, 7.6) cm].

Change to No. 7 needles and Aran patt:

1st row: (K1, p1) 0 (1, 2, 3, 4) times, * k1, (p1, c 4f) twice, p1, k1 **, p6, sl next st on cable needle and keep at back, sl next 2 sts on another cable needle and keep at front, k 2 sts, p1 from first cable needle, p 1 st, then k2 from second cable needle, p6; rep from * to ** once ***, p22, rep from * to *** once, (p1, k1) 0 (1, 2, 3, 4) times.

2nd row: (P1, k1) 0 (1, 2, 3, 4) times, * p1, k1, p4, k1, p4, k1, p1 **, k6, p2, k2, p2, k6; rep from * to ** once *** k1, (p3 tog, (k1, p1, k1) into next st) 5 times, k1; rep from * to *** once, (k1, p1) 0 (1, 2, 3, 4) times.

3rd row: (K1, p1) 0 (1, 2, 3, 4) times, * k1, p1, k4, p1, k4, p1, k1 **, p5, cr 2 over 1 b, p2, cr 2 over 1 f, p5; rep from * to ** once ***, p22; rep from * to *** once, (p1, k1) 0 (1, 2, 3, 4) times.

4th row: (P1, k1) 0 (1, 2, 3, 4) times, * p1, k1, p4, k1, p4, k1, p1 **, k5, p2, k4, p2, k5; rep from * to ** once ***, k1, ((k1, p1, k1) into next st, p3 tog) 5 times, k1; rep from * to *** once, (k1, p1) 0 (1, 2, 3, 4) times.

5th row: (K1, p1) 0 (1, 2, 3, 4) times, * k1, p1, k4, p1, k4, p1, k1 **, p4, cr 2 over 1 b, p4, cr 2 over 1 f, p4; rep from * to ** once ***, p22; rep from * to *** once, (p1, k1) 0 (1, 2, 3, 4) times.

6th row: (P1, k1) 0 (1, 2, 3, 4) times, * p1, k1, p4, k1, p4, k1, p1 **, k4, p2, k6, p2, k4; rep from * to ** once ***, k1, (p3 tog, (k1, p1, k1) into next st) 5 times, k1; rep from * to *** once, (k1, p1) 0 (1, 2, 3, 4) times.

7th row: (K1, p1) 0 (1, 2, 3, 4) times, * k1, (p1, c 4f) twice, p1, k1 **, p3, cr 2 over 1 b, p6, cr 2 over 1 f, p3; rep from * to ** once ***, p22, rep from * to *** once, (p1, k1) 0 (1, 2, 3, 4) times.

8th row: (P1, k1) 0 (1, 2, 3, 4) times, * p1, k1, p4, k1, p4, k1, p1 **, k3, p2, k8, p2, k3; rep from * to ** once ***, k1, ((k1, p1, k1) into next st, p3 tog) 5 times, k1; rep from * to *** once (k1, p1) 0 (1, 2, 3, 4) times.

9th row: (K1, p1) 0 (1, 2, 3, 4) times, * k1, p1 k4, p1, k4, p1, k1 **, p2, cr 2 over 1 b, p8, cr 2 over 1 f, p2; rep from * to ** once ***, p22; rep from * to *** once, (p1, k1) 0 (1, 2, 3, 4) times.

10th row: (P1, k1) 0 (1, 2, 3, 4) times, * p1, k1 p4, k1, p4, k1, p1 **, k2, p2, k10, p2, k2; rep from * to ** once ***, k1, (p3 tog, (k1, p1, k1) into next st) 5 times, k1; rep from * to *** once, (k1, p1) 0 (1, 2, 3, 4) times.

11th row: (K1, p1) 0 (1, 2, 3, 4) times, * k1, p1, k4, p1, k4, p1, k1 **, p1, cr 2 over 1 b, p10, cr 2 over 1 f, p1; rep from * to ** once ***, p22; rep from * to *** once, (p1, k1) 0 (1, 2, 3, 4) times.

12th row: (P1, k1) 0 (1, 2, 3, 4) times, * p1, k1, p4, k1, p4, k1, p1 **, k1, p2, k12, p2, k1, rep from * to ** once ***, k1 ((k1, p1, k1) into next st, p3 tog) 5 times, k1; rep from * to *** once, (k1, p1) 0 (1, 2, 3, 4) times.

13th row: (K1, p1) 0 (1, 2, 3, 4) times, * k1, (p1, c 4f) twice, p1, k1 **, p1, cr 2 over 1 f, p10, cr 2 over 1 b, p1; rep from * to ** once ***, p22; rep from * to *** once, (p1, k1) 0 (1, 2, 3, 4) times.

14th row: As 10th row.

15th row: (K1, p1) 0 (1, 2, 3, 4) times, * k1, pl, k4, p1, k4, p1, k1 **, p2, cr 2 over 1 f, p8, cr 2 over 1 b, p2; rep from * to ** once ***, p22; rep from * to *** once, (p1, k1) 0 (1, 2, 3, 4) times.

16th row: As 8th row.

17th row: (K1, p1) 0 (1, 2, 3, 4) times, * k1, p1, k4, p1, k4, p1, k1 **, p3, cr 2 over 1 f, p6, cr 2 over 1 b, p3; rep from * to ** once ***, p22; rep from * to *** once, (p1, k1) 0 (1, 2, 3, 4) times.

18th row: As 6th row.

19th row: (K1, p1) 0 (1, 2, 3, 4) times, * k1, (p1, c 4f) twice, p1, k1 **, p4, cr 2 over 1 f, p4, cr 2 over 1 b, p4; rep from * to ** once ***, p22; rep from * to *** once, (p1, k1) 0 (1, 2, 3, 4) times.

20th row: As 4th row.

21st row: (K1, p1) 0 (1, 2, 3, 4) times, * k1, p1, k4, p1, k4, p1, k1 **, p5, cr 2 over 1 f, p2, cr 2 over 1 b, p5; rep from * to ** once ***, p22; rep from * to *** once, (p1, k1) 0 (1, 2, 3, 4) times.

22nd row: As 2nd row.

23rd row: (K1, p1) 0 (1, 2, 3, 4) times, * k1, p1, k4, p1, k4, p1, k1 **, p6, cr 2 over 1 f, cr 2 over 1 b, p6; rep from * to ** once ***, p22; rep from * to *** once, (p1, k1) 0 (1, 2, 3, 4) times.

24th row: (P1, k1) 0 (1, 2, 3, 4) times, * p1, k1, p4, k1, p4, k1, p1 **, k7, p4, k7; rep from * to ** once ***, k1, ((k1, p1, k1) into next st, p3 tog) 5 times, k1; rep from * to *** once, (k1, p1) 0 (1, 2, 3, 4) times.

Rep above 24 rows until work measures 15 (16, 16½, 16½, 17) ins [38 (40, 41, 41, 43) cm], ending on wrong side.

Shape armholes: Cont in patt and cast off 3 (3, 4, 5, 6) sts at beg of next 2 rows, then dec 1 st each end of next row and every foll alt row until 96 (98, 100, 102, 104) sts rem. Cont straight until armholes measure 7 (7, 7½, 8, 8½) ins [17.8 (17.8, 19.1, 20.3, 21.6) cm], ending on wrong side.

Shape shoulders: Cast off 5 sts at beg of next 8 rows, then 5 (6, 6, 7, 7) sts at beg of foll 2 rows. Leave rem sts on a holder.

FRONT

Work as given for Back until armholes measure 5 (5,

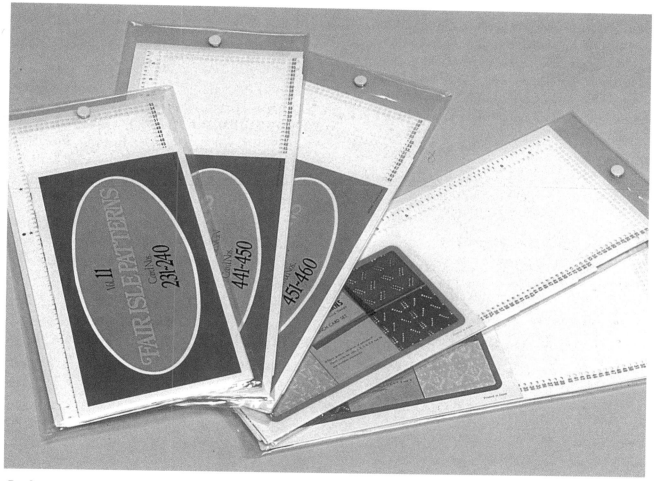

Predesigned punchcards for machine knitting. © Courtesy Brother Industries.

5½, 6, 6½) ins [12.7 (12.7, 14, 15.2, 16.5) cm], ending on wrong side.

Shape neck. Next row: Patt 38 (39, 39, 40, 40) sts, turn and cont on these sts only. Cast off 2 sts at neck edge on next row and foll alt row, then dec 1 st at same edge of every foll row until 25 (26, 26, 27, 27) sts rem. Cont straight until armhole measures same as Back armhole, ending at side edge.

Shape shoulders. Cast off 5 sts at beg of next and foll 3 alt rows. Work 1 row, then cast off rem sts.

Return to rem sts and sl middle 20 (20, 22, 22, 24) sts on a holder. Rejoin yarn to inner end and work to correspond with other side.

SLEEVES
With No. 9 needles cast on 52 (52, 52, 56, 56) sts and work in k1 b, p1 rib for 3 ins (7.6 cm). Change to No. 7 needles and Aran patt:

1st row: (K1, p1) 2 (2, 2, 3, 3) times, work from * to *** of patt once, (p1, k1) 2 (2, 2, 3, 3) times.

2nd row: (P1, k1) 2 (2, 2, 3, 3) times, work from * to *** of patt once, (k1 p1) 2 (2, 2, 3, 3) times.

Cont thus, omitting blackberry patt and working cable and diamond middle patt, inc 1 st each end of next row and every foll 6th row to 74 (76, 80, 82, 84) sts and taking the extra sts into the rib at each end. Cont straight until work measures 17 (18, 18, 19, 19) ins [43 (45.7, 45.7, 48.3, 48.3) cm] (or length required), ending on wrong side.

Cast off 3 (3, 4, 5, 6) sts at beg of next 2 rows, then dec 1 st each end of next 12 (10, 10, 8, 6) rows, then dec 1 st each end of every foll alt row until 48 sts rem. Cast off 3 sts at beg of next 2 rows, then 4 sts at beg of foll 2 rows. Cast off rem sts.

NECKBAND

First, join right shoulder seam. Rsf and with No. 9 needles, pick up and k 22 sts down left side of neck, k across 20 (20, 22, 22, 24) sts at middle front, pick up and k 22 sts up right side of neck and, finally, k across 46 (46, 48, 48, 50) sts at back neck (110, 110, 114, 114, 118 sts). Work in k1 b, p1 rib for 1½ ins (3.8 cm), then cast off ribwise.

TO MAKE UP

Join rem shoulder seam and neckband. Join side and sleeve seams. Set in sleeves. Press seams.

◆

Man's sweater

(See photograph page 65)

MEASUREMENTS

This garment is designed to be a generous fit in keeping with today's fashions.

Size		14	16	18	20	22	24
Fits chest	cm	90,	95,	100,	105,	110,	115.
	ins	36,	38,	40,	42,	44,	46.
Garment measures	cm	115,	119,	123,	127,	131,	135.
Length	cm	70,	70,	71,	71,	72,	72.
Sleeve	cm	48,	48,	48,	48,	48,	48

MATERIALS

Patons Totem 8 ply 50g balls. Quantity for the six sizes given: 25 25 26 27 27 28. Quantities are approximate as they vary between knitters. IMPORTANT! Use only the yarns specified for this garment. Other yarns may give unsatisfactory results.

ACCESSORIES

1 pair each 4.50mm (No 7) and 3.25mm (No 10) Milward Knitting Needles or sizes needed to give correct tension. A Cable Needle; 2 Stitch Holders.

ABREVIATIONS

"Cable B" = Slip next 3 sts on to cable needle and leave at back of work, K3, then K3 from cable needle; "Cable F" = Slip next 3 sts on to cable needle and leave at front of work, K3, then K3 from cable needle.

TENSION

21 sts and 28 rows to 10 cm over stocking st.

Check your tension carefully. If fewer sts, use smaller needles, if more sts, use bigger needles.

BACK

Using 3.25mm Needles, cast on 114 (118-126-130-134-138) sts.

1st row: K2, * P2, K2, rep from * to end.

2nd row: P2, * K2, P2, rep from * to end. Rep 1st and 2nd rows 13 times, then 1st row once. 30th row - Rib 9 (9-15-15-16-15), inc in each st to last 10 (10-14-14-16-15) sts, rib 10 (10-14-14-16-15) … 209 (217-223-231-236-246) sts. (NOTE - If this number of sts will not fit comfortably on needle, we suggest using a circular needle.) Change to 4.50mm Needles.

NOTE - This instruction has been written specifically for the stitch pattern given. Using any other stitch may result in a garment which is the wrong shape or size.

1st row: K1 (5-8-12-1-6), * P2, K2, P2, K6, P2, K2, P2, K9, rep from * to last 19 (23-26-30-19-24) sts, P2, K2, P2, K6, P2, K2, P2, K1 (5-8-12-1-6).

2nd and alt rows: Knit all knit sts and purl all purl sts as they appear.

3rd row: K1 (5-8-12-1-6), * P2, K2, P2, "Cable B", P2, K2, P2, "Cable B", K3, rep from * to last 19 (23-26-30-19-24) sts, P2, K2, P2, "Cable B", P2, K2, P2, K1 (5-8-12-1-6).

5th row: As 1st row. 7th row - K1 (5-8-12-1-6), * P2, K2, P2, "Cable B", P2, K2, P2, K3, "Cable F", rep from * to last 19 (23-26-30-19-24) sts, P2, K2, P2, "Cable B", P2, K2, P2, K1 (5-8-12-1-6).

8th row: As 2nd row. Rows 1 to 8 incl form patt. Cont in patt until work measures 44 cm from beg, working last row on wrong side.

Shape armholes: Keeping patt correct, cast off 12 (14-15-17-18-21) sts at beg of next 2 rows … 185 (189-193-197-200-204) sts. ** Work a further 66 (66-70-70-72-72) rows patt.

Shape shoulders: Cast off 13 (13-13-13-14-14) sts firmly at beg of next 6 rows, then 12 (13-14-15-13-14) sts at beg of foll 2 rows. Leave rem 83 (85-87-89-90-92) sts on a stitch-holder.

Opposite: A man's sweater. For instructions see pages 64-7. Pattern and photo courtesy Coats Patons.

FRONT

Work as for Back to **. Work a further 42 (42-46-46-46-46) rows patt.

Shape neck: Next row - Patt 71 (73-75-76-77-79), turn. *** Cont on these 71 (73-75-76-77-79) sts. Dec at neck edge in every row until 51 (52-53-54-55-56) sts rem. Work a further 3 (2-1-1-3-2) row/s patt.

Shape shoulder: Cast off 13 (13-13-13-14-14) sts firmly at beg of next and alt rows 3 times in all. Work 1 row. Cast off. *** Slip next 43 (43-43-45-46-46) sts on to stitch-holder and leave. Join yarn to rem sts, patt to end. Rep from *** to ***, working 1 extra row before shoulder shaping.

SLEEVES

Using 3.25mm Needles, cast on 58 (58-58-62-62-62) sts. Work 29 rows rib as for Back. 30th row: Rib 13 (13-13-4-4-4), * inc in next st, rib 0 (0-0-1-1-1), rep from * to last 14 (14-14-4-4-4) sts, rib 14 (14-14-4-4-4) ... 89 sts. Change to 4.50mm Needles.

1st row: P1, * K6, P2, K2, P2, K9, P2, K2, P2, rep from * to last 7 sts, K6, P1.

2nd and alt rows: Knit all knit sts and purl all purl sts as they appear.

3rd row: P1, * "Cable B", P2, K2, P2, "Cable B", K3, P2, K2, P2, rep from * to last 7 sts, "Cable B", P1.

4th row: As 2nd row. Keeping patt correct as for Back, as placed in last 4 rows, and working extra sts into patt as they become available, inc at each end of next and foll 4th rows until there are 125 (125-119-119-113-113) sts, then in alt rows until there are 151 (151-157-157-163-163) sts. Work 3 rows patt. Tie a coloured thread at each end of last row to mark end of sleeve seam. Work a further 10 (12-12-14-16-18) rows patt to sew to sts cast off at armholes. Cast off.

COLLAR

Using back-stitch, join right shoulder seam. With right side facing and using 3.25mm Needles, knit up 31 (31-30-31-33-32) sts evenly along left side of neck, knit across front stitch-holder thus: K1 (3-1-1-0-2), * K2 tog, rep from * to end, knit up 31 (31-30-31-33-32) sts evenly along right side of neck, then knit across back stitch-holder thus: K1 (1-1-1-0-0), * K2 tog, rep from * to end ... 126 (126-126-130-134-134)

sts. Work in rib as for Back until work measures 18 cm from beg. Cast off loosely in rib.

TO MAKE UP

It is not recommended that you press this garment, owing to the textured pattern. Using back-stitch, join left shoulder seam. Join side and sleeve seams (reversing seam for ¾ of rib for cuff) to coloured threads. Sew in sleeves, placing rows above coloured threads to sts cast off at armholes. Fold collar in half on to wrong side and slip-stitch in position. Press seams lightly. Turn back cuffs.

MACHINE KNITTING

A knitting machine is a real investment; you can save time by knitting garments much more quickly than you could ever knit them by hand; it is a profitable hobby to knit for friends, neighbours and even boutiques, who often call for exclusive garments which you will be able to produce; and you save money by knitting everyday garments for your whole family.

With practice and perseverance, anyone can use a knitting machine. After your initial lesson, you must start knitting and keep going. The more you knit, the easier it will become.

First, knit garments from easy-to-follow patterns, then turn your own ideas into exclusive creations. By that time, knitting for you will have become a real pleasure, not only satisfying but definitely a money-saving hobby that gives the added enjoyment of being able to wear one of your own creations with pride.

◆

The invention of the knitting machine

The art of knitting is older than written history and probably originated when man knotted grasses to make nets, a far cry from the variety of fabrics knitting machines produce today. In early times, knitting was mainly considered a pastime for men. However, it was not long before women took over the major role, very much to the frustration of one particular gentleman, Mr William Lee, a clergyman from Nottingham, England. His complaint, way back in 1589, was that his wife paid more attention to her hand knitting than to him and in an effort to solve his

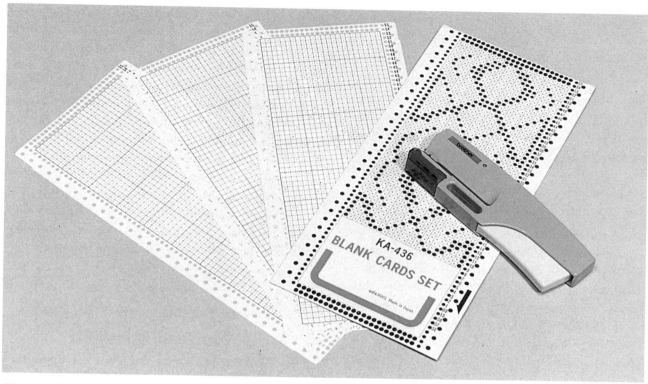

Blank cards and a puncher used to create individual designs for machine knits. © Courtesy Brother Industries.

problem he invented the first knitting machine. His idea was to turn knitting into an industry.

William Lee was unable to persuade Queen Elizabeth I or even her successor, James I of Scotland, to give him a patent for his invention, because they feared the economic effect the knitting machine would have on the livelihood of many women throughout England, who were hand knitting intricately patterned stockings which were the high fashion of those days. Even in France, William was unsuccessful and died without realizing his ambition. His brother James, however, returned to London and eventually, after many years' effort, established the hosiery industry in England.

Today not only hosiery but every other kind of garment has at one time or another been knitted on a machine or manufactured from knit fabric. The principle of William Lee's invention, the 'Knitting Frame', has not been changed and forms the basic principle of the highly developed warp knitting machines and the simple-to-use home knitters of today.

◆
Features of today's modern knitting machine

The knitting machine has become a must to many people who have found less and less time to produce the necessary garments for their families. The different knitting machines available today have their own special features and attachments. Before purchasing a knitter, you must consider what you will need from your machine as your experience and enthusiasm grows. Your basic requirements will be for a machine which will handle with ease the heavy yarns for the colder season as well as delicate cottons for warm summer days. You may also want a machine that will not only knit plain stocking stitch, but also beautiful, multi-coloured Fair Isle, lace patterns, cable stitch and Aran knitting.

It is important to choose the right machine: one that will give you the greatest versatility with the minimum amount of time-consuming effort on your part. The machine you choose should be light and easy to operate. It should knit textured patterns (tuck patterns) with just the touch of a button, knit multi-coloured Fair Isle patterns automatically.

There are many types of machines available today. The standard gauge knits from 2-ply to a fine 8-ply and the bulky or 'chunky' machine knits from 8-ply to 20-ply. Both types are available with either punchcard operated patterning devices or the more sophisticated built-in computer operated fully programmable types which have hundreds of built-in patterns in their memory.

Much machine lacemaking, up until a few years ago, consisted of lifting stitches by hand from one needle to another. The modern machine, which is able to knit real lace patterns quickly and efficiently with a lace carriage, is a must if you intend to use your machine fully. Most standard gauge machines now come with a lace carriage or have one available as an optional accessory.

One of the most popular accessories now available is the Garter carriage. This is manufactured by Brother Industries to fit all their later model knitting machines. This little wonder knits plain and purl on the main bed, knitting ribs just as easily as all combinations of plain and pearl to give Aran type designs, garter stitch, moss stitch, as well as being able to knit unaided as it chugs along by virtue of its inbuilt motor and negative row counter.

Another most important piece of equipment is a ribbing attachment. This can be purchased with the machine or at a later date. The ribbing attachment will enable you not only to vary your patterns considerably by giving you a choice of purl, as well as plain stitches for cable patterns and intricate Aran designs, but also to produce tight, neat rib bands.

You will not want to be packing and unpacking your machine continuously as you would when you have it set up on a table in the house. Therefore, you will need a good solid stand or table. One designed especially for the machine is always the most practical.

Take time to compare all the different brands of machines available. Ask for a demonstration and assure yourself that the machine will handle every weight of yarn and any type of pattern you may

desire. Make sure that free basic instruction as well as a regular supply of machine pattern books is regularly available. It is very important to purchase your machine from someone who can give after sales service, this means not only someone who can provide free lessons but who can also service your machine in the event that something goes wrong. With our new computerised machines they cannot be repaired by a handy person as the older, less sophisticated ones may have been. When you find the specialist who has the knitting machine with all these features and the after sales service to go with it, you may make your purchase with full confidence. In fact, you will be on your way to enjoying a very worthwhile and profitable hobby.

◆

Choosing the correct yarn for your garment

It is most important that you select the appropriate ply as well as the correct quality yarn for each garment you intend to make. For example, heavy wools make strong durable jumpers, but would be quite unsuitable for baby outfits. On the other hand, soft cuddly 3-ply wools would produce a flimsy ski jumper.

There are many wools and yarns available and these vary, not only in thickness but also in wearing and caring qualities. Imagine your disappointment when a nicely knitted lace jumper in cotton yarn is reduced to child size after the first wash. Or your smartest Fair Isle jacket is ruined because it was not dye-fast. Before you make each garment, consider the effort and time it will take to make and the wear and conditions it will be subjected to. You will then be able to choose the most suitable material, the wool or yarn of the correct thickness and quality to give your garment the longest life.

◆

Wool preparation

Knitting machine manufacturers have solved the problem of yarn tension by fitting an adjuster spring to the take-up rod, so that the yarn threaded through the spring is held with the same tension continuously, tight for thin yarn and loose for heavy yarns. Even with this adjustable tension you may still end up with loops at each end of the knitting or tight stitches in the centre of the row if the yarn does not feed into the adjuster spring evenly and without snags.

It is recommended that you knit from a cone or pre-wind your wool so that it can be drawn from the inside of the ball. In this way you can obtain the smoothest feed for your machine which will result in an even fabric being produced.

Some wools are already available wound on cones and still others are pre-waxed especially for use with home knitting machines. Waxing the wool prior to knitting is particularly important for 8-ply or double knitting wool. It smooths the fibres and binds them together. It also lubricates the yarn so that it moves through the needles more easily and helps to prevent needle breakage. If the yarn you choose has not been pre-waxed, rewind each ball, letting it run lightly over a piece of paraffin wax. A wool winder or a cone winder is available to make this operation simpler. Rewinding and pre-waxing is well worth the extra effort.

◆

Setting the size of your garment

You choose the number of stitches per row by selecting that number on needles forward from the 'out of work position' to the 'knitting position'. You also select the number of rows you knit with the aid of the row counter (r/c). However, the actual size of the garment will vary according to the tension to which you set the machine. You may like a nice tight tension for certain garments, while on others you may choose a loose tension for a bulky pattern. Therefore, to make sure that your garment turns out the right size with your choice of tensions, you must take that little extra time to knit your tension sample.

The tape measure becomes the main tool of trade. The measurements of the finished garment are always given in the knitting pattern and after making sure that those measurements are the ones you require, you should proceed to knit the following sample in the tension recommended for that yarn.

With the yarn you intend to use for your garment or the main yarn if your garment includes a

combination, knit a sample over 60 stitches for 60 rows with the tension recommended for that yarn. Let the knitting sample rest overnight or at least 6 hours to allow the yarn to 'pull back' to its original shape after being stretched across the machine in the knitting process. Once the sample has returned to the normal shape, you may count the number of stitches and rows you have over a square of 5 cm (2 inches by 2 inches) (diagram 53). It is necessary to tighten the tension if you have fewer stitches and fewer rows than the amount given under 'Tension' in your knitting pattern. If you have more stitches and more rows than the pattern states, loosen the tension.

The better knitting specialists can provide a gauge for measuring the tension sample. This consists of a 5 cm cut-out which when placed over the sample, makes checking the stitches and rows a simple operation.

After working out the right tension for your machine to give you the correct number of rows and stitches in the 5 cm square (2 in x 2 in), remember the tension number on your machine, as in the knitting pattern, that number is referred to as 'main tension' or 'tension for stocking stitch'. For ribbing, the tension can be varied according to the stretch required in the band, so try different tensions and use the one you prefer.

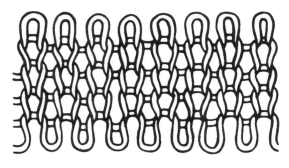

diagram 53

◆

Knitting from patterns or to your own designs

There is an interesting challenge in creating your own designs and patterns. However, hand knitting as well as machine knitting a garment is quite easy when you simply follow the instructions from the knitting pattern. Patterns can vary, but in all cases they will give you the number of stitches to cast on, the number of rows to knit and the point at which increasing and decreasing should take place.

Once you have perfected pattern knitting, before you know it you will be knitting your own designs. With a little experience, this will not be difficult. However at that stage you will realize the importance of the previously mentioned tension sample, because after taking the exact measurements for the garment you intend to knit, the number of stitches and rows have to be calculated. From your tension sample you will see how many stitches and rows you have to 5 cm. Simply multiply this by the measurement for the width and length of your intended garment and you will know the number of stitches and rows for the complete garment. The width of the shoulders and the depth of the armholes and neck will have to be calculated in the same way.

To illustrate these calculations, take as an example the back of a rib-finished jumper to fit a child with a 55 cm chest measurement. To make the jumper fit comfortably, we must knit it slightly larger than the actual chest measurement. This extra looseness can vary according to the thickness and style of the jumper, but a good average is 10 cm. This means that the measurement of our garment will be 65 cm, i.e. chest measurement 55 cm, plus 16 cm for comfort.

As the garment is made in two sections, a front and a back, we must divide this 65 cm by two, 32.5 cm per section.

From the pre-knitted tension sample, we know the number of stitches to each 5 cm. For our sample garment, we will say that there are 15 sts to each 5 cm. Therefore, we divide the 32.5 cm by 5 cm and multiply by 15 sts, giving us a total of 98 sts for the front of the garment as well as 98 sts for the back. Should you at any time require a 1 x 1 rib cast-on and your calculations give you an even number of stitches, simply add or subtract one stitch.

Now that we have arrived at the correct number of stitches to cast on, the next calculation will be for the length of the garment, in other words the number of rows. Our length measurement is taken in the centre of the child's back from the most prominent neck bone at the top to the point where we would like the

jumper to end. It is handy to know that jumpers with rib-bands 'ride up' with the movement of the wearer. Therefore, we allow a little extra length to compensate for this. For our example we will make our garment 45 cm. Now we must break this measurement up into the various sections for shaping, i.e. from the cast on to the end of the band, from the band to the armhole, from the armhole to the lower shoulder point.

To make these calculations, we again refer to our tension sample and the 5 cm gauge. We will probably find that there are 20 rows to each 5 cm of knitting. Therefore, to knit a 5 cm rib band, which is reasonable for a child, we would need to knit 20 rows.

The next measurement we require would be from the top of the band to the armhole. To allow for comfort, take this measurement to approximately 2 cm below the child's actual armpit. In our example, this measurement will be 25 cm. Therefore, to calculate the number of rows, we divide this 25 cm by 5 cm (our gauge) and multiply it by 20 rows, giving us 100 rows of knitting before we start to shape for the armhole.

The depth of the armhole is measured from 2 cm below the actual armpit to the lower shoulder point. In our example, we will take this as 13.5 cm. Again using the formula of dividing by 5 and multiplying by 20, we find that from the start of the armhole shaping to the start of the shoulder shaping, we will have to knit 54 rows.

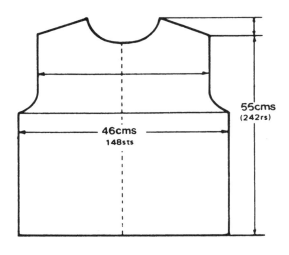

diagram 54

The height of the shoulder slope varies from person to person and children normally have very little shoulder slope compared to elderly people, for instance. Calculate the height of the shoulder slope by stretching the tape measure across the back from one shoulder to the other and measuring from the tape in the centre back to the neck bone mentioned previously. For our example, we will say that this measurement is 1.5 cm. Therefore, 1.5 divided by 5, multiplied by 20, equals 6 rows. This means that the shoulders of our jumper should slope over six rows.

To check our calculations, we add up the number of rows in each of the four sections and in our example they are 20 + 100 + 54 + 6 = 180 rows. Now by reversing our original formula, we multiply 180 by 5 and divide it by 20. This gives us 45 cm, which was the original centre back measurement calculated to give us a comfortable and well-fitting jumper.

These instructions may seem slightly complicated and involved, but after the experience of one or two garments, knitting your own designs becomes very easy and most rewarding to the creative operator (diagram 54).

◆

Knitting hints

Naturally, when shaping and casting off the various parts of your garment, you will follow the directions taught during your knitting lessons. These are usually the simplest procedures but often alternative methods can improve the look and fit of your garment. Look at the following suggestions:

TO OBTAIN A FULLY FASHIONED DECREASE
(diagram 55)

Transfer the second or third stitch to the adjacent inside needle, then move all the end stitches inwards to fill the empty needle and knit the rows your pattern states.

TO OBTAIN A FULLY FASHIONED INCREASE
(diagram 56)

Transfer the first stitch to the adjacent needle on the outside, then pick up the bar of the second stitch and hang it on to the empty needle. Knit the rows your pattern states.

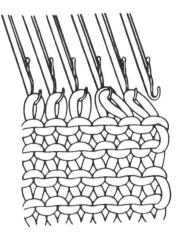

diagram 55

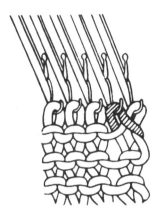

diagram 56

TO OBTAIN A FLAT CAST-OFF
(diagram 57)

Transfer the second stitch to the first needle, then transfer both stiches on to the empty second needle. Now cast off both stitches together. Continue this operation until the last stitch and fasten off. If casting off more than 3 or 4 stitches take the stitches behind the sinker posts so that the cast-off is not tight.

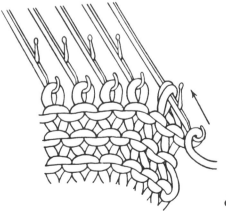

diagram 57

TO OBTAIN A SMOOTH SHOULDER SHAPING
(diagram 58)

Instead of casting off several stitches at a time, as many patterns advise, use the 'partial knitting method'. Bring those stitches to be cast off up to holding position (partial knitting). Place the return cams out of action and knit one row. Lay yarn under the first inner needle in the holding position to prevent a hole in the fabric and knit one row. Continue shaping shoulder in this way, finally releasing the return cams and knitting one row over all the shoulder stitches and cast off.

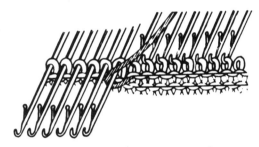

diagram 58

◆

Making up your garment

A jumper quickly and roughly sewn together has an amateur appearance, regardless of the good design and the perfect knitting. A little more care given to the making up will, on the other hand, give your garment that professional look.

Here are some finishing tips used by the professionals:

BACKSTITCHING
(diagram 59)

This is quite an acceptable method for joining sleeve and side seams. Hold the two parts with the right sides together and with matching yarn, backstitch closely to the edge. Do not pull the yarn too tightly as this may cause the seams to buckle.

MATTRESS STITCH METHOD
(diagram 60)

This is the best method for joining raglan seams or where an invisible seam is required. Hold the two parts with the right sides together and, with matching yarn in a tapestry needle, bring it under two threads between the first and second stitch on the right piece of material, then under the same two

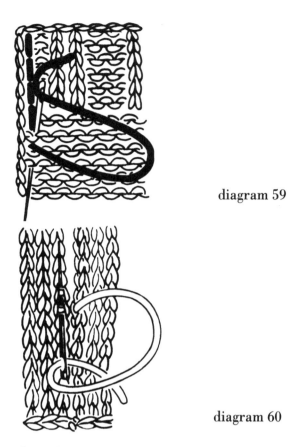

diagram 59

diagram 60

threads on the left. Move to the next two threads on the right, then the left and so on. As you are working from the right side of your knitting, you will be able to match the patterns or stripes perfectly.

GRAFTING STITCHES TOGETHER
(diagram 61)

To obtain an invisible seam while joining two equal ends of stocking stitch knitting, butt the edges together so that the stitches are opposite each other with the right side of each piece facing you. Bring the tapestry needle from right to left under the second stem of the first stitch and the first stem of the second stitch on one part. Then, under the

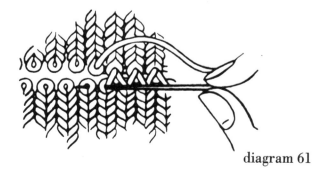

diagram 61

second stem of the first stitch and the first stem of the second stitch on the other piece of fabric. Continue in this way, from stitch to stitch, until the seam is closed.

WIND-ON METHOD
(diagram 62)

With the carriage on the right-hand side of the machine, bring forward the required number of needles for the cast-on. Starting with the left-hand needle, wind the yarn loosely in an anti-clockwise direction around each needle. Knit the first few rows slowly and carefully.

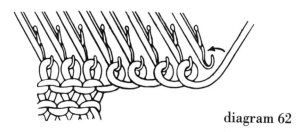

diagram 62

PICOT ROW
(diagram 63)

With your single transfer tool, transfer the second and every following alternate stitch to the next needle on the right. In other words, the 2nd, 4th, 6th, 8th and so on stitch is transferred to the 3rd, 5th, 7th, 9th needle and so on across the bed. Machines with a lace carriage will knit picot by transferring every second stitch automatically as the lace carriage is moved from left to right.

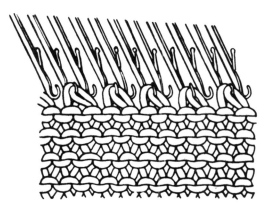

diagram 63

◆

Pressing your finished garment

To add that professional look to the garment and give it a smooth appearance, it will need just a touch with an iron. It is an important rule not to overpress knitwear. Heavy handed ironing can easily spoil the fluffy look of the synthetic and flatten the bulky or raised pattern in your wool garment. Some manufacturers help by giving ironing recommendations on the yarn label.

The best results are obtained by covering the garment with a damp cloth and pressing very gently, allowing the steam to penetrate thoroughly.

◆

Care of your machine

Although your garment is finished and you are ready to show it off, the job is not quite done. Your knitting machine, if it is to last a lifetime, will need a small amount of your personal attention. After every garment has been knitted, brush off the dirt and wool dust which has settled on the rails, needle beds and in the needle grooves themselves. Lift off the carriages, turn them over and carefully clean their undersides with a soft smooth rag, making sure not to snag or catch the springs or cams. Apply good quality, clean, light machine oil wherever your machine requires it. Your manual should point out the most important oiling spots.

Cover your machine or pack it away until you are ready to zoom into the tension sample for your next exclusive creation.

◆

Child's poncho

MEASUREMENTS
To fit 3 to 4 year old.

MATERIALS
5 ply crepe: 7 x 25 g balls m; 2 x 25 g balls c.

TENSION
14 sts and 20 rows to 5 cm (2 in).

PATTERN
Body pattern over 12 sts and 21 rows, Fair Isle pattern as per graph.

TO MAKE UP
Poncho is knitted in 4 parts.

Parts 1 and 2 (see graph for Fair Isle).
With waste yarn cast on 43 sts, k some rows in waste, then use ravelling cord for 1 row.

Change to m with main tension, k 6 rows. Work picot row, k 7 rows and close hem. Pull out ravelling cord and discard waste knitting.

Make row of holes by transferring 2nd and every foll 3rd st to adjacent needle, leave empty needles in B position (working position).

R/c on 0, inc 1 st on left end next and every foll alt row. At same time inc 1 st on right end next and every foll 4th row to row 80 on r/c. Cont shaping on both sides as before, at same time work Fair Isle pattern.

Cont shaping, with m, k 10 rows after completing patt. Make row of holes by transferring 4th and every foll 4th st to adjacent needle. Leave needles in B position. Knit 2 rows and cast off loosely.

Parts 3 and 4
K as part 1 and 2, reversing shaping.

TO MAKE UP
With fine back-stitch sew together the 2 short seams and the 2 long seams. Pull fringe through each hole on hem. Make string and pull through holes at neck and attach a tassel to each end of string. Press lightly.

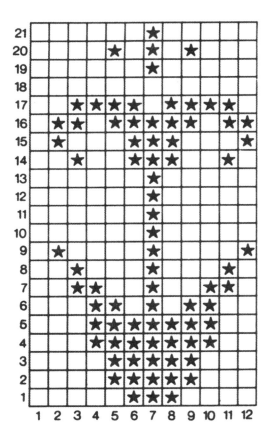

★ contrast color

ABBREVIATIONS FOR MACHINE KNITTING

k	knit, i.e. move carriage across needles to make a row	foll	following	patt	pattern
		trans	transfer	no(s)	number(s)
dec	decrease	st st	stocking stitch	dc	double crochet
inc	increase	sts	stitches	LC	Lace Carriage
r/c	row counter, counts each row automatically as you knit	cm	centimeter	incl	inclusive
		in	inch(es)	opp	opposite
m	main color	g	grams	req	required
c	contrasting color	approx	approximately	ravelling cord	strong nylon cord: when pulled, it separates waste knitting from main part
1st c	first contrast	rem	remaining		
2nd c	second contrast	cont	continue		
beg	beginning	tog	together	waste yarn	remnant of contrasting yarn
alt	alternate	rep	repeat		

A child's poncho to knit on machine. Instructions on pages 73-4.

Crochet

MATERIALS NEEDED

The only tool required is a crochet hook and the only basic material is some thread. However, several other items will be useful:

a tape measure

dressmaking pins and safety pins

clean bag to keep your work in

pencil and paper to keep a note of increases, decreases and number of rows worked

a variety of large-eyed sewing needles for making up (tapestry needles)

scissors.

CROCHET HOOKS

Crochet hooks are made of steel, plastic, alloy metal, composition or bone, and are usually 5 or 6 in (12.7 or 15.2 cm) in length.

Each hook is especially adapted for use with a certain size thread. The size of the hook used depends on the weight and type of thread you are working with, and the type of pattern you are using; crochet patterns usually instruct you as to which size the hook should be. To ensure correct results, it is important that you use the number hook specified in the directions. There are times when you don't necessarily have to use the precise hook quoted, but be sure to check your tension first by working a small sample in the stitch pattern. If you achieve the correct tension as given in the instructions then the size hook you use does not matter.

◆

Crochet hook sizes

From 1970 crochet hooks have been made according to the International Standard range of sizes. The following chart shows both the old aluminium sizes (for yarn) and steel sizes (for fine cottons) and their equivalent new sizes. Although the International Standard range provides enough sizes to work all patterns, it is advisable to check your tension before you begin any crochet work to ensure that the finished item is the correct size.

In the patterns throughout this section, the International sizes of crochet hooks are given. The chart below shows the equivalent sizes of hooks in all ranges.

Note: Old sizes may vary according to the brand of crochet hook. For instance, Aero size 10 and Milwards size 11 are both equivalent to the International Standard size 3.00.

International Standard size	Old 'cotton' (steel)	Old 'yarn' (aluminum)
	8	
	7	
	6½	
0.60 mm	6	
	5½	
0.75 mm	5	
	4½	
1.00 mm	4	
	3½	
1.25 mm	3	
1.50 mm	2½	
1.75 mm	2	
	1½	
2.00 mm	1	13 or 14
	1/0	13
2.50 mm	2/0	12
3.00 mm	3/0	10 or 11
3.25 mm		10
3.50 mm		9
4.00 mm		8
4.50 mm		7
5.00 mm		6
5.50 mm		5
6.00 mm		4
7.00 mm		2

Opposite: Crochet can create broad, colorful patterns in home furnishings.

HOW TO BEGIN

The basis of every crochet pattern is the chain stitch — one loop pulled through another loop. Repeat this operation for the length required. Use a large hook at first and fairly coarse thread to practice. Do the stitches again and again until you are familiar with them and can work quite quickly. Then you will be able to work any pattern given in a book.

◆

If you work with your right hand

Go straight through the steps given below and there you have all the hand positions at your finger tips. From there it is simple to learn the other stitches and make all the crocheted articles in this book.

STEP 1: MAKE A LOOP

1. Grasp thread near end between thumb and forefinger of left hand.

2. With right hand make a loop by lapping long thread over short thread.

3. Hold loop in place between thumb and forefinger of left hand (diagram 1).

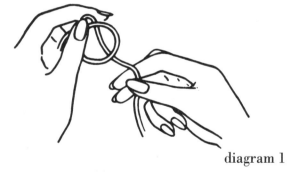

diagram 1

STEP 2

1. With right hand take hold of broad bar of hook as you would a pencil.

2. Insert hook through loop and under long thread. With right hand catch long end of thread (diagram 2). Draw loop though.

3. Do not remove hook from thread.

STEP 3

1. Pull short end and ball thread in opposite directions to bring loop close around the end of the hook, but not too tight (diagram 3).

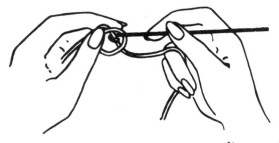

diagram 2

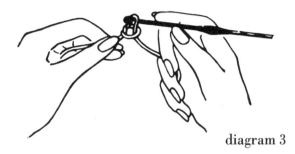

diagram 3

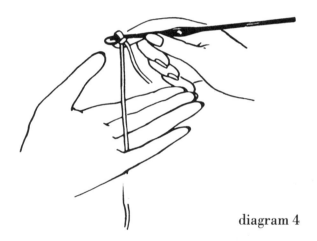

diagram 4

STEP 4: WHAT TO DO WITH THE LEFT HAND

1. Measure with your eye about 4 ins (10.1 cm) along ball thread from loop on hook.

2. At about this point insert thread between ring and little fingers, having palm of hand facing up (diagram 4).

STEP 5

1. Bring thread toward back, under little and ring fingers, over middle finger, and under the forefinger toward the thumb (diagram 5).

STEP 6

1. Grasp hook and loop between thumb and forefinger of left hand.

Opposite: Crochet yarns and hooks.

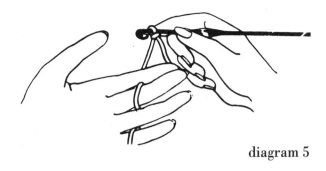

diagram 5

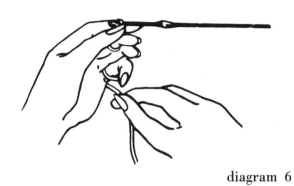

diagram 6

2. Gently pull ball thread so that it lies around the fingers firmly but not tightly (diagram 6).

3. Catch knot of loop between thumb and forefinger.

STEP 7: WHAT TO DO WITH THE RIGHT HAND
1. Take hold of broad bar of hook as you would a pencil.

2. Bring middle finger forward to rest near tip of hook (diagram 7).

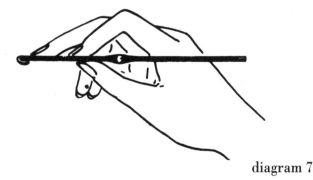

diagram 7

STEP 8: CHAIN STITCH (abbreviation — ch st)
1. Adjust fingers of left hand as in diagram 8 — the middle finger is bent to regulate the tension, the ring and little fingers control the thread. The motion of the hook in the right hand and the thread in the left hand should be free and even. Ease comes with practice.

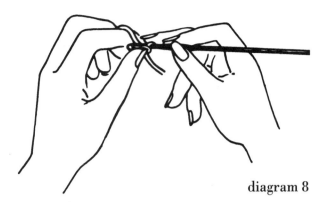

diagram 8

STEP 9
1. Pass your hook under thread and catch thread with hook. This is called 'thread over' (diagram 9).

2. Draw thread through loop on hook. This makes one chain (ch).

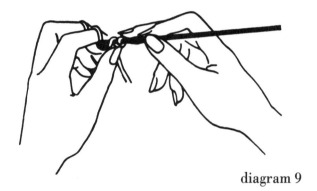

diagram 9

STEP 10
1. Repeat Step 9 until you have as many chain stitches (ch sts) as you need — 1 loop always remains on the hook (diagram 10).

2. Always keep thumb and forefinger of left hand near stitch on which you are working.

3. Practice making chain stitches until they are even in size.

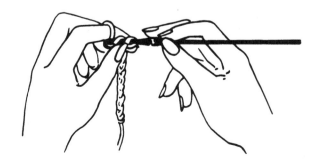

diagram 10

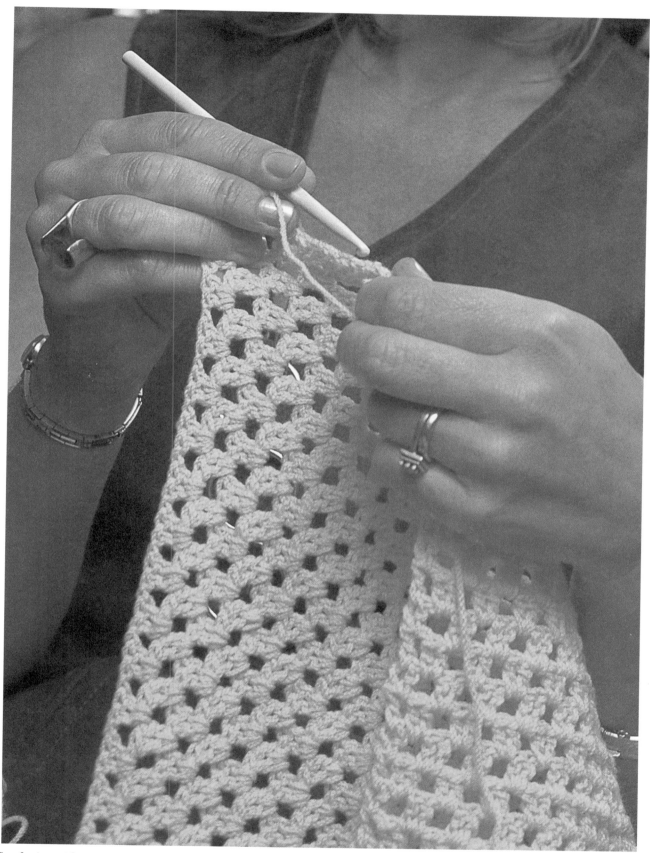

Crocheting with yarn.

◆

If you work with your left hand

Do exactly as the right-handed people on the preceding pages. Go through the steps below. Study each step very carefully and from then on you will be crocheting happily and correctly.

STEP 1: MAKE A LOOP

1. Grasp thread near end between thumb and forefinger of right hand.

2. With left hand make a loop by lapping long thread over short thread.

3. Hold loop in place between thumb and forefinger of right hand (diagram 11).

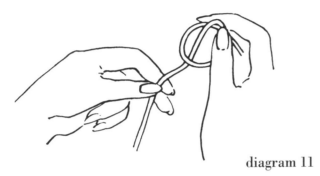

diagram 11

STEP 2

1. With left hand take hold of broad bar of hook as you would a pencil.

2. Insert hook through loop and under long thread. With left hand catch long end of thread (diagram 12). Draw loop through.

3. Do not remove hook from thread.

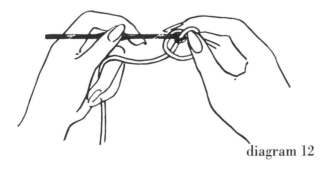

diagram 12

STEP 3

1. Pull short end and ball thread in opposite directions to bring loop close around the end of the hook, but not too tight (diagram 13).

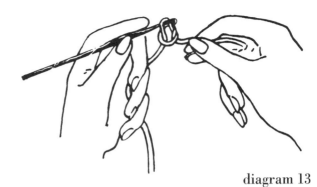

diagram 13

STEP 4: WHAT TO DO WITH THE RIGHT HAND

1. Measure with your eye about 4 ins (10.1 cm) along ball thread from loop on hook.

2. At about this point insert thread between your ring and little fingers, having palm of hand facing up (diagram 14).

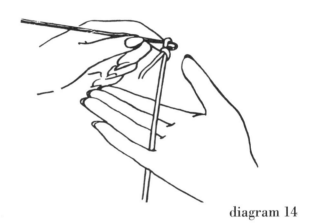

diagram 14

STEP 5

1. Bring thread toward back, under little and ring fingers, over the middle finger, and under the forefinger toward the thumb (diagram 15).

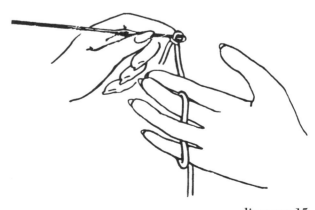

diagram 15

A lady's crocheted top.

STEP 6

1. Grasp hook and loop between thumb and forefinger of right hand.

2. Gently pull ball thread so that it lies around the fingers firmly but not tightly (diagram 16).

3. Catch knot of loop between thumb and forefinger.

STEP 7: WHAT TO DO WITH THE LEFT HAND

1. Take hold of broad bar of hook as you would a pencil.

2. Bring middle finger forward to rest near tip of hook (diagram 17).

diagram 16

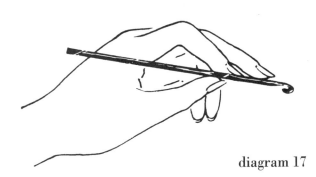

diagram 17

STEP 8: CHAIN STITCH *(abbreviation — ch st)*

1. Adjust fingers of right hand as in diagram 18 — the middle finger is bent to regulate the tension, the ring and little fingers control the thread. The motion of the hook in the left hand and the thread in the right hand should be free and even. Ease comes with practice.

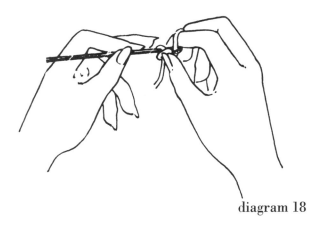

diagram 18

STEP 9

1. Pass your hook under thread and catch thread with hook. This is called 'thread over' (diagram 19).

2. Draw thread through loop on hook. This makes one chain (ch).

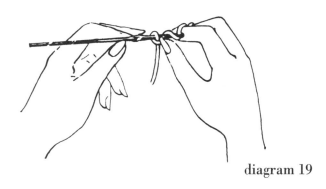

diagram 19

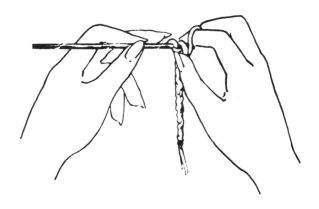

diagram 20

STEP 10

1. Repeat Step 9 until you have as many chain stitches (ch sts) as you need — 1 loop always remains on the hook (diagram 20).

2. Always keep thumb and forefinger of your right hand near stitch on which you are working.

3. Practice making chain stitches until they all even in size.

Right-handed people work from right to left. Left-handed people work from left to right. The directions for each stitch apply to both right- and left-handed people. All the illustrations of stitches shown on the following pages are in position for the right-handed person. So left-handed workers should follow the instructions as given, but read right for left, and left for right. To follow the stitch diagrams use a mirror to reflect them in reverse by placing the mirror to the left of each illustration.

SIMPLE STITCHES

These basic stitches are the foundation of all crochet work and once you have learned them you will be able to make attractive articles from the directions included in this book.

Note: In all crochet, pick up top loops of each stitch, unless otherwise instructed.

◆

Chain stitch

The basis of all crochet is the chain stitch. For details of how to make it see page 80.

◆
Slip stitch or single crochet

(see diagram 21)

This stitch can be used to give a firm edge, or for joining, fastening or repositioning the thread without making your work any longer. Insert the hook into the stitch to the left of the hook, catch the long thread and draw it through the stitch and the loop already on the hook. This forms a flat chain. (See also diagrams 44 and 45).

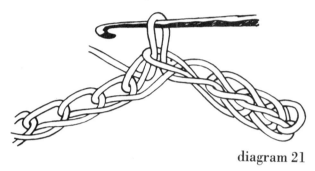

diagram 21

◆
Double crochet

(see diagrams 22 to 28)

Make a starting chain of 20 stitches for a practice piece and work some rows of double crochet.

FIRST ROW (1ST ROW)

Step 1: Insert hook from the front under the 2 top threads of 2nd ch from hook (diagram 22).

diagram 22

Step 2: Catch thread with hook — this is known as 'thread over' (diagram 23).

Step 3: Draw thread through chain. There are 2 loops on hook (diagram 24).

diagram 23

diagram 24

Step 4: Thread over (diagram 25) and draw through 2 loops — 1 loop remains on hook.

diagram 25

diagram 26

Step 5: You have now completed 1 double crochet (dc) (diagram 26).

Step 6: For next double crochet, insert hook under 2 top threads of next ch and repeat Steps 2 to 6.

Step 7: Repeat Step 6 until you have made a double crochet in each ch.

Step 8: At end of row of double crochets, 1 ch (diagram 27). The 1 ch enables you to turn your work more easily.

diagram 27

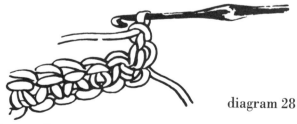

diagram 28

Step 9: Turn your work so that the reverse side is facing you (diagram 28).

◆
How to turn your work

In crochet a certain number of chain stitches are added at the end of each row to bring work in position for the next row. Then the work is turned so that the reverse side is facing the worker. You have noticed that in double crochet 1 ch only is used for turning. The number of turning chains depends upon the stitch with which you intend to begin the next row. Listed on page 94 are the turning chains for each of the basic stitches.

SECOND ROW (2ND ROW)

Step 1: Insert hook from the front under the 2 top loops of first stitch (st) — the last stitch made on previous row.

Step 2: Catch thread with hook ('thread over') and draw through st — 2 loops remain on hook.

Step 3: Thread over and draw through 2 loops — 1 loop remains on hook.

Step 4: For next double crochet, insert hook from the front under the 2 top loops of next st and repeat Steps 2 and 3.

Step 5: Repeat Steps 4, 2, and 3 until you have made a dc in each st, 1 ch and turn.

diagram 29

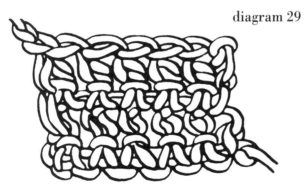

Step 6: Repeat Second Row until you are familiar with this stitch. Break off (diagram 29).

◆
How to 'break off'

Step 1: Do not make a turning chain at end of last row.

Step 2: Clip thread about 3 ins (7.5 cm) from work, bring loose end through the one remaining loop on hook and pull tightly (diagram 29).

◆
Half treble

(see diagrams 30 to 33)

Rows of half-treble crochet are worked as follows.

FIRST ROW (1ST ROW)

diagram 30

Step 1: Pass hook under the thread of left hand (this is called 'thread over' — diagram 30).

Step 2: Insert hook from the front under the 2 top loops (or threads) of 3rd ch from hook.

diagram 31

Step 3: Thread over hook and pull loop through chain (3 loops on hook), thread over (diagram 31).

Step 4: Draw through all loops on hook — 1 loop remains on hook (diagram 32). A half treble (hlf tr) is now completed.

Step 5: For next hlf tr, thread over, insert hook from front under the 2 top threads of next ch.

diagram 32

Step 6: Repeat Steps 3, 4, and 5 until you have made a hlf tr in each ch.

Step 7: At end of row, ch 2 (diagram 33) and turn.

SECOND ROW (2ND ROW)

Step 1: Thread over hook, insert hook from front under the 2 top loops of first stitch (st) — the last st on previous row.

The pansies decorating this knitted tea cosy are crocheted. Courtesy Avalon Craft Cottage.

diagram 33

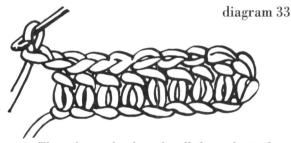

Step 2: Thread over hook and pull through stitch — there are 3 loops on hook; thread over and draw through all loops on hook.

Step 3: For next hlf tr, thread over hook, insert hook from the front under the 2 top loops of next st and repeat Step 2.

Step 4: Repeat Steps 3 and 2 until you have made a hlf tr in each st, 2 ch and turn.

Step 5: The turning 2 ch of each row does not count as a stitch on the following row.

Step 6: Repeat Second Row (2nd row) until you are familiar with this stitch. Break off at end of last row (diagram 29).

◆

Treble

(see diagrams 34 to 39)
Rows of treble crochet are worked as follows.

diagram 34

FIRST ROW (1ST ROW)

Step 1: Thread over, insert hook from the front under the 2 top threads of 4th ch from hook (diagram 34).

Step 2: Thread over and draw through st. There are now 3 loops on hook (diagram 35).

Step 3: Thread over (diagram 35) and draw through 2 loops — 2 loops remain on hook (diagram 36).

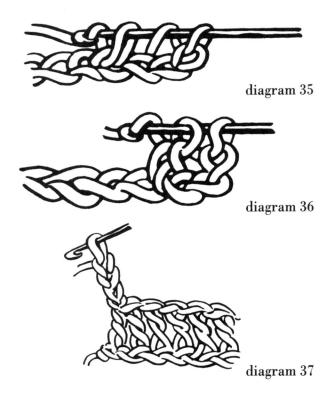

diagram 35

diagram 36

diagram 37

Step 4: Thread over again and draw through the 2 remaining loops — 1 loop remains on hook. One treble crochet (tr) is now completed (diagram 37).

Step 5: For next tr thread over, insert hook from the front under the 2 top loops of next st and repeat Steps 2 to 5 until you have made a tr in each chain.

Step 6: At end of row ch 3 (diagram 38) and turn.

Step 7: The turning 3 ch counts as the first tr on next row. Therefore the first tr of each row is always missed.

diagram 38

When working a dbl tr—thread over twice.

When working a trip tr—thread over three times.

When working a quad tr—thread over four times.

When working a quint tr—thread over five times.

Step 1: Thread over, insert the hook from the front under the 2 top loops of the 5th stitch from the hook (2nd stitch on previous row).

Step 2: Repeat Steps 2 to 7 of First Row.

Repeat the Second Row until you are familiar with this stitch. Break off.

diagram 39

◆

Double treble

(see diagram 40)

Pass the hook under the thread held in the left hand twice, insert the hook into the next stitch, thread over the hook and pull it through the stitch. There will now be four loops on the hook. Place the thread over the hook and pull it through two loops, leaving three loops, place thread over the hook again and pull through the next two loops. Place thread over the hook and pull through the last two loops.

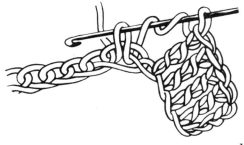

diagram 40

◆

Triple treble

(see diagram 41, page 90)

Pass the hook under the thread held in the left hand three times in succession, put the hook into the next stitch and draw the thread through. There will now be five loops on the hook. Place thread over the hook and draw through the first two loops (four loops on hook), thread over and draw through the next two loops (three loops), thread over and draw through the next two loops (two loops), thread over and draw through last two loops.

A crocheted wool scarf. Courtesy Avalon Craft Cottage.

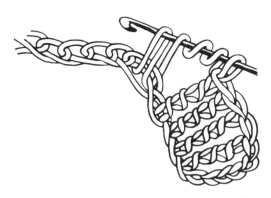

diagram 41

◆

Quadruple treble

(see diagram 42)
Pass the hook under the thread four times and complete in the same way as given for triple treble.

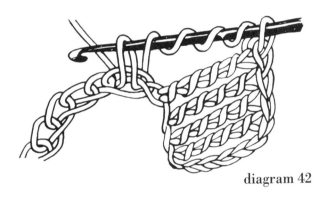

diagram 42

◆

Quintuple treble

(see diagram 43)
Pass the hook under the thread five times and complete in the same way as given for triple treble.

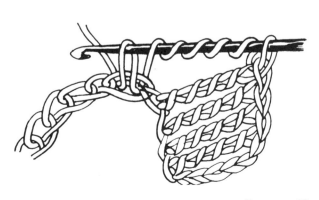

diagram 43

◆

Rounds of double crochet

(see diagrams 44 to 47)

Step 1: Make a chain (ch) of 4 stitches (sts). Join with slip stitch (ss) in 1st ch to form a ring (diagrams 44 and 45).

diagram 44

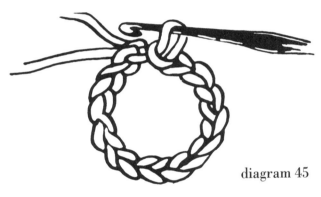

diagram 45

Step 2: 1st round (rnd): Make 8 double crochet (dc) in ring (diagram 46). Place a safety pin in the last dc of 1st rnd to mark end of rnd. Move the safety pin to the last dc of the following rnds.

diagram 46

Step 3: 2nd rnd: 2 dc in each dc of previous rnd. There are 16 dc on rnd (diagram 47).

*Left: Two simple
crocheted ladies'
hats. Courtesy Avalon
Craft Cottage.
Below: Delicate
crotchet work adorns
this lovely old
tablecloth.*

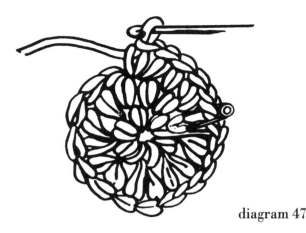

diagram 47

Step 4: 3rd rnd: * 2 dc in next dc — an increase made in last dc (diagram 47), dc in next dc. Repeat from * all round (24 dc on rnd).

Step 5: 4th rnd: * Dc in next 2 dc, 2 dc in next dc (increase made in last dc). Repeat from * all round (32 dc on rnd).

Step 6: 5th rnd: * Dc in next 3 dc, 2 dc in next dc. Repeat from * all round (40 dc on rnd).

Step 7: 6th rnd: Dc in each dc all round. Slip stitch (ss) in next 2 dc (diagrams 44 and 45). Break off.

Sometimes in the directions you will see the following phrases:

1. Repeat from * across.

2. Repeat from * all round.

3. Repeat from * 3 (or any number) more times.

In Nos. 1 and 2 follow the directions from the first to the last * (asterisk) completely across row or all round. In No. 3 follow the directions from the first * as many times as specified.

◆

Slip stitch

(abbreviation — ss)

It is not necessary to make a practice piece for slip stitch (ss) because it is seldom used except when an invisible stitch is required. When the directions say join, you always use a slip stitch. (See also diagram 21).

Step 1: Insert hook from the front through the 2 top threads of chain (diagram 44).

Step 2: Thread over and with one motion draw through chain and loop on hook — 1 loop remains on hook (diagram 45). This completes a ss.

diagram 48

◆

Rounds of half-treble crochet

(see diagrams 48 and 49)

Notice there is an extra loop directly below the 2 top loops of each hlf tr. Work only in the 2 top loops.

Step 1: Make a chain of 4 stitches (sts). Join with ss in 1st ch to form a ring (diagrams 44 and 45).

Step 2: 1st rnd: 2 ch, 11 half treble crochet (hlf tr) in ring (diagram 48).

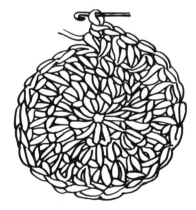

diagram 49

Step 3: Place a safety pin in the last hlf tr of 1st rnd to mark end of rnd. Move the safety pin to the last hlf tr of the following rnds.

Step 4: 2nd rnd: 2 hlf tr in each hlf tr all round (22 hlf tr on round).

Step 5: 3rd rnd: Hlf tr in each hlf tr all round (22 hlf tr on round).

A hat crocheted in thick, soft yarn. Courtesy Avalon Craft Cottage.

Step 6: 4th rnd: * Hlf tr in next hlf tr, 2 hlf tr in next hlf tr. Repeat from * all round (diagram 49) (33 hlf tr on rnd).

Step 7: 5th rnd: Hlf tr in each hlf tr all round.

Step 8: 6th rnd: 2 hlf tr in each hlf tr all round (66 hlf tr on rnd).

Step 9: 7th rnd: Hlf tr in each hlf tr all round. Ss in next 2 hlf tr (diagrams 44 and 45). Break off (diagram 29).

Step 10: If a larger circle is desired, do not break off but increase 9 hlf tr evenly on each rnd to keep work flat. Do not have increases fall over those of previous rnd.

Increasing

Specific instructions for increasing are usually given in individual patterns, but it is quite a simple matter, and consists of working two stitches into one stitch, instead of one. It can be done in nearly any part of the work, but preferably at the beginning or end of a row.

To increase several stitches make a chain equivalent to the number of extra stitches required, plus turning chain.

Decreasing

Instructions for decreasing are also usually given in individual patterns. One way to decrease is to miss a stitch of the previous row in the middle or at the beginning of a row, which shortens the length of the work, but you must be sure that the space is not too obvious. Another way to decrease is to work two stitches together. Do not finish either of the stitches but leave the last loop on the hook in addition to the loop already on the hook. Draw the thread through all the remaining loops which leaves a single loop on the hook.

When decreasing several stitches, if at the beginning of a row, slip stitch over the required number of stitches to be decreased. Work one or two chain stitches before continuing, according to the stitch being worked. When decreasing at the end of a row, work to within the number of stitches to be decreased and turn. Work back in the usual way.

Turning

A certain amount of chains are added at the end of each row to bring the work into position for the next row. The work is turned so that the reverse side is facing the worker. The number of turning chains differs according to the stitch with which you are about to begin on the following row.

Although the precise number of extra chain depends on which stitch you are working in, the following is a general plan to follow:

double crochet (dc)—1 ch to turn
half treble (hlf tr)—2 ch to turn
treble (tr)—3 ch to turn
double treble (dbl tr)—4 ch to turn
triple treble (trip tr)—5 ch to turn
quadruple treble (quad tr)—6 ch to turn.

Joining thread

Avoid making a join in the middle of a pattern and never make knots in your work. As the thread with which you are working is coming to an end, place the new thread along the top of the work and crochet a few stitches over this. Before the old thread has run out change to the new thread and work stitches over the old.

Finishing

Do not make any turning chain at the finish of the last row. Cut the thread leaving an end of approximately 3 ins (7.5 cm) from the work, and draw the end through the last loop on the hook and pull it tight. To hide the loose end, use a tapestry needle to darn it into the work.

Tension

Wrong tension can destroy the beauty of a pattern or create an ill-fitting garment. Tension in crochet, as in knitting, refers to the number of stitches and rows worked to each square inch of fabric. This measurement is achieved by the combination of a certain weight and type of thread with a suitable hook size, and it can be varied by changing the thread and/or hook used. The same pattern can be

A soft crocheted baby's blanket. Courtesy Avalon Craft Cottage.

worked in a variety of threads and hook sizes and an entirely different result is achieved.

Before you begin any pattern check that your work achieves the tension measurement quoted, otherwise your finished work will not be the correct size. To check your tension, work 4 ins (10.1 cm) of chain using the thread and hook size stated in the pattern, and make up a sample square of the stitch pattern [about 4 x 4 ins (10.1 x 10.1 cm)]. Lay it flat and, using a ruler or tape, measure across 1 in (2.54 cm) and mark this area with pins (see diagram 50). Count the number of stitches between the pins. If this comes to greater number than quoted in the pattern you are working too tightly, so make another sample but this time using a larger hook. On the other hand, if you have fewer stitches in your inch than quoted in the pattern, try working with a smaller sized hook. Make as many sample pieces with varying hooks as are necessary until you achieve the correct tension.

Repeat instructions in parentheses as many times as specified. For example: '(5 ch, dc in next dc) 5 times' means to make all in parentheses 5 times in all; '(1 tr into next tr, 1 ch) 3 times', means to make all that is in parentheses 3 times in all.

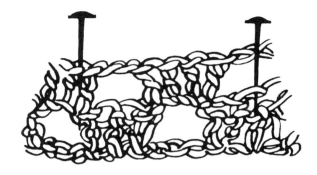

diagram 50

◆

Crochet threads

Crochet threads are made in a variety of sizes, twists, finishes, and hues to provide a suitable one for all types of crochet, from fine delicate laces to coarse heavy rugs. It is important to use the type designed for the article you are planning to make, as an article's beauty and usefulness depends greatly on the thread with which it is made. The finer mercerized threads are more effective for the delicate designs used for tablecloths, doyleys, runners, edgings, and accessories.

ABBREVIATIONS

alt	—alternate	quad tr	—quadruple treble
beg	—beginning	quin tr	—quintuple treble
blk(s)	—block(s)	r	—ring
C	—contrasting color	rep	—repeat
ch	—chain	rnd	—round
cl	—close (in certain patterns, where indicated, cl means cluster)	rw	—reverse work
		SC	—selected color
cont	—continue	sep	—separated
dc	—double crochet	sh	—shell
dec	—decrease	smp	—small picot
dbl tr	—double treble	sp(s)	—space(s)
ds	—double stitch	ss (or sl st)	—slip stitch
foll	—following	st(s)	—stitch(es)
gr(s)	—group(s)	thr	—through
hlf tr (or htr)	—half treble	tog	—together
in(s)	—inch(es)	toh	—thread over hook
inc	—increase	tr	—treble
lp(s)	—loop(s)	trip tr	—triple treble
M	—main color	yd	—yard
p	—picot		
patt	—pattern		
pc st	—popcorn stitch		

* (asterisk) ... repeat the instructions following the asterisk as many more times as specified, in addition to the original.

Ideas for crocheted doyleys.

If the exact thread given in a pattern is unavailable, be careful with your substitute thread, as an equivalent may not work up to exactly the same measurements. Therefore be sure to make a tension check (see diagram 50) before starting your work. (Yardage can also vary with different threads so you may need either more or less than what is specified in the pattern.)

It is important to purchase at the one time the entire amount of thread required to make the article as dye lots vary in the strength of the hue and you may be unable to obtain the exact dye lot if you return for extra thread at a later date.

◆

Common mistakes in crochet work

NOT KEEPING WORK STRAIGHT
Beginners have great difficulty in maintaining straight edges because they are doubtful as to which stitch to work into at each end of the rows.

AT THE BEGINNING
The turning chain must be counted as the first stitch, just as if it had been worked into the last stitch of the previous row, which means missing the top of the end stitch when going on with the row.

AT THE END
The turning chain counts as the first stitch at the beginning of a row, so the last stitch in successive rows must be worked into the top of the turning chain. Until you master this principle, count the number of stitches after each row to check that the right number has been worked.

VARYING THE TENSION
Your work should be uniform throughout, which means the tension should be the same, provided of course that you have used the same sized needles and the same thickness of thread. Crochet work should be fairly tight but the loops should run easily through the hook without sticking. Loose work stretches, while work that is too tight causes the thread to lose much of its elasticity.

KNOTTING THREAD
When any form of thread has to be joined it should never be knotted. It stretches the thread, and knots give the work an uneven surface. Join the thread by the method shown on page 94.

UNTIDY SEAMS
Hours of hard work on a garment or any other article can be wasted if you do not give it the special make-up it deserves. The manner in which a seam is joined is most important to the appearance of the finished article. An uneven seam will stand out, and such seams as those on the shoulder or any others which protrude, need maximum care. Methods for joining seams are described below.

◆

Finishing details
Careless finishing off can spoil any well-made crocheted article or garment. To have a neat, professional-looking article or garment, take time and care with correct pressing and making-up.

PRESSING
Always read any specific pressing instructions given in a pattern, for various threads require different treatments. Before you sew up the pieces of your finished article, press each piece separately. Pin out each piece of the work to its correct shape and size with the right side downwards and on a thick blanket; take care that the stitches and rows are running in straight lines. Always insert the pins from the outer edge towards the middle of the work, and the closer the pins are, the straighter the pressed edge will be. This is called blocking. Press the main part of the work with a warm iron over a damp cloth. When the steam has settled remove the pins. Be careful not to overpress the main part of the work as overpressing will flatten the fabric and could even destroy the character of the work, especially when it is a fancy pattern.

Many fibers should not be pressed, but so that you will have a perfect fit they should be blocked. Pin out as described above, then put a damp cloth over the fabric and leave it until the cloth is thoroughly dry.

MAKING-UP
Once the individual pieces of your work have been finished and, where necessary blocked and pressed, they are joined together. Make sure that all the ends of thread have been neatly darned into the work.

Crocheted bedspread worked in rows to make large squares.

A FLAT SEAM
Using the same thread as your garment or article has been worked in (or contrasting color of the same thickness) and a tapestry needle, stitch the pieces together with a flat seam.

To make a flat seam have right sides facing, and place the two pieces of work together, edge to edge. Put your left forefinger between these edges. Using an overcasting stitch draw the edges together over your finger. Move your finger along as you proceed.

TO CROCHET SEAMS TOGETHER
Using the same thread as your garment has been worked in and using a size smaller crochet hook than specified in your instructions, join seams by the double crochet method as shown on page 85.

◆

Keeping your work clean
If you don't take care to protect your work, and particularly with light-colored or white work, it will quickly get dirty.

When you are not using it keep it wrapped in a polythene bag or in a special bag made from cotton or linen material. Always wash your hands before you start work and try to keep your hands smooth as rough hands will make your work fluffy which could spoil the end product.

If the work you are doing is long, such as a scarf or a poncho, keep the part already worked rolled up so that it won't look dirty or worn before the garment is finished.

◆

Washing
Never allow crocheted work to get too dirty before washing. The first wash must be done carefully as this determines how the garment will look from thereon. Frequent washing (as long as it is carefully done) will never harm yarn, cottons or other fibers.

COTTON
Wash cotton items in warm water and soap flakes; squeeze gently to remove the dirt. In cases where the crochet is worked to a certain shape, such as in a circle, it may be necessary to pin it out again.

YARN
Wash wool items gently in warm water and a recommended washing detergent and rinse thoroughly in at least three changes of warm water. To prevent the garment (or any other article) from stretching out of shape while it is wet, always support it with both hands. Squeeze the garment gently after the final rinse, and roll it in a clean, dry, white towel without twisting. Leave it to dry flat on a clean towel, away from direct sunlight or strong artificial heat. Make sure it is in its correct shape and size. Once the garment is dry press it lightly on the wrong side with a medium hot iron over a damp cloth.

MAN-MADE FABRICS
Follow the same washing instructions as for yarn. Fibers such as Courtelle, Acrilan, Tricel, Nylon or Orlon do not need pressing.

WHITE ARTICLES
These articles can easily lose their whiteness and become an unattractive yellow hue. This is often due to the washing water being too hot, which will also shrink any wool material. Work up a good lather in warm water and gently move the garments around in the suds, squeezing them carefully (do not rub) and give each part equal treatment. Rinse in clean warm water.

COLORED ARTICLES
Colors can run so the water should be cooler than for washing whites.

If the crochet requires any stiffening, dip it into a thin solution of starch, pin out on a clean board with rustless pins and leave to dry.

◆

Drying
To ensure that the garment, or any other article, retains its correct shape take care when drying it. Never wring it out as this harms the texture of the material. Remove the article from the washing water and put it on a clean, dry towel and press out the moisture.

Never hang any garment to dry, for the weight of the wet material will pull the garment out of shape. Lay it out flat on a clean towel and allow it to dry in the air or in a moderately warm room.

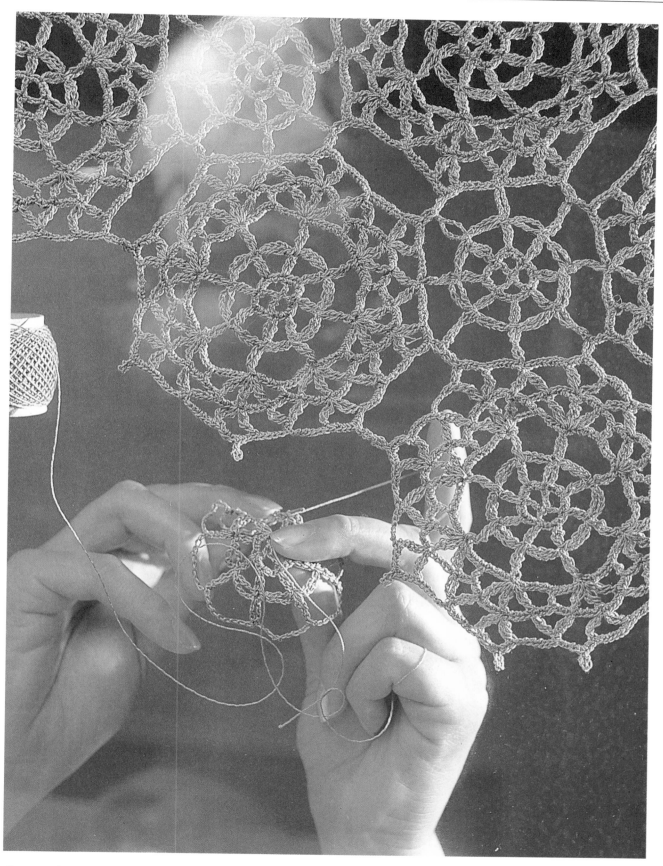

Creating the motif for the table runner, the instructions for which are on page 103.

◆
Definitions

CHAIN (ch)
A series of loops forming a chain, used at the start of every crochet pattern.

DOUBLE CROCHET (dc)
A stitch formed by the double action of the crochet hook. It can be made in two ways: as a flat surface, or as a ridged surface.

DOUBLE TREBLE (dbl tr)
The thread is wound twice around the hook instead of once.

FASTENING OFF
Finishing off stitches at the end of a piece of work.

FILET CROCHET
A particular technique of crochet based on forming designs from a series of solid and open squares, called 'blocks' and 'spaces'. The effect of this work is similar to lace or net, and makes attractive edgings for many household items.

PICOT
A small loop of twisted thread, one of a series forming an edging to lace, etc.

SLIP STITCH
A stitch formed by passing the hook through the stitch and drawing it through both loops on the hook.

TENSION
The number of stitches/motifs/patterns given to each square inch or inches as stipulated in the pattern.

TREBLE (tr)
Ordinary treble stitch, made by winding the thread once around the hook before putting it into the stitch. See page 87-88.

TRIPLE TREBLE (trip tr)
An elaborate form of treble, where the thread is wound three times around the hook before the hook is inserted in the stitch below.

MOTIFS

Motifs are small crocheted squares or circles which form the basis of many delightful articles, large or small, which can be crocheted for the home. Motifs may be used as medallions, mats, tablecloths, rugs, bedspreads, trolley mats, cheval sets, runners, etc. They can be either sewn together or crocheted together as the last row or round is worked.

◆
Round motif tray cloth

MATERIALS
Coats Mercer-Crochet No. 20 (20 gram), 3 balls selected color; crochet hook No. 1.25 (if your crochet is loose use a size finer hook, if tight use a size larger hook).

TENSION
Size of motif = 2½in (6.4 cm) in diameter.

MEASUREMENT
15 in x 20 in (38.1 cm x 50.7 cm).

ABBREVIATIONS
See page 96; cl — cluster.

FIRST MOTIF
Commence with 6 ch, join with a ss to form a ring.

1st row: 6 ch, into ring work (1 dbl tr and 3 ch) 7 times, 1 ss into 4th of 6 ch.

2nd row: 1 ss into next sp, 4 dc into same sp, 4 dc into each sp, 1 ss into first dc.

3rd row: 4 ch, * 1 tr into next dc, 1 ch; rep from * ending with 1 ss into 3rd of 4 ch.

4th row: 1 dc into same place as ss, 1 dc into next sp, 1 dc into next tr; rep from * ending with 1 dc into next sp, 1 ss into first dc.

5th row: 4 ch leaving last lp of each on hook work 1 dbl tr into each of next 3 dc, thread over and draw through all lps on hook (3 dbl tr cluster made), * 6 ch, 4 dbl tr cl over next 4 dc; rep from * ending with 6 ch, 1 ss into top of first cl. Fasten off.

SECOND MOTIF
Work as first motif for 4 rows.

5th row: 4 ch, 3 dbl tr cl over next 3 dc, 3 ch, 1 ss into any lp on first motif, 3 ch, 4 dbl tr cl over next 4

Close-up of round motif for tray cloth.

dc on second motif, 3 ch, 1 ss into next lp on first motif, 3 ch, 4 dbl tr cl over next 4 dc on second motif and complete as first motif.

Make 6 rows of 8 motifs, joining each as second motif was joined to first, having 2 free lps between joinings of motifs.

FILLING

Commence with 7 ch, 1 ss into first free lp on any motif, 6 ch, 1 dc into first ch worked, (6 ch, 1 ss into next free lp on same motif, 6 ch, 1 dc into same place as last dc, 6 ch, 1 ss into next free lp on next motif, 6 ch, 1 dc into same place as last dc) 3 times, 6 ch, 1 ss into next free lp on same motif, 6 ch, 1 ss into same place as last dc. Fasten off.

Fill in all spaces between motifs in same manner.

Damp and pin out to measurements.

◆

Motif table runner

(see photograph, page 101)

MATERIALS

Coats Mercer-Crochet No. 20 (20 gram), 5 balls selected color; crochet hook No. 1.25 (if your crochet is loose use a size finer hook, if tight use a size larger hook).

MEASUREMENT

12 in x 36 in (30.5 cm x 91.4 cm).

TENSION

Size of motif = 4½ ins (10.7 cm) in diameter from picot to picot.

ABBREVIATIONS

See page 96; cl — cluster.

FIRST MOTIF

Commence with 8 ch.

1st row: 1 tr into 8th ch from hook, * 4 ch, 1 tr into same place as last tr; rep from * once more, 4 ch, 1 ss into 4th of 8 ch.

2nd row: 1 dc into same place as ss, * 5 dc into next sp, 1 dc into next tr; rep from * ending with 5 dc into last sp, 1 ss into first dc.

3rd row: 4 ch, 1 dbl tr into same place as ss (starting cl made), * 5 ch, 1 dbl tr into 5th ch from hook, miss next 2 dc, leaving last lp of each on hook, work 2 dbl tr into next dc, thread over and draw through all lps on hook (2 dbl tr cl made), rep from * omitting cl at end of last rep, 1 ss into first dbl tr.

4th row: 4 ch, 1 dbl tr into same place as ss, * 11 ch, 2 dbl tr cl into next cl, rep from ending with 11 ch, 1 ss into first dbl tr.

5th row: 1 dc into same place as ss, * 11 dc into next 11 ch lp, 1 dc into next cl, rep from * omitting 1 dc at end of last rep, 1 ss into first dc.

6th row: 4 ch, 1 dbl tr into same place as ss, 4 ch, 2 dbl tr cl 4 ch and 2 dbl tr cl into same place as last dbl tr, * 4 ch, miss next 5 dc, 1 dc into next dc, 4 ch, miss next 5 dc, into next dc work (2 dbl tr cl, 4 ch) twice and 2 dbl tr cl; rep from * ending with 4 ch, miss next 5 dc, 1 dc into next dc, 4 ch, 1 ss into first dbl tr.

7th row: 1 dc into same place as ss, * (4 dc into next sp, 1 dc into next cl) twice, 3 dc into each of next 2 sps, 1 dc into next cl; rep from * omitting 1 dc at end of last rep, 1 ss into first dc.

8th row: 4 ch, 1 dbl tr into same place as ss, * 6 ch, miss next 4 dc, into next dc work 2 dbl tr cl, 6 ch and 2 dbl tr cl, 6 ch, miss next 4 dc, leaving last lp of each on hook, work 2 dbl tr into next dc, miss next 6 dc, 2 dbl tr into next dc, thread over and draw through all lps on hook (joint 2 dbl tr cl made); rep from * omitting joint cl at end of last rep, 2 dbl tr cl into next dc, 1 ss into first dbl tr.

9th row: 1 dc into same place as ss, * 6 dc into next sp, 1 dc into next cl, 4 dc into next sp, 5 ch, 1 ss into last dc (picot made), 3 dc into same sp, 1 dc into next cl, 6 dc into next sp, 1 dc into next joint cl; rep from * omitting 1 dc at end of last rep, 1 ss into first dc. Fasten off.

SECOND MOTIF

Work as first motif for 8 rows.

9th row: 1 dc into same place as ss, * 6 dc into next sp, 1 dc into next cl, 4 dc into next sp, 2 ch, 1 ss into corresponding picot of first motif, 2 ch, 1 ss into last dc worked on second motif, 3 dc into same sp, 1 dc into next cl, 6 dc into next sp, 1 dc into next cl; rep from * once more and complete as for first motif.

Make 3 rows of 9 motifs, joining adjacent sides as second was joined to first.

FILLING

Work as first motif for 2 rows.

3rd row: 4 ch, 1 dbl tr into same place as ss, * 6 ch, 1 ss into joining of 2 motifs, 6 ch, 1 ss into top of last cl, 5 ch, 1 dbl tr into 5th ch from hook, miss next 2 dc, 2 dbl tr cl into next dc, 5 ch, 1 ss into dc on top of joint cl of motif, 5 ch, 1 ss into top of last cl on filling, 5 ch, 1 dbl tr into 5th ch from hook, miss next 2 dc, 2 dbl tr cl into next dc; rep * from omitting 2 dbl tr cl at end of last rep, 1 ss into top of first dbl tr. Fasten off.

Fill in all sps between motifs in same manner.

Damp and pin out to measurements.

◆

Crochet motif tablecloth

MATERIALS
Coats Mercer-Crochet No. 20 (20 gram), 25 balls selected color; crochet hook No. 1.25 (if your crochet is loose use a size finer hook, if tight use a size larger hook).

MEASUREMENT
45½ ins (115 cm) square.

TENSION
Size of motif = 3½ ins (8.8 cm) square.

ABBREVIATIONS
See page 96; cl — cluster.

FIRST MOTIF
1st row: Commence with * 4 ch 1 dbl tr into 4th ch from hook (a starting cl made); rep from 4 times more, turn.

2nd row: * Leaving the last lp of each on hook work 2 dbl tr into top of 2nd starting cl made thread over and draw through all lps on hook (a 2 dbl tr cl made), a starting cl, a 2 dbl tr cl into top of first starting cl made, a starting cl made, a starting cl, a 2 dbl tr cl into base of first starting cl, turn.

3rd row: 2 starting cls, miss first 2 dbl tr cl, a 2 dbl tr cl into next 2 dbl tr cl, a starting cl, a 2 dbl tr cl into next 2 dbl tr cl, a starting cl, a 2 dbl tr cl into base of next starting cl, turn.

4th row: As 3rd row, do not turn.

5th row: 1 dc into top of last cl made, 6 ch a 2 dbl tr cl into base of same cl, 6 ch, miss next starting cl, a 2 dbl tr cl into top of next 2 dbl tr cl, 6 ch, 1 dc into base of same cl, (6 ch, a 2 dbl tr cl into base of next 2 dbl tr cl) twice, 6 ch, 1 dc into top of next starting cl, 6 ch, a 2 dbl tr cl into top of next starting cl, 6 ch, a 2 dbl tr cl into top of next 2 dbl tr cl, 6 ch, 1 dc into top of next starting cl, (6 ch, a 2 dbl tr cl into top of next 2 dbl tr cl) twice, 6 ch 1 ss into first dc.

6th row: 1 dc into same place as ss, * (7 dc into next lp, 1 dc into next cl) twice, 7 dc into next lp, 1 dc into next dc; rep from * 3 times more omitting 1 dc at end of last rep, 1 ss into first dc.

7th row: 1 dc into same place as ss, 1 dc into each dc, 1 ss into first dc.

8th row: 15 ch, 1 trip tr into same place as ss, * (miss 3 dc, 5 dbl tr into next dc, miss 3 dc, 1 dbl tr into next dc) twice, miss 3 dc, 5 dbl tr into next dc, miss 3 dc, into next dc work 1 trip tr 10 ch and 1 trip tr; rep from * 3 times more omitting 1 trip tr 10 ch and 1 trip tr at end of last rep, 1 ss into 5th of 15 ch.

9th row: 7 ch, * leaving the last lp of each on hook work 1 dbl tr into each of next 5 ch, thread over and draw through all lps on hook (a 5 dbl tr cl made), 10 ch, a 5 dbl tr cl over next 5 ch, (3 ch, 1 dbl tr into next st, 3 ch, a 5 dbl tr cl over next 5 dbl tr) 3 times, 3 ch, 1 dbl tr into next st, 3 ch; rep from * 3 times more omitting 1 dbl tr and 3 ch at end of last rep, 1 ss into 4th of 7 ch.

10th row: 3 dc into first lp, into next cl work 1 dc 3 ch and 1 dc (p made), * into next lp work 5 dc 5 ch and 5 dc, p into next cl, (3 dc into each of next 2 lps, p into next cl) 4 times; rep from * 3 times more omitting 3 dc and p at end of last rep, 1 ss into first dc. Fasten off.

SECOND MOTIF

Work as First Motif for 9 rows.

10th row: 3 dc into first lp, p into next cl, 5 dc into next lp, 2 ch, 1 ss into corresponding 5 ch lp on first motif, 2 ch, 5 dc into same lp on second motif, (1 dc into next cl, 1 ch, 1 ss into corresponding p on first motif, 1 ch 1 dc into same cl on second motif, 3 dc into each of next 2 lps) 4 times, 1 dc into next cl, 1 ch, 1 ss into corresponding p on first motif, 1 ch, 1 dc into same cl on second motif, 5 dc into next lp, 2 ch 1 ss into corresponding 5 ch lp on first motif, 2 ch, 5 dc into same lp on second motif and complete as First Motif. Make 13 rows of 13 motifs joining each as second motif was joined to first. Where 4 corners meet join 3rd and 4th corners to joining of previous corners.

Damp and pin out to measurements.

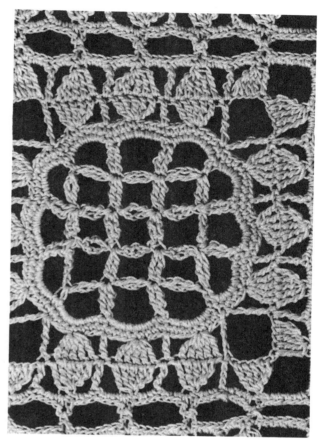

Above: Close-up of stitch pattern for table cloth motif (see opposite and this page).

◆

Filet doyley — flower motif

Stitches used: chain stitch (ch), slip stitch (sl) single crochet (sc). Insert the hook in 1 ch, yarn over, draw yarn through stitch, yarn over, draw yarn through 2 loops on hook.

Double crochet (dc): yo, insert hook in 1 ch, yo, draw through st, twice (yo, draw through 2 loops on hook). Net stitch: follow chart.

One space = 2ch, skip 2 st, 1dc in next st.

One block = 1 dc in next 3 st.

Double picot = (1 sc, 5 ch) x 2 in same st, and 1 sc.

MATERIALS

Cordonnet Special DMC Art. No. 151 2 balls white 5200, crochet hook No. 0.75 Continental.

Chain 237 and continue according to chart. Begin 1st row with 1 dc in the 9th ch after the hook and with 3 ch in following rows. End rows with 1 dc in the 3rd

Key to chart
☐ 2ch, skip 2 st, 1dc in next st.

☒ 1 dc in next 3 st.

ch of preceding row. On completing final row do not break thread. Begin border.

1st row: 1 ch, 6 sc in the corner round and 3 sc in the following rounds, except in the corners where 9 sc. End with 3 sc in the last corner and 1 sl st in the ch.

2nd row: 1 ch, 1 sc in the next st, 3 sc in the next st, 1 sc in the next st except in corners where 3 sc. End with 1 sl st in the ch.

3rd and 4th rows: 1 ch, then 1 sc in each st except in the corner st where 3 sc. End as 2nd row.

5th row: 1 ch, turn work and continue as 3rd row.

6th row: 1 ch, 1 sc in the next 6 st, 8 1 double picot in the next st, 1 sc in the next 6 st, 8 1 double picot in the next 6 st, * 1 double picot in the next st, 1 sc in the next 6 st *, repeat from * to * right along side ending with 1 sc in the last 4 st and 1 double picot in the central corner st. On the next edge, 1 sc in the next 4 st then repeat from * to * as first side. End with double picot in last st and 1 sl st in ch.

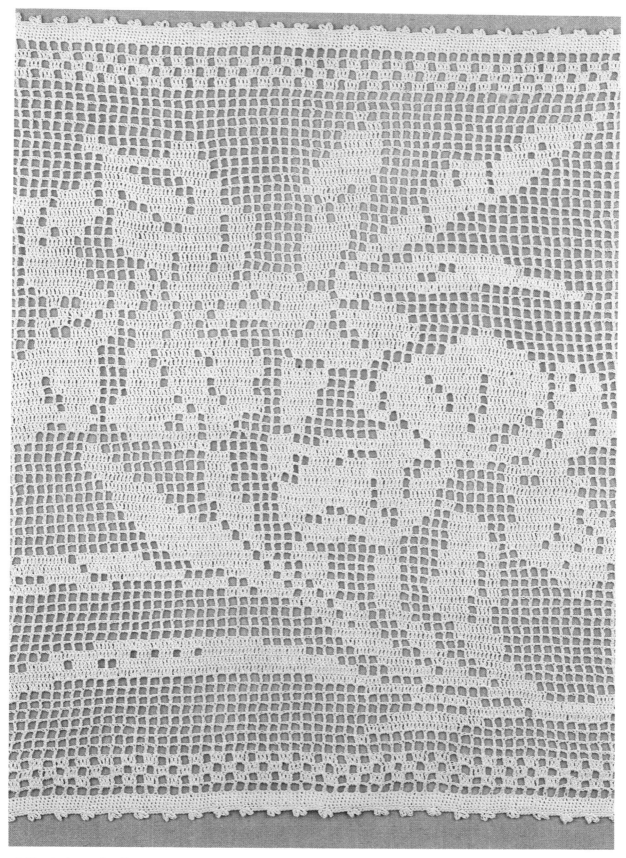

A filet doyley with a flower motif worked in cotton thread. For instructions see pages 105-6.

◆

Crocheted cushion cover

MATERIALS

Cebelia Cotton No. 10 by DMC, 4 balls white 5200, a piece of pink satin 40 cm x 80 cm, synthetic stuffing, a No. 1.25 crochet hook.

FRONT

Crochet 4 identical squares. For each one, ch 8 and close into a ring with 1 sl st in the 1st ch. Work around following chart. On completion of final row, break the thread. Join the four squares with 1 row sc, inserting the hook in 1 st on each square.

BACK

Chain 8 and close into a ring with 1 sl st in 1st ch. Work around.

1st row: 2 ch, 3 times (2 ch, 1 tr in ring), 2 ch and 1 sl st in 2nd ch.

2nd row: 3 ch, 1 tr in 2nd ch at point of sl st, 3 times (1 tr, 2 ch and 1 tr in the following round, 2 ch and 1 sl st in next 2 st), 3 times (1 tr, 2 ch and 1 tr in the following round, 1 tr in the next 3 st), 1 tr in following round, 2 ch and 1 sl st in 3rd ch. Continue, increasing 2 tr at each end of row. On completing 53rd row, work 1 row sc with 5 sc in corners, then stop.

TO MAKE UP

Fold satin in half, right sides together, baste and sew sides, leaving an opening for turning. Fill with synthetic stuffing and stitch closed. Slip stitch three sides of the crochet squares together, place satin 'pillow' inside, and slip stitch the remaining side closed.

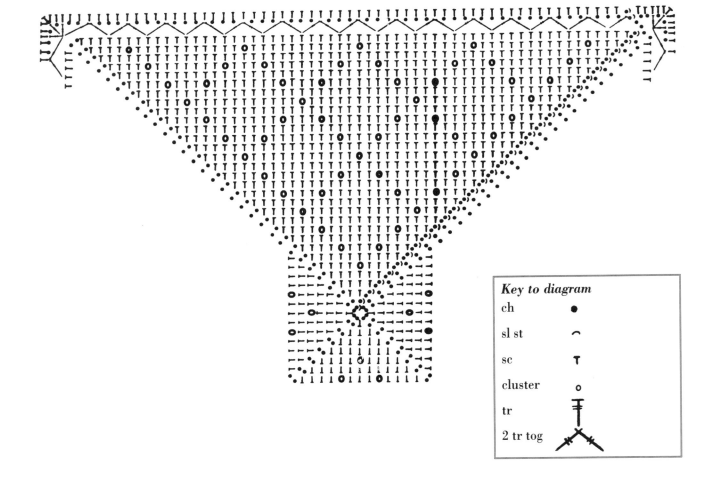

Key to diagram	
ch	●
sl st	⌒
sc	⊤
cluster	o
tr	⊤
2 tr tog	⅄

A cushion cover finely worked in crochet. Instructions on page 108.

◆

Crocheted trim for hand towels

Finished measurements of trim 5.5 cm x 57 cm

STITCHES USED

Chain stitch (ch), single crochet (sc). Insert the hook in 1 ch, yarn over, draw yarn through stitch, yarn over, draw yarn through two loops on hook. Double crochet (dc): yo, insert hook in 1 ch, yo, draw through st twice, (yo, draw through two loops on hook).

MATERIALS

1 ball white 5200 Cebelia cotton No. 30, DMC Art. 167, one white hand towel, 57 cm wide, one No. 1 Continental crochet hook.

METHOD

Chain 33 and work the following chart. On completing final row (of chart) repeat from 2nd row, repeating these 14 rows 7 times in all, then ending with 1st row. Crochet a second trim as above.

Fasten threads and iron. Using running stitch, attach each length in the desired position to the right side of the towel.

Pick up from 2nd row.

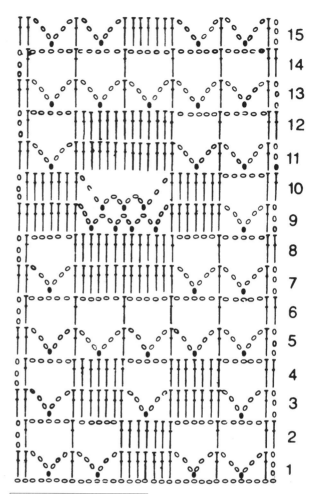

Key to diagram	
ch	o
sl st	⌐
sc	●
dc	↑

A pattern for decorating hand towels. For instructions see opposite page.

◆

Diamond crocheted trim
for hand towels

Finished measurements of trim 5.5 cm x 50 cm.

STITCHES USED

Chain stitch (ch), single crochet (sc). Insert the hook
in 1 ch, yarn over, draw yarn through stitch, yarn
over, draw yarn through two loops on hook. Double
crochet (dc): yo, insert hook in 1 ch, yo, draw
through st twice, (yo, draw through two loops on
hook).

MATERIALS

1 ball white 5200 Cebelia cotton No. 30, DMC Art.
167, one white hand towel, 50 cm wide, one No. 1
Continental crochet hook.

METHOD

Chain 232 and work the following chart. Begin the
first row with 1 ch and 1 sc in the 2nd ch after the
hook. Make a second length as above and then iron
both pieces lightly. Attach each one using running
stitch to the right side of towel.

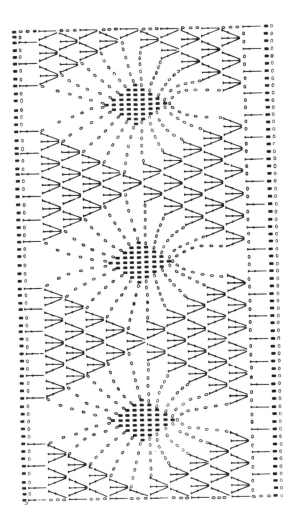

Key to diagram

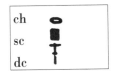

ch	
sc	
dc	

Repeat from * to *

Opposite: A diamond pattern for decorating hand towels.
For instructions see this page.

◆

Collar and trimmings for child's dress

MATERIALS

Coats Chain Mercer-Crochet No. 20 (20 gram), 1 ball selected color; crochet hook No. 1.25 (if your crochet is loose use a size finer hook, if tight use a size larger hook); a dress.

MEASUREMENT

Depth of collar = 1½ ins (3.8 cm).

ABBREVIATIONS

See page 96.

COLLAR

(2 sections)

Commence with 17 ch.

1st row: 1 hlf tr into 8th ch from hook, (2 ch, miss 2 ch, 1 tr into next ch) twice, 2 ch, miss 2 ch, 1 dbl tr into next ch, 1 ch, turn. The first sp made on each alternate row forms the heading.

2nd row (right side): 1 dc into first st, (2 dc into next sp, 1 dc into next st) 4 times, 5 ch, turn.

3rd row: Miss first 3 dc, 1 hlf tr into next dc, (2 ch, miss 2 dc 1 tr into next dc) twice, 2 ch, miss 2 ch, 1 dbl tr into next dc, 1 ch, turn.

4th row: As 2nd row working last dc into 3rd of 5 ch.

Rep last 2 rows for length required from middle front to middle back of neck having an uneven number of rows of sps and omitting turning ch at end of last row. Fasten off.

EDGING

With right side facing attach thread to 3rd foundation ch to right of first hlf tr worked, 1 dc into same place as join, 2 dc into same sp (1 dc into base of next st, 2 dc into next sp) 3 times, 1 dc into base of next st, do not turn, 1 dc over same dc row-end, * 3 dc over next row-end, 7 ch, remove lp from hook, insert hook into first of 3 dc and draw dropped lp through, into 7 ch lp work 1 dc 1 hlf tr and 7 tr, 5 ch, 1 ss into last tr (5 ch, 1 ss into same place as last ss) twice (a triple p made), into same ring work 6 tr 1 hlf tr and 1 dc, 1 ss into last dc before lp, 1 dc over next dc row-end, 2 dc over next row-end, 5 ch, 1 ss into

last dc (a p made), 1 dc over same row-end, 1 dc into next dc row-end; rep from * omitting 2 dc a p and 2 dc at end of last rep, 1 ss into next dc. Fasten off.

TRIMMING (make 6)

Commence with 9 ch, join with a ss to form a ring.

1st row: Into ring work 2 dc 1 hlf tr 7 tr a triple p 6 tr 1 hlf tr and 2 dc, 1 ss into first dc. Fasten off.

Damp and pin out to measurements.

Place headings to wrong side of next edge and sew neatly in position. Place trimmings centrally on front of dress and sew in position.

Close-up of pattern in dress trimming.

Opposite: A traditional crocheted rug from the 1920s.

◆
Bedspread

(not illustrated in colour)

MATERIALS

Coats Chain Mercer-Crochet No. 20 (20 gram), 50 balls Main color, 35 balls 1st contrasting color, and 35 balls 2nd contrasting color; crochet hook No. 1.00 (if your crochet is loose, use a size finer hook, if tight use a size larger hook).

MEASUREMENT

13 motifs x 16 motifs = 79⅝ ins x 98 ins (202 cm x 249 cm).

TENSION

Size of motif = 6⅛ ins (15.5 cm) square.

ABBREVIATIONS

See page 96; M — Main color; C — contrasting color.

FIRST MOTIF

Using M commence with 12 ch, join with a ss to form a ring.

1st row: 11 ch, 1 dbl tr into same place as ss, * 1 dbl tr into each of next 2 ch, into next ch work 1 dbl tr 7 ch and 1 dbl tr (a V st made); rep from * omitting V st at end of last rep, 1 ss into 4th of 11 ch.

2nd row: 4 ch, * 1 dbl tr into each of next 3 ch, V st into next ch, 1 dbl tr into each of next 3 ch, 1 dbl tr into next 3 ch, 1 dbl tr into each of next 4 dbl tr; rep from * omitting 1 dbl tr at end of last rep, 1 ss into 4th of 4 ch.

3rd row: 4 ch, 1 dbl tr into each of next 4 dbl tr, * 1 dbl tr into each of next 3 ch, V st into next ch, 1 dbl tr into each of next 3 ch, 1 dbl tr into each of next 12 dbl tr; rep from * omitting 5 dbl tr at end of last rep, 1 ss into 4th of 4 ch.

4th row: 4 ch, 1 dbl tr into each of next 8 dbl tr, * 1 dbl tr into each of next 3 ch, V st into next ch, 1 dbl tr into each of next 3 ch, 1 dbl tr into each of next 20 dbl tr; rep from * omitting 9 dbl tr at end of last rep, 1 ss into 4th of 4 ch.

5th row: 4 ch, 1 dbl tr into each of next 12 dbl tr, * 1 dbl tr into each of next 3 ch, V st into next ch, 1 dbl tr into each of next 3 ch, 1 dbl tr into each of next 28 dbl tr; rep from * omitting 13 dbl tr at end of last rep, 1 ss into 4th of 4 ch.

6th row: 4 ch, 1 dbl tr into each of next 16 dbl tr, *1 dbl tr into each of next 3 ch, V st into next ch, 1 dbl tr into each of next 3 ch, 1 dbl tr into each of next 36 dbl tr; rep from * omitting 17 dbl tr at end of last rep, 1 ss into 4th of 4 ch. Fasten off.

7th row: Attach 1st C to middle ch of any V st, 11 ch, 1 dbl tr into same place as join, * 4 ch, miss 3 ch, (1 dbl tr into each of next 4 sts, 4 ch, miss 4 sts) 5 times, 1 dbl tr into each of next 4 sts, 4 ch, miss 3 ch, V st into next ch; rep from * omitting V st at end of last rep, 1 ss into 4th of 11 ch.

8th row: 6 ch, * miss 3 ch, V st into next ch, 2 ch, miss 3 ch, 1 dbl tr into next dbl tr, thread over hook twice, insert hook into next ch and draw thread through, thread over hook and draw through 2 lps, thread over hook, miss 2 ch, insert hook into next ch and draw thread through (thread over hook and draw through 2 lps) 4 times, 3 ch, 1 tr into middle point of cross (cross completed), (1 dbl tr into next dbl tr, 2 ch, miss 2 dbl tr, 1 dbl tr into next dbl tr, a cross st over next 4 ch) 6 times, 1 dbl tr into next dbl tr, 2 ch; rep from * omitting 1 dbl tr and 2 ch at end of last rep, 1 ss into 4th of 6 ch. Fasten off.

9th row: Attach 2nd C to middle ch of any V st, 11 ch, 1 dbl tr into same place as join, * 3 ch, miss 3 ch, (1 dbl tr into next dbl tr, 2 dbl tr into next sp, 1 dbl tr into next dbl tr, 3 ch, miss next cross st) 7 times, 1 dbl tr into next dbl tr, 2 dbl tr into next sp, 1 dbl tr into

Close-up of stitch pattern in bedspread motif.

next dbl tr, 3 ch, miss 3 ch, V st into next ch; rep from * omitting V st at end of last rep, 1 ss into 4th of 11 ch.

10th row: 5 ch, * miss 3 ch, into next ch work 1 tr 5 ch 1 ss into 5th ch from hook (6 ch, 1 ss into 5th ch from hook) twice and 1 tr (a p lp made), 2 ch, miss 3 ch, (1 tr into next dbl tr, miss 1 ch, a p lp into next ch, miss 1 ch, 1 tr into next dbl tr, 2 ch, miss 2 dbl tr) 8 times, 1 tr into next dbl tr, miss 1 ch, a p lp into next ch, miss 1 ch, 1 tr into next dbl tr, 2 ch; rep from * omitting 1 tr and 2 ch at end of last rep, 1 ss into 3rd of 5 ch. Fasten off.

SECOND MOTIF

Work as First Motif for 9 rows.

10th row: 5 ch, * miss 3 ch, 1 tr into next ch, 5 ch, 1 ss into 5th ch from hook, 3 ch, 1 ss into corresponding p on First Motif, 2 ch, 1 ss into 2nd of 3 ch, 6 ch, 1 ss into 5th ch from hook, 1 tr into same ch on Second Motif, 2 ch, miss 3 ch, * (1 tr into next dbl tr, miss 1 ch, 1 tr into next ch, 5 ch, 1 ss into 5th ch from hook, 3 ch, 1 ss into corresponding p on First Motif, 2nd ch, 1 ss into 2nd of 3 ch, 6 ch, 1 ss into 5th ch from hook, 1 tr into same ch on Second Motif, 1 tr into next dbl tr, 2 ch, miss 2 dbl tr) 8 times, 1 tr into next dbl tr, miss 1 ch, 1 tr into next ch, 5 ch, 1 ss into 5th ch from hook, 3 ch, 1 ss into corresponding p on First Motif, 2 ch, 1 ss into 2nd of 3 ch, 6 ch, 1 ss into 5th of 6 ch, 1 tr into same ch on Second Motif, miss 1 ch, 1 tr into next dbl tr, 2 ch; rep from * to * once more and complete as First Motif.

Make 13 rows of 16 motifs joining adjacent sides as Second Motif was joined to First (where 4 corners meet, join 3rd and 4th motifs to ss at joining of first 2 motifs).

Damp and press.

An attractive crocheted bedspread in very large squares.

Sewing

A PERSONAL MEASUREMENT CHART

If you plan to make your own clothes or those of your family, it will be so much easier if you know your figure and pattern type. It is a good idea to take measurements before buying each pattern. The diagrams given show a women's figure, but the principles of fitting and sewing apply equally to men's and children's clothing.

It is necessary to take certain measurements and these are shown in diagram A. Those numbered 1, 2, 3, and 4 are the body measurements on which your pattern type and size are based. Record all your measurements on the chart, right. When you start on your first project, shop for your pattern design using your newly taken bust (chest), waist and hip measurements.

The back waist length measurement is the clue to your figure type: the bust measurement is the key to your correct size for all garments except skirts, slacks, and shorts; for these garments buy by waist measurement. You should buy the same size pattern for a coat or jacket as for a dress or blouse.

1. Bust or chest (around fullest part, tape slightly raised over shoulder blades)	
2. Waist (comfortably, at natural waistline)	
3. Hips [around largest part, about 9 ins (22.9 cm) below natural waistline]	
4. Back neck to waist (from prominent bone at neck base to natural waistline)	
5. Shoulder to bust (from neck base at shoulder to bust point)	
6. Front waist length (from back of neck over fullest part of bust to waistline)	
7. Sleeve length, a. Shoulder to elbow (take with arm bent); b. Elbow to wrist	
8. Back skirt length (from natural waistline to bottom of skirt down middle)	

When a pattern includes more than one type of garment, such as a wardrobe pattern or top and pants pattern, purchase by bust measurement. If bust and hip measurements require two different sizes, pattern alterations are easier to make in the hip area.

For skirt and pants patterns, buy the size shown on the measurement chart according your waist measurement unless your hip measurement is larger than shown for that size. In that case, select size by hip measurement and adjust the waistline.

6. Back neck to front waist length

4. Back neck to waist length

5. Shoulder to bust

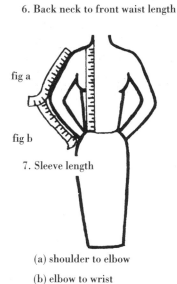

fig a

fig b

7. Sleeve length

(a) shoulder to elbow

(b) elbow to wrist

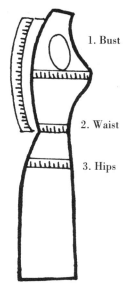

1. Bust

2. Waist

3. Hips

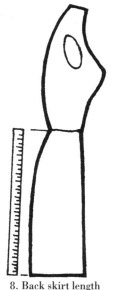

8. Back skirt length

Opposite: A girl's dress made with contrasting trim enhanced by machine embroidery. © Courtesy of Brother Industries.

Pay heed to a pattern envelope. It has a wealth of important information. In addition to sizing facts it tells you what type of fabric is suitable and how much to buy, and all the extras you'll need, so that you'll be able to get everything in one trip.

Some tools you should invest in at this point are good, sharp dressmakers' shears, dressmakers' pins, tracing carbon and tracing wheel (for marking darts).

If this is to be your first sewing project you'll find firmly woven cottons or blends the easiest fabrics to work with. Allow yourself plenty of space in which to work, with a big cleared table for cutting out on. You may find that the floor, covered with an old clean sheet, is more convenient.

◆

A sewing time-saver

If you must make a good garment in a hurry, look for a pattern with few design details. Patterns such as "Simplicity Jiffy" are designed for quick and easy sewing, with a limited number of pieces.

Choose a fabric that doesn't need an underlining, a style which has facings as opposed to bindings or fancy collars that may require handwork. Look for raglan or kimono sleeves. Avoid handwork wherever possible. Pin baste sparingly at the notches. Do as much work as you can by machine while the dress is still in its flat stage. Sew pockets and trims to the front. Put slide fasteners and any trims to the back, then join front to back.

Modern sewing machines make home sewing easy. One of the newest models saves lots of hand-sewing with its chain-stitch tacking that pulls out invisibly after fitting. It also makes buttonholes easier than ever — a special cam makes buttonholes any size with perfect stitch width and spacing.

◆

Make your pattern a personal fit

Perfect fit in a garment means personal fit. After you've taken accurate body measurements, the next step is to compare your dimensions with the pattern's "body" measurement, and then to adjust the pattern accordingly.

A proper fitting bodice, be it dress, tunic, or blouse, means darts pointing to the fullest part of the bust, comfortable sleeves, and an absence of unsightly wrinkles and pulls. Enter your measurements on the chart, below, then the measurements stated on the pattern. The difference between the two figures is the amount you must adjust.

Measurements	Mine	Pattern	Adjust
(a) Bust (chest)			
(b) High bust			
(c) Waist			
(d) Hips			
(e) Back waist length			
(f) Front waist length			
(g) Shoulder length			
(h) Back width			
(i) Sleeve length			

◆

How to adjust

If your pattern style has no waistline seam you will find the waistline indicated at the middle back. Draw a line at right angles to the middle back across to the side seams. Do the same for the front pattern piece at the waist. Diagrams 1 and 2 show you how to mark your pattern clearly to correspond with the measurements taken on your own body.

Using the figures in the adjust column, make any needed alterations in this order: shoulder length, back width, back waist length, front waist length, waist, hips, sleeve length. Reposition darts if necessary.

No garment fits as snugly as the tape measure. There is some ease or "squirming room" added to every pattern to ensure wearing comfort, and some patterns include additional ease for fashion effects. To preserve the style, refer to the measurement chart and the differences between yours and the pattern's "body" for any adjustments needed.

Exquisite detail in heirloom baby clothes. Courtesy Elna Australia.

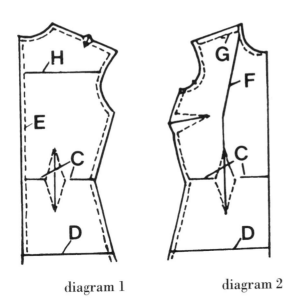

diagram 1   diagram 2

TO NARROW SHOULDERS

Just above armhole notch, clip pattern to seam line. From midpoint of shoulder seam, cut to armhole seam just above the pin. Place paper beneath and lap cut edges the needed amount. Fasten to paper. Draw new shoulder line as shown by broken line (diagram 3).

TO WIDEN SHOULDERS

Just above armhole notch, pin pattern to seam line. From midpoint of shoulder seam, slash to armhole seam slightly above pin. Spread pattern over paper to needed amount. Fasten. Draw a new cutting line as shown by broken line (diagram 4).

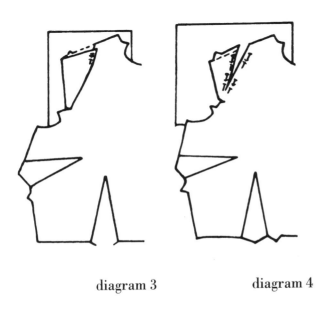

diagram 3   diagram 4

TO SHORTEN BACK

At middle back bodice, measure up from waistline amount needed to shorten. Do the same at the middle of the waistline dart. Draw a line between these two marks. Taper it to nothing at the sides (diagram 5).

TO LENGTHEN BACK

At middle back bodice, measure down amount needed to lengthen. Draw a line. Extend darts to drawn line (diagram 6).

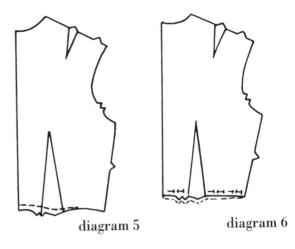

diagram 5   diagram 6

TO SHORTEN SLEEVE

Measure up from the shortening line on the pattern the needed amount. (Above and/or below, as needed. Middle dart of three should come at the elbow.) Draw line. Fold pattern on shortening line. Bring fold up to drawn line and fasten. Draw new cutting line (diagram 7).

TO LENGTHEN SLEEVE

Cut pattern apart on lengthening line (one above, one below elbow), place paper under the pieces. Spread pattern to wanted length. Draw new cutting line (diagram 8).

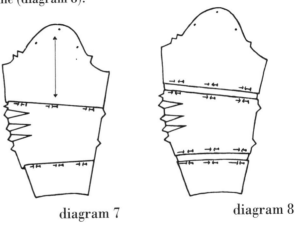

diagram 7   diagram 8

TO ADJUST WAIST

For a small increase, add adjustment to side seams (diagram 9). For a large increase, add to side seams and make darts smaller (diagram 10).

For a small decrease in waist, take in on side seams (diagram 11). For a large decrease, take in on side seams and make darts larger (diagram 12).

TO WIDEN HIPLINE

At side seams of front and back, add quarter the needed amount from waist to lower edge. To restore original waist, increase width of darts nearer the side seams the same amount added at side (diagram 13).

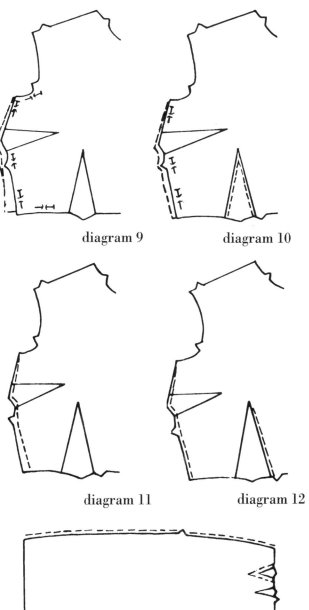

diagram 9   diagram 10

diagram 11   diagram 12

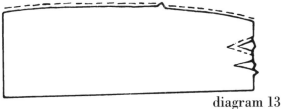

diagram 13

◆

How to fit pants

How closely pants fit is mostly a personal matter, but always consider the activities for which the pants will be worn.

For accuracy of measurements you'll need an unstretchable tape measure and some string. Wear normal undergarments and tie the string snugly around your waist. Place your measurements in the inches (centimeters) column of the chart below.

Measurements	Inches (cm)	Minimum ease	Totals
Hips		+2 in (5.1 cm)	
Crotch depth		+ ½ - 1 in (1.3 - 2.54 cm)	
Waist to knee		None	
Knee to ankle-bone		None	
Crotch Seam		+1½ in (3.8 cm)	
Back crotch length		+1 in (2.54 cm)	
Front crotch length		+ ½ in (1.3 cm)	
Waist		None	
Thigh girth		+ 2 in (5.1 cm)	
Knee girth		+ 2 in (5.1 cm)	

HOW TO MEASURE HIPS:

Around body, at fullest area (diagram 14, fig 1).

CROTCH DEPTH:

Sit on a hard chair, feet flat on the floor (very important) and measure from waist to chair (diagram 14, fig 2).

WAIST TO KNEE; KNEE TO ANKLE-BONE

Along outside of one leg (diagram 14, fig 1).

CROTCH SEAM

Run tape measure from waist in back, between legs, to waist in front (diagram 14, fig 3).

FRONT CROTCH LENGTH

With tape in same position as for crotch seam,

measure from waist string in front to a spot in the middle of inside leg, as close to body as possible.

BACK CROTCH LENGTH

Subtract front crotch length from crotch seam measurement.

WAIST

Around natural waistline, snug enough to get one finger underneath (diagram 14, fig 1).

THIGH GIRTH; KNEE GIRTH

Around leg at fullest part of thigh and knee (diagram 14, fig 1).

Fill out the "totals" column on the chart by adding the "inches" and the "minimum ease" columns. For crotch depth, add ½ in (1.3 cm) ease if the hips are 36 ins (92 cm) or less, 1 in (2.54 cm) if hips are 38 ins (97 cm) or more.

The "totals" column now gives you the minimum measurements for your pants pattern at each of these points.

Purchase the pattern closest to your hip measurement.

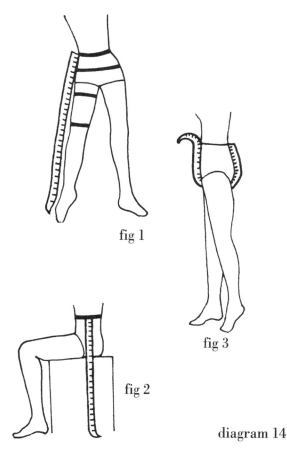

fig 1

fig 2

fig 3

diagram 14

◆

To adjust pattern

Open out your pattern and draw a line, if not already on your pattern, from the crotch point at inside seam, at right angles to the grain line, to side seam (diagram 15a). This line should be indicated on both front and back main pattern pieces.

The pattern crotch depth is measured from this line where it meets side seam to waist seam (diagram 15a). Compare this to your crotch depth marked on the chart.

Adjust length from waist to knee, or knee to ankle, by inserting paper strips to lengthen (diagram 15b) or making tucks to shorten (diagram 15c). Make identical alterations on front and back pattern pieces.

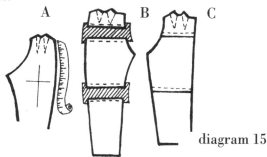

A   B   C

diagram 15

Next adjust both back and front crotch lengths to measurements in "totals" column. To shorten crotch, see diagram 16a. To lengthen crotch, see diagram 16b.

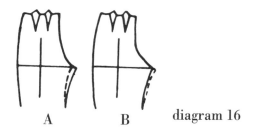

A   B   diagram 16

If your waist is smaller than the pattern measurement, divide the difference by the number of darts back and front and make each dart larger by this amount. If your waist is larger, decrease darts by the same method, or eliminate a dart on each side.

Adjust thigh or knee girth by adding width on leg side seams front and back (diagram 17a) or subtracting width on the leg side seams front and back (diagram 17b).

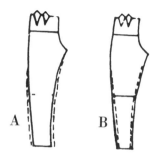

diagram 17

Avoid baggy-seated pants by pinning waistband around you before stitching it to the pants. Pin the pants to the band, raising or lowering them until you get a smooth, professional "hang." When you have them looking right, check for sitting comfort, adjust them if necessary, and stitch them up.

Much of the style in pants today is located below the knee, where the pants flare or not. Sometimes the flare is subtle. To help you predict just how your pants will look when made, measure the width of the leg at the hem (both pattern pieces). Straight pants will be 17 ins to 21 ins (43 to 53.3 cm), more than 28 ins (71 cm) is a prominent flare, anything in between is considered a moderately-flared pants leg style.

◆

How to fit culottes

Culottes or divided skirts have proved to be versatile and useful additions to the wardrobe. The amount of fullness is simply a matter of personal preference, and fitting them is easy once you have mastered pants. To alter culottes at the waist, crotch, or hips, simply use the methods shown for pants.

◆

Making a jumpsuit
or boilersuit fit

Jumpsuits are the now and future fashion, and in order to be the most flattering and comfortable they must fit you to a T — from your shoulders through your waist and crotch, down to your ankles. None of us is perfect, so our shoulders, waist and crotch don't always fall just where the pattern dictates they should. That can be remedied, however. Here's how you should go about it.

To start, buy the jumpsuit pattern by your bust measurement. Then take the following measurements and enter them on the chart below, after tying a

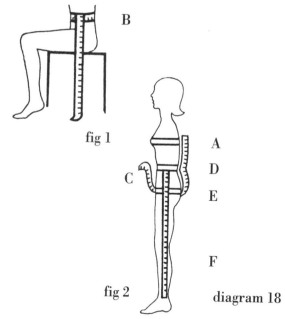

diagram 18

string tightly around your middle to pinpoint your waistline: back waist from highest prominent neck bone to waist as in diagram 18, fig 2 (A); crotch depth as in diagram 18, fig 1 (B); front and back crotch, as in diagram 18, fig 2 (C and D); hip at the fullest point (diagram 18, fig 2, E) and waist to ankle (diagram 18, fig 2, F).

For B, sit on a hard chair and measure from the string around your waist to the chair. Add ½ in (1.3 cm) ease for figures with 36 ins (91 cm) hips or less, 1 in (2.54 cm) for figures 37 ins (94 cm) or over through the hips. To determine C and D, measure your crotch from front waist to back waist, between your legs. This is the total crotch measurement. Then measure from your waist in front to a point between your legs, close to the torso, where you want the inside leg seam. This is measurement C. Subtract this from the total crotch measurement for D. Add 1 in (2.54 cm) ease to C, 2 ins (5.1 cm) ease to D. When you have completed these measurements, record them. Now you're ready to adjust the pattern pieces.

On the front and back pattern pieces, mark the crotch depth by drawing a line from the crotch points to the side seams, at right angles to grain lines (diagram 18, fig 3). Mark the waistline in this manner, also. Measure the pattern from the waist to crotch as side seams (2). Check 2 against B (your measurement plus ease) and adjust the pattern accordingly, as shown in diagram 18, figs 4 and 5.

Compare C to 3 (front crotch seam, not shown here, as only back pattern pieces are illustrated) and D to 4, and lengthen or shorten the crotch seam lines tapering the new inside leg seams (diagram 18, figs 4 and 5).

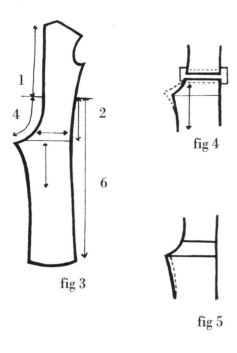

fig 3

fig 4

fig 5

diagram 18

Body measurements are given on the pattern envelope and ease is included for each particular style. Check your measurements for A, E, and F and make necessary adjustments at 1, 5, and 6.

Once you've gone through this process your next jumpsuit will be easy to alter.

	Inches/centimeters	Ease
1. Back waist	A	
2. Crotch depth	B	½ - 1 in (1.3 - 2.54 cm)
3. Front crotch	C	1 in (2.54 cm)
4. Back crotch	D	2 in (5.1 cm)
5. Hip	E	
6. Waist to ankle	F	

SEWING TERMS

Special terms are often used in directions for making up a garment. Some apply to fabrics and the way to cut them, others apply to methods of sewing. It is a help to know what they mean.

SELVAGE
The narrow, woven edge on lengthwise sides of a fabric (diagram 19).

GRAIN
The direction of the threads of a fabric (diagram 19).

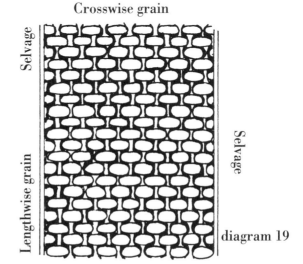

diagram 19

LENGTHWISE GRAIN
The threads that run up and down the fabric parallel to the selvage.

CROSSWISE GRAIN
The threads that run across the fabric from selvage.

ON GRAIN
A fabric is "on grain" when lengthwise and crosswise threads run perpendicular to each other to selvage.

OFF GRAIN
A fabric is "off grain" when crosswise threads are not at right angles to selvage edge and fold.

BIAS
Any direction away from the straight lengthwise or crosswise grain.

TRUE BIAS
The diagonal line formed when a fabric is folded so crosswise threads run in the same direction as the lengthwise threads (diagram 20).

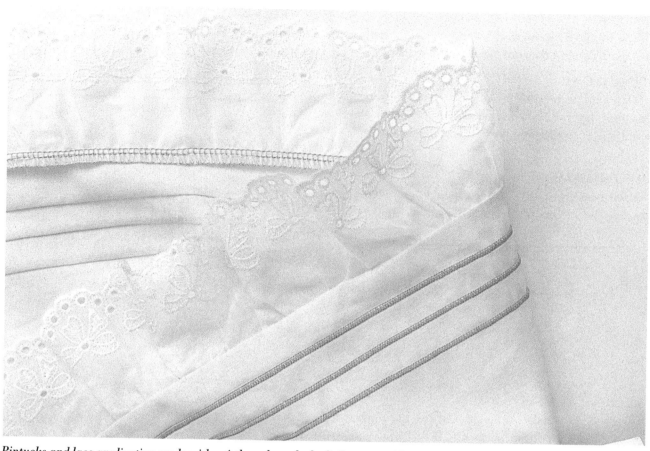

Pintucks and lace application made with a 4-thread overlock. © Courtesy of Brother Industries.

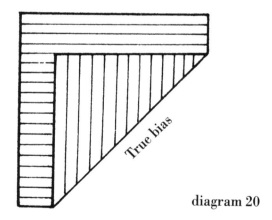

True bias

diagram 20

NAP

"With nap" refers to fabrics such as corduroy, velveteen, satin, and fleece, and to fabrics with a one-way design. These require a special cutting layout with all pattern pieces laid so their tops point in the same direction (diagram 21).

"Without nap," pattern pieces can be placed either direction on fabric.

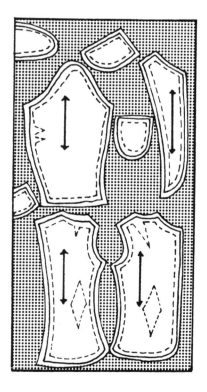

diagram 21

BASTING

Is used to hold two or more pieces of fabric together temporarily until they are permanently stitched.

PIN-BASTING

Holding fabric together by pins. Use enough pins to keep two layers of fabric from slipping. Place pins at right angles to edge and on seamline. Remove as you stitch.

HAND-BASTING

To sew temporarily by hand with long even, uneven, or diagonal stitches (diagram 22).

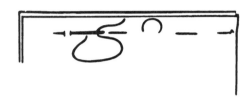

diagram 22a

MACHINE-BASTING

To sew temporarily by machine using the longest stitch. Useful for fitting garments. Before removing, clip top thread every few inches and pull out bottom thread.

BASTE-STITCH

To machine-baste as described above to mark the position of such things as buttonholes. Baste-stitch on the wrong side over the markings using contrast thread and the stitches can be seen on the right side. Remove as soon as they have served their purpose.

EVEN BASTING

Make stitches and spaces even about ¼ in (0.6 cm).

UNEVEN BASTING

Make stitches ½ in (1.3 cm) long and space between less than this.

diagram 22b

COMBINATION BASTING

Make a long stitch; then several short stitches, continue for series.

diagram 22c

DIAGONAL BASTING

Useful for slippery fabrics and basting small sections of material together. Take long diagonal stitches.

diagram 22d

REGULAR STITCHING

This refers to the length of the machine stitch used in stitching your garment. About 12 stitches to the inch (4 to the centimeter) is the usual length. Try different lengths on a scrap of your fabric as stitch length may have to be varied.

BACKSTITCHING

This stitching is used to secure thread ends at the beginning and ending of a line of stitching. Place the needle in the fabric about ¼ in (0.6 cm) from the edge and stitch backwards to the edge; then stitch forward. At the end of a stitching line, stitch backwards for about ¼ in (0.6 cm) (diagram 23). If your machine does not reverse stitch, leave the needle in the fabric at the end of the stitching; lift the presser foot and turn the fabric around on the needle. Lower the presser foot; stitch over the first stitching.

Opposite: Pillow with pintucking, lace entredeux and ruched panel. Courtesy of Elna Australia.

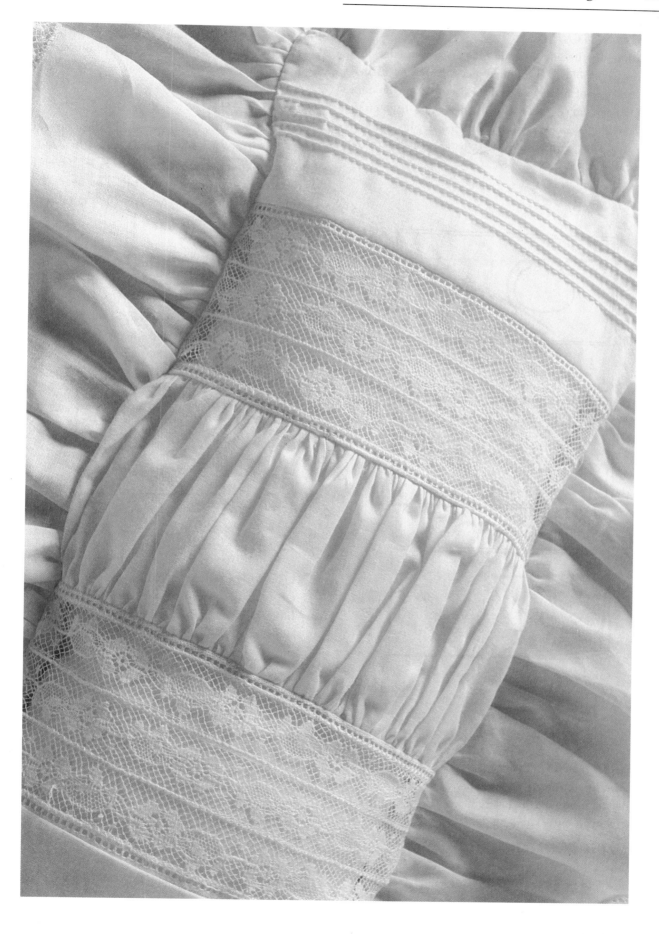

STAY-STITCHING

A line of stitching done on bias or curved edges that are to be joined to another piece. Stitch on a single thickness of material, ½ in (1.3 cm) from the edge. (On deep curves, such as necklines, stay-stitch on the seam line, ⅝ in (1.5 cm) from the edge. Stay-stitching holds the fabric so that it does not stretch in handling.

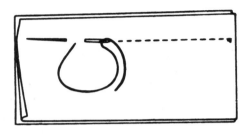

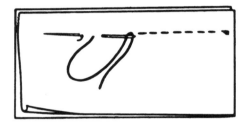

diagram 23

PLAIN BACKSTITCH

Take one running stitch, then take a stitch back, placing needle at the beginning of the first stitch and bringing it out a stitch ahead.

HALF BACKSTITCH

Take a long running stitch. Place needle half-way back and bring out two stitches ahead.

TOPSTITCHING

Stitching made on the outside of a tailored garment close to a seam line, or if used as a trim, ¼ in (0.6 cm) or more from an edge.

GATHERING

Controls fullness by drawing up fabric on a line of stitches. Use a medium long machine stitch and stitch on seam line. Sew the second row ¼ in (0.6 cm) from the first within seam allowance. For heavy fabrics, such as corduroy or velveteen, hand-gather using stitches ¼ in (0.6 cm) long.

SLIP-STITCHING

An "invisible" hand-sewing for finishing hems or facings, and interfacings in tailoring. On hems or facings, pick up one thread of the garment. Take ⅛ in (0.3 cm) stitch through fold of top fabric. To join edges, slip needle in fold of one edge, then in the other (diagram 24). Do not pull stitches tight.

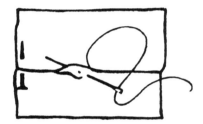

diagram 24

WHIP-STITCHING

Is used to join two pieces of fabric together, such as belts where stitches need to be invisible. Hold the edges of two pieces of ribbon together or the belt fabric and its lining. Turn both fabrics to the right side and stitch as shown (diagram 25).

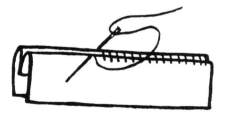

diagram 25

EASED SEAM

Extra length in one seam edge which is to be joined to a slightly shorter edge. The back shoulder seam is often slightly Longer than the front shoulder seam.

TO EASE IN

Matching the longer seam to the shorter without gathers or puckers.

EASE-STITCHING

Rows of stitching of about 12 stitches to the inch (4 to the centimeter) used to control the ease when there is more than just "slight" fullness, such as at the top of sleeves. Put one row on the seam line and the other in about ¼ in (0.6 cm) from the first inside the seam allowance. Draw up the threads from both ends to distribute the fullness evenly.

CLIP

To cut into the seam allowance from edge to seam line. Clip a seam at ½ in (1.3 cm) intervals on inward and outward curves so a curved seam on neckline or collar will lie flat. Before clipping, make a row of machine stitching on the seam line to strengthen it.

SLASH

On heavy fabric a curved dart is "slashed" open through the fold edge after stitching so it will lie flat. The opening in a long sleeve is "slashed" between the stitching lines.

TRIM

Reduces bulk of fabric. Trim a seam to make it narrower. "Trim" off corners to remove the fabric that would bunch when collars and fronts are turned (diagram 26).

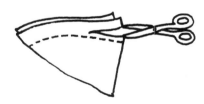

diagram 26

GRADE

Trim seam allowances on heavy fabrics in different widths to reduce the bulk and give a flatter, smoother look.

CATCH-STITCH

Hand-sew one section of a garment to another with a few loose stitches. For final finish, catch-stitch neckline facing to the garment at the shoulder seams.

KNOW YOUR FABRICS AND FINISHES

The right fabric can make all the difference to a garment and it can do wonders for your figure. Spend a little time in choosing the fabric for your next piece of sewing.

Fabrics are woven from yarns: yarns are spun from fibers. Fibers used for fashion fabrics are natural (animal and vegetable) or man-made synthetic.

Among natural fibers there are:

COTTON

A vegetable fiber from seed pod of cotton plant and may be long or short staple.

LINEN

The vegetable fiber from the leaves of the flax plant.

SILK

Natural animal fiber from cocoon spun by the silk worm.

WOOL

Natural animal fiber from the fleece of sheep. Also included in the yarn "family" are alpaca and angora goat fleeces, and camel and llama hair, as well as vicuna, cashmere, and mohair.

Man-made fibers come in two groups:

CELLULOSE GROUP

Includes rayon, acetate, and triacetate. Processed from the natural fibrous sections of wood pulp. Although they have a natural base, chemistry is used to produce the artificial fibers.

SYNTHETIC GROUP

A term used generally for all man-made fibers; strong, resilient, stable fibers that are chemically created, such as nylon, polyester, and acrylic.

◆

Fabric terms

BLEND

A yarn or fabric that combines the best qualities of two or more fibers, natural or man-made, or a combination of both.

BONDED

(1) Non-woven fabrics made by pressing fibers together with a special bonding solution to hold the fibers together.

(2) The term applied to a single piece of fabric made by bonding two fabrics together, back-to-back, with an adhesive of resin or glue. Fabric-to-fabric bonding produces a new material. Often woven and knit fabrics or laces are bonded to tricot knit or taffeta for self-lining; coating fabrics are bonded to interlining to retain shape; two-face fabrics are bonded to make them reversible or with a layer of filling for extra warmth; open weaves to cotton backing for easy handling.

BOUCLE

Any fabric made from irregularly twisted yarns; woven or knitted. The small loops give a nobbly, uneven surface texture.

COARSE/ROUGH

Fabrics with this texture are generally made of very thick and uneven yarns, or a combination of bulky yarns with smooth yarns. The result is a coarse, textured look. They may be sturdy fabrics with mixed color effect as in tweeds and hopsacks or all one color as in homespun or burlap.

CORDS/RIBS

These fabrics have a definite raised cord or ribbing on the surface, produced by alternating fine yarns with coarse yarns in a plain weave. Bedford cord has a heavy lengthwise rib; cotton broadcloth, poplin, faille, and ottoman have crosswise ribs produced by heavy crosswise yarn.

CREPE

A plain weave fabric with a crinkled or grainy surface formed by weaving various combinations of highly twisted yarns. The surface textures range from a fine, flat grain to a pebbly effect. Georgette and crepe de chine are sheer crepes; polyester crepe is drip-dry; some heavy crepes have a satin back finish.

CRINKLED

Fabric with a permanently wrinkled or puckered effect may be done chemically or with heat setting. Seersucker, with crinkled stripes, is made by weaving some threads slackly, others tightly. The blistered surface of plisse and the crepe-like crinkle of cotton georgette are produced by chemical and heat treatment of the fabric.

These surfaces may also be embossed by using hot rollers, although this crinkle is not permanent. Woven crinkles are more lasting but may be flattened in ironing.

DOUBLE-FACED

Double cloth fabrics with two right sides that can be used either side. Sides usually contrast in weave, design, or color for fashion interest. Two layers of the same fabric may give double weight and extra stability, and eliminate the need for linings and facings. Double-faced fabrics are generally of three types:

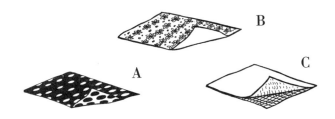

diagram 27

(1) Woven

More than one set of warp or filling yarns is used to create a two-layered fabric with an interwoven design holding the two layers together. Design and color are exactly reversed on each side. These fabrics have both sides woven together (diagram 27a).

(2) Bonded

Two separate fabrics are first woven then joined back-to-back with an adhesive. This creates a lined effect or a reversible fabric, e.g., tricot-backed jersey (diagram 27b).

(3) Connected with binding thread

Double-faced fabrics are joined with a separate binding thread between the layers. This may easily be clipped so fabric will separate for sewing concealed seams (diagram 27c).

EYELET AND EMBROIDERY

Any fabric may have embroidery or decorative needlework designs applied by hand or machine. Eyelet has open-work patterns with machine-embroidered buttonhole stitch on edges. Embroidery can be delicate or bold in design and color in all-over or border patterns.

Opposite: A selection of fabrics, woven and knitted.

FELT
Non-woven fabric that is made of matted fibers of yarn, fur or mohair. It has a dull, flat finish. Short fibers are matted by combination of heat, moisture, and pressure.

JACQUARD
Fabrics with special weaving pattern that produces an elaborately woven design. Damask patterns in a satin finish contrast with a dull ground. Brocade has heavy raised designs on a contrasting surface, often using metallic threads.

KNITS
Fabric made by interlocking loops of one or more yarns. Main types are double knits and warp knits. Single knits, such as tricot, drape softly but do not hold their shape as well as the double knits. Double knits look nearly the same on both sides, are firmer than jersey, yet still supple. Knit fabrics are made of all fibers and blends, often in textures and patterns. They have a natural stretch or elastic quality. Weights vary from gossamer to heavy coating weights. Novelty knits include multi-colored patterns, blistered, and pile surfaces. There are also jacquards, velours, ribbed ottomans, and brocades.

LACE
This "fabric" is an open fabric in which a delicate network consisting of a web of fine threads is formed into a design. Lace may be hand or machine-made from almost any fiber. When a motif is outlined with cord it is called re-embroidered lace.

ALENCON AND CHANTILLY
Light, delicate laces; usually a floral design on a fine net background.

GUIPURE
Coarser, stronger lace with geometric designs or floral motifs; usually cotton without mesh background.

LAMINATED
Term usually applied to fabric that is joined to a backing. Synthetic foam provides insulation and warmth with little weight or bulk and keeps garment shaped and wrinkle free.

LUSTRE
Surface sheen on some fabrics increases light reflection on surface threads. A process of mercerization of fabric or yarns such as chintz, polished cotton, or sateen. The satin weave may produce this sheen, as in satin sateen, and taffeta, where warp threads predominate over weft.

NAPPED
Fibrous surface is given to fabric. Some of the hairy or downy fibers are brought to the surface and then are either brushed for a soft effect or pressed flat to give a sheen. Napped fabrics, such as yarn face cloth, fur fabrics, doeskin, and suede cloth, reflect light differently when slanting up than when slanting down, so all pieces of a garment must be cut with the nap running in the same direction.

SLUBBED
Fabrics having a roughness or unevenness in their weaves. The yarns have natural thick-and-thin areas (slubs), such as in silk doupion, honan, and tussah. The "slubs" may occur at random or regular intervals. Linen has a slightly slubbed effect due to occasional thicker places in the yarn. Rayon fabrics are often made with yarn slub to give the effect of a natural unevenness. "Linen-look" or "silk-look" fabrics are often synthetic without any natural fiber in them.

PILE
Fabrics are woven with an extra set of Looped yarns. The threads forming the pile are woven over cutting wires. When withdrawn they cut the loops to form tufts on velvet, velour, and velveteen. Corduroy has fine-to-wide wales. "Deep-pile" fabrics are especially thick, usually of man-made fibers and often imitate animal fur. Terrycloth is a cotton pile fabric with long uncut loops.

PIQUE
Medium to heavyweight corded cotton cloth woven with lengthwise or crosswise ribs, or both. Pin-wale pique has very fine wales running lengthwise; wide-wale is similar. Patterned piques: waffle pique has a woven honey-comb check; birdseye is a closely spaced, diamond-shaped design. Sculptured cottons with novelty patterns are sometimes called piques.

Opposite: The modern sewing machine is capable of a wide array of stitches. The articles in this photograph feature the stitches shown in the detailed photographs on page 137. © Courtesy of Brother Industries.

PLAIDS

Pattern of colored stripes crossing each other at right angles, printed or woven in any fabric, natural or synthetic.

BALANCED PLAID (OR EVEN)

The plaid design is exactly the same on both lengthwise and crosswise directions. They are the easiest plaids for sewing.

UNEVEN PLAID

One in which the design is not the same in both lengthwise and crosswise directions. They are the most difficult plaids to use.

PRINTS

A general term given to any fabric that has a printed pattern or design applied to a plain fabric after it is woven.

QUILTED

Two layers of fabric stitched together with padding between. Stitching may be done by hand or machine. Very often a pattern, such as diamond-shaped, scroll, or circle is used, or a floral motif is outlined.

SHEER

Thin fabric with a transparent quality, generally a plain weave made from any fiber. Sheer fabrics may be soft and fluid or crisp.

SOFT SHEERS

Have very little body, such as chiffon.

SEMI-SOFT SHEERS

A heavier type of sheer, such as voile, lawn, dotted Swiss batiste, muslin.

CRISP SHEERS

Easiest to handle because they have a crisp, durable finish, such as organdie, organza.

STRETCH

Specially constructed yarns woven in fabric to allow it to give with body movement then bounce back into shape. Stretch qualities add comfort, lengthwise stretch for slacks and ski pants, crosswise stretch for blouses and jackets.

TWEED

Sturdy fabric of rough textured appearance and often with a mixed color effect, but may be plain colors, checks, and plaids. Usually made of yarn, but cotton, silk, and synthetic tweeds are available.

TWILLS

Woven diagonal lines appearing on fabric face. The basic twill runs up from left to right in a diagonal line. Variations include the herringbone formed by reversing direction of the twill at set intervals. Diagonal weaves are seen in rugged cotton denim, suit weights for tailoring, such as gabardine, and lightweight surah.

VINYL

Fashion "fabric" in clear film, printed or plain, is popular for rainwear and other garments because it is permanently waterproof. Vinyl films may be fused to a knit or woven backing for flexibility. Patent vinyl is shiny. Embossed vinyl with woven or knitted back simulates reptile skins and leather.

VINYL-COATED FABRICS

A base fabric, such as a printed or solid plain-weave cotton is coated with a thin layer of vinyl. Choose simple pattern designs with few seams and details. Raglan sleeves are best.

◆

Finishes

Treatment applied to a fabric to add to its comfort and ease of care or to enhance its appearance or feel is called finish. Finishes of some kind are applied to most fabrics; "special" finishes add qualities the fiber may lack and makes them perform more effectively. The three basic finishes are termed:

Non-durable

Lasts only until the first washing or dry cleaning.

Durable

Lasts through several washings or cleanings.

Permanent

Effective for life of fabric and garment.

Here are the "special" finish terms most generally used on fabrics.

COLORFAST

This term means that colors do not noticeably change for the life of the fabric. Colors should not rub off and should resist fading from laundering, dry cleaning, sunlight, perspiration, or ironing.

CREASE RESISTANT/WRINKLE RESISTANT

Finish applied to cotton, linen, and rayon to resist creases and help the fabric to shed wrinkles.

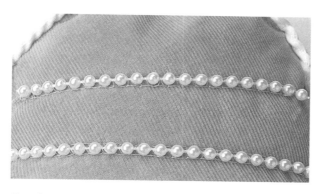

Pearl sequence stitch using a presser foot.

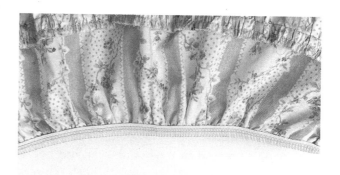

Taping stitch using a presser foot.

Piping stitch using a presser foot.

Blind stitch using a presser foot.

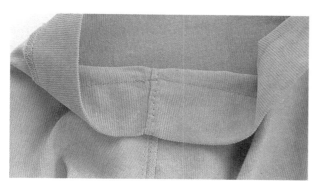

Double chain stitch.

An S-thread overlock stitch.

Narrow overlock stitch.
All photographs © Courtesy of Brother Industries.

Narrow overlock stitch with a rolled edge stitch.

DRIP-DRY

Minimum-care finish for fabrics which after washing, and without wringing are hung on a hanger to "drip dry." Garments, after laundering, should have a minimum of wrinkles and cottons require little or no ironing.

DURABLE PRESS

The most advanced in wash-and-wear finishes; it keeps creases in and wrinkles out through repeated washings. In ready-to-wear fashions it enables the fabric to be permanently pleated or creased when heat-setting is applied after the garment is made. It was first used for men's slacks to keep creases in. Garments treated with this finish no longer need to be ironed. Durable-Press or Permanent Press finish is available on piecegoods, 100 percent cotton and cotton/polyester blends. They need modified sewing techniques to prevent puckering along seam lines and zip closures.

STAIN AND SPOT RESISTANT

This finish has previously been used on home furnishing fabrics, but is now often applied to fashion fabrics. Stains caused by water and oily substances will not penetrate the fibers and can be wiped off with Scotchgard or Zepel.

SHRINKAGE CONTROL

Treatments to fabric to remove most of its tendency to shrink. "Residual shrinkage" is the percentage of shrinkage left in the fabric after application of a shrinking process.

PRE-SHRUNK

Will not shrink more than 3 percent.

SANFORIZED®

Finish applied to pre-shrunk cotton or linen, guarantees less than 1 percent shrinkage in length or width.

WASHABLE

Term describing fabrics which will not noticeably fade or shrink when they are washed. Directions are usually given for hand or machine washing and correct water temperature. Special processes applied to all-yarn fabrics now make them completely machine washable.

WASH-AND-WEAR

Various finishes that are applied to fabrics which require little or no ironing after laundering come under this heading. With crease resistant finishes, the amount of pressing necessary varies from "no-iron" to "touch-up" depending on fiber content, durability of finish, and the appropriate laundering method. Minimum care finishes give a fabric a wearable appearance after laundering, with little ironing or finishing.

WATERPROOF

This finish creates a smooth, unbroken fabric surface so no moisture or air can penetrate it; usually it is a coating of rubber, resin, or plastic, such as vinyl, to close spaces between yarns. These fabrics do not "breathe" and can be uncomfortable to wear.

WATER-REPELLENT/RESISTANT

Finish applied to fabrics to make them resist penetration by water, but air can still pass through the fabric. This fabric can "breathe" and is more comfortable to wear. Spray-on finish is available in cans.

HOW TO SEW FASHION FABRICS

Choose your fabrics carefully, making sure they suit both your pattern and your figure. A fabric can make you appear larger or smaller, taller or shorter, older or younger.

There is a world of new fabrics that add to the pleasure of creative sewing. Deep-pile, vinyls, bonded, and stretch fabrics take their place beside the classic favourites of knits, plaids, and stripes, lace, sheer, printed, and pile fabrics. There are leathers and suedes, real and imitation. They all add up to the wonderful world of fashion fabrics.

Each fabric needs some special handling, so here are the extra pointers you need to sew them successfully:

1. Always check the back of the pattern envelope for fabric and yardage suggestions. You will find a wealth of information there on suitability of fabric to the design. Some designs are made only for knit fabrics. "Simplicity" patterns, for instance, have a rule guide on the envelope for the amount of stretch needed in your fabric to make a successful garment.

2. Choose fabric carefully and follow instructions for

preparation, cutting, sewing, pressing, or care in making up a garment.

3. If your fabric has special texture interest or design, choose a simple pattern style that will show the fabric to best advantage, for the fabric itself is all-important.

If, however, your fabric is one of the simpler types, this is your chance to use a more detailed or tailored pattern, with lots of seaming, to add interest.

4. Always make any necessary alterations on the pattern before cutting fabric. This will avoid changes after the garment is cut and stitched.

5. Use fine pins, sharp shears and needles.

6. Along the cutting edge of Simplicity patterns are printed # which are called notches. They indicate where parts of the garment are to be matched and joined as the garment is constructed.

Cut notches outwards (never in); for double or triple notches, cut across top of notches on solid line.

7. Some pattern designs need a shaping material such as underlining, or lining (some laces and sheers, for example). In other cases, an underlining or lining is left to you, the type depending on your choice of fabric.

If an underlining or lining is needed, cut garment and lining from the same pattern piece. Treat the two pieces as one, baste fabric and underlining together, then sew as one. Linings are made separately and joined at the major seams, such as the waistline, for a finished look inside the garment.

8. Before stitching, always test the sewing machine setting on a folded scrap of fabric. Check to be sure the needle size, type of thread and stitch length are suitable for the fabric to be sewn. Make any adjustments to stitch length, and tension.

9. Layer bulky seams enclosed inside a collar, cuff, or facing, to reduce bulk. The seam allowances are trimmed in different widths, with one seam allowance narrower than the other. The seam allowance next to the outside fabric should be the widest to prevent a bulky ridge from showing after pressing.

10. Press as you sew. Correct pressing shapes a garment and makes it look professionally made.

◆
Stretch fabrics

Stretch in a fabric means it gives with body movement, adds comfort, shape retention, wrinkle resistance, and longer wear. Specially constructed yarns woven into fabric make it stretch when pulled — then bounce back into shape.

There are three types of stretch fabrics:

Filling (horizontal) stretch
Crosswise from selvage to selvage. Used for blouses, shirts, dresses, jackets, and skirts.

Warp (up and down or vertical) stretch
Lengthwise or parallel to selvages. Best for pants.

Two-way stretch
In both directions. Up to now, used mostly in swimsuits and foundation garments.

Stretch is being applied to an ever-widening range of fabrics, lightweight batistes, broadcloth, pique, and seersucker; firmly woven denims, gabardines, yarn flannels, poplins, twills, corduroys, and tweeds. Far greater comfort and freedom of movement in all types of fashion come with introduction of stretch fabrics.

PURCHASING FABRIC

Test the direction of the stretch to be sure it is that needed for garment. Pants may be made from a filling stretch fabric if it is wide enough to lay pattern along crosswise grain. In this way, stretch will still run from waist to ankle.

PATTERNS

Use patterns for stretch fabrics in your usual size. Make pattern alterations in the usual way. Pants should have a stirrup under the foot.

HANDLING

If not labelled "pre-shrunk," shrink fabric by steam pressing. Use heat setting suitable to fiber content. Press lightly and lift iron to avoid stretching fabric. Before cutting, lay the fabric smooth and flat for about 24 hours.

LAYOUT

Place pattern on the fabric so that stretch runs in the required direction: across the shoulders for blouses, shirts, dresses, and jackets; from waist to ankle in pants, slacks, or shorts; from side to side in skirts. Lay waistband in non-stretch direction.

CUTTING
Avoid stretching the fabric as you work. Roll or fold excess so it is all on table and do not let fabric hang over edges of cutting table. Place pins perpendicular to stretch direction.

SEWING MACHINE
Pressure
Medium to light.

Stitch length
Short — 14 to 15 stitches per inch (5 to 6 per centimeter).

Needle
Fine to medium — size 11 to 14.

Thread
Textured nylon or nylon threads have more "give" with stretch seams than mercerized. With a straight stitch and nylon thread maintain stretch in the seams by stretching fabric slightly as you stitch. Reinforce the seam with a second row of stitching sewn close to first, a small zigzag stitch allows greater stretch in seams. Experiment first with test threads to be sure stitching won't break when seam is pulled.

SEWING TIPS
Interfacing
May be used as usual on garment where stretch is not important.

Lining
If needed, use only a stretch lining or bias-cut tricot. Lining must stretch in same direction as outer fabric. Do not sew lining into side seams — join to garment at neck and waistline seams.

Slide fastener
Hand-baste in position. Ease fabric, do not stretch. Sew fastener in by hand or machine. Keep opposite seam firm for length of fastener so both sides will hang in same way.

Buttonholes
Make them perpendicular to stretch direction. Strengthen with a small patch of iron-on or firmly woven interfacing.

Hems
Zigzag stitch ¼ in (0.6 cm) from edge or use bias seam binding. On heavier fabrics, stitch ¼ in (0.6 cm) from edge or overcast. Loosely slipstitch hem in place.

PRESSING
Use steam or setting suitable to fiber content. Lift iron to avoid stretch or pull on fabric.

◆

Bonded fabrics
Bonded fabrics have a lining permanently fused to the woven or knitted outer fabric. The added body creates a stable fabric structure and wrinkle resistance; fabrics will not stretch or fray, need no interfacing or interlining, and little pressing. The smooth, silky backing adds new comfort and a lining to fabrics such as yarn flannel, jersey, and lace.

PURCHASING FABRIC
Check for a straight grain. These fabrics cannot be easily straightened if bonded off grain.

PATTERNS
Simple patterns are best. Remember some bonded fabrics are soft, some stiff, some fine, some bulky.

HANDLING
The fabrics are pre-shrunk, stable, and firm. Fabrics cannot be straightened, cut garment following lengthwise grain or rib: crosswise grain may not be straight but appearance or wear of garment will not be affected.

CUTTING AND MARKING
Place pattern on right side of fabric where grain line shows.

Cut single thickness for best results. For pieces cut on fold: cut first half, flip pattern over on fold line; cut other half.

If possible, cut garment and facing in one to eliminate seam.

Mark with tailor tacks.

SEWING MACHINE
Tension and pressure
Medium to light.

Stitch length
Medium to long.

Needle
Fine to medium — size 11 to 14.

Thread
Use any suitable for outer fabric content.

Modern sewing machines usually have a special stitch setting that sews stretch into the seams of knitted fabrics.

SEWING TIPS
Hand-baste and fit to avoid stitch marks. No seam finish is needed if fabric does not ravel.

Darts
Press darts flat.

Seam finishes
Some fabrics are springy, press open and topstitch close to seam line. Or, trim one edge close to seam line, press and stitch other edge over it — this prevents seam allowance from rolling.

Facings
On heavy fabrics, reduce bulk by using a lining fabric for facings. Or substitute a braid-trimmed edge.

Buttonholes
Reinforce with strips of lightweight fabric.

Hems
Hem tricot-bonded garments through lining only.

PRESSING
Use steam or dry iron at heat setting suitable for outer fabric. Test before pressing garment. Use dry or damp press cloth to protect tricot lining.

◆

Knitted fabrics

Knitted fabrics are made in a variety of fibers — natural and synthetic — and lend comfort and a fluid elegance to every fashion. Some are sold in tubular form; others are sold flat.

Single knits drape softly. Double Knits are not difficult to handle. They are in double stitch and firmer, yet still flexible; they tailor beautifully and usually do not need underlining.

PURCHASING FABRIC
The lengthwise rib is the "straight-of-grain." Check to be sure rib is not severely twisted out of line. It is better not to buy fabric with a prominent weave if it is more than ½ in (⅓ cm) off grain: it cannot be straightened.

Weight can be your guide in choosing knit jersey: fine for blouses; medium weights for dresses; heavy weights for suits and coats.

Lining slim skirts and completely underlining the loose knits helps them retain their shape.

PATTERNS
The pattern envelope will guide you with knit fabric suggestions.

"Designed for Knit Fabrics Only" styles are for stretchable, unbonded knits. These patterns have little or no ease and often darts may have to be omitted. For a good-loooking garment, use a knit with lots of stretch, or "give," for these styles. At times patterns will include one or two views for stretchable knits only, while other views will be for woven fabrics and knits that are firm and stable or bonded.

"Ideal for Knits" styles have the usual amount of ease and fit equally well in woven fabrics. Use a knit that's firm and stable, or one that's bonded, for these styles.

PREPARATION
All knit fabrics, except tricot-backed jersey should be pre-shrunk before cutting.

If using a tubular knit, cut along one rib close to the fold line to open it.

Check "grain" of fabric; pull gently on bias to straighten.

Press out folds of tubular knit. If folds will not press out completely place pattern on fabric so creases will not be prominent on finished garment.

CUTTING OUT
Look closely at right side of knitted fabric before pinning pattern pieces to it. Align lengthwise pattern marking with lengthwise rib.

Lay fabric flat on sewing table, avoid stretching while planning and cutting. Remember knits stretch more in width than in length.

Since some patterns include views for both stretchable and stable knits, check to make sure you use the correct layout and pattern pieces. Some tricots, jerseys, and stretch terries curl up at the edges, making layout tedious. In these cases it is easiest to lay out the pattern on the wrong side of the fabric and to place plans at right angles to the seam lines.

SEWING MACHINE

Tension
Medium to light.

Stitch length
12 - 15 per inch (4 - 6 per centimeter), or a small zigzag.

Needle
For lightweight knits — size 11 (fine); Double and heavier knits — medium size 14.

Thread
Terylene, nylon, or mercerized cotton, depending on fibrous content of knit.

SEWING TIPS

In lightweight knits
Stay-stitch shoulders, neckline and reinforce shoulder and waistline with pre-shrunk woven seam tape to prevent stretching.

Interfacing
Use on faced edges and under buttonholes to reinforce. Also waistbands.

On bulky knits
Cut facing of lining fabric.

Lining
Cut lining pieces same as garment. Wrong sides together, stitch knit to lining pieces ½ in (1.3 cm) from edge and sew as one fabric. For skirt and one-piece dress, make lining separately. Join to bodice at neckline and armhole; and at waistline. At hem, finish lining separately, about 1 in (2.54 cm) shorter than dress. Knits do not ravel so special seam finishes are not needed.

Make tailor's hem
Let garments hang a day before hemming. Pink, machine edge — stitch raw edge of hem; catch loosely to garment.

To hold an A-line shape at the hem of a dress or skirt, a layer of lightweight woven interfacing cut on the bias should be used to back the hem. Cut bias strips 1 in (2.54 cm) wider than, and the length of, the hem; pin to wrong side of hem, the lower edge ½ in (1.3 cm) below hem fold. Baste to garment, then follow the steps for a catch-stitched hem. Remove basting stitches.

To make a catch-stitched hem, finish the raw edge with a row of machine stitches, either straight [about 10 stitches to the inch (4 to the centimeter)] or zigzag. No hem tape, other than a stretch lace type for purely decorative purposes, is required. Baste hem in place ¼ in (0.6 cm) from raw edge. Fold hem back ¼ in (0.6 cm) on the wrong side and catch-stitch loosely to garment. Press hem lightly.

Set-in sleeves
With the side seams open and the garment flat, pin sleeve to garment at underarm, notches, shoulder seam, and a few strategic places here and there in between to distribute the ease. No basting is necessary. Sew sleeve to the garment, stretching as you sew. Sew the side and sleeve seams in one continuous stitching line.

Slide fasteners
Setting the slide fastener in the fabric by hand works best on stretchable knits. Here is a quick way to position the fastener. Use transparent adhesive or masking tape to hold the fastener and seam allowances in position. Hand pick the fastener. Use silk buttonhole twist or embroidery thread and take tiny backstitches. Work from bottom of fastener to neckline.

Knit slacks
To prevent baggy knees in slacks made from stretchy knits, borrow this idea from the makers of expensive imported knit slacks. Sew pieces of lightweight, non-stretch fabric in the seams of each leg at the knee.

Although slacks from polyester or yarn knit will hold a heat-set crease, those from cotton knits resist neat creases. So the answer to this problem is the stitched-down crease. First fold the finished slacks so side seam and inner leg seam meet. Press crease on the front only, stopping about 6 ins (15 cm) from the waist. Baste crease. stitch by machine as close to the edge of the crease as possible. Remove basting stitches.

PRESSING
Press with lengthwise rib. Lift and lower iron; do not stretch or pull fabric.

◆

Nylon jersey

CUTTING
Use fine pins, place in seam allowance possible.

SEWING MACHINE

Tension

Loosen tension of upper and bobbin heads.

Stitch length

Use about 12 stitches per inch (4 per centimeter).

Needle

Sharp, fine — size 11. Change the needle when it becomes dull. Hold fabric taut in front and behind presser foot as you stitch to help prevent puckers.

SEWING TIPS

Pin-baste in seam lines to prevent pin marks from showing. Stitch at a slow, even speed to prevent puckering.

Hems

Stitch or zigzag edge. Hand-sew hem loosely to prevent puckering.

◆

Sheers

Sheer fabrics are always firm favorites for "special" occasions. In both bouffant and slim styles sheers impart a graceful feeling, an enchanting feminine look.

There are three types of sheer fabrics:

Soft and fluid sheers such as chiffon.

Semi-soft sheers such as voile lawn, dimity.

Crisp sheers such as organdie. Crisp sheers are easiest to handle.

PURCHASING FABRIC

Sheers can be lined or worn with a separate slip. (Sleeves and upper bodices can remain unlined.) Choose linings carefully to give depth, interest or opaqueness to sheer fabric. Wide hems and double hems add body. Allow 3 ins (7.5 cm) hem on straight skirt, 2 ins (5 cm) on full skirts. If not allowed for on your pattern, be sure to purchase enough fabric to allow for a deep hem.

PATTERNS

Patterns designed for sheers are best, as they include all instructions for that final finish.

Tucks are easier to make on the crisp sheers.

Select a pattern with as few seams as possible.

HANDLING

Sheers have a tightly woven selvage which may cause the fabric to "buckle." If so, clip through the entire depth of the selvage every few inches (8 cm).

CUTTING AND MARKING

Soft sheers may shift, so pin to tissue paper to prevent the fabric from shifting. Cut with very sharp shears. Remove the paper, then mark construction details.

When possible, cut full gathered skirts on the crosswise grain to eliminate some seams.

Sleeves are generally cut from a single layer of fabric.

Using sheer alone, eliminate facing at neckline, sleeves, or armholes and use a French binding of self material.

Take a ¾ in (2 cm) bias strip of the fabric, fold it in half lengthwise, and lightly press. Taking ⅛ in (0.3 cm) seam allowance on the cut edges, baste the double bias to right side of neckline ¼ in (0.6 cm) lower than the finished neckline is to be. Slightly stretch bias as you baste. Machine stitch, turn bias to wrong side of dress and slip-stitch folded edge to stitchline.

On the full soft sheers a wide hem is often used. On circular skirts a narrow hem. Straight and A-line skirts have the normal 2¼ in (5.6 cm) hem.

SEWING MACHINE

Tension

Average to loose, depending on fabric and thread.

Stitch length

About 14 - 16 stitches per inch (5 to 6 per centimeter).

Needle

Very fine — size 9 to 10.

Thread

Fine thread, suitable to fabric or mercerized cotton thread.

SEWING TIPS

Soft sheers

To prevent marring surface when sewing, stitch against strips of tissue paper, handling paper and fabric as one.

Seams and seam finishes

(1) Double stitched seam. Stitch a plain seam. Make a second row of stitching about ⅛ in (0.3 cm) from the seam line, within the seam allowance. Trim seam close to this stitching.

(2) Make a narrow French seam. First, with wrong sides together, sew the seam ¼ in (0.6 cm) outside the stitching line (within the seam allowance). Trim the seam allowance to ⅛ in (0.3 cm); press, turn to wrong side and stitch again ¼ in (0.6 cm) from edge encasing the raw edges. Press to one side.

(3) The almost-invisible seam. (a) Right sides together, stitch ⅛ in (0.3 cm) from seam line within the seam allowance. (b) Fold and press both layers of seam to one side along stitching line. Stitch again, close to folding edge. (c) Trim off seam allowance close to stitching. (d) Turn seam to wrong side; stitch close to edge.

Buttonholes

Machine buttonholes are usually best on sheers.

Hems

Turn hem to inside; turn edge under ¼ in (0.6 cm) and stitch. Slip-stitch hem in place.

Double fold hems

Turn hem up desired depth; turn up again so raw edge is in fold.

Narrow hem

Fold fabric to wrong side ⅛ in (0.3 cm) outside marked hemline and press. Stitch as close to the edge as possible. Trim off excess fabric close to stitching. Turn the stitched edge to the wrong side again; press. Stitch again close to edge. For a circular skirt use a narrow, hand-rolled hem.

◆

Lace

Lace lends its special charm to clothes. Laces vary from heavy cotton to delicate silk and nylon, and yarn. Despite the fragile look, lace often masks strength, wrinkle resistance, and ease-of-care.

PURCHASING FABRIC

Weight and type of lace, all-over pattern, a one-way, or panel design are important considerations.

Net makes the lace design stand out; an opaque underlining eliminates transparency. Sew lightweight laces to the underlinings for body and support. Make linings from fine silk for softly-draped lines, taffeta for crisp bouffant effects, organza for a semi-sheer look. Bonded laces where lining is fused to lace are available.

Not all laces need to be underlined. You can make a separate matching or contrasting slip.

Jackets and coats can be lined in the usual way.

PATTERNS

The right pattern will show the lace to best advantage. Look for simple lines, and use a minimum number of seams and darts to keep lace motif intact.

CUTTING AND MARKING

Place pattern pieces carefully to show lace design at its best.

If matching is needed, match at seams and front openings.

Cut underlining pieces from the same pattern as the garment. For more formal designs, leave sleeves and upper part of bodice unlined, or use chiffon or net for underlining upper bodice.

In facings in heavy laces, cut from lining fabric. For unlined or sheer garments, cut from matching net. An elegant finish is achieved by edging with binding cut from chiffon or satin.

For lined garments, mark construction details on the wrong side of the lining pieces only. For unlined laces use tailor tacks.

SEWING MACHINE

Tension
Slightly loose.

Pressure
Adjust to fabric.

Stitch length
Medium to long — 15 stitches per inch (6 per centimeter).

Needle
Fine — size 11.

Thread
Mercerized, nylon, or silk, depending on fabric.

Opposite: Beautiful lace, old or new, gives a classic look to garments.

SEWING TIPS

Construction linings
With right side of lining and wrong side of lace together, sew along all edges except hem, and treat as one fabric when putting garment together. All seams will be hidden.

Darts
Stitch lace-and-lining fabric together down the middle line of the dart to hold in place.

In unlined heavier laces darts are easier to stitch if slashed open first to within ⅝ in (1.5 cm) of point. Stitch; press edges open, trim back to ¼ in (0.6 cm).

Hold lined heavy laces together with a line of machine stitching through outline of dart. Stitch dart and finish.

Seams
Stitch fine laces over tissue paper.

Seam finishes
For laces with opaque linings, use a plain seam; pink, stitch, or overcast edges. For unlined laces stitch on seam line then stitch, or zigzag ¼ in (0.6 cm) from seam line within seam allowance. Trim close to stitching and press to one side.

Armhole seams
Make second row of stitching ¼ in (0.6 cm) from seam line in seam allowance. Trim, press.

For gathered or soft-pleated skirts
Stitch side seams of lace and lining pieces separately. Then place right side of lining to wrong side of lace. Join together along upper edges and along seam line of left side opening. Gather or pleat as if one fabric. Hem lining and lace separately.

Facings
In underlined garments, hand-sew facing edges to lining only. Finish edges of net facings with row of straight or zigzag stitching.

Slide fasteners
Stitch lace-and-lining fabric together along seam lines at fastener closing. Insert fastener using hand stitches for a more invisible closure.

Buttonholes
Machine buttonholes are best. Some sewing machines have a special cam for making buttonholes on lace.

Hems
With underlined garments trim underlining so edge comes to crease of hem and finish edge with seam tape. Catch hem to underlining.

In unlined garments, make hem by:
(1) Running a line of machine stitching ¼ in (0.6 cm) from trimmed raw edge of lace. Hand-stitch hem in place. (2) Finishing edge with zigzag stitch then hand-stitch in place. (3) Or, turn edge up ⅝ in (1.5 cm) and stitch ¼ in (0.6 cm) horsehair braid through hem allowance and skirt. Trim lace close to braid.

PRESSING
Set iron for fiber content of fabric. Press from wrong side with lace over dowel to prevent back flattening.

Leather and suede fabrics
Animal skins are fashionable. They come in smooth, supple leather and napped suede. These skins make fashion garments of classic and lasting beauty.

PURCHASING SKINS
Leather and suede are bought by the skin. Choose skins uniform in weight and hue.

Buy your pattern first and lay out pattern pieces to determine how many skins you will need.

Interfacings are important for holding shape.

PATTERNS
Patterns should be simple with straight lines, few seams, darts and details.

CUTTING
Avoid waste in cutting. Trim pattern seams ⅜ in (1 cm) to reduce bulk.

Eliminate seams if possible — such as straight middle back seam. A complete paper pattern for front and back should be cut and used.

Lay skins flat. Place the complete pattern on a single layer of skin to plan your cutting out.

If skin is not wide enough to make a complete front or back, cut two separate pieces and seam in the middle. Add seam allowance when cutting.

Smooth leather: place pattern pieces all lengthwise or crosswise on right side of skins. Suede: cut with tops of all pieces pointing to neck of the skin, so that "nap" will lie in the same direction.

Pin marks will show, so hold pattern pieces in place with weights or tape pattern to skins.

Mark darts, sewing details with chalk on wrong side.

Extend front interfacing to armhole for strength.

Cut facings from skins or lining fabric. Or, line to edge with taffeta to reduce bulk.

SEWING MACHINE

Tension

Balanced, slightly loose.

Pressure

Light; adjust to weight of skins.

Stitch length

Long — 7 - 10 stitches per inch (3 to 4 per centimeter).

Needle

Use a special wedge-shaped machine needle for stitching leather.

Thread:

Heavy-duty mercerized or synthetic.

SEWING TIPS

Needle marks will show. Stitch with care to avoid ripping. Do not stretch as you stitch.

Darts

Stitch, slash, flatten, glue in place.

Seams

Avoid pins. Use paper clips to hold layers together. Do not backstitch; tie thread ends.

Stitch seams

Press seams open and flatten with a mallet. Then glue seams flat. Spread a thin line of fabric glue or rubber cement over stitches on both sides of seam line; press seam open, using brown paper "press cloth." On curved seams, cut out small "Vs" before finishing so that seam will be flat.

Attach lining to facing

(1) Bind facing with bias tape and hand stitch lining to binding. (2) Or, glue lining under edge of facing.

Buttonholes

Always test first on scrap of leather. (1) Use bound buttonholes on soft leather. (2) Machine buttonholes

— stitch rectangle close to slash marking. Stitch again just outside this first row — slash.

Hems

Make 1 or 2 in (2.54 or 5.1 cm) wide. Turn up then glue and hammer lightly in place.

PRESSING

Do not use steam. Press with warm dry iron over a dry press cloth or brown paper.

◆

Vinyl fabrics

The look of beautifully tanned leathers has been faked so expertly in ways that only an expert tanner can tell the difference. They are being used for dresses, suits, pants, capes, jackets, and a whole range of accessories.

PURCHASING FABRIC

There are three basic types of leather-like fabrics:

Vinyl surface with a cotton backing has smooth or antiqued finishes. They are light in weight, often machine washable.

Cotton canvas, with a resin or plastic-coated outer surface, is washable, and can be dry cleaned. It may be ironed lightly and carefully on the wrong side.

Nylon knit has an embossed surface to look like soft, sleek kid. This can be washed and pressed very lightly.

PATTERNS

When you begin working with these fake leathers, choose a simple pattern. Raglan or kimono sleeves are the easiest.

CUTTING AND MARKING

Interlinings are recommended in buttonhole and neckline area.

Cut single thicknesses only.

Linings are used in jackets and coats for comfort.

Keep the fabric rolled until ready for use to prevent creasing.

Pin the fabric in seam allowances only, as pin marks show.

SEWING TIPS

A medium tension and light pressure will do for the machine.

As fabrics respond differently to machines, test first

before doing the seams.

Use a tailor's hem or rubber cement to fix the hemline.

◆
Mohair fabrics

Softly spun mohair is strong and lustrous. Classic sportswear and separates, dresses, jackets, and coats look great in this fabric.

Mohair may be woven or knit, looped or brushed, and is often combined with other fibers in fabrics that are bulky but lightweight.

PURCHASING FABRIC
Buy yardage given for fabrics "with nap" — refer to back of pattern envelope.

Knit mohair
Dry clean only, do not steam press or sponge in preparing fabric for cutting, during making up or in care of garment.

Underline with firm backing or, for a soft effect, use lightweight fabric such as thin silk.

PATTERNS
Simply styled lines complement the bulky fabric. Avoid pleats. Select pattern with minimum of seams.

CUTTING
Refold knit mohair to avoid the original pressed-in side creases used in manufacturing.

Use nap layout — with loops or nap running down.

Do not stretch fabric as you cut.

Mark with tailor tacks.

SEWING MACHINE
Tension
Loosen tension upper and bobbin threads.

Stitch length
Average — 12 stitches per inch (4 per centimeter).

Needle
Medium — size 14.

Thread
Mercerized.

SEWING TIPS
Stitch slowly and carefully to avoid catching loops on presser foot. Stitch with tissue paper placed between both sides of fabric and machine.

Seams
Overcast, bind, or zigzag seam edges.

Bound buttonholes
To hold shape, back with a matching firm fabric. For corded buttonholes, interface strips that cover cord with same backing.

PRESSING
Use a dry iron and very little heat. Never steam press; steam will shrink the fabric and flatten the texture of the surface.

◆
Diagonal fabrics

Diagonal fabrics have a prominent twill weave. Woven diagonal lines of the same or contrasting color appear on fabric surface. They require no special sewing tips, but the pattern and proper cut are all-important. Diagonals cannot be matched when a bias seam is used.

PURCHASING FABRIC
Remember that many twill weaves — such as gabardine, silk surah, and denim — are so closely woven that the diagonal line is not prominent. But some of these fabrics may show a color difference between pieces joined on the bias.

PATTERNS
Check back of pattern envelope — some designs are marked "not suitable" for diagonal fabrics.

Simple styles, slim skirts, few seams, set-in sleeves, and straight underarm darts are best.

When using prominent diagonals avoid bias seams, long bias darts, wide A-line or gored skirts, long kimono sleeves, and deep V-necklines.

CUTTING
If pattern is carefully selected you can follow the regular cutting layout. Experiment with placing collars, waistbands, pockets, and other trimming details to see which way you want the diagonal lines to run.

For definite diagonal pattern, cut garment so diagonal lines run from upper left side towards lower right in garment front, and from upper right to lower left in garment back. The diagonal continues around figure in same direction.

A beautifully made dress for a little girl. The detail shows the smocking on the bodice. Courtesy Avalon Craft Cottage.

Chevron

You can form chevrons if the fabric is identical on both sides. Open fabric to its full width. Measure pattern pieces being used for chevrons to determine length. Cut this length twice. Place the right side of one piece against the wrong side of the other. Place your pattern pieces on the double layer following pattern layout.

◆

Nap and pile fabrics

Both nap and pile add a special look to a fabric, giving it a feeling of warmth and luxury.

Napped fabrics — such as yarn broadcloth and fleecy fabrics — have had fibers raised from the body of the cloth. These are brushed for soft effect or pressed flat to give a sheen.

Pile fabrics are woven with an extra set of looped yarns; these are clipped to form the special textures of fabrics such as corduroy, velveteen, and velvet.

PURCHASING FABRIC

Buy the yardage given on your pattern envelope for fabrics "with nap." The pattern will include a layout for napped, pile, or any fabric which must be cut with the tops of all pieces pointing in the same direction.

PATTERNS

Choose a simple design that will emphasize the fabric. Look for minimum of seams, darts, and tucks.

CUTTING AND MARKING

Pile reflects light differently when it slants up and when it slants down. Run your hand along the grain. The nap running down has a smoother feeling and lighter, shinier look. Nap or pile running up has a rougher touch, richer color.

In general, cut napped fabrics (such as yarn broadcloth) with nap running down. Corduroy cut this way wears longer.

For richer color cut most pile weaves such as velvet and velveteen, with nap running up.

Important

The nap on all pieces must run in the same direction. Place pattern pieces on fabric with tops all pointing the same way.

Cut velvet, velveteen, and corduroy with right sides on outside to prevent the pile from matting together. The corduroy rib also is easier to follow.

To prevent velvet from slipping, pin the fabric edges together before placing the pattern. On delicate fabrics pin in seam allowances only.

Baste with silk thread to prevent marks when it is removed.

SEWING MACHINE
Tension and pressure
Light.

Stitch length
About 10 stitches per inch (3 to 4 per centimeter).

Needle
Fine.

Thread
Mercerized for corduroy, velveteen; silk or mercerized for wools, velvets.

SEWING TIPS
Seams
Use silk thread to baste before machine stitching to prevent slippage and puckered seams. Always sew in the direction of nap or pile.

Seam finishes
Turned edges leave press-marks on right side. Pink or overcast seams or zigzag raw edges. Bind seam edges that ravel in seam tape.

Gathering
Hand-gather with ¼ in (0.6 cm) stitches and ¼ in (0.6 cm) spaces. To keep threads from breaking, use silk, nylon, or heavy-duty thread on corduroy.

Facings
Use lightweight fabrics such as organza or taffeta for velvets and velveteens, and lightweight cotton for washable garments.

Hem and facing finishes
Pink and stitch or zigzag raw edge or stitch bias, seam binding to edge; loosely catch hem to garment as for tailor's hem.

PRESSING

To open seams in velvet, stand iron on end and place a damp cloth over it. Hold the wrong side of the velvet by the seams and run along the covered iron.

◆
Faked furs

Cleverly faked — you would take them for real, the latest designs in these deep-pile fabrics bring the luxury look of fur into every woman's wardrobe. This year's fashion "animal kingdom" fabrics include leopard, pony, zebra, lamb, and tiger. The pile is usually synthetic with either a knitted or woven backing of cotton, acrylic, or other fiber.

PURCHASING FABRIC
Follow yardage charts and layouts for fabrics "with nap." Read labels: some of these pile fabrics may be washed; others must be dry cleaned.

PATTERNS
Simple designs (with few seams in coats, jackets), accessories, and a fashion favourite — sleeveless pop-overs. Avoid collars, set-in sleeves or buttonholes, and inset pockets.

CUTTING
When using double width fabric cut pattern in one piece to eliminate straight middle back seams. If possible, cut straight facings in one with garment or from lighter weight matching fabric. If suitable, bind edges with braid.

Place pattern on wrong side with tops of all pattern pieces in same direction. Cut so pile runs down. With very deep pile, cut in single layers. Pile may be easier to handle if you cut with a razor blade from the wrong side, as for fur.

SEWING MACHINE
Tension
Loose.

Pressure
Light.

Stitch length
8 - 10 stitches per inch (3 to 4 per centimeter).

Needle
Medium size.

Thread
Mercerized cotton thread.

SEWING TIPS
It helps to hand-baste fabric to prevent "creeping" and puckering while machine stitching.

Seams
Stitch in direction of pile wherever possible. Reinforce points of strain with seam tape. Use pin to lift pile caught in stitched seam to right side.

Facings
Where facings do not show use taffeta facings to eliminate bulk of deep pile fabrics.

Darts
To finish, cut open and press flat, using tip of iron only.

On deep pile use bias hem facing and catch-stitch hem to backing. For other piles finish raw edge with stretch lace seam binding. Overcast catching seam binding to backing.

PRESSING
Prevent flattening of pile by placing it pile side down on velvet board, with press cloth over backing. Steam lightly, holding iron above fabric. If two pile sides (such as front facing) must be pressed, turn one end of a terry towel up over facing.

HOW TO PRESS NAPPED FABRICS
For fabrics with a brushed nap, press in the direction in which the nap runs. Use a light pressure and a slightly damp press cloth with a dry iron. After pressing, brush lightly with the nap.

For fabrics with unbrushed nap place a piece of wool fabric over the ironing board. Place right side of the garment against the yarn. Press on the wrong side. While the fabric is still steaming, brush with the grain of the fabric.

HOW TO PRESS PILE FABRICS
The best results are obtained by using a velvet pressing board or, as it is often called, a needle board. This is a heavy backing canvas covered with wire bristles called "needles." Place the pile side against the needles and press lightly; the needles prevent the pile being crushed.

If the garment has a facing of pile fabric, place in between two velvet pressing boards or turn one end of the board over the facing. Use a steam iron or damp cloth with dry iron over the top board.

As an alternative to a velvet board, stand a dry iron on its heel; place a damp press cloth over the wrong side of the fabric and pass the garment back and forth over the iron so the steam penetrates the pile.

Another substitute is to lay the fabric pile side down over a heavy terry towel (or a pad covered with a towel) and press lightly with a steam iron or a damp cloth.

◆

Glamor fabrics

There is nothing more feminine or more elegant to wear for summer's special occasions than the glamor fabrics. They range from the sheers (which we've already covered) to the lustrous sequined or metallic finishes.

Sequined fabrics

After cutting, catch ends piece of chain stitch with which sequin strips are sewn to fabric, either by hand or by stay-stitching on the machine.

Stitch slowly and keep extra needles close at hand. You may break a few. When it's necessary to remove some sequins (as at slide fastener seam allowances) cut through each sequin up to the hole only, and pull off. Do not cut retaining threads. Do not press.

Metallic brocades

Test the effect of heat on a sample fabric (some metallics may melt). Use warm, dry iron and press cloth, with light pressure, from the wrong side.

To keep the presser foot of your machine from slipping beneath the threads that "float" over many metallic brocade surfaces, sew over strips of tissue paper.

TIPS FOR A GOOD-LOOKING GARMENT

◆

Seams and seam finishes

Seams and seam finishes are mostly determined by the fabric and their use on the garment. Standard seam allowance on patterns is ⅝ in (1.5 cm) wide.

PLAIN SEAM

Most common on firm fabrics and lined coats. With right sides together stitch seam and press open (diagram 28).

OVERCAST SEAM

Single for fabric edges that fray. Tack, stitch and press seam open. Overcast each edge, taking up about ⅛ in (0.3 cm) of the fabric (diagram 29).

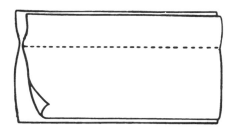

diagram 28

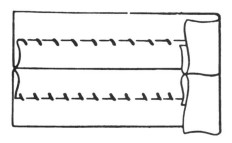

diagram 29

OVERCAST SEAM

Sew double for armholes, waistline seams: neaten together. Tack and stitch seam. Overcast edges together and press to one side (diagram 30).

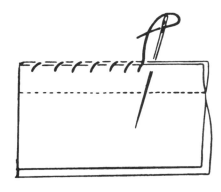

diagram 30

PINKED SEAM

For non-frayable fabrics — yarn, silk, velvet. After seam is stitched finish edges with pinking shears. Press seams open (diagram 31).

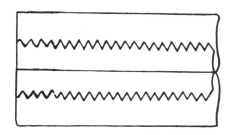

diagram 31

MACHINE FINISHED EDGES

For non-bulky fabrics that ravel: stitch seam, turn, and stitch raw edges, press seam open (diagram 32).

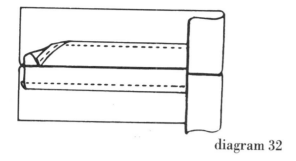

diagram 32

BOUND SEAMS

For unlined jackets and coats: stitch and press seam open. Tack binding to cover each raw edge then stitch through all layers (diagram 33).

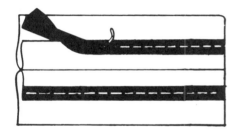

diagram 33

DOUBLE STITCHED SEAM

For sheer fabrics: stitch an ordinary seam. Make a second row of stitching close to the first. Trim close to second stitching (diagram 34).

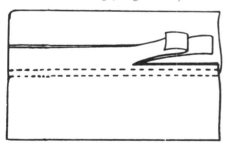

diagram 34

FRENCH SEAM

For washable sheers. Wrong sides together make seam half depth of seam allowance. Trim close to stitching. Turn to wrong side, crease along seam and stitch enclosing edges (diagram 35).

FLAT FELLED SEAM

Stitch plain seam on right side. Trim one edge to within ⅛ in (0.3 cm) from stitching. Turn in other edge and topstitch it over trimmed edge (diagram 36).

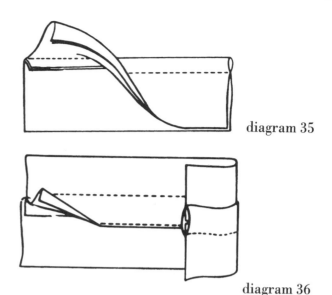

diagram 35

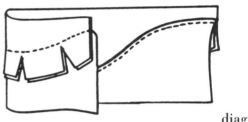

diagram 36

TOPSTITCHED SEAM

For decoration. Stitch and press both edges to one side. Clip curved seam edges. Topstitch even distance from seam line on outside (diagram 37).

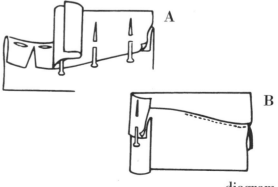

diagram 37

LAPPED SEAM

Turn under seam allowance of top piece and press. Match seamed edges on wrong side.

(a) Pin at right angles to folded edge.

(b) Topstitch close to turned edge on outside (diagram 38).

A

B

diagram 38

◆

Hems

All eyes will be focused on your hemline. Different skirts need different hems. (See diagrams 39 to 45.) For lightweight fabrics use the slip-stitched hem; for heavyweight fabrics or those that ravel easily use the taped hem. For firmly woven fabrics and knits use the catch-stitch hem.

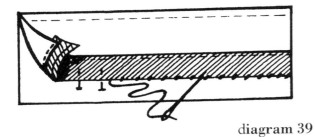

diagram 39

To prepare

Have hem marked with pins parallel to the floor. Turn up along pins, matching seams. Press, avoiding pins. Baste close to fold, taking pins out as you go. Mark depth of hem plus ¼ in (0.6 cm) with chalk or pins. Trim surplus.

TAPED HEM

Sew bias tape ¼ in (0.6 cm) from edge, easing tape slightly. Pin in place. Hem tape to garment invisibly.

CATCH-STITCH HEM

Work from left to right. Take one thread in hem by inserting needle right to left, then one in garment. Keep loose.

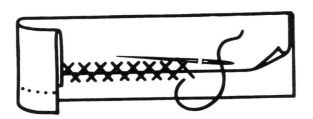

diagram 40

FRENCH DRESSMAKER HEM

Overcast hem edge, drawing up any fullness. Press hem. Turn overcast edge back ¼ in (0.6 cm). Work left to right slipstitch loosely catching one thread of skirt and one of hem.

diagram 41

SLIPSTITCHED HEM

Measure width of hem required. Tack along turning. Turn under raw edge and stitch, then pin. Take tiny stitch in garment and slip needle along folded edge of hem to make stitch.

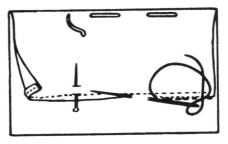

diagram 42

CIRCULAR HEM

Turn hem and tack along turning. Gather edge so hem will lie flat. Stitch one edge of binding to hem. Hem other edge to garment.

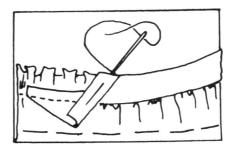

diagram 43

HEM IN PLEATED SKIRT

Seam inside a hem must be flat. Press open. At edge of pleat, overcast seam edges together above hem, clip at top of hem and press seam open below clip.

Opposite: Brilliant buttons provide elegant or whimsical fastenings for clothes.

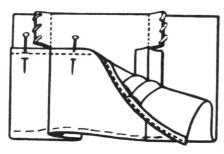

diagram 44

PLAIN HEMMING

Fasten thread under fold; take a tiny stitch in garment and bring needle through edge of fold. On dresses space stitches farther apart.

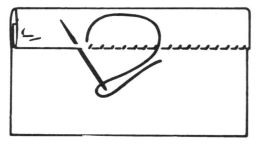

diagram 45

◆

Buttons and buttonholes

Buttons are styling touches that make a big difference. They deserve careful thought and careful sewing, too. It's wise to buy a button comparable in size to the one sketched on the pattern envelope, since it is the designer's choice and will fit the buttonholes marked on the pattern. Buttons should slip through the buttonhole easily and smoothly.

Buttonholes are usually ⅛ in (0.3 cm) longer than the diameter of the button. A button 1⅛ in (2.9 cm) diameter needs a 1¼ in (3.2 cm) buttonhole. This is the general rule for thin, flat buttons. When very small buttons are used, then the difference would be less. When a thick or heavy fabric is used for a coat and the button is covered in the same fabric, then a slightly larger buttonhole would be needed. It is a good idea to make a test buttonhole for a thick button on a scrap of the fabric. Cut a slit in the fabric the diameter of the button and increase the length of the opening until the button slips through easily. Use this measurement for the buttonhole on the garment.

TYPES OF BUTTONHOLES

There are two kinds of buttonholes, bound and worked. Bound buttonholes have the edges finished with fabric; worked buttonholes have the edges finished with thread. Those parts of the garment where buttonholes are used should be interfaced for firmness and strength. Stitching must begin and end exactly on lines indicating the ends of the buttonholes.

Worked buttonholes may be done by machine or by hand. Machine-made flat buttonholes save many hours of work and are satisfactory for most garments. Hand-worked buttonholes have an eyelet at the end of the buttonhole; this tailored buttonhole is used on men's clothing and top coats. Mark the buttonhole and punch a hole at the outer end with a stiletto. Cut on line for buttonhole and overcast edges of buttonhole and eyelet. For extra strength work the buttonhole stitches over a cord and finish the inner end with a bar tack. A corded buttonhole will also wear better than a buttonhole made without it. Work over the edges with buttonhole or blanket stitches keeping them close together. If you insert the stiletto from the right side every few stitches it will help to keep the fabric turned under, making it easier to shape the eyelet and work the buttonhole stitches.

PLACING BUTTONHOLES AND BUTTONS

Simplicity patterns clearly mark buttonhole locations with a printed line. If, however, you lengthened or shortened your pattern you must re-space the buttonholes. On a bodice, keep the top buttonhole in its position on the pattern so that the neckline closure is not changed. Also keep the lowest buttonhole where it is relative to the waistline and belt. Then evenly space the remaining buttonholes between these two positions. All areas containing buttonholes should be interfaced. Baste it to inside of garment section on which buttonholes are to be made. Transfer all markings to right side of fabric with basting stitch in contrasting thread.

On garments that close at middle front, the horizontal buttonholes usually extend ⅛ in (0.3 cm) over the middle line towards the outer edge. (See diagram 49 for marking buttonholes and buttons.) Coat buttonholes extend ¼ in (0.6 cm) over the middle line. This allows for shank of button and for garment to close on middle front.

On Simplicity patterns buttons used with horizontal holes are sewn on the underwrap in line with the buttonhole and exactly on the middle front or back line (diagram 46). If the buttonhole is vertical, mark

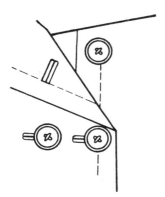

diagram 46

the upper end on the underwrap and sew the button ⅛ in (0.3 cm) below this mark. When the closing is an off-center one or the buttonhole is slanted, place top wrap over underwrap; match middles and pin closed. Place a pin through the end of the buttonhole nearest the edge if it is horizontal or through the upper end if it is vertical. Middle of button is placed ⅛ in (0.3 cm) from pin — away from the outer edge if horizontal, down from top if vertical. If the buttonhole is slanted, put the pin through the end nearer the outer edge, and place the button ⅛ in (0.3 cm) from the pin. If the buttonhole slants up towards the edge, the button goes ⅛ in (0.3 cm) from the top of the buttonhole (diagram 47); if it slants down towards the edge, ⅛ in (0.3 cm) from the bottom of the buttonhole (diagram 48).

Buttonhole making is easy if you have a modern sewing machine — neat, accurate buttonholes of every size can be made with a minimum of effort.

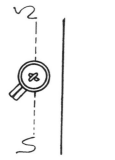

diagram 47   diagram 48

BUTTONS AND BUTTONHOLES

Cut a test buttonhole in scrap of fabric. Mark buttonhole with basting in contrast thread.

diagram 49a

Accurately space buttonholes.

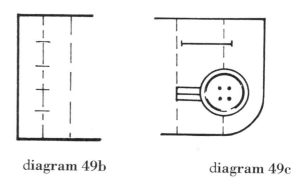

diagram 49b   diagram 49c

Sew button under outer end of buttonhole. Mark position with a pin.

Place pin on top of flat buttons while sewing. Wind thread around to form stem. Fasten off securely.

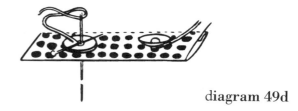

diagram 49d

Fabric loops

Cut true bias ¾ in (1.9 cm) wide. Turn one end of fabric to right side and sew end of cord to it. Fold fabric and stitch with cord inside. Turn loop right side out by pulling cord through. Sew loops to edge of garment. Stitch facing over ends of loops to neaten.

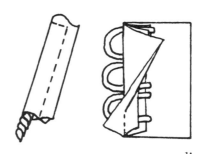

diagram 49e

HOW TO CHANGE THE SIZE OF BUTTONHOLES

Vertical buttonholes may easily be lengthened or shortened for use with larger or smaller buttons. This is done at the lower end of the buttonhole. To make a horizontal buttonhole smaller, simply shorten from the inner end until it is ⅛ in (0.3 cm) longer than the button size you plan to use. Do not change button sizes too drastically with horizontal buttonholes as the buttonhole length is allied to the width of the underlap and the facing.

Never lengthen a buttonhole so far inward that it extends beyond the edge of the underlap or the facing; nor extend a buttonhole too close to the outer edge. The edge of the button should be at least ⅜ in (1 cm) from the opening.

If the buttonhole needs to be lengthened only ⅛ in or ¼ in (0.3 cm or 0.6 cm), it may be done easily by extending both ends of the marked buttonhole one half the extra amount. If this cannot be done you will need to make a wider underlap. However, you must decide to do this before cutting out the garment so that the underlap can be cut wider to take the larger buttonhole.

Remember: on lightweight fabrics and children's clothes, the width of the underlap is only a few inches (8 cm), so do not increase the button size more than ⅛ in (0.3 cm) beyond the size suggested on the Simplicity pattern.

◆

Button shanks or stems

Buttons should not be sewn down flat to the garment with firm thread; there should always be a shank or stem to allow the button to ride smoothly in the buttonhole when it is buttoned.

Some buttons come equipped with their own shank (see diagram 50), others may not (see the tunnel button, diagram 51).

To add a shank to a button, make a stitch on the right side of the fabric where the button is to be sewn. Bring the needle through the button. Then place a pin or match across the top to allow for extra "play." Continue sewing back and forth over the pin (diagram 52) in any way desired (see four suggested ways in diagram 53). Remove the pin and wind the thread firmly around the threads under the button,

forming the shank. Draw the needle to the wrong side of the fabric and fasten the thread with several stitches to make it absolutely secure. (See diagrams 54 and 55 for bound and worked buttonholes.)

diagram 50   diagram 51

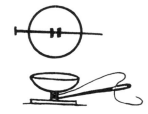

diagram 52

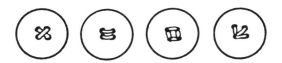

diagram 53

BUTTONHOLES

Making

Cut a strip of fabric 1¾ in (4.4 cm) wide and 1 in (2.54 cm) longer than buttonhole marking. Tack in middle over mark, right sides together. Stitch ⅛ in (0.3 cm) above and below tacking, and across the ends.

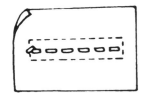

Slash between stitchings to within ⅛ in (0.3 cm) of ends. Clip ends diagonally stitching at corners. Turn strip to wrong side through opening.

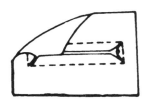

Fold strip back over buttonhole. Allow ends to meet to form a binding on outside. Tack. Stitch points at ends of opening to inside of binding. Sew strip invisibly to stitching.

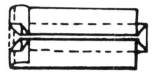

Slash garment facing under buttonhole opening. Turn in cut edges and slipstitch to binding.

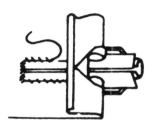

Finished buttonhole on the outside.

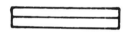

diagram 54

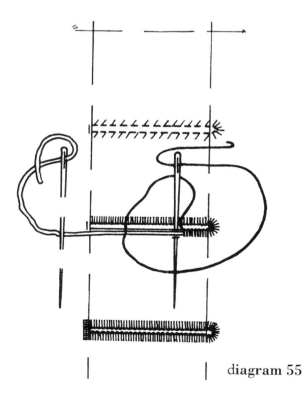

diagram 55

LIGNE GAUGE

Ligne sizes are the standard measurement of button sizes. In the chart are equivalent measurements in both metric and imperial. For buttons that are not round, measure the length of the largest diagonal.

Ligne	mm	Inches
14L	9	Just under 3/8
16L	10	3/8
18L	11.5	7/16
20L	13	1/4
22L	14	9/16
24L	15	Just under 5/8
26L	16	5/8
28L	18	11/16
30L	19	
32L	20	Just over 3/4
36L	23	7/8
40L	25	1
44L	28	1 1/8
48L	30	1 3/16
54L	34	1 3/8
60L	38	1 3/4
70L	44	1 3/4
80L	51	2
90L	57	2 1/4
100L	63	2 1/2

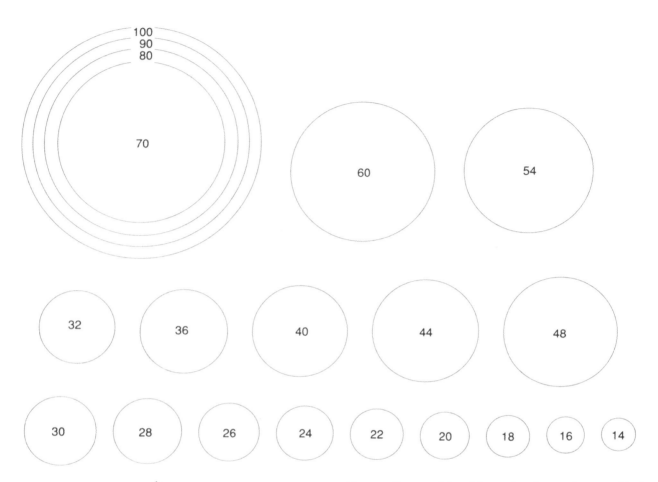

Collars and necklines

Neckline treatments can turn an otherwise plain garment into an interesting one. Necklines may be finished with collars (see diagram 56 for attaching a collar with bias) or with facing if the garment is collarless (diagrams 57 to 59).

Pin collar and facing with right sides together. Tack and stitch around outside edge. Trim seam to make less bulky.

Turn collar to right side, tack edge and press. Tack collar to garment on right side. Turn under seam allowance on front lap of garment. Next turn underlap hem allowance back over ends of collar; pin. Tack bias to neck edge extending ends over the hem. Stitch in position. Markings on Simplicity patterns make it easy.

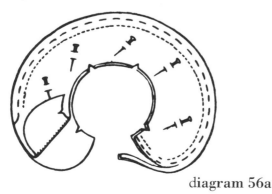

diagram 56a

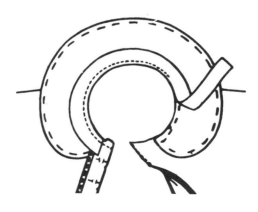

diagram 56b

Two different styles of collars for ladies' dresses. Courtesy Elna Australia.

Turn the hems and facing to inside. Fold bias strip over turnings, sew in position. Tack hems in place with invisible stitches.

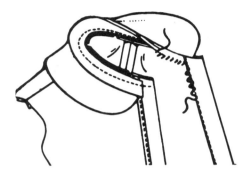

diagram 56c

FACED OPENING

Fold in side and lower edges of facing; stitch. Place on garment, right sides facing. Run a V stitching to outline opening. Slash between stitchings.

Turn facing to wrong side; slip stitch.

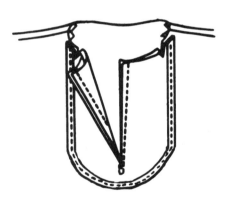

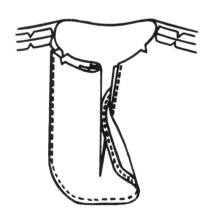

diagram 57

BIAS BINDING

Fold fabric so crosswise edge runs parallel to selvage. Mark width of strips with chalk, cut along bias fold and markings.

Place the right sides together with straight edges parallel and bias edges at right angles. Stitch, then press open.

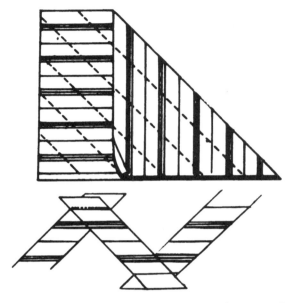

diagram 58

BIAS FACING FOR V-NECK

Stitch 1½ ins (3.8 cm) width bias strip to neck edge, right sides facing. Begin and end strip at point of V, ends overlapping. Stitch ends at point.

Trim surplus bias strip and press seam open to make it sit well.

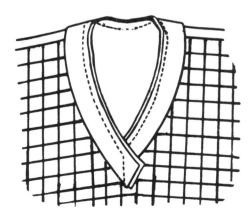

diagram 59a

Turn facing to inside of garment. Tack and stitch around neckline. Turn raw edge under and stitch. Do not stitch to garment, catch down only at shoulder seams.

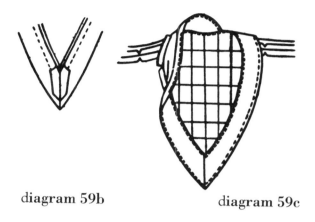

diagram 59b   diagram 59c

Inserting a slide fastener

If you follow diagram 60 carefully you'll find the plain seam system is easiest every time.

Press under seam allowances on openings. Pin fastener with right side against wrong side of garment, keeping edges of opening at middle of fastener on outside.

Remove pins. Turn garment to right side. Baste through seam allowance, garment and tape. Shape top of opening to take the tab.

Machine close to tacking, garment and tape, keep two sides even. Remove tacking. Press.

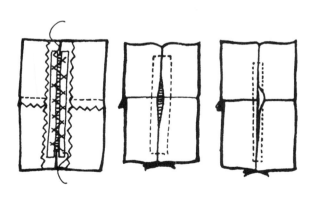

diagram 60

Tricks of tailoring

If you're planning to sew one of the new soft suits, one of the new-length jackets, remember that this type of garment needs an extra something — tailoring.

In making any tailored garment your first consideration is the shrinkage of the fabric. Unless it is marked pre-shrunk you would be wise to shrink all fabrics before using them.

Wet a strip of sheeting the length and width of your fabric. Place this on your material and roll them together, the sheet inside. Leave for two to eight hours, or overnight, before removing the sheet.

Press the damp fabric with a hot iron over a dry pressing cloth. The fabric should be face downwards and you press slowly, working straight down the grain, never diagonally. Do not allow the iron to rest for long in one place: it may imprint the fabric. Continue pressing until fabric is dry.

Underlining and interfacing will make all the difference to your garments. Underlining fabric, which is cut from the same pattern pieces as the outer fabric, improves the look of any garment. Choose a weight of underlining that is not too heavy for the outer fabric or it will spoil the line. For jackets and vests, unbleached muslin is perfect. Interfacing used between the facing and outer fabrics gives shape to fronts, collars, lapels, and edges.

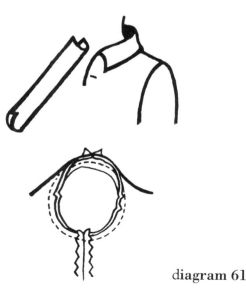

diagram 61

Woven materials, such as canvas, have a lengthwise and crosswise grain. Non-woven linings are fibers pressed together, they have no grain, and may be used in any direction.

Front interfacings are stitched to the seam lines of the garment pieces.

Slip-stitch bias strips of interfacing to the hemlines of cuffs and jacket bottoms to form edges and hold the shape.

Always stitch seams in the direction shown by arrows on your pattern. In this way you are sewing with the grain and you prevent wobbly, taut, or puckered seams.

Test the grain by running your finger down the cut edge of a seam. If the edge remains flat you are moving in the direction of the grain. If the threads ruffle, you are moving against the grain.

If the seam is curved, sew in the direction in which you can follow the grain line longest.

One of the most important areas of professional tailoring is the care taken with seams.

Before stitching, clip interfacing ¼ in (0.6 cm) away from the corners.

After stitching, clip away seam allowances of interfacings to the seam line.

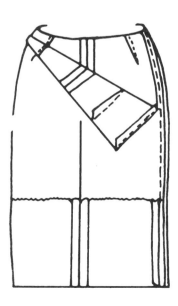

diagram 62

Trim other seam allowances so that the bulk of the seam is layered and evenly distributed.

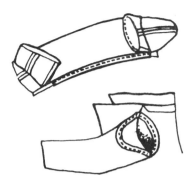

diagram 63

Clip away excess fabric where seams cross and be sure to trim fabric away at corners to make a sharp point.

Always press as you sew, using a steam iron.

Just before stitching the lining into the jacket, press the whole garment carefully from the right side, using a well-padded board and pressing cloth to avoid putting a shine on the fabric.

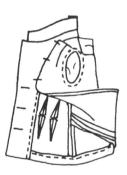

diagram 64

To get the smooth rounded top to sleeves, cut a 2 in (5.1 cm) strip of soft wool fabric on the bias or a piece of non-woven interlining. Fold the strip in half lengthwise and stitch it in with the sleeve between the notches, folded edge towards the sleeve (diagram 61).

Clip and layer seam allowance then press firmly, but lightly, into the top of the sleeve. Lining covers the inside seams. Use lining fabrics that agree with cleaning rules for outer fabrics.

Shrinkage percentage should also agree. We have all had the experience at some time or other when the lining has shrunk and ruined the shape of a favourite garment. (See diagram 62 for placement of lining in a skirt; diagram 63 for lining in sleeves; diagram 64 for lining in a jacket.)

◆
How to set in a sleeve

With wrong side of garment towards you, set sleeve in, matching notches and underarm seams marked on Simplicity patterns. Pin sleeve to armhole easing in fullness across top.

Tack and stitch sleeve in armhole.

Place top of sleeve over your tailor's cushion and press through a damp cloth. Shrink out any fullness in sleeve cap by pressing sleeve and armhole seams together from sleeve side. Overcast.

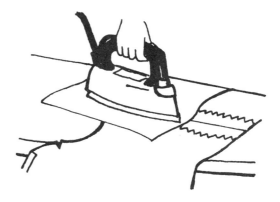

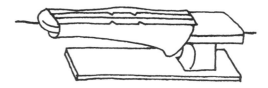

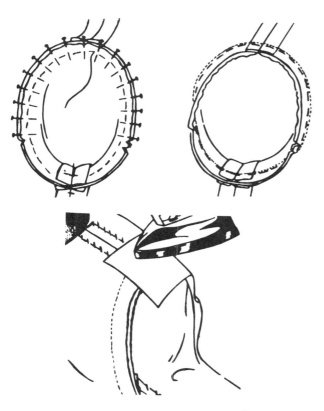

diagram 65

Use a small brush to open seams. Press over a dry cloth or a slightly dampened cloth. This is good for tailored wool garments.

A tailor's cushion for pressing armhole seams and shrinking out the fullness at the top of sleeves is an important aid. Sew two 12 in (30.5 cm) ovals together and stuff with wadding until very firm.

◆
How to press

Press each seam as you sew. This is essential to allow other seamed pieces to lie flat when joined and so make a better garment.

Press sleeves on sleeve board for perfect results. Use board also when pressing awkward seams and small darts.

diagram 66

THE FINISHING TOUCHES

To help you stitch better and to sew the most for your money, keep abreast of all the latest developments and discoveries in the sewing world, and brush up on techniques that fashion brings to the fore.

You will find many advances in sewing machines. In the modern ranges machines will do fancy stitches, tacking, and buttonholes, with stitch selectors adjustable for every fabric. Some convert to free-arm for sewing those intricate parts on collars, cuffs, sleeves, legs of pants, and children's clothes.

◆

How to gather the waist of a dress

There are three ways to get pretty gathers at the waistline of a one-piece dress: by inserting elastic into a casing; by stitching elastic directly to the dress; by using elastic thread.

When the pattern you choose specifies the casing method, the casing will be either an actual pattern piece or a strip of bias tape. For this type of gathering, insert "heavy-duty" or "strong stretch" rayon elastic into the casing. The pattern will indicate the width needed.

Elastic in a casing often tends to "roll" or a bunch gathers in spots. To avoid this and to have good distribution of fullness, place four vertical lines of stitching to anchor the elastic, through the elastic and the garment (the length of these stitching lines should be the same as the width of the elastic used). Place two rows of stitches in the back and two in front.

To avoid fullness in the middle front, gathers can be distributed to either side of the middle front of the garment and held by these anchoring stitches — each midway between the middle front and a side seam.

When you plan to shirr an area of a dress by stitching elastic directly to the garment, purchase elastic that is a combination of nylon and rubber, the width indicated in the pattern. This elastic has a softer stretch than rayon elastic and is easier to sew on. It is sometimes called "lingerie" elastic and gives the best results in this type of shirring.

Mark the stitching lines on the wrong side of the garment. Cut the length of elastic specified in the pattern, divide the elastic and the stitching line into quarters or eighths, depending upon the length of the area to be shirred. Allow ½ in (1.3 cm) of elastic at each end for finishing.

Pin the elastic to the garment stitching line at these points. Stitch, either with a zigzag stitch or a large straight stitch [8 - 10 stitches to the inch (3 to 4 to the centimeter)]. Stretch the elastic between pins as you go, using both hands, stretching both in front of and in back of the presser foot. Fasten elastic ends securely (diagram 67).

diagram 67

Another way to gather fabric is with elastic thread. This method is pretty when you wish several rows of close-together shirring.

Select a 10 - 12 to the inch stitch length (4 to 5 to the centimeter). Wind the elastic thread by hand on to the bobbin. Use mercerized cotton for the top thread. Be sure to test the fullness on a swatch of your fabric since each fabric reacts differently.

Mark the first stitching line with basting. Stitch on the right side of the garment (so the elastic thread will be on the wrong side). When you stitch additional rows, hold the fabric already shirred flat, by stretching it both in front and in back of the presser foot (diagram 68). Spacing of rows may be judged by the edge of the presser foot. At the end, tie elastic and needle threads together.

Opposite: Flat trimming, ribbons and simple appliqué enhance this child's outfit. Courtesy Avalon Craft Cottage.

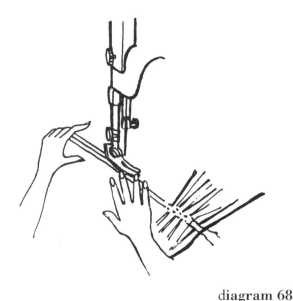

diagram 68

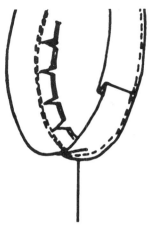

diagram 69

◆

How to finish sleeveless garments

To give shape, body, and a smooth line to a sleeveless armhole, it must be interfaced and understitched.

Use the facing pattern for the interfacing (the facing and interfacing can be cut out at the same time). Stitch the underarm seam of the armhole interfacing, press open, and baste the interfacing to the armhole edge on the wrong side of the bodice.

Construct the armhole facing. Machine stitch ¼ in (0.6 cm) from the outer edge. To finish this edge, pink, hand overcast, machine zigzag, or turn and stitch. A pretty, and personal, touch is to finish the facing edges with lace or trimming. Pin and stitch the facing to the armhole edge, right sides together, matching notches and underarm seams.

Trim the interfacing close to the line of stitching. Trim facing to within ¼ in (0.6 cm) of the seam line, and clip at intervals along the curves. To hold the facing neatly in place, understitch it by stitching on the right side of the facing, very close to the seam line, through the facing and the seam allowances (diagram 69). The facing will turn easily and lie flat. Trim interfacing even with the finished edge of the facing. Press and slip-stitch to the underarm and shoulder seams.

◆

Topstitching

Topstitching is a distinctive detail currently decorating dresses with bold, curving seams, and sharply tailored garments. You can add topstitching to a garment either by machine or hand.

Choose a heavy thread of the same type as the fabric. If you are topstitching cotton or linen, use heavy-duty thread. If you are topstitching silk or yarn, or linen that will not be washed, use silk twist (remember that silk dyes aren't always colorfast in hot water).

To topstitch by machine on yarn or silk, or linen to be dry cleaned, put silk twist in the upper threading of your sewing machine. You need not waste it in the bobbin as it will not show. Use a size 16 needle (which will take the thicker thread). Loosen the top tension a bit, so that no part of the bobbin thread will show through on the top, and use a long stitch. If you find that silk twist will not go through the top threading of your machine, put it in the bobbin and do your topstitching from the wrong side of the garment.

If you are working on cotton fabric, sew two rows of heavy-duty thread right on top of each other. This will give the appearance of one row of somewhat heavier thread.

Topstitching by hand is called hand-picking. Baste the line to be stitched with fine thread. On this stitching line, bring needle through to the surface from underneath, take a backstitch, picking up

approximately one yarn of fabric. Bring needle
forward and up through fabric about ½ in (1.3 cm)
from the backstitch. Continue with a backstitch then
forward (diagram 70) until you have finished.

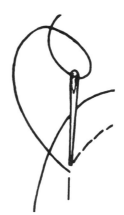

diagram 70

*A simple child's apron put to practical and decorative use.
Courtesy Avalon Craft Cottage.*

◆
Adding special trims

GATHERED LACE

Gathered lace trim is easy to make this way. Put buttonhole twist in your bobbin; use the longest basting stitch. After stitching the length of lace to be gathered, tie the thread ends at one end of the lace into a loop and slip it over the sewing machine spindle. Back away from the machine, lace in hand, until it is taut. Then, pulling on the bobbin thread, push lace up into the gathered length you wish and proceed exactly as the pattern tells you.

RHINESTONES

Rhinestones by the yard come slipped on to twill tape. The double and triple rows are best used on straight areas. The single row is pliable enough for curved areas.

When working with this tape, cut it about 1 in (2.54 cm) longer than you need. Slip off ½ in (1.3 cm) of rhinestones at either end and tuck the excess tape under the rhinestones as you attach them, by hand, stitching through the tape between each one of the stones.

FEATHERS

Feathers can be attached to a finished dress. Mark the feather line with thread tracing. Then, working from the wrong side, slip-stitch through the fabric and around the "spine" of the feathers. This way you won't have to wander through feathers looking for spine and stitchline.

PICOT EDGING

Picot edging is easy to use and adds a pretty finish to a lace dress. Press hems of sleeves and skirt. Trim away all but ¼ in (0.6 cm), baste the edging to the skirt of the dress, covering the raw hem edge, with the picot edging peeking out. Machine stitch.

GLITTER BY THE YARD

When adding glitter by the yard to a finished garment slip-stitch it first along the outer curve of an area, then ease it in on the inner curve. Finish off ends by removing jewels from the seam allowance area and turning under before stitching in place.

FRINGE

This can be inserted into seams by machine very easily. It needs care, as it has a tendency to come off its woven binding. Stabilize the cut end with ordinary adhesive tape as soon as you cut it to avoid this happening.

If you find fringe becomes tangled or gets in your way as you sew, place tissue paper over it as you work. It can easily be torn away when you have finished.

◆
Adding ribbons and braids

A neat mitred corner is often the difference in a professional or a non-professional trim. When you trim a skirt with embroidered ribbon or a wide braid trim, and must turn a corner, the trims must be mitred, as they have no "give."

Stitch trim, on both sides, down to the corner. Then fold ribbon back on itself and to the side, making a right angle. Press to make a diagonal crease on wrong side. Stitch along the diagonal crease through ribbon and garment. Then stitch along edges to the next corner.

An easy way to get rickrack attached in a straight line is to draw a guideline with a pencil on the right side of the fabric (the marks will be covered). Roll the rickrack up on a pencil and begin stitching the loose end in place, with a straight line of stitching through the middle of the rickrack. As you stitch, unroll it a bit at a time. This method keeps you from having a tangled mass of rickrack in your lap.

For an instant scalloped edge, apply scalloped braid in much the same way as you apply rickrack, stitching straight across braid at edge away from scallop.

There's a trick to sewing grosgrain ribbon on without puckering — which it is apt to do. Baste it in place with diagonal stitches (which hold more securely than running stitches). When stitching in place, sew both edges in the same direction. This will keep it flat and eliminate puckering that may occur if it is stitched down one side and up the other.

If the garment to be trimmed will be washed, remember to pre-wash both fabric and trim, as they may have different degrees of shrinkage.

Sewing for gifts or your own convenience is a pleasurable activity. © Courtesy Coats Patons.

Dyecraft

GENERAL TECHNIQUES

◆

Guide for dyecraft

• Cover all surfaces with plastic or paper to protect against splatters.

• Wear rubber gloves and an apron.

• Wash all fabric first to remove sizing. Always work on wet fabric laid on a large flat surface. Cover surface with a plastic sheet.

• Pots. Mix dye solutions in pots large enough to hold complete bundle with room for stirring. Don't use Teflon pans.

• Always shake liquid dyes well. Add a little liquid detergent if the water is hard.

• All dye solutions should be kept simmering (not boiling) over low heat throughout the dyeing procedure. This ensures the brightest hue possible.

• When using undiluted liquid dye in squeeze bottles, heat bottles of dye in hot water bath for most vibrant hue.

• Pour-on dye technique tends to be messy. Work on a smooth non-absorbent protected surface. Keep damp sponge handy to wipe excess dye. Remove any stains with household bleach.

• When using pour-on technique, there will be some splatters onto the white fabric. These will be covered by the final darker dye solution.

• Dyeing time varies with each item. Leave fabric in simmering dye solution for at least 20 to 30 minutes. Heavy fabrics and fabric with thick folds require an extra 10 minutes dyeing time. Remember that fabric looks much darker when wet … it gets lighter as it dries. If possible, test dye on a piece of scrap fabric.

• Stir fabric in dye solution to ensure even dyeing.

• After dyeing remove fabric from solution and squeeze to remove excess dye. Rinse under cold, running water while still tied until water runs clear. Re-rinse without ties.

• Remove bands and rinse again.

• Use spin cycle on washer or wring out excess moisture.

• Drip-dry in protected area until fabric is just damp, then iron. Cover ironing board with a cloth to protect it from wet dye. Or, dry fabric in dryer.

• Laundering: wash dyed garments separately in cool water to protect colors and other washables.

◆

How does tie-dyeing work?

The basic principle of tie-dyeing is to keep the color from penetrating the portion of material that is tied. What is tied does not dye.

As long as the tied areas are tight, and the fabric is not allowed to soak in dye for too long, the dye will not have a chance to penetrate the material in the unexposed areas and a definite pattern will result. The ties may be made with string, rubber bands, or elastic.

Tie-dyeing is not a complicated process at all. A piece of fabric is knotted, twisted, bunched, gathered or pleated and tied at intervals with rubber bands, or string of some sort. Then it is dipped in dye — some people use store-bought dye and others concoct their own — which doesn't penetrate into the areas that are tied.

All commercial dyes give full instructions in the use of their products. So just follow the directions pertaining to the kind of fabric you are using. Water for the dye solution can be hot or cold, but be sure to have a container large enough so that the material is not crowded. Allow about three gallons (13.5L) of water for each three yards of fabric.

Not all fabrics are suitable for tie-dyeing. Some synthetics such as polyesters and acrylics do not "take" the dye, so a small area should be tested beforehand. Cut a small piece from the hem, seam or pocket. Then dye it to determine the end result. For really exciting results use satin acetate, rayon, velveteens, velvets, and silks.

Dramatic dyed works by Paul O'Connor, finalist in the 1988 and 1989 Hoechst Textile Award. Courtesy Hoechst Australia Ltd.

Nylon jersey and nylon tie-dye well and natural fibers, silks, cottons, and wool items are excellent for dyeing. The material must be washed so that the sizing is removed. It is a good idea to dip the material in vinegar after it has been dyed to ensure that the colors will not fade.

SEVEN BASIC METHODS OF TYING THE MATERIAL.

1. Tie a tight knot with the fabric itself. This makes an irregular shadowy string.

2. Fold the fabric lengthwise or across in pleats like a paper fan and tie in a long tube. This makes long, streaky stripes.

3. Fold both lengthwise and across, then tie. This makes irregular checked patterns.

4. Fold a square of fabric like an envelope, corners to middle, several times and tie in one or two places. This is a good procedure to begin experimentation.

5. Take a point of the fabric and begin tying, gradually taking in more fabric. By tying two or more bands around a circularly gathered portion of cloth, circles and rings called rosettes are formed.

6. Sketch a simple pattern on the material, stitch around the outlines with a strong thread, draw up tightly and wrap string around drawn up parts.

7. Tie some objects in the cloth. This makes the most novel designs and is excellent for experimental purposes.

Keep in mind, however, that these are the basic ties and many variations are possible on all of the above mentioned methods. If just basic methods alone are used, they should be used in pleasing combinations or in pre-planned repeat design patterns.

The use of repeat design, pleasing combinations patterns, and experimental ties is generally the most self-satisfying means of working with tie-dyeing since the mere reproducing of one method or another can become boring.

◆

Materials needed

A piece of fabric, or a clean garment. Choose white or light-colored material.

Liquid dye, available in most supermarkets, department, and variety stores. RIT liquid dyes were used in all models demonstrated in this chapter.

A container for every color of dye you plan to use.

Rubber bands. Wide elastic bands are better than string for tying as the tension prevents dye penetrating beneath the tie.

Rubber gloves, if you want to keep your hands free from dye.

Plastic bags or plastic wrapping to protect the parts of the cloth you don't want touched by dye.

Squeeze bottle or medicine dropper for spotting or for splatter effects.

◆

Method

Start with your fabric and your choice of colors. Choose colors that blend well together, as the edges of the colors merge. You can get any color you want by mixing undiluted liquid dyes.

THE BASIC KNOTS

Wash the fabric and make all the knots on the wet fabric on a flat surface. You fold and bind the material into the design you want, remembering that where the rubber band or plastic bag touches, the dye won't. There are five basic knots: rosette, donut, stripe, gather, and two-color effect. Of course you may want to experiment with designs yourself but it is advisable to master these well-known techniques first.

1. ROSETTE KNOT

Pinch fabric up, secure with rubber bands. For sunburst, as shown add more ties (diagram 1).

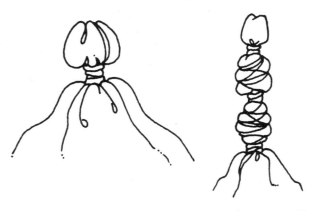

diagram 1a   diagram 1b

Fabric dyed by Lesley Baldwin. Courtesy Hoechst Australia Ltd.

2. DONUT KNOT

Pick up the fabric in one hand and grasp it part-way down with the other, so that you have a circular puff of material above your hand. Don't try to keep the puff too small. Poke the puff in the middle and grasp the middle with your hand at the bottom of the puff. Wrap a rubber band around the whole thing, being sure to get the middle of the puff caught in the band. Now make little donut puffs all over your fabric — wherever you want a design — and dunk the whole thing in the dye (diagram 2).

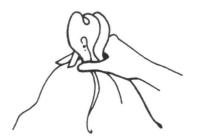

diagram 2a

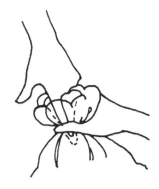

diagram 2b

diagram 2c

3. STRIPE

This is one of the easiest patterns, and one of the most striking, especially on soft fabrics. Lay the fabric out straight and mark where the stripe is desired. Gather the fabric between thumb and forefinger. Now, wrap rubber bands wherever you want a "stripe." Immerse the whole thing in a dye, or put half in one color and half in another, or try getting the color between every stripe a different color (diagram 3).

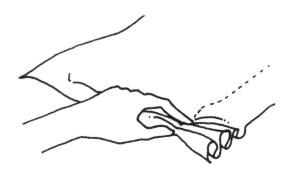

diagram 3a

diagram 3b

4. GATHERING

Gather entire piece of fabric into both hands. Secure with rubber bands (diagram 4).

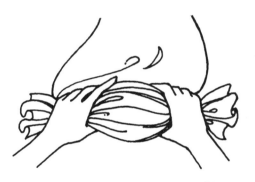

diagram 4a

diagram 4b

5. TWO-COLOR EFFECT

Fold fabric lengthwise, gather through middle and tie. Immerse up to the tie in one color, then other side in another color (diagram 5).

Intense color in fabric dyed by Martien van Zuilen. Courtesy Hoechst Australia Ltd.

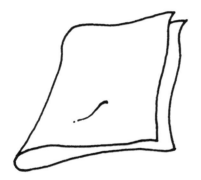

diagram 5a

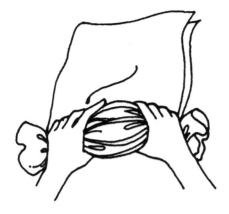

diagram 5b

diagram 5c

◆

Spotted cushion cover

DYEING THE FABRIC

It is important to have the dye very hot before you immerse the fabric, so keep your dyes simmering on the stove (but do not boil) all the time you are working. Dyeing time varies with each article but generally 15 to 20 minutes is enough. However, for some of the heavier fabrics such as denim, canvas or sailcloth, allow an extra 10 minutes dyeing time. It is better to simmer the fabric for too long than not long enough, for the longer you simmer the faster the color will be. However, be sure to follow all special "care of the fabric" rules when dyeing.

As fabrics are several shades darker when they are wet it is a good idea to test the color on a small piece of scrap fabric first so you will know the time needed to get the desired shade.

Once you have this shade of color squeeze the excess dye from the article and rinse it thoroughly under cold running water before untieing. Then take off all the rubber bands and rinse again in cool water until the water is clear. If you want to "set" the dye, rinse again in a strong vinegar-water solution.

Allow the fabric to drip-dry and iron it while it is damp.

Note

If your tie-dye knots are made with the bands well apart you will get muted designs. If you tie the looped bands close together, the design will be more precise.

STEP-BY-STEP GUIDE TO TIE-DYING

(Illustrated by Carol Dolighan of "Untied," Edgecliff, NSW. Dyes courtesy of RIT Dyes.)

MATERIALS

½ yd, 36 in (50 cm, 90 cm) yellow rayon velvet; RIT liquid dyes — Kelly green and dark green; rubber bands; rubber gloves; large container.

MEASUREMENTS

To fit an average sized cushion — 18 x 18 ins (46 x 46 cm).

METHOD

1. Wash fabric to remove sizing.

2. Lay damp fabric out flat.

Three beautiful lengths of fabric and an intriguing pattern dyed by Ruth Belfrage. Courtesy Hoechst Australia Ltd.

3. Tie rosette knots over entire surface of material (see Step A). The knots should be tied approximately 2 ins (5.1 cm) apart (see Step B).

4. Submerge damp tied material into dye bath with enough hot water to cover and ¼ cup of Kelly green dye (see Step C).

Step B

11. Remove rubber bands and rinse fabric in cold running water until the water runs clear.

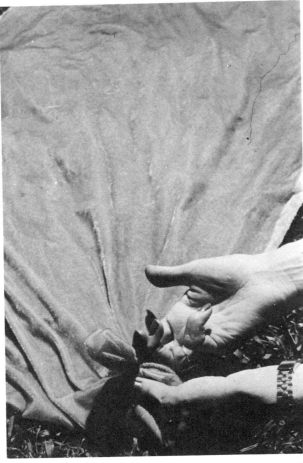

Step A

5. Simmer for 45 minutes, making sure that you stir it regularly.

6. Remove fabric from dye bath and rinse it in cold water.

7. Wind rubber bands on each side of existing rubber bands.

8. Submerge article into dye bath of ¾ cup of dark green dye and with enough water to cover.

9. Simmer for 45 minutes, stirring regularly.

10. Remove fabric from dye bath and rinse it in cold water.

Step C

Angela Leany's winning entry for the 1989 Hoechst Textile Award. Courtesy Hoechst Australia Ltd.

◆
Tablecloth

MATERIALS

1½ yds, 54 in (1.4 m) calico; RIT liquid dyes —
yellow, tangerine, and cocoa brown; rubber bands;
large container; rubber gloves.

MEASUREMENT

54 ins (137 cm) diameter.

METHOD

1. Cut calico into a circle 54 ins (137 cm) diameter.

2. Wash material to remove sizing.

3. Submerge damp material in a dye bath consisting
of enough hot water to cover and ½ cup yellow dye.
Simmer for 30 minutes, stirring frequently.

4. Remove material from dye bath and rinse in cold water.

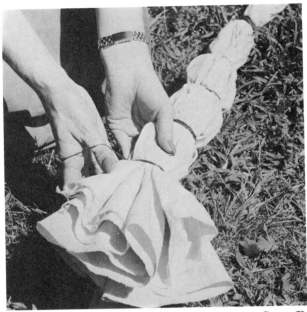

Step B

5. Make a large rosette knot. Secure it with rubber
bands (see Steps A and B).

6. Submerge tied material in dye bath consisting of
enough hot water to cover and ½ cup tangerine dye
(see Step C).

7. Simmer in dye bath for 30 minutes.

8. Remove from dye bath and rinse in cold water.

9. Wind rubber bands between the existing bands
(see Step D).

10. Add ½ cup cocoa brown dye to tangerine dye
bath.

Step A

Step C

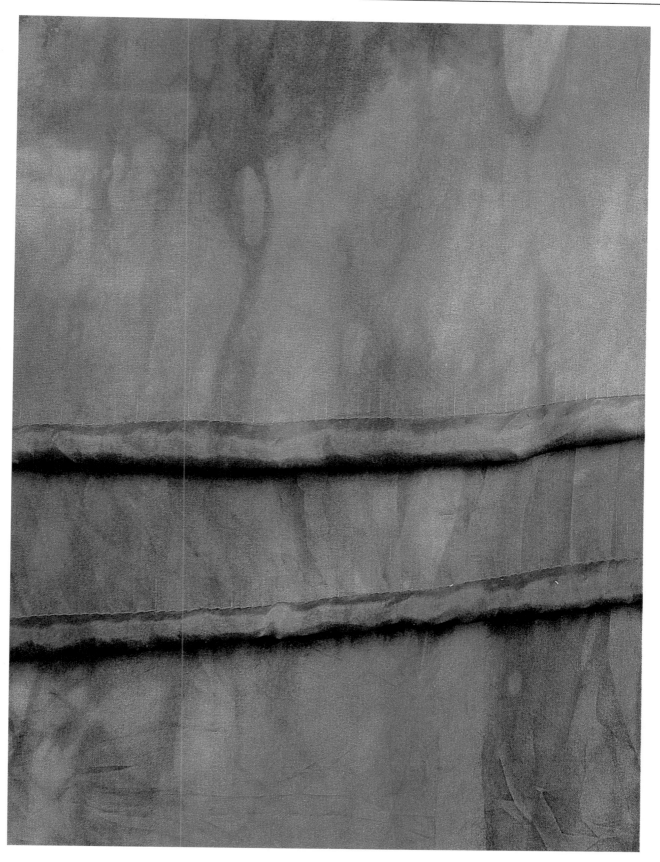

Moody colors from Judith Prescott. Courtesy Hoechst Australia Ltd.

11. Submerge tied article in dye bath and simmer for 30 minutes, stirring regularly.

12. Remove from dye bath and rinse in cold water.

13. Remove rubber bands and rinse article in cold running water until the water runs clear.

14. You can iron the tablecloth while it is wet, but it can be just spread out to drip dry (see Step E).

Step D

Step E

◆
Checked cushion cover

MATERIALS
⅔ yd, 36 in (65 cm, 90cm) white rayon velvet; large container; rubber bands; rubber gloves; RIT liquid dyes — yellow, tangerine, gold, and dark brown.

MEASUREMENT
18 x 24 in (46 x 61 cm).

METHOD
1. Wash fabric to remove sizing.

2. Lay damp fabric out flat.

3. Pleat material every 5 in (12 cm) from selvage to selvage.

4. Drip undiluted yellow dye in 1 in (2.5 cm) strip down middle of the material lengthwise, making sure that the dye penetrates through all the folds.

5. On each side of yellow strip drip bright orange (intermixed color from one part yellow to one part tangerine.

6. Pleat material in 3 in (7.6 cm) folds down its length, following the strips of bright orange.

7. Wind rubber bands over entire yellow and bright orange area.

8. Rinse bundle under warm water to remove excess dye.

9. Using a squeeze bottle, drip undiluted gold dye into middle of both unbanded corners.

10. Protect with rubber bands across ends.

11. Submerge article into dye bath consisting of enough hot water to entirely cover fabric and 1 cup dark brown. Simmer for 45 minutes, stirring regularly.

12. Remove from dye bath and rinse in cold water.

13. Remove bands and rinse under cold running water until the water runs clear.

14. Hang up article and allow to drip dry.

Opposite: The winner of the 1992 Hoechst Textile Award was Penelope McKeown with this dyed installation for a stairwell.

◆
Wall Hanging

MATERIALS

1⅓ yds, 36 in (1.55 m, 90 cm) white rayon velvet; RIT liquid dyes: royal blue, evening blue, scarlet, fuchsia; RIT color remover; rubber bands; large container.

MEASUREMENT

434 in long x 36 in wide (1111 cm x 91 cm).

METHOD

(illustrated on pages 187 and 189)

1. Wash velvet to remove sizing.

2. Fold damp velvet in half with selvages together.

3. Start at the selvage side and drip undiluted evening blue dye across fabric (see page 187, step 1).

4. Pleat evening blue section in small folds (see step 2).

5. Wind rubber bands around each edge of the evening blue section (see step 3).

6. Protect entire evening blue section with heavy plastic and secure with rubber bands (see step 4).

7. Sprinkle large drops of raspberry on section above evening blue (see step 5). Raspberry is a color mixed with 1 part scarlet and 1 part fuchsia dye.

8. Tie small rosette knots with rubber bands over entire section dripped with raspberry. Cross the rubber bands over top of knots (see step 6).

9. Wind more rubber bands in between these knots (see page 189, step 7). Make dye bath with enough hot water to completely cover article and add 1 cup royal blue dye. Simmer for 20 minutes.

10. Wrap heavy plastic around entire knotted section. Secure with strong rubber band (see step 8).

11. Submerge article in royal blue dye bath. Simmer for 60 minutes, stirring regularly.

12. Remove article from dye bath. Rinse off excess royal blue dye.

13. Remove plastic from raspberry section.

14. Make a solution of 2 quarts (2.3 L) of hot water and 3 tablespoons color remover. Simmer for 10 minutes.

15. Dip knots into color remover for 4 or 5 minutes until color has been lightened to a soft apricot shade (see step 9).

16. Rinse knots in warm soapy water.

17. Remove bands from knots. Rinse this section in cold water.

18. Remove plastic and bands from evening blue section. Rinse this section in cold water.

19. Rinse entire piece of velvet in cold running water until water runs clear

20. Spread article and allow to drip dry.

TO MAKE WALL HANGING

Sew 1 in (2.5 cm) hems top and bottom and put a wooden rod trhough each. Attach a cord to the top rod to suspend the hanging.

BATIK

Batik is a method of resist dyeing or printing fabric, the origin of which cannot exactly be traced. However, archaeological research suggests that it pre-dates the Christian era. The Egyptians and Persians seem to have worn garments with colored designs probably achieved by this or a similar method. In Asian countries it has been a common form of craft and art amongst the Malay, Japanese, Chinese, and Indonesians. It has also been used in the Pacific Islands and New Zealand.

Batik is actually a Javanese word applied to the wax resist technique of pattern dyeing on cloth as practiced there. The technique is to use hot wax to cover those parts of the cloth not required to take the dye, then the whole fabric is dipped in the dye vat — this operation is then repeated according to the number of colors in the pattern.

Although batik is mainly done on fabric, the principle has been applied to other media such as bark, paper, etc. The basic idea is simple. A substance that clings to material and also resists the liquid of a dyeing medium is used to separate or block out areas of cloth. The cloth is dyed and set. The resist medium is removed, leaving the patterned fabric. Rice starch was used as a resist medium, and is still used today in many places. It may have been

Opposite: Tie-dying a fabric length for a wall hanging. Instructions this page.

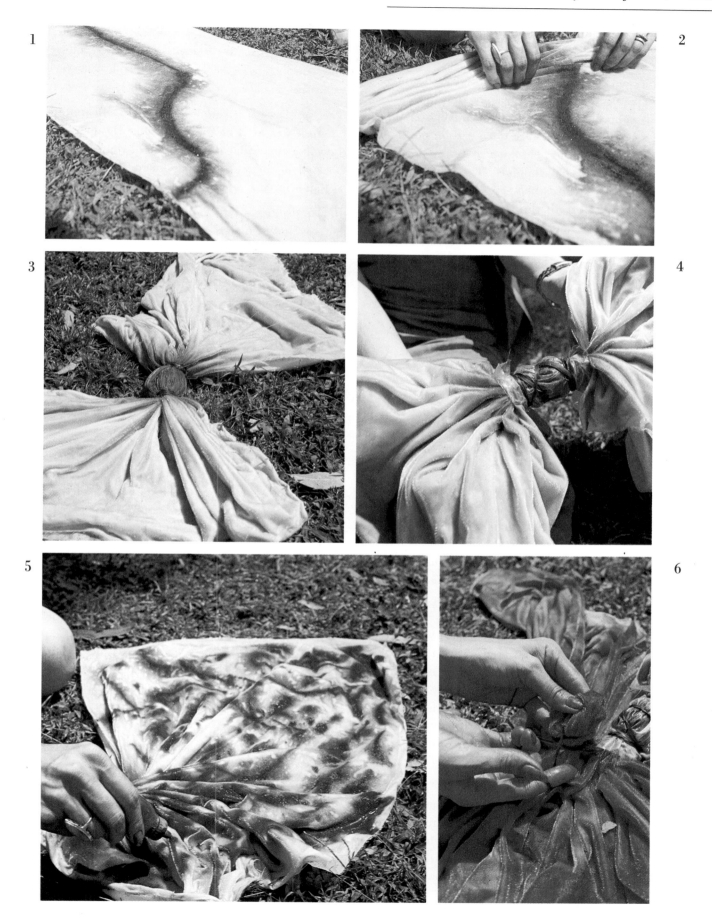

the forerunner of the more reliable wax which is now used as the principal resist material.

The garments so dyed were generally free-flowing, rather like the sarong and toga as we know them, so that the pattern was uniform (or repetitive) over the whole area. The fabrics were often cotton, muslin, and calico. Each country has adopted its own designs and motifs as well as techniques. The early artists were influenced by birds, flowers, butterflies, shells, fish, animals, and all things of natural beauty surrounding them, and recorded these in the batik art form. Religious law forbids Moslems from representing any living beings, so they stylized their designs. Other ideas made use of geometric figures, formal and abstract; of symbols current in the local cults, myths, or religion, or of simple spontaneous choice. If you look closely at some of the more modern national batiks you will still see the basic pattern designs representing local birds, foliage, etc.

Each country, within its own culture has developed a distinct form of the craft. The Indians have their paisley patterns, the Africans symmetrical tribal motifs, the Japanese and Chinese their delicate oriental abstracts.

In Java, the batiked garment was a status symbol and its making a courtly art. Just as the Scots developed clan tartans and the houses of aristocracy their coats of arms, the nobility in Java had its own designs, motifs, and colors. As time passed, it increased in popularity and became a sort of national costume for men and women alike. In about the 16th century, the Dutch brought the batiks to Holland. Batik then spread throughout Europe where the beauty of the craft aroused great interest, so velvet velours and similar luxurious materials were used. This was a big development from using the simpler cotton and muslins of the East. Batik offered a new medium for the artists to experiment with, and this they did, bringing new, exciting, and original techniques and effects to the craft.

The word "batik" is Javanese, derived from "mbatik," meaning writing or drawing. Calligraphy has always been an art form, particularly with the Chinese and Japanese. The actual word "batik" may not have been applied to the craft until fairly recently in its development. Resist media was probably first applied freely by hand, then with a stick similar to the first drawing or writing instruments. Later, the tjantings and tjaps were used. Now, all sorts of implements such as brushes and home-made printing blocks are used.

The tjap has been traced back to the 15th century where it was used in Madras, India. However, the Javanese claim that they introduced copper blocks for applying the wax to the cloth and this was known as tjap printing.

In tjap printing a type of metal stamp is dipped into hot wax and then placed on the fabric, leaving a wax pattern to resist the dye. The tjap itself is a beautiful work of art and is usually made of intricately patterned copper. Obviously, the tjap cuts the working time immensely since it prints a large area at one time. Another successful method of using a genuine tjap can be done by making a stamp pad of jute fiber wrapped in a muslin bag. Saturate this thoroughly with melted wax, and keep it hot in a frypan or in a pot over heat. The tjap is then pressed on the pad where it absorbs the wax, and it is then applied to the fabric in a repeat pattern.

The traditional tjanting is a small copper vessel (sometimes brass is used) with a bamboo handle and a projecting spout for applying the wax. Sometimes there are as many as six spouts. When using a tjanting for batik dyeing the cloth is carefully washed and soaked so that the right texture and surface is achieved. It is then hung over a frame. Sometimes the artist will sketch the design on with charcoal but most use only their tjantings and rely on visual memory. The area to be dyed is outlined and patterned with tjanting. The rest of the surface is covered with wax. The tjanting is dipped in a pot of melted wax until the cup-like form is filled. After wiping off the excess, the spout is drawn across the fabric as though one were as writing or drawing. In fact it is held in much the same way as one holds a pen. This leaves the wax pattern on the fabric. When empty or cold, the tjanting is dipped again into the wax and the process is continued. The cloth is turned over and the process repeated on the other side. Then the cloth is immersed in cold water until the wax hardens, and is later dipped in the dye vat. The wax is removed, leaving exposed other areas of the cloth to be dyed different colors by the same method.

Final steps for the wall hanging (see page 186).

◆
Basic requirements
for batik work

The waxes, dyes, materials, and equipment used in these projects are all simple to use, inexpensive, and readily available. Many fabrics can be used for batik but the fabric must be dyeable. Colored fabric may be used but the background will change the effect of the dye hues. All fabric should be of natural origin, i.e. no synthetic fibers or treatments should be used when using wax cold water dyes. Synthetic fibers can be used, but the methods necessary to work on them are very involved and impractical for hobby work.

Any fabric used must be washed before waxing to allow for shrinkage, and also to remove any starch or sizing that is often applied to fabrics to stiffen them. There are various ways of waxing the fabric so the wax is free to penetrate the fabric but these will be described in detail with each project. Since the properties of each fabric are different, they are waxed with slightly different techniques and methods. Sometimes, if the material is very thick, both sides of the fabric need waxing. On silk it is rather a simple matter for, as on thin cotton, the wax penetrates very easily.

There are many wax recipes all with varying proportions of beeswax, resins, and paraffin. A crystalline wax such as "Batik-Magik" is simple and more convenient to use since it is a complete formula in itself. No mixing is necessary, and it is readily available at craft shops. The Dylon "Cold Water Dyes" and the I.C.I. "Procion M" dyes are easy to use, extremely colorfast, and also readily available.

There really is no exact temperature to recommend when melting wax for doing batik, since once again the temperature depends on the thickness of the material, how absorbent the material is and the method of wax application being used. Largely, the object is to apply the wax so that it penetrates the fabric. The waxed portions then resist the dye color.

Dyeing techniques and recipes vary according to the dye being used and are described in detail.

The vessels used for dyeing can be plastic, enamel, wood, or copper; a plastic bucket or enameled basin is economical and convenient.

There are many methods for removing the wax. Sometimes several methods are used on the same batiked piece of work. Each project in this chapter describes in detail the method and techniques used from start to finish.

Various methods of batiking fabric have been used intentionally. Many different types of fabrics, dyes, and projects have been chosen to encourage you to try your hand at it. Once you start, you will realize the infinite scope and uses of batik work. This craft is much easier and more enjoyable than is generally believed and you can become as intricately involved with techniques as you like. You surely will find ways to incorporate batik with any of the other crafts with which you may already be familiar.

Always start dyeing with the lightest color, and work up to the darker ones. When washed and dried the parts to remain yellow are waxed in, and then the cloth is dipped into orange-red dye. This process is repeated until the cloth is white, yellow, orange-red, and brown.

Here is a simple guide to color schemes. The primary colors are red, yellow, and blue. To make orange, use yellow and red. To make green use yellow and blue. To make purple use red and blue. To make brown use red, yellow, and blue. Infinite variations on these colors can be obtained depending on how much of each color you use in your mix.

In batik dyeing always dye the lightest color first and go on up the scale to the darkest color. You will have many surprises when dyeing your fabric, most of them exciting and delightful.

The charm of batik is that it is creative and can be completely individual. You can have your very own designs, colors and patterns. In fact, a batik can never be exactly reproduced.

Opposite: A work by Paul O'Connor, a finalist in the Hoechst Textile Award. Courtesy Hoechst Australia Ltd.

◆

Abstract flowers on brown background

MATERIALS

Cotton material, batik wax, dye, salt, washing soda, bristle brush, wax pot, heat source, plastic bucket, large pot. Optional: old picture frame, tjanting.

METHOD

If you decide to plan and draw your own design, then draw it on paper first, preferably with a felt tipped pen. Tape it onto the back of your cloth and hold it up against the light. Perhaps taped against a window will make it easiest to see and handle. Then you can trace onto your fabric with a soft lead pencil. Otherwise, you can draw directly on the fabric itself with a very soft lead pencil; hard lead pencil marks are very difficult if not impossible to remove.

It is wise to work out the color scheme of your design on paper. Remember the color scheme of one dye over another — as in the sample piece (see page 190). A 1 in (2.5 cm) flat brush cut down to a point in a taper is one of the most useful implements for waxing. To taper, dip the brush in wax, let cool, and cut the diagonal with scissors. This shape will enable you to wax in small dots and lines or wide stripes and other shaped areas.

APPLYING THE WAX

Tacking the fabric to an old picture frame is a convenient way to keep the fabric free from touching anything underneath. With the fabric well stretched across the frame, wax in all the white areas with the brush. Use the pointed end of the brush for the large dots. Dip the fabric into the first and lightest dye bath. Rinse, dry, and tack it back onto the frame for the next waxing. You will notice that in some places the shades of a color vary. This variation is achieved by using thicker and thinner amounts of wax on the fabric. The thinner the wax, the more chance there is for penetration of the dye. With a tjanting, wax in very wavy thin lines.

To use a tjanting, heat a pot of wax, dip the tjanting into it, hold it there for a few moments to warm up the entire metal area of the tjanting. From painful experience, I recommend that you use a cloth to wipe the bottom of the tjanting as soon as you remove it from the pot; otherwise you will have drip marks over your fabric. Then slowly hold the point of the tjanting against the fabric and move it along in the pattern you desire, as though you were writing. If the wax no longer penetrates the fabric, it is time to dip it into the wax pot again and repeat the same process before continuing the waxing.

DYEING THE FABRIC

When the fabric is ready for the first dye bath, remove it from the frame and immerse it. When rinsed and dried, tack it to the frame again. In places where the wax starts to dissolve or crack, it can now be re-waxed where wanted, to retain some color as well as to avoid too much crackle. This gives each color several shades. As you can see, where some of the wax is left thin, there are tinges of blue in amongst the colors and some of the yellows have a greenish tinge, so although only three dye baths are used in this case, yellow, orange-red, and blue, the result is a combination of varying shades of yellows and slight greens, with several depths of color of orange, and some tinges of blue and brown.

Boil off the wax as in previous projects. This piece is mounted on pineboard.

◆

Two-piece dress

MATERIALS

A piece of pure cotton fabric, "Batik-Magik" wax, I.C.I. "Procion M" dyes, salt, washing soda, piece of plastic, rubber gloves, wax pot, heat source, plastic bucket, large pot.

METHOD

First, ensure that the fabric is thoroughly washed, dried, and pressed. With this particular design of overall crackle, you can either cut your pattern in advance before it is sewn and then wax and dye it, or you can sew it first and then wax it, etc. Otherwise, you can simply batik lengths of fabric and decide on the style and pattern later on. Perhaps to start with, it would be wisest to choose simple styles of clothing until you are familiar with the effects possible with batik.

TO OBTAIN THE OVERALL CRACKLE

These are two ways of getting the overall crackle: either use a large brush and paint in the entire fabric

Batik flower shapes on a brown background. Instructions opposite.

with wax, or heat enough wax so that you can dip the fabric into it until it is entirely covered. For this technique there is no frame or pinning needed. Hold the fabric over the pot with a wooden spoon until the hot wax has stopped dripping. When cool enough to handle, enclose both parts in a plastic bag and put it in the refrigerator to cool. When cold, remove the fabric from the plastic bag and crackle it with your hands; do some places more heavily than others to make various patterns.

DYEING THE FABRIC

Put the dyes with warm water into a bucket, add five tablespoons of common salt, plus two level teaspoons of the dye powder.

Place the fabric in this solution for 5 to 10 minutes, then dissolve two tablespoons of washing soda in very hot water and add to the solution. It is best to leave the fabric in the dye bath a further 15 minutes at least. Since "Procion" dyes air set, lay the fabric on plastic to dry overnight. Then rinse it thoroughly.

REMOVING THE WAX

When so much wax is used, rather than press the fabric first, simply heat it in a large pot of water with a little washing soda. Skim the wax off as it rises to the top of the pot. Since the fabric must be completely covered with water, be sure to add more water when necessary. Domestic plumbing cannot cope with any wax whatsoever, therefore when skimming off your wax, collect it onto absorbent paper towelling, or put it into a disposable receptacle.

When all the wax is removed, wash the fabric in the washing machine with ordinary detergent.

◆

Continuing with batik

In some countries, Easter eggs are waxed and dyed in the same way as we would do fabric. The results are beautiful.

Effective results can be achieved using white candles to draw on white paper. Paint over this with diluted inks or water paints. The inks, of course, will be resisted by the candle marks, and suddenly the original colorless wax marks become a pattern against the darkened background.

Old and tired clothing can be brightened up, either by tie-dyeing or batik. Wax can also be dripped and splattered onto a fabric to create a modern and simple design.

You can use the batik principle for letters and words just as well as designs, which can be fun on T-shirts for club names, slogans, etc.

Batik drapes, lampshades, room dividers, all manner of clothing, place mats, toys, cravats, ties as well as background mounting pieces for other types of work can all be done in batik.

You can probably think of many more uses for this medium. While experimenting you may discover new techniques. Why not try making some of your own printing blocks? Try sticking some pins in the top of a cork and dip that in your wax and print. How about removing the entire lid from a can and using the edge of the can for a circle pattern? Some of your cookie cutters will also do an excellent job. Stencils can also be used. Why not batik or tie-dye some of your old sheets and pillow slips to brighten them up? If you do ceramics, for example, why not try tiles on a batik background?

We know embroidery fits in well with batik. Copper shim and enameled pieces can also be interestingly used in conjunction with batik.

The possibilities are unlimited. All you need to do now is simply collect your materials and start work; in no time you will be able to enjoy the delightful experience of having a white piece of fabric one moment and a colored pattern the next — all achieved by your own hand.

◆

Batik and tie-dye scarves

MATERIALS

Silk fabric, batik wax, dye, vinegar, washing soda, bristle brush, thread, rubber gloves, wax pot, heat source, plastic bucket, large pot. Optional: a piece of plastic; rubber bands.

METHOD

Tie-dyeing is essentially what the name implies. Fabric is actually tied, knotted, folded, sewn, and bound in different ways to act as a resist to dye for creating patterns. The exposed pieces of fabric accept dye solutions; the tied and knotted parts do not. Hot or cold dyes may be used.

When batik patterns are combined with tie-dying, it is necessary to use cold water dyes. Either batik a pattern on the fabric and then tie or knot it, or else complete the batiking process and then start the tie-dyeing patterns. In this latter case, hot water dyes may be used, since there is no longer any wax on the fabric. The fabric itself can be knotted at intervals and then placed in a dye bath. The knotted portions of the fabric will not be penetrated by the dye, whereas the exposed portions will receive the dye.

Beautiful use of gold in a dyed work by P. Bygott. Courtesy Hoechst Australia Ltd.

This is what creates the relief pattern. If more than one color is wanted, rinse after the dye bath and tie again amongst the other knots, or else undo the knots, allow to dry and re-knot the fabric again before the next color is used, depending on which effect you prefer.

For tying the fabric, cotton, linen, waxed thread, or rubber bands are used. Bind the thread around the fabric at varying intervals (see diagram). For a marble pattern, scrunch up the entire piece of material into a ball and wind the thread round and round till most of it is covered, before placing it into the dye bath. For individual patterns, such as circles, pick up the fabric, perhaps in the middle, and start to bind the thread around it, leaving no spaces between the rows of thread. Secure the ends of the thread. This procedure is repeated at intervals, down the fabric. Vary the amount of

binding and spaces to produce different sized circles, etc. Rubber bands can also be used for binding fabric, instead of thread.

Sometimes, for an interesting effect, place a piece of plastic over an area of fabric and then bind it tightly with a rubber band before immersing in dye. This method, done at random over a piece of fabric, creates an interesting type of pattern. Techniques for tying other more specific patterns and shapes are discussed earlier in this chapter.

The general principles of dyeing are the same as for batik. Wash and dry the fabric. Rinse well between dye baths. The coloring systems and principles are the same. Try all types of natural fabrics for tie-dyeing; each one produces its own individual effect. Shirts, T-shirts, socks, sheets, cotton jeans, and other ready-made articles are also excellent to use for tie dyeing.

Spinning and Weaving

SPINNING

◆

The spindle

(see diagrams 1a, b)

The spindle is the most ancient device for spinning; it consists of a smooth, wooden stick with a wooden disc fitted to it about 1 in (2.5 cm) from the lower end. A notch is cut in the stick about ½ in (1.3 cm) from the top. A length of wool thread is fastened to the shaft just above the disc, passed over the edge of the disc and fastened round the bottom of the shaft then taken up over the edge of the disc and fastened to the notch at the top of the shaft. The spindle is now held upright, suspended from the thread, and can be spun by twisting between fingers and thumb.

Join a piece of teased yarn to the thread at the top and hold this between the fingers of the left hand. Spin the spindle with the right hand and the thread will begin to twist.

Yarn is formed by this spinning motion pulling the loose wool yarn into the thread between finger and

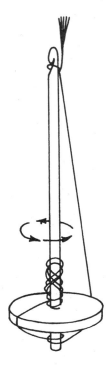

diagram 1b

thumb. The length of the thread gradually extends and lowers the spindle to the floor.

When the spindle reaches the floor the thread is slipped off the notch and the bottom of the shaft and wound on to the shaft of the spindle above the disc.

A sufficient length of thread is left to set the spindle up again and the procedure is repeated until the spindle is full. Then the thread is eased off the spindle and skeined for further treatment, such as scouring and dyeing.

◆

The spinning wheel

The spinning wheel is the traditional form of spinning equipment and consists of a foot treadle, a wheel, and a number of parts with such interesting names as "Mother of All," "Maidens," "Bobbins," "Lazy Kate," "Niddy Noddy," and "the Flier". Good spinning is an even feed of yarn into the spinning head; feet, and hands must be in complete rhythm.

The wheel is set up by tying a length of wool thread round the bobbin, the yarn is then carried over a hook on the flier and passed through a hole in the

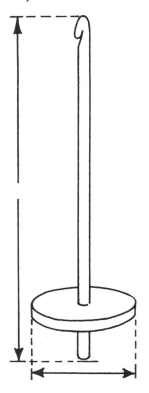

diagram 1a

Spinning and weaving are rewarding home activities. The wooden loom shown is for tapestry weaving.

spindle. Tease the end of this thread and place beside it a teased piece of yarn held between finger and thumb.

Start the wheel and slowly let the yarn twist and with the right hand pull out a few inches (9 cm) of yarn to the thickness required. The twist will pick up and the thread will feed through the left hand into the spinning head. Continue to do this until the bobbin is filled.

Shift the feed to another hook as each section of the bobbin fills.

Full bobbins are removed and placed on the Lazy Kate and when this is filled the yarn is skeined on the Niddy Noddy. Tie the skein tightly at four points before removing from the Niddy Noddy.

This yarn may now be scoured ready for knitting or weaving, and is called homespun.

WEAVING

Hand weaving is a centuries-old craft which has become popular again. It is a craft that can be fun for children as well as adults and lets everyone develop their own creative talents.

While early weavers used the fabrics they made mainly for warmth, today's weavers are making attractive fashion accessories, such as belts, bags, and ties, and adding brightness to their homes with such things as wall-hangings, cushion covers, and bedspreads.

Weaving depends on the use of two sets of threads. One set, known as the warp threads, is fastened in the weaving frame, usually a loom; these run lengthwise to the piece that is being woven. The other threads, called the weft, run under and over the warp creating the woven pattern.

Various threads may be used in weaving to give different effects. Some are knitting yarn, cotton, flax, string, raffia, rushes, rayon thread, or metallic threads.

Experimenting with different types of thread is part of the fun of weaving interesting and unusual designs. Choose threads with the article you are making in mind. Be practical, and if it is for general use, choose threads that will give good wear.

◆
Weaving terms

Certain terms are used in weaving. Here are some:

WEAVING
Weaving is a combining of threads, carried out in a frame called a loom. Darning a hole is the simplest form of weaving.

LOOM
Loom is the framework on which weaving is undertaken.

WARP
The fixed threads that run lengthwise to the piece that is being woven on the loom is the warp.

FRAME
A frame carries the warp thread.

HEDDLE
Heddle consists of a piece of string tied round every second warp thread and these, in turn, are secured to a stick. They form a clear passage between the alternative warp threads.

SHED
Shed is the tunnel formed by raising every second thread of the warp: one set of warp threads is raised and the other set depressed to allow passage of the shuttle with the weft.

WEFT
Weft is the thread that is woven in and out of the warp threads to make the cloth.

SHUTTLE
Shuttle carries the supply of weft thread. Thread is wound round the shuttle and passed through the shed to lay the weft.

BEAMS
Beams enable a greater length of web to be woven than can be held on the frame. Usually two rollers are used: one carries the made warp, the other the finished cloth.

REED
Reed is a series of metal wires held in the frame and used for spacing the warp and pushing the wefts into place after the shuttle has passed through the shed.

Bags made with handspun and woven yarn. Courtesy Avalon Craft Cottage.

◆
A simple loom

(see diagrams 1 to 5)

The simplest form of weaving is done on a cardboard loom. This is suitable for beginners.

To make a cardboard loom you will need a piece of heavy cardboard, say 6 or 8 ins (15 or 20 cm) long and 3 or 4 ins (7 or 10 cm) wide. You will need another strip the same length as your first piece and about ½ in (1.3 cm) wide, to make the needle.

Make an uneven number of marks opposite each other along each of the short sides of the piece of cardboard about ¼ in (0.6 cm) apart. Next, cut a shallow notch in the edges of the card opposite each mark. Punch holes in diagonally opposite corners of the card (diagram 1).

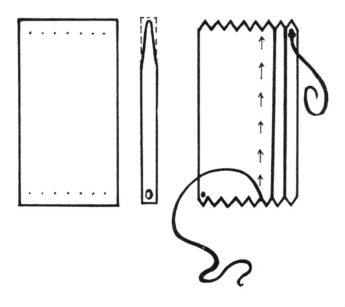

diagram 1   diagram 2

To make your needle, take the piece of cardboard ½ in (1.3 cm) wide and punch a hole in one end to take the thread, then shape the other end to a point. Round off any sharp edges to allow easy passage of the needle through the threads.

Your small loom is ready. For thread use string, yarn, heavy cotton or a soft cotton thread called "dish cloth cotton".

Pass the thread through the hole at the top of the card and knot the end. Wind thread around the cardboard going through all the notches. The loose ends of yarn are tied together at the back (diagram 2). These are the warp threads.

Thread the needle with a different color yarn about 1 yd (91cm) long. Beginning at one end of the loom, pass the needle with weft thread over and under the warp threads. When you reach the end of the warp go back in the other direction, reversing the over and under movement. Continue until you have woven 1 or 2 ins (2.5 or 5 cm) of cloth. This over-and-under weave is known as tabby weave.

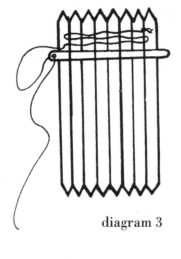

diagram 3

diagram 4

Tabby weave is one of the simplest patterns to weave (diagram 3) and is the most useful of all weaves. Such fabrics as calico, muslin, hopsack, tweeds, and some Scottish tartans can be made in this basic tabby weave.

When weaving is completed, cut off the end of the weft thread and tuck it into the warp. Cut the warp

*A handwoven coverlet.
Courtesy Avalon Craft
Cottage.*

*Handwoven silk stoles by
Mary Williams. Courtesy
Craft Australia.*

thread in the centre of the back and remove the cloth from the loom. Gather several warp threads together and knot as close to the weave as possible. Continue until all the threads are knotted. Trim the fringes to the same length. You now have a bookmark ready to be used (diagram 4).

Card looms are invaluable for teaching the rudiments of weaving, but adults will find frame looms improvised from picture or window frames useful for coarse weaving, such as tapestries and rugs. For heavy rug weaving needing a very strong loom, a wire bed frame is excellent.

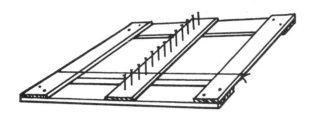

diagram 5

The frame loom is a wooden frame with a thin slat of wood nailed top and bottom to raise the warp threads clear of the frame The slats have a series of saw-cuts or nails (diagram 5). The warp threads are wound around the nails or across the serrations, and pass up and down the face of the frame, or completely around the frame.

The slats at top and bottom of the frame lift the warp threads above the face of the frame so there is less strain on the warp when the shed is made. One set of warp threads sinks, the other set rises, sharing the stretch. Note that a shuttle replaces the needle used with the card loom.

These looms can be adapted to take a warp twice their length by winding each warp end separately around the loom and knotting the ends together.

As weaving progresses the work is pulled downward, so exposing more warp at the front of the loom. The saw-cuts or nails at the bottom of the loom must be omitted.

To space the warp, use an independent piece of wood as long as the width of the loom, containing a row of

nails protruding equidistant above the board in a straight line. One or more warp ends are placed in each space between the nails. As well as spacing the warp, this board is drawn forward after each row to push the weft close up to the preceding rows.

When making the warp allow 1 to 4 ins (2.5 to 10 cm) to the yard for shrinkage and approximately 1 to 2 ins (2.5 to 5 cm) for shrinkage sideways, as the weft thread will tend to pull the work inward.

A good deal depends on the type of yarn used; some tend to shrink more than others. More yarn is needed for the warp than for the weft, and this should be kept in mind when calculating the quantities of yarn needed. The weft takes about three-quarters of that needed for the warp.

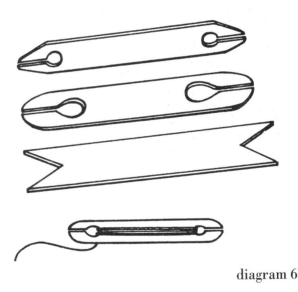

diagram 6

A stick shuttle is the most suitable for use with simple looms. These are made from smoothed hardwood ⅛ to ¼ in (0.3 to 0.6 cm) thick, 1 in to 1½ ins (2.5 to 3.8 cm) wide and slightly longer than the distance between the first and last warp threads of the work. Small ones can be cut from firm cardboard (diagram 6).

For fine weaving, table looms and treadle looms are mainly used, and there are many varieties of each .

A good loom isn't cheap. A table loom will be useful for scarves, tray cloths, table mats. The treadle loom is for large lengths of material.

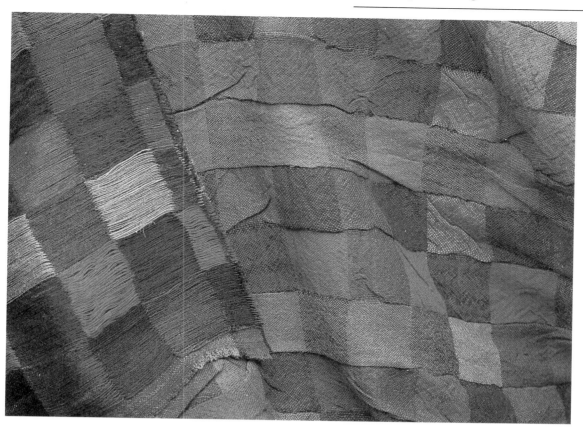

Work by the weaver Liz Williamson, winner of the Hoechst Textile Award in 1983 and 1989. Courtesy Hoechst Australia Ltd.

Of the smaller, easily handled looms, the Inkle loom is one of the simplest. It is the perfect medium for making belts, head and neck bands, and braids that are restricted in width.

Other looms are used for more complicated patterns, and to introduce greater textural variety into woven cloth.

Tapestry looms are used for the type of weaving where openly spaced warp threads are entirely hidden by the weft and also for wall panels used as mural decoration where the weft is used to completely cover the warp. Tapestry weaving techniques allow great freedom in design and choice of threads in creating individual pieces.

The Handweavers and Spinners' Guild of Australia provides help and information to members on spinning and weaving.

◆

Tapestry weaving

Tapestry is simple weaving in which the warp does not show. The design is formed entirely by the weft, which is beaten down to hide the warp completely. Although the Incas and the Chinese began with it independently, tapestry weaving came to us from the Egyptians; wall paintings show tapestries being woven along the Nile from 3,000 B.C. The oldest extant tapestry is from the tomb of Thotmes III, which was made in 1,500 B.C., the yarns used being linen and wool yarn. The Coptic Egyptians continued the tradition tapestry and had a golden period of tapestry weaving around 500 A.D. When the Arabs moved on after their invasion of Egypt they took this art west to the Atlantic, north into Spain and France, and eastward to Syria, Persia, and Turkey.

A 9 in (23cm) box loom for the beginner. It does tabby weaves and is suitable for making scarves, place mats and other simple woven pieces to your own design. Courtesy Woman's Day.

This tapestry weaving by Mary and Larry Beeston is made with a fine linen (invisible) warp and a wool weft. Courtesy Craft Australia.

Rugmaking

♦

1. Wool yarn

Strands of wool yarn, cut to the same length are required to produce the pile of the rug. These can be cut to any length between 2 and 6 ins (5 and 15 cm) depending on whether a low plush pile effect, or a loose shaggy pile is desired. The pile produced is slightly less than half the length of the strand, as each strand is hooked through the backing producing two ends in the pile of the rug.

Among the best yarn in the world for the making of rugs and carpets generally is that produced in New Zealand. The breeds of sheep, the excellent pasture land and the climate combine to produce a long, strong, resilient staple yarn which is ideal for use in making floor coverings that will look and wear well.

The yarn goes through a series of processes after the sheep has been shorn, to prepare it for use in hooking through the rug screen.

First, the raw, greasy yarn is sorted into grades by highly skilled operators. It is then scoured in what is effectively a giant washing machine and dryer. By gently washing, combing, and rewashing the yarn, it is eventually clean and dry, ready for spinning.

In the spinning process, the yarn is first combed into narrow ribbons, about ¾ in (2 cm) wide. These ribbons, knowns as condensor slubbings, are then twisted together at high speed to form individual strands of yarn. Normally between two and six strands of yarn are twisted together to form a suitable yarn for carpets and rugs; 4-ply yarn (that is, four strands twisted together) is most suitable for use in hand-made rugs. The yarn is then wound into hanks, ready for dyeing.

Dyeing yarn in hank form is a modern method which is both quick and effective. Up to 4,000 lbs (1.8 t) of yarn can be dyed at once, in giant vats. The yarn is stirred around to ensure penetration of the dye and then dried. It is then ready for cutting and packaging into the required forms.

Yarn for kitset rugs is precut into the length required and packaged in a cylindrical form in cellophane, each wrapper containing 1 oz (25 g) (about 320 strands of yarn).

♦

2. Backing material

The backing material into which the yarn is hooked is a mesh webbing material known as the "canvas". The rug-makers of ancient times had to weave their own canvas as well as prepare the yarn for their rugs, but modern techniques have eliminated this tedious task for today's rug-maker. Canvas screens are manufactured specifically to cater for the rug-making craft.

The two most important aspects of the canvas screen are its stability, and its firmness to give support and durability to the finished rug. The canvas is woven in such a way as to produce small squares evenly throughout its area. The most suitable size for the squares is ¼ in (0.6 cm) square, making 16 squares to 1 square inch (2.5 per square centimeter). This allows ample room to hook the yarn through the mesh and still gives very adequate coverage to the pile of the finished rug. Very rigid manufacturing specifications are followed to ensure the stability of each square in the mesh, thus giving the full canvas true and exact dimensions.

Finishing the canvas by the application of sizing gives it sufficient firmness to form a sound backing for the rug. In making the rug, constant handling of the canvas can make it limp unless adequate sizing is applied.

♦

3. Design

(see diagrams 1 to 3 overleaf)

Once the canvas has been purchased (or made) the design can be applied to it. Choice of design is influenced by the purpose for which the rug is

Basic equipment to make a hooked rug.

intended when finished, the method of making it, the size, and general suitability to its future surroundings.

In general, when people are designing their own rugs they tend to use too many colors and make patterns which are too complicated for the rug-making technique to be used. Simple geometric patterns such as stripes, lines, checks, circles, and curves make the best rug designs. It is important to keep in mind that the design should be worked so that the rug looks good from any angle.

Today the rug-maker can buy prepared designs on the canvas, ready to be worked. These pre-packed kits include a complete guide to the making of the rug.

In this case the design is printed onto the screen in the colors desired in the rug. There is no limit to the style of design or the number of colors which can be used, provided sufficient of the one design are produced to make an economic run for the manufacturer. Pre-packed kitset rugs are available in a wide range of sizes, shapes, and designs, and featuring numerous color schemes.

Very careful use of dye chemicals is necessary, as some chemicals will tend to break down the sizing already applied to the canvas, making it weak and susceptible to tearing when the rug is being hooked. The inks must be colorfast, they must impregnate the canvas sufficiently to provide the design, and must not rub off when the canvas is being worked.

The last method of applying the design is by silk screening, which is a sophistication of a simple transfer process. The design is transferred onto a silk backing

diagram 1

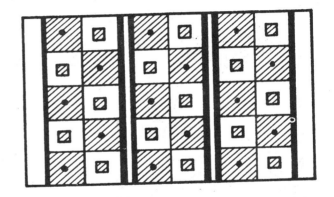

diagram 2

diagram 3

A simple hooked rug in colorful squares.

which is stretched onto a frame. One silk screen is made for each color in the design. All of the areas that are not to be printed are blocked out with a varnish-type material which does not allow the inks to penetrate. The inks are placed within the frame of the screen and drawn across the silk with a squeegee, printing the desired color onto the canvas. Using the silk screens for each color in the design, successively, produces the canvas printed with the design in its colors.

◆

4. Rugmaking tools

The only tools required are a pair of scissors (or a sharp knife), yarn, a latch hook or a punch needle. For hundreds of years, rugs were woven by using only hands and fingers but today it is normal to use a hooking tool or a punch needle. The most suitable hooking tool is that illustrated (see diagram 4).

This tool has a fixed hook at the top and a swinging latch just below this hook. It is simple to use and very effective in producing tight, even tufts in the pile of the rug.

diagram 4

METHODS OF RUGMAKING

◆

1. Punch needle

This method requires a special punch needle on stencilled jute canvas (hessian), and a continuous thread (skein yarn is used). The threaded needle is pushed through the stretched jute on the wooden rug frame from the wrong side leaving loops of the yarn on the right side. These loops form the pile of the rug and can be cut or not. A variety of traced jute canvas designs are available.

TO WORK THIS METHOD (see diagram 5)
1. Stretch the jute canvas tightly over a wooden rug frame or any other open frame of solid wood, and secure with drawing pins along the four sides. Work the design from the traced side of the jute.

2. Thread yarn into the needle. The yarn must enter

the needle at the top and protrude 1 in (2.5 cm) through the needle eye.

3. Hold the needle like a pencil (see illustration, right). Push through the jute canvas as far as the shoulder then withdraw the needle without lifting the point above the level of the material, otherwise the stitches on the wrong side will be loose.

4. Insert the needle again in the same way about 3/16 in (0.5 cm) further along. It is not necessary to work in rows but always have the grooved side of the needle point facing the direction in which you are working and the yarn threading through freely.

5. As each small section is worked, cut the loops with sharp scissors. To define a clear outline around important parts of the design the outer edge of the design may be clipped closer.

6. When each section is completed move the frame to an adjacent part.

FINISHING
If your finished piece is intended as a floor rug you will need to back it. As the pile is not knotted, it is desirable to bond the underside by coating it with thin adhesive or glue before lining or binding.

diagram 5

Opposite: A knotted rug made by Solvig Baas Becking. Photograph by Alana Harris, Courtesy Craft Australia.

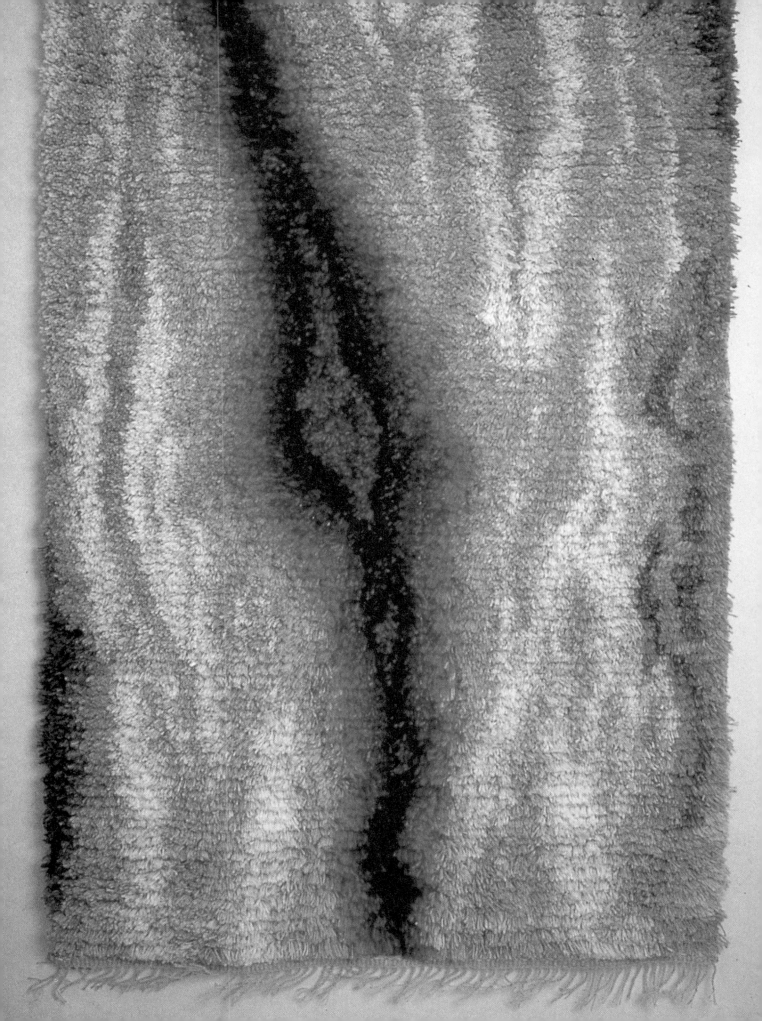

If your design is being used as a wall hanging, then use linen thread and stitch a 1 in (2.54 cm) hem down the long sides. Fold and stitch the hems top and bottom and insert dowelling of suitable size. The dowelling in the lower hem will add weight to the work so that it will hang better.

Another method is to place a piece of soft wood or straw board on the wrong side of the design. Stretch and staple the surplus jute evenly to this, working on each side alternately until the jute has been attached firmly and the corners are neatly folded. The staples can then be covered with tape to neaten the sides.

◆

2. Latchet hook

This method requires a stencilled canvas with the design traced ready for working, a latchet hook and pre-cut packs of rug yarn. Each stencilled canvas includes instructions showing how to work the rug, the colors and amounts of yarn needed.

If you want to make up your own original design, plain check canvas can be purchased by the yard from any department store. Allow approximately six 2 oz (50 g) packets of pre-cut rug yarn for each square foot of canvas.

BEGINNING THE RUG
Fold back about 2 ins (5 cm) of canvas upward across the width at the starting edge. Work knots through the double thickness to give a neat, strong edge. It is a little difficult at first, but the trouble is well worth taking. This is also repeated at the end of the rug.

ENDING THE RUG
Fold over 2 ins (5 cm) of the canvas as at the beginning and work through the double thickness once more. Note, however, that oval, circular and semi-circular rugs cannot be worked in this way. In this case, when the rug is finished the surplus canvas is cut off, leaving a small edge which is turned under and bound with carpet braid or webbing.

THE WORKING POSITION (FOR THE FIRST METHOD)
To be comfortable when working it is easier to sit at a table with the working end of the rug facing you. Work from left to right in rows across the width of the canvas, do not work separate blocks of pattern or color, and as the rug progresses, let the completed fabric come forward onto your knees. Put a fairly heavy weight on the canvas to resist of the pull of knot making.

HOW TO MAKE THE KNOT: FIRST METHOD
(see diagram 6)

1. Select strand of yarn to match color of hole at lower right corner of canvas. Loop it under shank of hook just in front of bend. Hold yarn in place with index finger (a).

2. Fold canvas back along first line of design. Push hook through first hole passing it through both layers of canvas until latch is through (b).

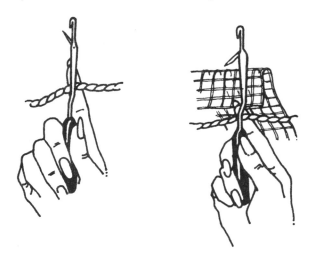

diagram 6a   diagram 6b

3. Pull hook back until latch is vertical. Grasp both ends of yarn with free hand. Bring yarn over hook behind latch and hold between latch and hook (c).

diagram 6c

4. Pull the hook toward you, holding on to yarn until the latch closes (d).

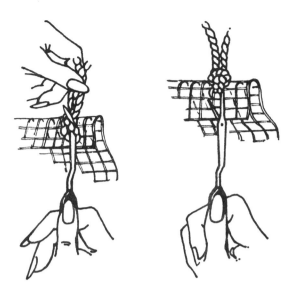

diagram 6d

diagram 6e

5. Release yarn. Draw hook with ends of yarn back through loop (e).

6. Tug ends toward you to tighten knot. Continue in this manner across first row, then across each row above (f).

diagram 6f

TO MAKE THE KNOT: SECOND METHOD
(see diagram 7)

1. Place yarn, doubled equally, on shaft of hook. Insert hook under the double thread of canvas with hook turned to left (a).

2. Twist cut ends of loop behind the latch and across under the hook (b).

3. Pull hook through loop, bringing cut ends with it (c).

4. Give a slight pull to make the knot firm (d).

Pile worked by the second method lies the opposite way from that worked by the first method.

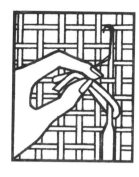

diagram 7a

diagram 7b

diagram 7c

diagram 7d

FINISHING

To make the surface flat and even, go over the rug carefully with a pair of scissors to clip off any long ends of pile. Then give the rug a good shake and wipe it over with a damp cloth to remove fluff and any loose ends.

BACKING

It is not really necessary to back rugs under normal wearing conditions. However, if the rug is to lie on an uneven floor where there is a risk of chafing the strands of yarn, backing may be a good idea.

BINDING

This is preferable to backing and gives a neat finish to the selvages. Binding is not essential but it is usually desirable to finish the edges of rugs with a binding stitch using, for example, Turkey rug yarn in skeins. Cut packs cannot be used. To complete a rectangular rug 27 x 54 in (69 x 140 cm) it would be necessary to purchase two skeins of yarn to match the background color of the rug.

BINDING STITCH

(see diagram 8)

First, oversew both ends of the rug. Then bind selvages with oversewing. With the wrong side facing, darn in end of yarn and make some upright oversewing stitches as shown, then insert needle in 1st hole and bring toward you, go over the 4th hole and bring toward you, go over the 4th hole back to 2nd, forward to 5th, and so on.

BINDING SHAPED RUGS

Binding is necessary when rugs are not rectangular in shape as it is impracticable to make a proper selvage by folding over the canvas and working through the double thickness. The surplus canvas should be cut off to within 2 ins (5 cm) of the rug, the remainder should then be turned under. Pin on 2 in (5 cm) wide matching carpet braid to the outside edge of the rug and then stitch it with strong carpet thread. Then press it flat onto the back of the rug — a warm iron may be necessary to flatten the folds. Finally, stitch the inner edge of the binding to the back of the fabric, putting in darts where required, to keep the edge flat.

FINISHING

1. With the rug flat, sew binding to canvas along outer edge of hooked area. Work around corners to allow for mitering. Square corners can be made if preferred. Keep binding and canvas flat.

2. Fold unworked edge of canvas to back of rug. Trim excess canvas away so that it is slightly narrower than width of binding and baste in place.

3. Turn binding to back of rug and sew in place, mitering or squaring corners.

4. Clip any uneven ends.

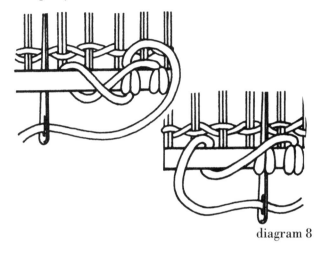

diagram 8

CARE FOR YOUR RUG

1. To remove grit, the vacuum cleaner can be used on the back of the rug.

2. If possible, shake off dirt when rug is dry.

3. Hand-hooked rugs, wall hangings and pillows should be dry cleaned.

4. Fluff your rug every few months. Wet a large Turkish towel and wring out all excess water. Place rug and damp towel in your dryer and fluff for about 20 to 25 minutes. This will remove any loose dirt and dust.

◆

Cross stitch floor rug

To make a rug about 1 x 1.5 yds (1 x 1.5 m)

MATERIALS

2 yds (1.75 m) of 45 in (115 cm) wide double thread rug canvas to a gauge of 10 holes to 3 in (7.5 cm). Rug yarn or 12 ply yarn. For this size rug, you will need about 40 balls of yarn, each of 27.5 yds (25 m) (quantity may vary slightly according to the tension of stitches), in colors according to your choice; a round-end needle with a large eye; felt pen for

marking canvas; any design suitable for cross stitch, or graph paper and colored pencils.

Cross stitch patterns are generally associated with sampler stitching, napery, or clothing decoration. They can also be used most effectively to create a stunning floor rug. The base material is rug canvas, which can be obtained pre-printed or plain. Plain canvas can be adapted for any counted cross stitch design. Please allow for a 1 in (2.5 cm) border right around the design.

METHOD

Before you begin, measure the area for the design, and mark an outline around the design area with a felt pen or tape. Trim any excess canvas, allowing four "holes" or about 1 in (2.5 cm) hem on each edge. Fold this hem area underneath and overcast with the color chosen for the edging and border.

Stitch your design in cross stitch over one pair of threads. Work from left to right along the row, beginning from lower left hole to upper right hole, until the color changes. Work back along the row from right to left, ensuring that the stitches all cross in the same direction. Work one color throughout, before commencing the next color.

The rug does not have to feature an overall pattern, but can show a combination of designs according to your choice. It is a good idea to plan ideas and place on graph paper, and if required, mark them on the canvas.

Circular rug is worked in black and white.

Patchwork

PATCHWORK TECHNIQUE

Patchwork is closely allied to appliqué (a method of applying one piece of material on another to form a pattern) but it does not require as much embroidery skill. However, intricate designs can be created and many interesting, attractive, and useful articles can be made using patchwork.

Most people who sew hoard odds and ends of fabric that are too pretty to throw away and yet not large enough to make anything practical. So if you have numerous pieces of fabrics (closely woven cottons are ideal), why not turn them into a piece of patchwork? But you must be careful in the way you arrange the various colors and patterns so that you achieve a good design.

Beyond the ability to cut and use a needle, patchwork demands no specific skill. It is a restful and pleasant recreation and once started it is like a jig-saw puzzle: hard to put down.

Handmade patchwork has an advantage over needlework since it needs little equipment and may be carried around in a small space. It only becomes unwieldy when nearing completion.

◆

Materials

The tools for handmade patchwork are simple: needle, thread, pins, scissors, templates, scraps of paper, and material.

You can also apply the following instructions to patchwork that is joined by machine.

To keep your pieces all the same size you will need a template, which will enable you cut accurate paper shapes — the basis of all good patchwork. The templates should be cut from a stiff, firm material, otherwise they will lose their shape after a certain amount of use. Very stiff cardboard or thin metal is preferable. The size and shape are entirely a matter of choice, depending on the size of the work you have in mind and the material available. The more

accurately you cut these, the smoother your finished patchwork will be.

Templates may be almost any geometric shape, but for the beginner the hexagon is the easiest and most commonly used to make an effective series of patterns in a variety of colors.

Draw on paper a hexagon, each side measuring 2 in (5 cm). Inside this draw a hexagon, each side 1½ ins (3.8 cm). Glue to firm cardboard. Leave to dry. (See diagram 1.)

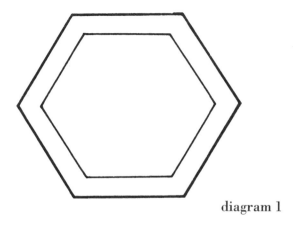

diagram 1

With a sharp razor blade cut round the inside line of the hexagonal shape to make the window. This enables you to see that your template has been placed on the straight of the fabric. Now cut around the larger outline and the template is complete.

The best fabrics to use for patchwork are silk, satin, and cotton that will not fray badly. Rayons are not successful since they fray and do not keep their shape.

◆

Method

Patchwork may be done in several ways:

1. By repeating one shape which must be geometrical so that it will fit into the next.

2. By repeating a design made up of several different shapes.

Opposite: Very colorful patchwork created to give a 'country' look

3. Mixing dissimilar shapes (see diagram 2), giving a crazy effect. Usually the pieces are arranged on a background of some cheap material, in as interesting a way as possible. One patch will overlay the next; the overlapping edge is turned under and hemmed down to the one beneath. All pieces are tacked into place before hemming. The edges are neat and an embroidery stitch such as feather stitch or herringbone can be added for emphasis.

diagram 2

4. Squares of material with patchwork designs already worked on them are joined together, sometimes with strips of contrasting material in between.

Note
Your patchwork will look more attractive if plain and patterned fabrics are combined; the contrast gives emphasis to the design.

◆

Geometrical patchwork

In pieced patchwork the shapes are geometrical and probably the most popular are hexagons, diamonds, squares, and triangles. All templates should be very carefully made as the slightest inaccuracy will throw them out of balance and your pieces will not fit together.

Geometric shapes are easy to make and need only a ruler, compass, and protractor to draw. Use strong scissors to cut from cardboard so that you have clean edges, and metal shears for metal templates.

In this type of patchwork each piece is sewn to the

next with small oversewing stitches. This method is particularly attractive for cushion covers and quilts, although a lining is needed to hide raw edges. If the quilt is quilted, an interlining will be needed.

◆

To prepare a patch

Cut a good number of paper patterns from your template. Next cut the patches from the material. Be sure to cut with the straight thread of the material, then place the paper pattern in the middle of the wrong side of the patch.

Carefully turn the hem of the patch over and tack to the paper with just enough stitches to make sure the corner folds are securely held down. Cut thread, leaving about ½ in (1.3 cm). (See diagram 3.)

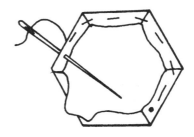

diagram 3

To join patches (see diagram 4), arrange them in the desired pattern, face uppermost. Join by holding two patches together, wrong sides out with the edges to be sewn, held neatly together. Oversew them evenly; do not crowd the stitches as this is apt to cause a ridge and weaken the seams.

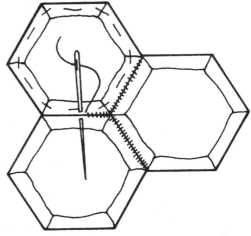

diagram 4

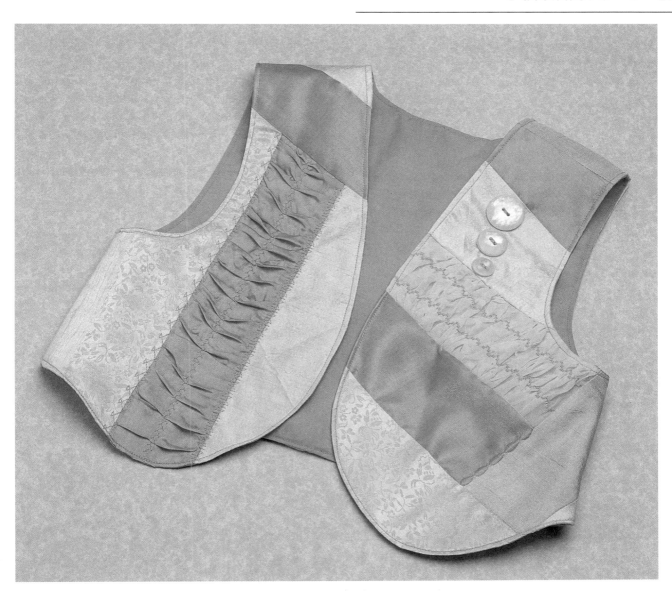

A pretty girl's waistcoat, patched in complementary fabrics and colors. Courtesy Avalon Craft Cottage.

When a large enough piece has been completed, lay work face downward on the table and remove tacking threads and papers. Be sure to leave the papers in the pieces to which others have to be joined.

◆

Lining

Almost all patchwork needs a lining and this must be chosen to suit the article to be lined, both for its texture and its tone. For lining linen and cotton, use lawn; for gingham, use poplin.

Note
Before lining the patchwork, work any decorative stitches over the seams.

PATCHWORK CUSHIONS

All the cushion patterns given can be sewn by machine. Make a paper or cardboard pattern of the patches you will need from the diagram to size.

Before cutting any fabric patches from patterns, test their accuracy. Reassemble the pattern pieces into the original design — the edges should meet perfectly without gaps or overlapping.

Choose firm fabrics that do not fray. Wash and press new fabrics. Lay fabric out flat, wrong side up, place pattern on fabric and trace around it with a pencil. When you have marked all the patch pieces you need, cut out each patch ¼ in (0.6 cm) away from the marked (stitching) line.

◆

Round cushion with square middle

MATERIALS

Small quantity of four contrast colored fabrics; 19.5 x 19.5 ins (50 x 50 cm) backing fabric; 15 ins (40 cm) of 1 yd (90 cm) wide fabric for frill; 1 in (2.5 cm) of 1.5 in (4 cm) wide lace; filling.

SIZE

18 ins (45 cm) in diameter excluding frill.

METHOD

Cut four frill pieces 4 ins (10 cm) by 1 yd (90 cm) long. Cut out patches according to instructions (see diagram). Sew the two patches of each quarter circle together. Sew quarter circles together in pairs then sew semi-circles together. Finish as for log cabin cushion from * to end.

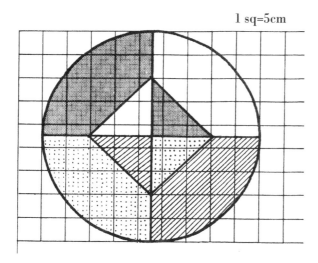

1 sq=5cm

◆

Patchwork log cabin cushion

MATERIALS

Small quantity of five fabrics with the same color base and four fabrics with contrast color base; 19.5 x 19.5 ins (50 x 50 cm) backing fabric; 15 ins (40 cm) of 1 yd (90 cm) wide fabric for frill; 3.25 ft (3 m) of 1.75 in (3 cm) wide lace; stuffing.

SIZE

Approx 19.5 x 19.5 ins (50 x 50 cm) excluding frill.

METHOD

Cut four frill pieces 3 ins (8 cm) wide by 1 yd (90 cm) long. Cut out patches according to instructions keeping the light colors towards the middle and the dark to the edge. Sew patches together from the middle square out to the edge in a spiral manner. * Cut backing piece out the same size as patchwork. Gather up lace to fit edge of patchwork and stitch over seamline, right sides together.

FRILL

Join short edges of frill pieces together to form a continuous piece. Narrow hem one long edge of frill. Gather up the other long edge of frill to fit edge of cushion. Pin frill to patchwork piece matching raw edges, right sides together and stitch.

Place patchwork and backing pieces together, right sides together and stitch around edge, leaving a small opening for turning. Turn through to the right sides and press. Fill cushion with stuffing and slip stitch opening closed.

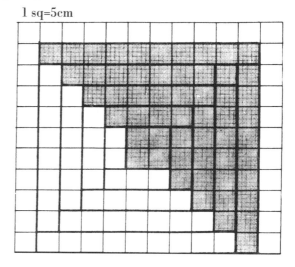

1 sq=5cm

◆

Round cushion with eight segments

MATERIALS

Small quantity of eight contrast colored fabric; 19.5 x 19.5 ins (50 x 50 cm) backing fabric; 15 ins (40 cm) of 1 yd (90 cm) wide fabric for frill; 1 in (2.5 cm) of 1.5 in (4 cm) wide lace; filling.

SIZE

18 ins (45 cm) in diameter, excluding the frill.

Square patches machine sewn to make a baby's cot cover. Courtesy Avalon Craft Cottage.

METHOD

Cut four frill pieces 4 ins (10 cm) wide by 1 yd (90 cm) long. Cut out patches according to instructions. Sew patches together in pairs, then sew the pairs together and then the two semi-circles together. Finish as for log cabin cushion from * to end.

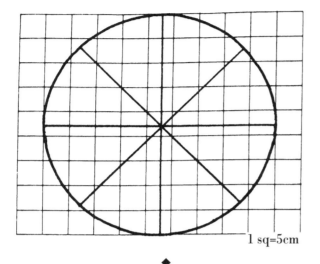

1 sq=5cm

◆

Patchwork star cushion

MATERIALS

Small quantity of four contrast colored fabrics; 19.5 x 19.5 ins (50 x 50 cm) backing fabric; 3.25 ft (3 m) of 2.5 in (6 cm) wide lace; stuffing.

SIZE

18 x 18 ins (45 x 45 cm).

METHOD

Cut out patches according to instructions. Sew triangle patch pieces together to make squares, join squares into rows, then rows together to complete the block. Sew border pieces around the edge. Cut a backing piece the same size as the patchwork piece. Gather up lace to fit the edge of patchwork and stitch over seamline of border, right sides together.

Place patchwork and backing piece together, right sides together and stitch around edge, leaving a small opening for turning. Turn through to the right side and press. Fill cushions with stuffing and slip stitch the opening closed.

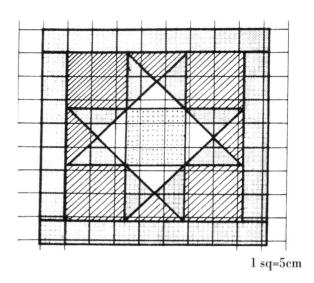

1 sq=5cm

HOW TO MAKE A PATCHWORK COVERLET

◆

How to cut patches

If you want the larger hexagonal patches, the outside edge of your template (see page 216) is the guide for drawing the paper pattern. Add an allowance for turnings when cutting the fabric. For smaller patches use the inside "window" shape. Cut your papers to this small inside size and your fabric to the outside edge size.

◆

To make

STEP 1:

Gather scraps of fabric together, select your color range, press the chosen scraps and work out your color scheme.

STEP 2:

Make the paper pattern, using any firm paper. Draw round the outside of your hexagonal template, holding the sharp pencil upright, so that you draw accurately against the edge. (If you slope your pencil you will get a fractional difference in the paper sizes. This makes it impossible to sew the patches up neatly. You can't cheat at patchwork, so take care with this part.)

Opposite: Miner's bedspread, early 1900s.

STEP 3:

Next, make the fabric shapes, placing the template on the wrong side of the fabric on a hard surface. Through the "window" you will see when the pattern is nicely centered and straight with the grain or selvage. Now draw round the template with a colored pencil indicate exactly where you should place the paper pattern on your fabric patch. Draw another pencil outline just under half an inch (1 cm) outside the first to give a turning line all round.

STEP 4:

Cut out the patch round the outer line. Start by cutting your middle patch and the first ring of six patterned patches round it, in your chosen colors.

STEP 5:

Now place a paper pattern on the wrong side of the fabric patch over the penciled lines. Hold the pattern flat and turn the surplus edges in a single hem over the paper, being careful to make six neat corners, then tack through paper and fabric, keeping the patch neat and taut (diagram 3, page 218).

STEP 6:

With firm stitches oversew (on the paper sides) one side of the middle patch to one side of a patterned or colored one. Add the next patterned or colored patch to the next side edge until all the sides of the middle patch have another patch joined to them (diagram 4, page 222).

STEP 7:

Join up the six radiating seams and you have your patchwork well begun and by now you will see the next step.

STEP 8:

Make a whole series of these motifs. Then, when you think you have enough, lay them out on the floor or a broad table and arrange them into a pleasing design.

STEP 9:

Start joining these large motifs together in the same way as you did the single patches.

STEP 10:

When you have completed your patchwork to the required size you will need single patches to finish the shape.

STEP 11:

Add a plain border of fabric as a final finish.

QUILTING

Patchwork is a technique that is often used when making quilts. Quilting is discussed in the next chapter, Embroidery, on pages 274-5.

Embroidery

HISTORY OF EMBROIDERY

Creative embroidery has been used as a decoration throughout the ages. Fragments of stitches have been found on early leather and cloth materials, and it has been depicted on primitive sculpture and paintings.

One of the earliest known pieces of embroidery was a twining stitchery incorporated with weaving. It was done with the fingers while the weaving was still on the loom. Much later, embroidery was widely used for religious purposes and during the 13th century, for instance, in England, beautiful church vestments were embroidered with a couching stitch which completely covered the garment.

Early needles were made of bone or ivory but with the development of the steel needle there flourished an era when garments and furnishings were very richly decorated. Mary, Queen of Scots created beautiful embroidery while she was held prisoner by her cousin Elizabeth. Much of her work, which included the embroidered hangings and covers for her four-poster bed, chair, and curtains, has been preserved to this day. She had previously studied embroidery in Europe and kept her own designers.

In the great homes beds were the first items to be decorated. The hangings around the four-poster beds were a necessity and not just for decoration, for in spite of the fires it was cold and draughty in those large rooms. Later on, tapestries and chairs were richly embroidered. A competent embroiderer was a permanent member of the household staff. Designs used at this time were variations on the Tree of Life, Jacobean, and Elizabethan scroll.

After 1750, when Robert Adam designed embroidery for his furniture, pure silk was used entirely. Previously, a fine 2-ply yarn was used. Later silk was combined with yarn and worked on a quilted background. When English ladies settled in America, they took their designs, needles, and materials with them. Their style of work soon changed, however, and they began to design from items they saw around them. Their hangings and chair covers, as well as their petticoats, dresses, and purses, and their husbands' waistcoats, were embroidered with grapes, chickens, sheep, flowers, and even pine trees. Many more stitches were introduced: buttonhole, Roumanian, herringbone; block shading, and French knots. They experimented with materials and designs and made their dyes from natural fibers. The designs were mainly light and joyous and embroidery became a folk art. This trend also occurred in Europe with each country building up its own tradition of stitches and design.

Many beautiful stitches were developed in China and Pakistan, where the embroidery work was very fine and close; whole pieces were worked in one stitch turning with the design and motive, and covering the whole garment. The Chinese worked in delicate silk threads and fabrics and to this day they have preserved the perfection of fine satin stitch, and the Pekinese and Chinese knot stitch.

In England, embroiderers began to work on fine Indian linen using chain, touches of stem, satin, and pulled stitch. In the 18th century, popular motifs were fruit and flowers worked in fine crewel yarns in colors of pale blue, leaf green, and dusty pink, using the stem and fishbone stitch, with long and short shading.

When printed cottons came to England, interest in embroidery declined as bright prints took the place of beautiful handworked pieces. Embroidery was only done by professionals and it was costly.

By the beginning of the twentieth century embroidery had almost vanished as a craft. Several attempts were made to revive interest in the craft for its own sake, but there was little response, apart from ecclesiastical work. However, some interest did spread to the Scandinavian countries, then to Germany and eventually back to England where much of the contemporary embroidery style showed a traditional Nordic influence.

Opposite: Thread in bright floral colors. Courtesy Coats Patons.

In later years stamped linens came into favor, although the cottons and designs were limited. In the last decade or so there has been a return to creative design and today many fine pieces are being worked and interest in embroidery is widespread.

◆

Canvas embroidery

Canvas embroidery, sometimes called needlework tapestry, is the art of stitching with the needle and thread upon canvas in such a way that the whole piece is covered.

When canvas embroidery first became popular, the designs were fine and delicate with a skilful blending of various stitches. Tent stitch was used to keep the fine line of the design, otherwise the nature of the canvas could produce a heavy and restricted design. But the prevalent use of square stitches, which were thought to be the most suitable for canvas work, caused designs to be executed in a rigid, rather angular manner. This greatly restricted the mode of expression in design.

This restricted style has completely changed and today canvas work is lively and creative although still using many of the conventional stitches.

Canvas work reached its peak in the late 16th to the 18th centuries. The works of this period show a clarity of line and interpretation of the design. This, however, was lost after tent stitch was rejected and too many square stitches were used. In the early twentieth century uninspired copies in silk and yarn, of floral and landscape paintings, became popular.

In our modern approach to canvas work the value of tent stitch in keeping a clear outline has been realized. Different stitches are also used for a textured effect as well as for shape. There is no need for canvas work to be a rigidly naturalistic interpretation of growing things. It is better to stylize designs and to think of them as shapes and tones. However, the designs must follow the laws of nature.

Canvas work is slow work, but it can be done a little at a time whenever the opportunity arises. There is virtually no limit to the articles which can be made with canvas work, and some of the most popular are hangings, pictures, small furnishings, handbags, chair seats, and coffee table tops.

When you are working with canvas, it is important that you note the texture that occurs with the change of stitch and to keep working in the same direction when you are stitching. Tent stitch, for instance, has quite a different texture when sewn vertically than when done horizontally. This can be used to advantage, however, for adding interest to backgrounds.

◆

Needleweaving embroidery

Needleweaving is a very old craft dating back to the time of the early Egyptians; many early pieces have been found in Egyptian tombs. It was done with a needle and was mostly used for costume decoration. Later it was used for wall hangings and religious purposes.

Coptic needleweaving was thought to be done with a shuttle. The cloth was woven with threads left loose to be embroidered later. The needleweaving was done on the top threads while the ones behind were left loose. This technique differed from the threading in special threads which was done with the great classical tapestries of Europe during the Middle Ages.

Contemporary needleweaving has developed from Finland, Denmark, Norway, and Turkey. Within these countries each style was distinct and rather formal. Gradually there was greater freedom in the work and much contemporary work is like a painting in scope and design.

Old embroidery that features the domestic values of a bygone era.

CURRENT TRENDS

Different styles of embroidery, depending on the materials available and on the local culture, have developed throughout the world. Since World War II there has been a great revival of interest in creative embroidery. Design is more important and has followed the general trend towards simplification and greater freedom. In some instances many crafts are combined in one piece of work. New materials and techniques have allowed a fresh approach to established technical methods. It is a time for creativity and experimentation which gives vitality and variety to the work being produced today.

◆

Materials and threads

Make sure you choose materials suitable for the use of the finished article as well as for the type of embroidery to be worked. However, many successful pieces of embroidery have been done with unconventional materials as a background and also as threads. So you can experiment, but only the finished work will tell how successful your experiment has been.

In your choice of materials so much depends on the type of work you are doing. For an everyday dress or a fun table cloth, for example, a good quality casement cloth, unbleached calico, or a sturdy cotton may be used. Linen, which is generally the most useful of the embroidery fabrics, should always be good quality.

A wide range of background material is available. Embroidery linen can be purchased in white and several light shades. This linen should be used for very fine or drawn thread work. Many dress materials, and several types of soft furnishings and curtain materials are suitable for embroidery and are available in wonderfully exciting colors. I suggest you watch the sales for remnants.

Embroidery canvas can be purchased at the embroidery counter of any big department store. It is natural or beige colored and is identified by the number of squares to the inch. Some canvas has a double strand while another has a single thread; a very fine, single thread white canvas is also available.

There is an endless range of silk, cotton, rayon, and yarn working threads in wonderful colors and varying weights and thicknesses. Knitting and embroidery cottons are called perle and have a lustre.

It is impossible to say how much thread is used in any one work. All threads and yarns are bought either in skeins or balls. Sometimes just a thread of one color or a thickness is used. If it is a large piece of needleweaving, for instance, at least half a ball could be used. It is a good idea to build up your collection of yarn by buying odd balls at the end-of-season yarn sales while a particular color or texture is fashionable. Buy balls of perle knitting cotton at the beginning of the knitting season so that you can build up a good selection of different colors and thicknesses.

For decorative purposes there are beads of all shapes and sizes, many varieties of sew-on crystals (jewels), and even shells, pebbles, and feathers have been used as part of a design.

There is no limit to your resources if you want to experiment. However, avoid using too many different textures in the one piece. The background texture is very important as well as the color. Many modern furnishings are lively and suitable as long as they harmonize with the threads you are using. If the material has an unstable weave, it can be backed with a strong cotton and vilene. Sometimes both have been used to give substance, for example, to a hanging.

◆

Equipment

The tools you need for embroidery are few and inexpensive. Have a special place to keep your equipment together, preferably in a workbox or a basket, but a small cupboard with a drawer to hold your designing things is good, too. Keep an assortment of small boxes for threads, beads, etc. Place your tools together in one place where they are easily accessible.

To keep your work clean and fresh, have a bag made from washable material which will hold your work when you are not busy on it. Embroidery should be spotless, so always wash your hands before you start work.

Simple and attractive canvas embroidery. Courtesy Coats Patons.

Ordinary sewing scissors are usually too large and clumsy for most embroidery work. A good pair of slender, sharp, pointed embroidery scissors (like surgical scissors) is essential.

A box of lace pins and a pincushion are necessary. Lace pins are very fine and will not mark fine silks, although they are inclined to bend if the material is too tough.

For design you will need tracing and plain white paper; colored tissue papers and some watercolor paints; squared or graph paper for working out canvas designs.

A watercolor brush, Nos. 0 or 1, for transferring the design by the "pricking and pouncing" method; pencils; thimble; tape measure with metal ends; tailor's chalk; a plastic square (a ruler with the

square at one end); and various needles—crewel needles are long with sharp points and large eyes to take the thicker thread easily, chenille needles also have sharp points but are shorter and thicker, tapestry needles have blunt points, and bead needles are long and thin with a long, thin eye to carry the thread.

◆
Design

There are several ways of obtaining a design for embroidery.

Commercial transfer designs and traced needlework designs already done on the fabric are available, you can draw your own design, or if you are very experienced, you can create a design from the embroidery stitches as you work.

TRANSFER DESIGNS

If you use transfer designs, pick out a pattern which is suited to the fabric and to the type of embroidery you intend doing. Then make sure that the transfer is correctly ironed onto your material so that you will have a clear outline for your work.

TRACED NEEDLEWORK DESIGNS

Although these designs are sometimes called stamped linens, they can be on a variety of fabrics. These traced designs on the fabric are available complete with illustration of the finished worked item, plus details of the design, how to do it, what stitches to use, what colors and threads to use, and any other relevant technical details for the particular item to be worked.

YOUR OWN DESIGN

A creative embroiderer can work out exciting designs for herself or himself. Design is just simply good arrangement and organization and provides the artistic groundwork or basic construction for your work. Embroidery aims to represent, not imitate. So try to keep your design as stylized as possible while following the laws of nature. There are two basic ways of designing: one is by lines and the other by mass.

When planning your design consider the size and proportions of your work. Cut out shapes in paper and move them around until you achieve the effect you like. Consider the materials you will be using and the type of embroidery you wish to do. If it is to be free needleweaving, you can suggest the pattern with tacking.

For interesting patterns look around you. In the

*Creative embroidery featuring original designs.
Courtesy Coats Patons.*

garden, for instance, look at the veining on leaves, the petals of flowers, the colors and patterns of rocks, and the bark of trees. Note the various shades of green that go with different colored flowers.

For formal designs for canvas or shaded work, use tissue paper to plan your design. Move it about as before, but overlap the edges so you get the tone. Tear the paper for blurred edges.

APPLYING THE DESIGN TO THE FABRIC

To transfer your design to the material to be embroidered you first trace your design onto thick tracing paper. Put the tracing (or drawing) on a thick, soft pad of material and prick the design outline or other guide lines with a large darning needle. The holes should be very close and even. Place the pricked design in position over the material and secure with pins.

Take a pad (which you have made previously from porous material) filled with either talcum powder (for use on dark material) or powdered charcoal (for light colors). Puff the pad along the holes. Carefully

remove the paper and the outlines will be clearly shown in lines of tiny dots. To "fix" these dots, go over them with a fine-pointed watercolor brush dipped in a contrasting watercolor—be careful not to use too much water or the powder will run.

If your design is a free one, however, you will only need some guide lines which can be just tacked into position.

If you wish to add embroidery to a fluffy sweater or dress, or a very fine silk that will mark or will not take the dots, try this method. Draw or trace the design on organdie or any other transparent material. Tack the design inside the item to be embroidered, with the right side placed against the wrong side of the item. As the design is on see-through material, it can still be clearly seen. Tack with small, neat stitches around all the lines. This will show the tacked design clearly on the right side of the garment. It can be embroidered on the right side of the garment and the tacking and the design on the transparent material cut carefully away from the inside (see diagram 1).

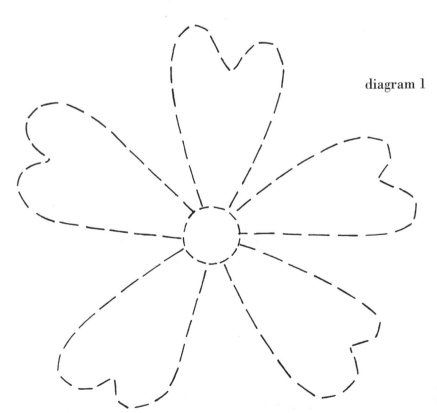

diagram 1

Opposite: Choosing thread colors is a pleasure with today's range. Courtesy Coats Patons.

BUILT-UP EMBROIDERY PATTERNS

This method of producing designs is to draw the motifs straight onto the material and build them up with the stitchery. This is best suited for very simple designs in which straight lines or circles are used. They are very suitable as dress trimmings or for decoration on small household goods, such as luncheon mats or napkins. You build up the patterns by adding one stitch to another until the desired effect is achieved.

◆

Color

Give careful consideration to color when you are planning your embroidery. Remember that the background is part of your color scheme, whether it is a tone of the colors to be used or a contrast. A small color wheel showing matching colors and their contrasts is most useful.

◆

Embroidery stitches

You must know your embroidery stitches thoroughly. Never try to work a stitch with which you are not familiar straight onto a piece of embroidery or even onto your sampler, or you could spoil the work. Always do some practicing first on another piece of scrap material. When you master a stitch, work it onto your sampler which you can then use as a reference notebook.

MAKING A SAMPLER (see diagram 2)

Early "samplers" were associated with little cross-stitch pictures grandma used to hang on the wall. The scene was usually a small house, sometimes with small figures in the garden, and flowers and trees in pots, all surrounded with a floral border. As well, there was a short verse or motto. This, however, was not a true sampler, and thus the name "examplar", meaning an example of the work. The early "samplers" were handed down from generation to generation and were greatly treasured. They were not planned pieces of work, but were used to teach a young girl her stitches and they were added to as she studied her craft, and so they became her needlework reference notebook, for they were really "samples" of different stitches.

This is a good idea to follow today, or at least with a few of the most used stitches. It gives you practice in working the different stitches really well.

Linen is the best material to use, for the weave is straight, which helps to keep the rows of stitching straight. A good size is about 9 x 12 ins (23 x 30 cm). It is important that the stitches be neat and even. Draw a thread to get the edges straight and then hem the linen to stop the edges from fraying.

Do not try to learn all the stitches at once. Practice two or three at first, then do some embroidery using these stitches. Practice another stitch, use this in your next work, and so go on gradually until you

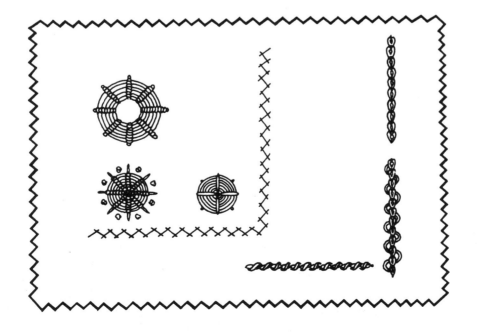

diagram 2

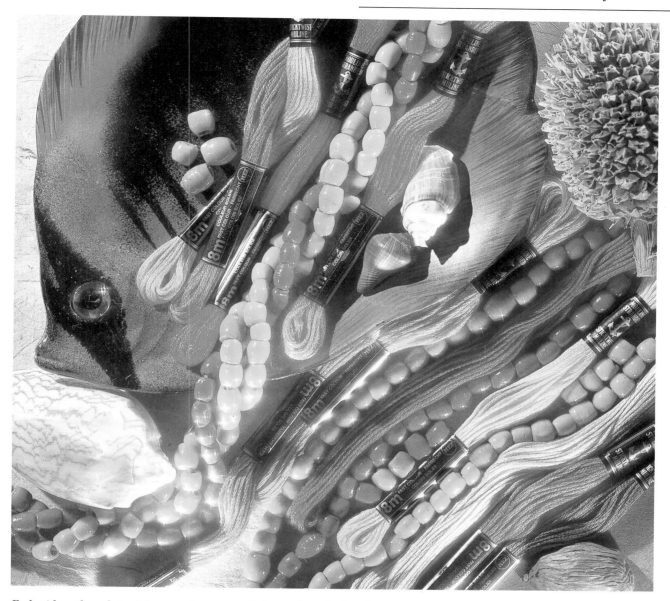

Embroidery threads in rich natural tones recall the sundrenched outdoors. Courtesy Coats Patons.

White on white: an age-old choice for table linen.

have thoroughly mastered a large number of stitches. When learning stitches, try them on your practice piece first and when you have mastered them add them to your sampler.

CHAIN STITCH (see diagram 3)
The basic chain stitch is one of the simplest ways of following a line. Bring the needle and thread out at the top or beginning of the line at A. Holding the thread down with the left thumb, insert needle again in the same hole A and come out at B. Loop the thread under the needle from left to right. Draw through. Insert the needle at B inside the loop, in the same hole, keeping the thread down to the left. Come up at C, loop the thread under the needle, and draw through. There are many variations of this stitch.

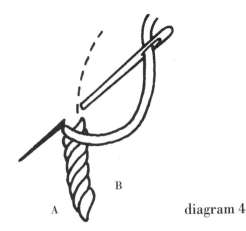

HERRINGBONE STITCH (see diagram 5)
As an embroidery stitch, herringbone may be worked as a decorative line or it can be used as a filling stitch. It is usually worked from left to right on two imaginary parallel lines. The thread is crossed between the stitches. Bring the needle and thread out on the lower line at A, take it to the upper line. Put the needle in at B in a short stitch coming out at C. Cross and bring it down to the lower line. Go in at D, coming up again at E.

diagram 3

STEM STITCH (see diagram 4)
The stem stitch consists of a long step forward on the front of the fabric and a short one at the back. The width of the line is governed by the slant of the needle as it picks up the material. If worked at an angle to the traced line the stem will be thicker. The thread must be kept to the same side of the needle while working.

Bring the needle up at A and down at B. The thread always emerges on the left side of the previous stitch. The stitches can be turned to follow the line. This stitch is used for flowers, stems, outlines, etc., and also as a filling, the rows of close stem stitch being worked around the shape until it is filled in.

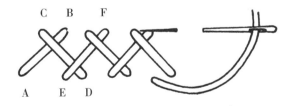

diagram 5

LAZY DAISY STITCH (see diagram 6)
This popular stitch is used for small flowers or leaves in designs embroidered in outline. It is also known as a detached chain, for it is really a form of chain stitch in which each link in the chain is detached from the others and secured with a small extra stitch.

Work it in the same way as the chain stitch (diagram 3), but fasten each loop at the bottom with a small stitch.

This beautifully intricate design in a piece of old embroidery would have taken careful planning.

diagram 6

FEATHER STITCH (see diagrams 7a and 7b)

This is an effective stitch which gives an open, rather lacy result. It is ideal for finishing hems or edges of embroidered work. As well, it is popular for simple decoration on children's clothes where it has been used for smocking. It is basically a buttonhole stitch, with the stitches below each other at an angle instead of alongside.

As this stitch must be evenly worked, lace pins are useful for marking an imaginary line to work along, and these pins can be withdrawn as you work. Stitch first to the left and then to the right (diagram 7a) at different levels, placing your needle at a slight angle towards the guide line, which it will touch at the bottom of the stitch. Remember to always keep the thread under the needle.

Diagram 7b shows double feather stitch in which

three stitches are taken to the right and three to the left, alternately.

WHEAT EAR STITCH
(see diagrams 8a, b, c, d, e, f)

This decorative stitch can be used for veining on large leaves, or for working ears of corn, and for borders on children's clothes. It is a combination of lazy daisy and fly stitch worked together to make a wheat ear formation.

This stitch is best worked between two imaginary parallel lines which have been tacked or pinned in. Make the ears of the stitch first with two stroke stitches. Bring the thread through in the middle of the lines and pick up a horizontal stitch from left to right, inserting the needle in the left-hand line and bringing it out immediately opposite on the right-hand line (diagram 8a). Pull the thread through and insert the needle again where the thread came out, bringing it out immediately below this point (diagram 8b). This last stitch should be the same size as the two stroke stitches. Next, slip the needle under the stroke stitches from right to left (diagram 8c).

Finish the wheat ear by picking up a diagonal stitch parallel with the first stroke stitch (diagram 8d). The first stroke stitch of the next wheat ear is made by

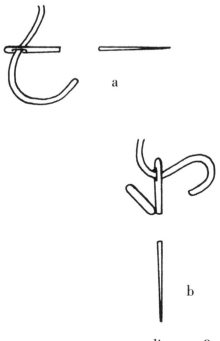

a

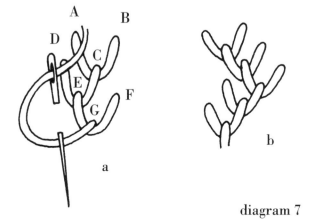

diagram 7

b

diagram 8a & b

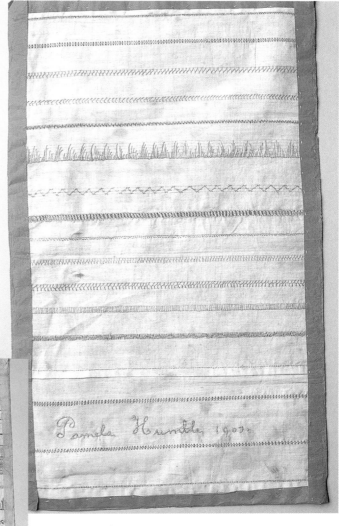

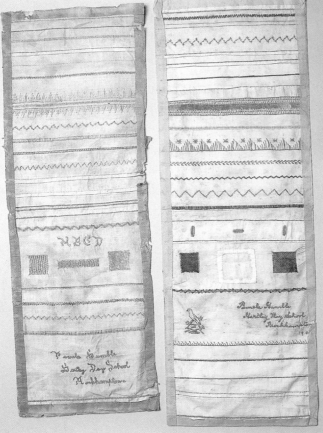

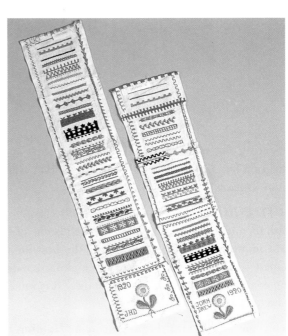

Three examples of traditional sampler work from the past.

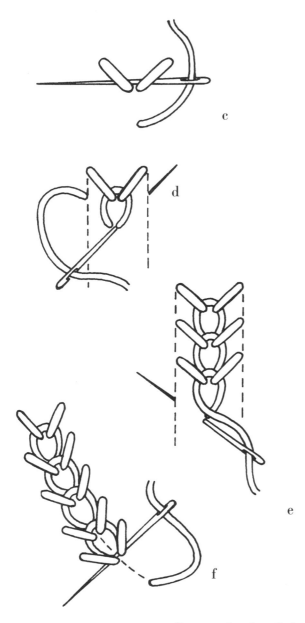

diagram 8c, d, e & f

diagram 9

inserting the needle at the base of the last loop (diagram 8e). Continue in this way for further wheat ears (diagram 8f).

BUTTONHOLE STITCH (see diagram 9)

With its numerous variations, this stitch is one of the most important in embroidery. It is the best-known looped stitch and can be used for making borders and edges as well as for outlining shapes. It is worked from left to right.

Bring the needle and thread out at A. Holding the thread with the thumb, insert the needle at B. Come out above A at C, drawing the needle out over the thread coming from A to form a loop.

SIMPLE BUTTONHOLE LACE STITCH
(see diagrams 10a, b, c)

This stitch can be worked from left to right, or right to left. Working from left to right, bring the needle through on the line of stitching and insert it vertically, a little to the right, picking up a small amount of fabric the width of the stitching. Pass the loop of thread under the point of the needle and pull the needle through (diagram 10a).

Many variations can be worked by changing the length of the stitches such as working one short and one long as in diagram 10b, or two long and three short as in diagram 10c.

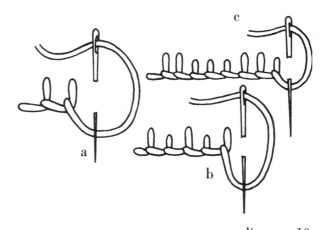

diagram 10

Stem stitch is used to create the stems in this old embroidery work.

CRETAN STITCH (see diagrams 11a, b, c, d)
A variation of buttonhole, Cretan stitch is taken from Eastern embroideries. It may be worked with the stitches close together to form a solid border or leaf filling, or openly as a thin braid-like border. In each case the stitch is worked between two invisible or imaginary parallel lines.

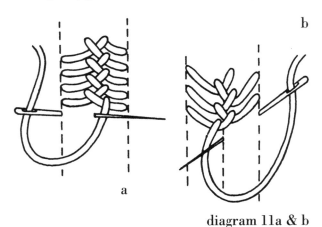

diagram 11a & b

Closed Cretan
Bring the thread through a little to the right of a central line and pick up a horizontal stitch, from left to right, bringing the needle out the same distance

from the central line, on the left, as the thread is on the right (diagram 11a). With the thread under the point, repeat this procedure to the right.

The stitch may be varied by spacing the stitches a little and by bringing the needle out on the middle line each time (diagram 11b). In this case the needle is inserted at an angle.

Open Cretan
This may be worked vertically as closed Cretan, or horizontally, as shown in diagram 11c. The method is the same and the needle comes out a little to each side of the middle line. The length of the stitches may be varied, as in diagram 11d, to be more decorative.

ROUMANIAN STITCH (see diagrams 12a, b, c)
This stitch is a quick filling, which takes less time than satin stitch; it is used for broad outlines and fillings, particularly flower or leaf shapes. The thread is worked across the shape to be filled and then tied down with a small slanting stitch. Work from top to bottom.

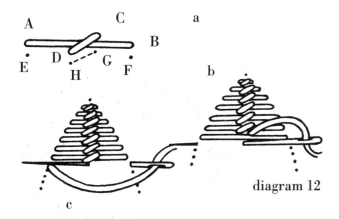

diagram 12

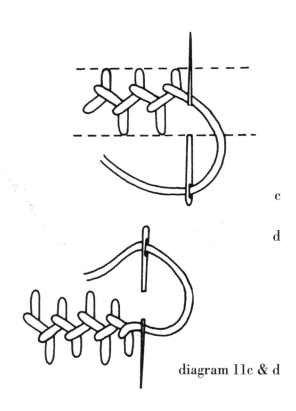

diagram 11c & d

Bring the needle and thread out on the left at A. Go in at B and come out at C, not quite halfway between A and B. Pull through. Take a small diagonal stitch over the laid thread to D, holding it in place. Come out at E and go to F coming out at G, and so on. This stitch is usually worked with the threads close together. The size of the middle crossing stitch can be varied, either to make a longer oblique stitch or a small straight stitch.

SATIN STITCH (see diagrams 13a, b, c)
This is a most useful embroidery stitch, and the most important of all filling stitches. It is used for filling when an all-over effect is desired, such as in flower

The principal stitch used in these two works is satin stitch. Courtesy Coats Patons.

embroidery. Satin stitch is a series of stroke stitches worked closely together and side by side; they can be straight or slanted. If the stitches are too long they tend to pull and do not wear well. In this case it is better to use Roumanian stitch which is anchored in the middle. For a flat appearance, work onto the fabric. For a raised appearance, a running stitch may be worked over the area first.

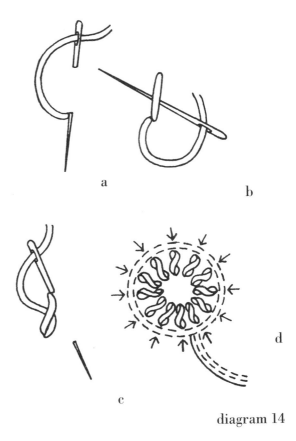

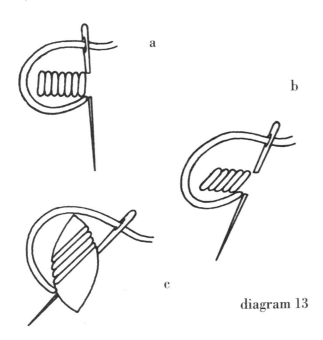

diagram 13

diagram 14

for the beginning of the next stitch (diagram 14c). Keep the twist loose enough by holding with the thumb when bringing the thread up at C.

LONG AND SHORT SHADING STITCHES
(see diagrams 15a, b, c, d)
This variation of satin stitch is used to obtain shaded effects either by the direction of working the stitch or by the use of graduated colors of thread (diagram 15a). It was exquisitely worked in Chinese and Japanese silk embroideries. It is useful for filling large leaves, where satin stitch cannot be used.

The first row of stitches is one long and one short stitch, worked as satin stitch is worked, so there is a smooth outer edge and a broken inner one (diagram

Bring the needle and thread through to the right side on one edge of the outline to be filled, and put it in again exactly opposite on the other edge of the outline, making a straight line of thread across the space. Bring the needle up again as near to the start of the first stitch as you can, put it in again beside the end of the first stitch. Continue in this way until the space is filled.

TWISTED SATIN STITCH
(see diagrams 14a, b, c, d)
This particular type of satin stitch is most attractive if worked in a circle, perhaps as a circular border for other stitches.

Bring the needle and thread out at A and in at B (diagram 14a). Go back to A and pull the thread through. Slide the needle and thread under A to B without picking up the material and pull gently through (diagram 14b). Insert the needle at B (not in the same hole, but a little above) and come out at C

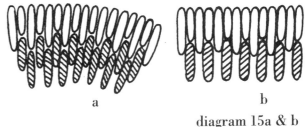

diagram 15a & b

This lovely work is partly created with short and long shading stitches. Courtesy Coats Patons.

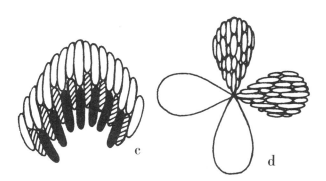

diagram 15c & d

worked at right angles to each other. It is useful for working leaves and if the stitches are of equal length it can also be used as a border.

This stitch can be worked between two parallel lines or within an outline with the stitches close together or wider apart.

15b). The following rows have stitches of equal lengths to fit into the broken line so that the long and short effect is maintained.

The last row of stitches completes the outline and is the same as the first, but in reverse. If the motif is shaped then the stitches must fit the shape as in diagrams 15c and 15d.

FISHBONE STITCH (diagram 16)
Similar to flat or satin stitch, but the stitches are

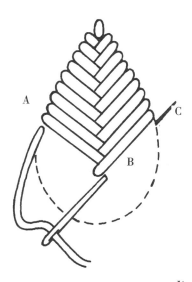

diagram 16

To work close fishbone stitch, start at the top and work towards the base. Use a single middle guideline and work each stitch alternately just to the side of the line. Bring the thread out on the left-hand line. Move down diagonally to the middle and insert the needle to the right of the middle line, picking up a diagonal stitch to the right-hand line. Repeat this procedure to the left.

CORAL KNOT (see diagrams 17a, b)

This simple line stitch looks like a beaded thread. It is useful for distinctive outlines, and particularly for petal or leaf shapes. It is worked from right to left on an imaginary line, which can be straight or curved, or downwards.

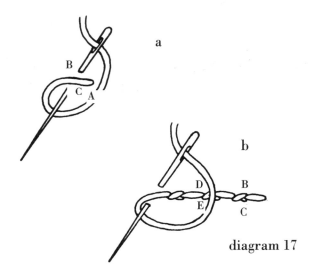

diagram 17

Bring the needle and thread from the back of the work along the line at A and hold the thread with the left thumb along the line. Take a stitch under the thread and through the material B–C and pull taut to form a knot (diagram 17a). Repeat the procedure along the line (diagram 17b).

FRENCH KNOT (see diagrams 18a, b, c, d)

This popular stitch has many uses. French knots, varying in number according to the size of the flower, make good centers for blossoms. Sometimes whole decorative outlines are worked in rows of French knots, which gives a beaded effect. Simple trimmings can be made with this stitch used in fillings of shapes, or scattered over the surface of the design.

Bring the needle and thread out at A. Hold the thread taut with left thumb, about 1 in (2.54 cm)

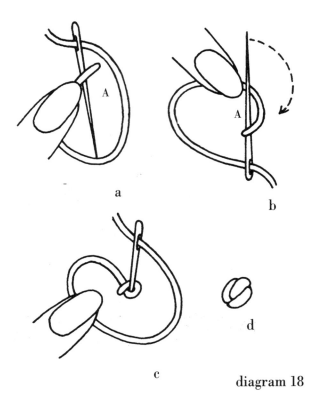

diagram 18

from A, slip the point of the needle under the thread (diagram 18a). Hold the thread firmly and rotate the point of the needle three or four times around it clockwise (diagram 18b). The needle should be pointing upwards with the twisted thread wound around it. Hold the twisted thread firmly on the needle. Snug the twists neatly, but not too tightly. Insert the point of the needle through to the back of the material and keep the left-hand finger on the twists as the thread is pulled through (diagram 18c). It takes a little practice to get a really firm knot (diagram 18d).

CHINESE KNOT (see diagrams 19a, b, c)

This very old stitch was used in ancient Chinese embroideries. It is rather like the French knot, but it has a little tail. The Chinese knot, when worked as a filling, with each stitch facing exactly the same direction, is very effective.

Bring the needle and thread out at A. Hold the thread down to the left with the thumb and circle it upwards, then pass the needle behind the thread without picking up the material (diagram 19a). Take a small stitch inside the loop from B to C. The thread is behind the upper part of the needle, but in front of the lower. Snug the thread and pull through

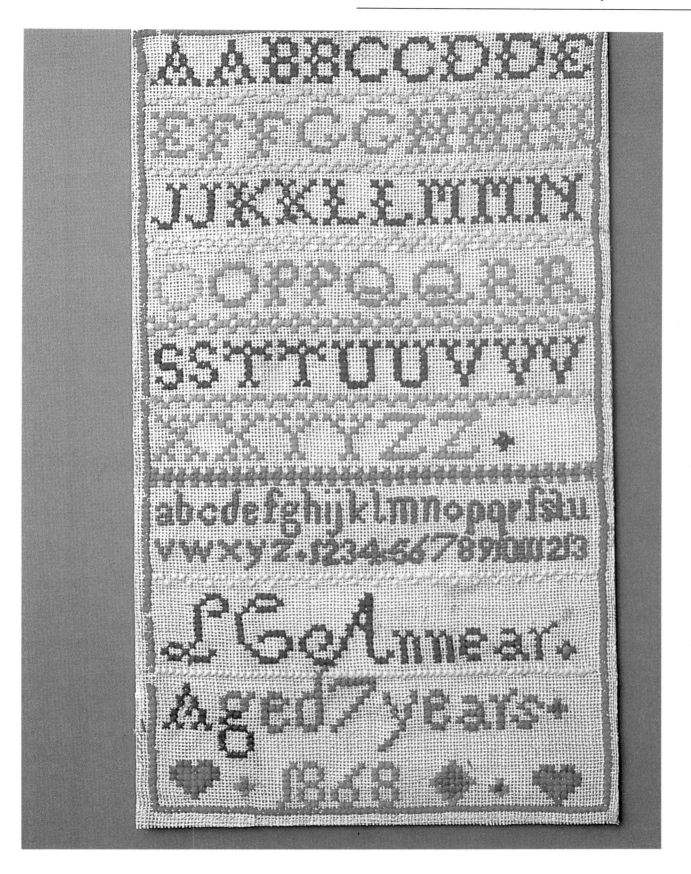

An example of traditional sampler work from the past.

(diagrams 19b and 19c). Start again at A, holding the thread down and circling it upwards, and so on. Make each stitch close together so that the knots lie side by side. If using these knots as a filling the knots can be staggered most effectively.

The stitches form rows of short lines on the back of the work.

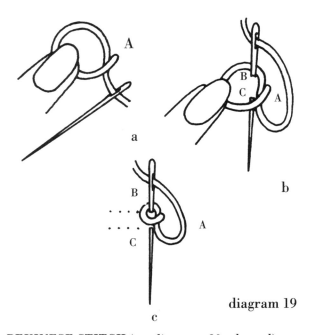

diagram 19

PEKINESE STITCH (see diagrams 20a, b, c, d)
This stitch is also a Chinese one and can be used as a filling or an outline. It can be worked in single or double lines. The lines can be back-to-back and laced together most effectively to form a border, or they can be straight or curved and are most useful for creative work. It is an interlaced stitch worked on spaced backstitches or even running stitches, with a distinctive texture. It is worked from left to right in two rows. The underneath row is the running or backstitch and the interlacing is worked on the first row. The interlacing is also worked from the left.

Bring the needle and thread out at A and thread through a second stitch between B and C. The stitch does not go through the material, so the stitches are held while the thread is being laced. The needle is held vertically (diagram 20a). The next stitch comes from between B and C on the top side of the row and is looped round and brought down through A and B (diagram 20b). The needle goes up from between A,

across B, and up between C and D (diagram 20c). It goes down again between B and C in the same stitch as the previous one, and so on (diagram 20d).

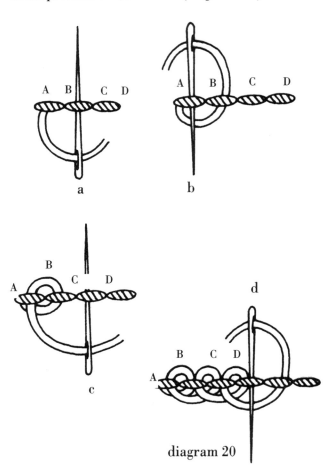

diagram 20

COUCHING (see diagram 21)
Couching stitch is a method of attaching gold bullion or lurex threads that do not go through the material. The thread is laid along the line of design on the surface of the background and is then held down with bar stitches worked across the thread at even intervals with a fine thread in either small straight or slanted stitches. These stitches can match the laid thread or they can be a contrasting color or texture. Couching can be used as a bold outline or as a close

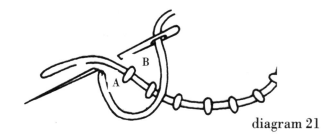

diagram 21

Simple canvas work. Courtesy Coats Patons.

filling. When used as a filling the threads can turn and follow the design.

ALGERIAN EYE STITCH
(see diagrams 22a and 22b)

This is an Italian stitch which, when worked side-by-side in several rows with several colors, makes an exciting border. It also looks wonderful if the crosses overlap slightly.

To form the star (diagram 22a), start in the middle, bringing needle out at A. Insert needle at B, come out at C, and go over back to A. Go under and out at D, over and back in at A, under and out at E, and back in at A. Come out at the middle of the new star, either to the right or below the first star. Continue in the same way, with the arms meeting (diagram 22b).

CLOUD FILLING (see diagram 23)
The small stitches of the first row run up and down and are not like the usual small running stitches. The

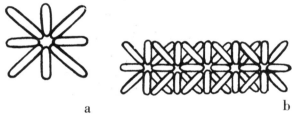

a   b

diagram 22

needle comes out at the bottom of the stitch (A) and goes back in above at B. The needle comes out again (C) and in again at D to the end of the line, where the stitches are worked checkerboard fashion. With a contrasting color and a tapestry needle, thread through these stitches from right to left. Repeat each row with the threading stitches linking together through the small straight stitches.

CHEVRON STITCH (see diagrams 24a and 24b)
This stitch is used for line borders and fillings. It is worked from left to right between two parallel lines much in the manner of herringbone. To avoid making the stitches too large, place your lines 1/4 in (0.6 cm) apart or even less.

Bring thread out on lower line on left side, insert needle slightly to the right on the same line and take a small stitch on the left, coming out halfway between the stitch being made (diagram 24a). Insert needle on

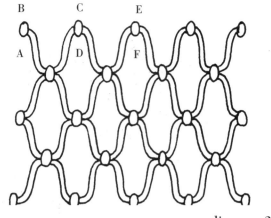

diagram 23

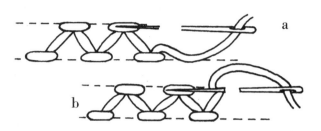

diagram 24

the upper line slightly to the right and take a small stitch to the left (A). Insert the needle again on the same line slightly to the right and take a small stitch to the left, coming out at the middle (B) (diagram 24b). Keep working in this way, alternately, on upper and lower lines.

BACKSTITCH (see diagram 25)
An elementary stitch used in embroidery and in plain sewing. It is popular for outlines which require a definite, although not smooth, look and for indented outlines, as it goes round curves. It is a favorite stitch for quilting.

Hold the work so that the outline to be backstitched is across the fingers. Bring the needle and thread out at A and take a small backstitch to B, coming out at C. Go in at A, the previous hole; A–B should equal C–A. Continue in this way, alternating a short backstitch on the surface with a double length one underneath. All the backstitches should join neatly, and be worked so that they do not pucker the material.

RUNNING STITCH (see diagram 26)
This stitch is the simplest and quickest of all to do and is the basis for many variations. It is used as an

The outer edge of this traditional linen embroidery shows the use of cloud filling.

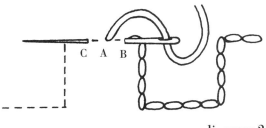

diagram 25

outline or as a filling to make texture. Work from right to left. Start with a knot on the wrong side. The stitches must be of equal length, with equal spaces between them. Start from the right side and make a row of stitches. Bring the needle and thread out at A, in at B, out at C, in at D, and so on.

SPIDER WEB STITCH

(see diagrams 27a, b, c, d, e, f)
Both types of the spider web stitch can be effective

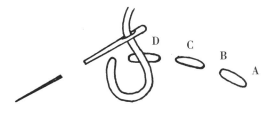

diagram 26

for centers or fillings, and for original borders on table linen or on clothing. As well, this stitch can be worked closely, in different sizes in combination with other stitches.

Spider web stitch worked on table linen should be in fine perle cotton and have 16 spokes instead of eight. However, the number of spokes is governed by the size and thickness of thread used.

There are two ways of working the stitch, both are done with a tapestry needle. One is woven, the other is whipped. The woven stitch must be worked on an uneven number of straight stitches while the whipping is done on an even number.

For the woven stitch on an odd number, a "Y" shape is made. Bring the needle up at A and down at B, leaving the thread slack enough to be caught by the

needle coming up at C. It goes down again at D (diagram 27a). If five stitches are required, bring the needle up at E, down at F, and out near the middle again (diagram 27b). The stitches are woven around the middle, under and over the straight stitches (diagram 27c).

The whipped spider web is started with four stitches crossing the middle of an imaginary circle. Start at

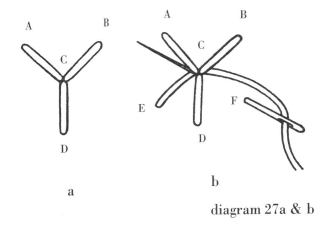

diagram 27a & b

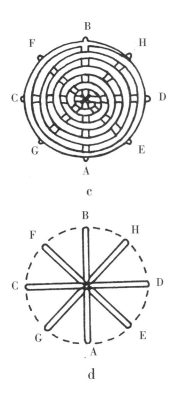

diagram 27c & d

A, go down to B, up at C, and down at D, up at E, down at F, up at G, down at H. This makes eight spokes on which to whip (diagram 27d). Keep the stitches slightly relaxed and bring the needle up in the middle. This stitch must be loose enough to allow the middle to be raised a little when you are working. If the needle is brought up between A and E, go back over and under E and A, repeat with G and A (diagram 27e). Continue working in this manner, going back over one stitch and under two, until the circle is filled (diagram 27f).

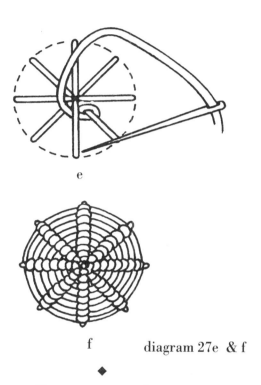

e

f

diagram 27e & f

◆

Canvas stitches

CROSS STITCH (see diagrams 28a, b, c, d)
One of the best-known canvas stitches. Cross-stitch embroidery has been used for centuries by rural people in Europe for decorating clothing, furnishings, and church vestments. Today it is used mainly for decorating household linens, and children's clothes.

When working cross stitch in rows it is quicker and nearer to work it from left to right, making one stroke parallel to the next, to the end of the row (diagram 28a). Then come back along the same row to make the crosses (diagram 28b). Make sure the crossing of the stitches is the same throughout the work.

An alternative way is to work each cross so that each cross stitch is completed before you go into the next

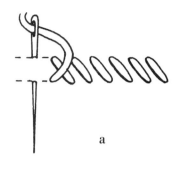

a

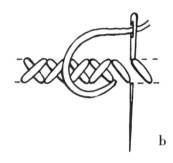

b

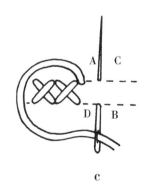

c

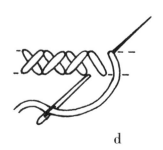

d

diagram 28

(diagram 28c). Bring the thread through at the top left of the stitch (A) and insert it again diagonally at the opposite corner (B). Make a vertical stitch to the right top (C), and complete the cross by inserting the needle at the bottom left (D), taking it diagonally across (diagram 28d).

CROSS STITCH WITH SATIN STITCH FILLING
(see diagram 29)

The combination of these stitches makes an unusual filling. Work the crosses detached leaving a space between each stitch the width of the cross stitch. Work the second row with the crosses underneath the spaces left in the first row. When the area is complete, add three short horizontal satin stitches to each space between the cross stitches.

DARNING (NEEDLEWEAVING) (see diagram 30)
A most useful and yet decorative method of work

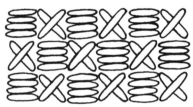

diagram 29

which can make many interesting patterns to cover backgrounds and large areas. There are two types of darning: running stitches are taken across the material, often with no regularity; pattern darning, where the threads of the material are taken up in a regular design.

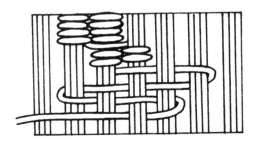

diagram 30

FLY STITCH (see diagrams 31a and 31b)

This stitch, sometimes also called tied or Y-stitch, has many uses as a simple hem or edge finish, or to build up borders in combination with other stitches.

It is wise to tack in guide lines, for its beauty lies in its evenness.

Bring the needle out at top left, hold thread down with left thumb, insert to the right on the same level a short distance from where it came out and make a small stitch downwards to the middle. With the thread below the needle, pull through and insert the needle again below at the middle (A) and come out ready for starting the next stitch. Fly stitch can be worked singly in horizontal rows, as in diagram 31a,

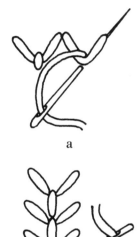

a

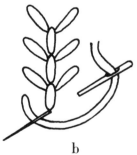

b

diagram 31

or vertically, as in diagram 31b.

TENT STITCH (see diagrams 32a and 32b)
An important stitch for canvas work, it is also sometimes called petit point or tapestry stitch. It is used for fine work on single mesh canvas and was worked for the background of the canvas purse.

Make sure every row is worked in the one direction from the same side so that the texture will not alter.

The diagonal method of working is stronger and does not pull the canvas out of shape.

The horizontal method shown here is more suited for small shapes. On the wrong side you will have long diagonal stitches (diagram 32a). Work from right to left and make a small sloping stitch over the crossing of two threads and pick up two threads diagonally (diagram 32b).

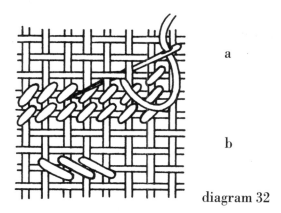

a

b

diagram 32

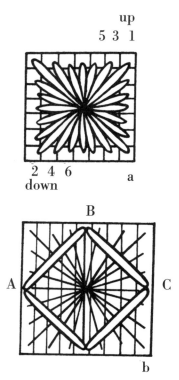

a

b

diagram 33

RHODES STITCH (see diagrams 33a and 33b)

This interesting and unusual stitch is usually worked on canvas, but it would also be attractive with heavy embroidery.

It is a square stitch with seven stitches crossing each other to make a square (diagram 33a). The stitches are longer where they form the corners. When the square is completed it is caught with four diagonal stitches to hold it (diagram 33b).

◆

Sampler

Measurements for embroidered section: 11 x 10 ins (27 x 26 cm)

Stitches used: Cross stitch in 2 ply, to a gauge of 18 st per inch (7 st per cm).

MATERIALS

20 ins (50 cm) of 51 in (130 cm) wide white Feinada cloth, 14 count, Art. 3706, Embroidery frame, size 24 round-end needle, 1 piece stiff cardboard 11 x 10 ins (27 cm x 26 cm), a frame, DMC Mouline Special embroidery cotton Art. 117 in the following colors and quantities:

3705	pink	2 skeins
3706	pink	2 skeins
3348	pale green	1 skein
3363	dark green	1 skein
792	blue	1 skein

METHOD

Cut out a 20 x 20 in (50 x 50 cm) square of cloth. Embroider motif following chart. When starting work, do not knot the thread. Leave 1 in (2.5 cm) "tail" and run under the first embroidered stitches.

To make up: Frame finished sampler.

For cross stitch instructions, see page 253.

Key to diagram

3705	✗
3706	•
3348	*m*
3363	╱
792	*ℓ*

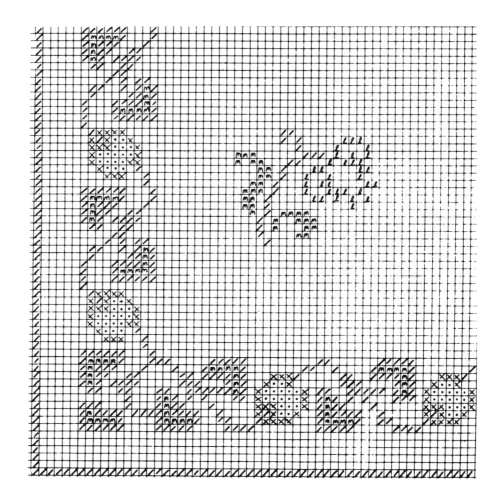

A traditional cross stitch sampler to make. Instructions opposite.

◆
Baby layette

MATERIALS

Anchor stranded cotton: 2 skeins gorse yellow 0300; 1 skein each geranium 06, kingfisher 0158, and forest green 0213. (Use two strands for French knot and three strands for the rest of the embroidery.) Baby garments similar to those in the picture, fine weight vilene or other bonded fiber interlining, Milward international range crewel needles No. 8 for 2 strands, and No. 7 for 3 strands.

METHOD

The full size drawing gives the complete motif and shows the position of the initials. Trace motif and initials (if desired) onto vilene using this drawing. Trace one motif for each article to be embroidered. DO NOT CUT OUT SHAPE. Place in desired position on right side of garment. Work embroidery through vilene and fabric following the diagram and key to diagram. For details of stitches see pages 234–55.

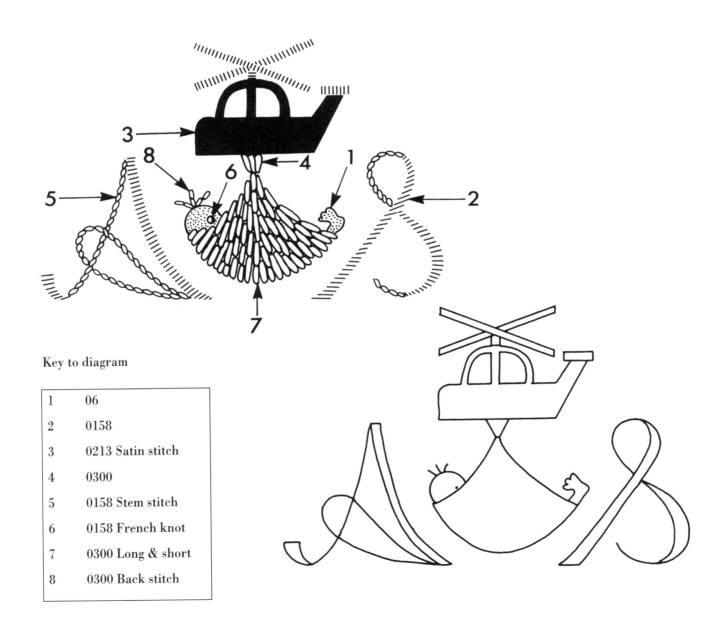

Key to diagram

1	06
2	0158
3	0213 Satin stitch
4	0300
5	0158 Stem stitch
6	0158 French knot
7	0300 Long & short
8	0300 Back stitch

A baby's layette with charming embroidered motif. Instructions on opposite page. Photograph courtesy Coats Patons.

◆
Embroidered tray cloth

A simple but delightful design that can be worked in less than 5 hours.

This design is specified for cross stitch embroidery over 8 threads.

MATERIALS

1 tray cloth or plain white tea towel, 1 embroidery hoop, Mouline special embroidery thread DMC Art 117, 1 skein of each of the following colors: 817, very dark coral red; 801, dark coffee brown; 910, dark emerald green; 3078, very light golden yellow; 61, variegated gold.

METHOD

Place the fabric in the embroidery hoop. Refer to the chart for placement of the colors and design, and begin working the pattern in cross stitch from the middle, towards the outside of the hoop. Stitches can be worked individually or in rows.

For further details on cross stitch techniques, see page 253.

Key to diagram

817	v. dark coral red	●
801	dark coffee brown	O
910	dark emerald green	X
3078	v. light golden yellow	✷
61	variegated gold	Y

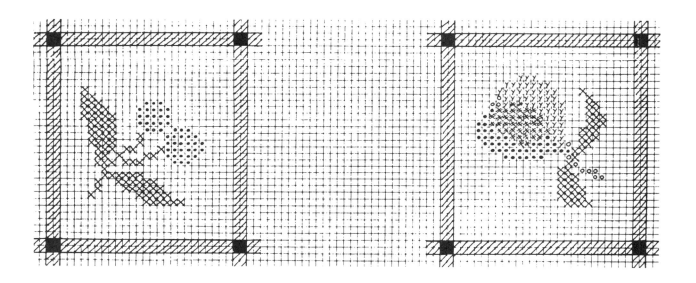

An embroidered traycloth. Instructions opposite.

◆
White cloth with cross stitch squares

Stitches used: Cross stitch and backstitch using three threads.

MATERIALS
4.6 ft (1.4 m) of DMC Aida cloth, 14 count, Mouline Special cotton DMC Art. 3706, white, and also the following colors and quantities: 796, medium Delft blue (4 skeins); and 798, dark Delft blue (3 skeins).

METHOD
Begin by embroidering Motif 2 (see chart) in the middle of the cloth. Then embroider 8 motifs in a diamond pattern around the central motif.

After completing the embroidery, iron your work carefully using a pressing cloth. Sew a ½ in (1.5 cm) seam, using small stitches.

1   2

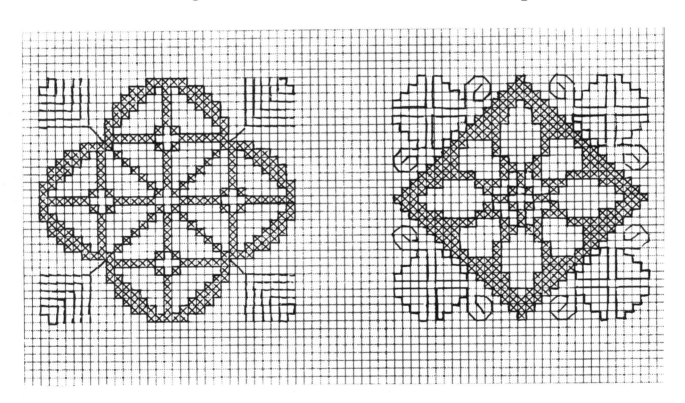

Key to diagram

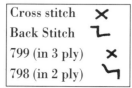

Cross stitch	✕
Back Stitch	⌐
799 (in 3 ply)	✕
798 (in 2 ply)	⌐

These cross stitch motifs add a special touch to a plain tablecloth. Instructions opposite.

◆

Cross stitch tablecloth

MATERIALS

Anchor stranded cotton

2 skeins each: Parma violet (0108 and 0109), cinnamon (0369 and 0371), olive green (0844), and apricot (4146).

1 skein each white (01), gorse yellow (0300), tangerine (0313), terra cotta (0336 and 0337), olive green (0843), mist green (0859 and 0861), and antique gold (0891).

Use 3 strands throughout. 4½ ft (1.3 m) square natural evenweave embroidery fabric 29 threads to 1 in (2.5 cm). Coats bias binding to match 0369 (sufficient to fit circumference of tablecloth). Milward international range tapestry needle No. 24.

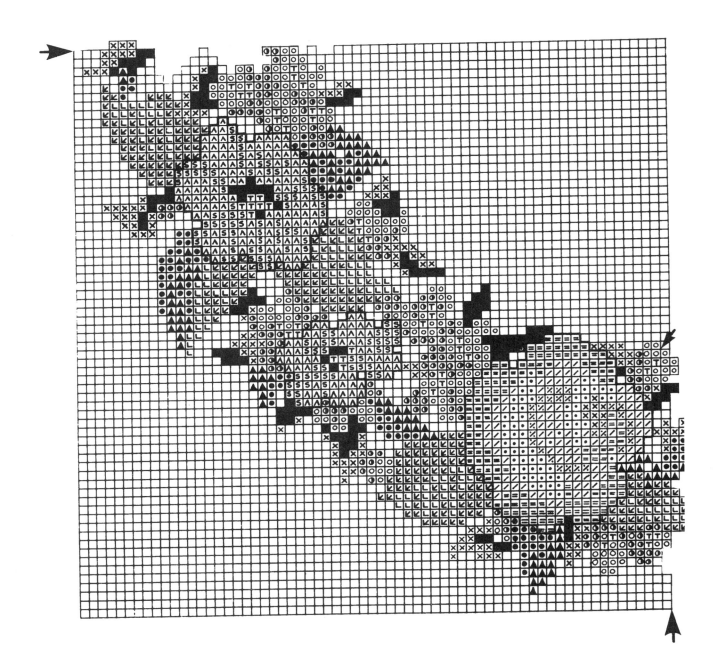

METHOD

Mark the middle of fabric lengthwise and widthwise with a line of basting stitches. The diagram gives one-quarter of the complete design center indicated by large black arrows which should coincide with the basting stitches. The design is worked in cross stitch over 3 threads of fabric and it is important that the upper half of all crosses should lie in the same direction throughout. Commence the design at small black arrow 108 threads down and 3 threads to the left of crossed basting stitches and work the given quarter following the diagram and key to diagram. To complete, turn fabric one-quarter to the right and work each of the remaining three-quarters in the same way. Press embroidery on the wrong side.

TO MAKE UP

Mark a circle 26 ins (65 cm) in diameter on the wrong side of fabric and cut round outline. Bind raw edge.

Key to diagram	
01	- ⊡
0108	- ◙
0109	- ◑
0300	- ⊼
0313	- ⊤
0336	- ⊿
0337	- ▨
0369	- ☒
0371	- ■
0843	- �
0844	- ◿
0859	- ◪
0861	- ◙
0891	- Ⓢ
4146	- ▣

◆

Appliqué

Appliqué is a method of applying one piece of material onto another to form a pattern. This work gives great scope for the imagination as there is an immense range of beautiful materials which can be arranged in a variety of ways to produce interesting designs.

There are many kinds of appliqué, but no strict rules must be followed for this work as the styles can be interchanged most effectively. For the embroiderer this is a great area for experiment.

Design for all appliqué should be simple with each piece of material making a good shape in itself as well as in relation to the other parts of the pattern.

Once you have worked out a design, you trace the design onto tracing paper, then transfer the various sections of the design to the appropriate material chosen for the applied pieces. Mark the straight grain of the material on the paper, so that when the applied pieces are tacked onto the background the grains of each will match. Cut out each piece, leaving 1/4 in (0.6 cm) turnings where necessary. Take care that you are accurate with the shape in each piece of material cut out, or your design will lose its original quality. Once you have cut out the pieces, trace the design onto the background material, and lightly mark in the main outlines. Place the pieces in position, pin them to the background and finish the work with embroidery stitches.

MACHINE EMBROIDERY

◆

The sewing machine

Most sewing machines can be used for some type of machine embroidery, from the simple straight stitch machine to the modern fully automatic models with embroidery cams. The straight stitch machine is very limited; if you want to try all types of embroidery a "swing needle" is essential. This means that the needle moves not only up and down to make a stitch, but also from side to side. This movement makes the zig-zag or satin stitch, opening up a completely new type of embroidery. On the more practical side, too, the zig-zag stitch is an essential part of modern dressmaking. On knitted and stretchy fabrics, the zig-zag stitch will stretch with the fabric instead of breaking and on linen and rayon, which fray a lot, a zig-zag over the edge will fix the threads in position. There are many other advantages on the modern automatic sewing machines, such as buttonholing and invisible hemming, but here we are concerned with the capabilities for embroidery of such machines.

There are one or two important points to check if you are purchasing a machine which you are going to use for machine embroidery as well as everyday sewing.

Most important is the tension on the machine. On some machines, it is necessary alter the tension for freehand work or darning. Try to avoid such a machine, because when you wish to revert to normal sewing, readjusting the tensions can be difficult. On my own machine, a Bernina, it is possible to sew on all thicknesses of fabric, from heavy tweed and leather to the finest sheers, with no change of tension and the machine is ready at any time for freehand embroidery.

In preparing the machine for freehand sewing, you need to lower the feed teeth and remove the sewing foot; another point to check is the ease of lowering the feed. On some machines, it is necessary to use a cover plate over the feed. You can still use this type of machine for freehand work, but may encounter some difficulty when using very fine fabrics. Check that a zig-zag cover plate is provided with the machine, as you may have to purchase one as an extra. Ease of removing the foot also adds to the versatility of the machine. If you are not sure of these points on a particular model, look at the instruction book under "Darning", as the settings for darning are similar to those for freehand embroidery. Lastly, make sure that the lever for changing the width of the zig-zag stitch is easily moved with one hand as you are stitching.

◆

Equipment

EMBROIDERY FRAMES

These frames or hoops are easily obtainable from the needlework department of most large stores. Sizes range from 3 to 11 ins (7.5 to 28 cm) in diameter. For practicing you will find the 5 in (12.7 cm) or 7 ins (18 cm) frames the most convenient. Binding the inner ring with bias tape helps to prevent marking on shiny fabrics and makes it easier to keep the fabric taut.

SCISSORS

A large pair for cutting materials and a small pointed pair for cutting threads and trimming around applied fabrics.

THREADS

Machine embroidery cottons are finer than ordinary sewing cottons, more economical and give a better finish to your work. The cotton comes in various thicknesses, but only two are readily available; these are No. 30 (the thicker of the two) and No. 50. If embroidery cotton is not available then No. 50 sewing cotton is the next best thing. The usual cotton used by the home dressmaker is a 40 thread which is too heavy for any zig-zag sewing.

The following gives some idea of cotton thickness and the correct needle to use. This is most important in all sewing if you want the best possible results.

40 sewing cotton	90 needle (16)
50 sewing cotton	80 or 90 needle
30 embroidery cotton	80 or 70 needle
50 embroidery cotton	70 needle (11)

Frames for machine embroidery. © Courtesy Brother Industries.

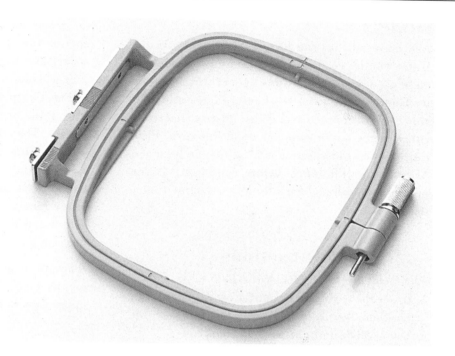

FABRICS

Any material that can be stretched tightly in the frame can be used as a background for machine embroidery; this includes everything between medium-weight yarn to sheer fabrics and net. However, when practicing, do use an easy material— either evenly woven cotton or a soft fine yarn. Plain calico or old soft sheeting is ideal for the beginner. Always press the fabric before you begin. As you progress you will find a use for all sorts of interesting scraps.

◆

Instructions

PREPARATION OF THE MACHINE

1. Lower the feed teeth or put the zig-zag cover plate in position. Details of how to do this for your own machine will be in the instruction book.

2. Remove the sewing foot. If the foot is held in place by a large screw remove this completely as it obstructs the view of your work.

3. Thread the machine top and bottom with a matching cotton. This is most important as different thicknesses of thread can affect the tension of the stitch.

There are a number of important points to remember concerning cottons and threading. A sharp needle is essential and you must match the size of the needle to the thickness of thread you intend using. Many of the difficulties associated with the tension on sewing machines are caused by the use of inferior threads and incorrect needles. Use the thread and needle guide given earlier in selecting your needle and make sure you are using the system of needle recommended for your own machine. Have a number of spare bobbins on hand so that you never need to wind one thread on top of another. Few things are more annoying than the belief that you have begun to sew with a full bobbin only to run out of thread halfway through your work.

4. If your machine is a free arm model, always use the extension table when doing free-hand embroidery.

Almost any fabric may be used successfully for machine embroidery providing it is stretched tightly in an embroidery frame. This is most important as

the frame takes the place of the feed and foot in moving the material and making a stitch. If the material is not taut all over the surface of the frame, your machine may fail to pick up the bobbin thread and miss a stitch. Having pressed the fabric well, lay it over the outer ring of the frame on a firm flat surface. The fabric should be held tightly all around when the inner ring is pressed into position. The screw on the outer ring should be adjusted so that the fabric is taut and the threads straight when the inner ring is in position. Tightening the screw afterward does not have the same effect. (See diagram 1.)

Place the embroidery frame so that the fabric is flat on the bed of the machine with the inner ring uppermost. Bring the bobbin thread to the surface of

Diagram 1: Embroidery frame used to keep the fabric taut. The inner ring is slightly lower to keep the fabric pressed against the machine.

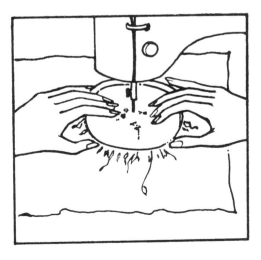

Diagram 2: The correct position of the hands on the embroidery frame.

Examples of fine work embroidered with a sewing machine.
© Courtesy Brother Industries.

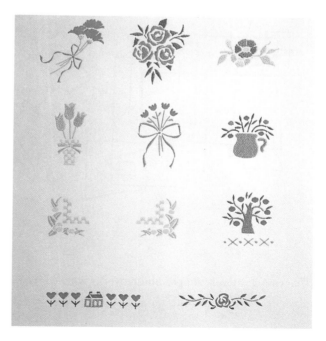

the work and holding both threads put the needle down into the material where you wish to begin your stitching. If you rest your elbows on the table you will find that this position leaves your wrists free to control the frame (diagram 2). Run the machine at an even pace and move the frame with both hands.

Practice drawing simple shapes and some of the filling stitches illustrated (diagram 3), varying the stitch length by the movement of the frame and the speed of the machine. As you gain more confidence you will find that the faster you run the machine the easier it is to move the frame. When you start to experiment with the zig-zag patterns you must control the frame with the left hand only, leaving the right hand free to use the stitch width control. Moving this lever to the widest stitch and back to straight stitch as you sew is the basis for all the zig-zag and satin stitch patterns.

Do not be discouraged if you don't get exactly what you want when you start; you will probably use a lot of fabric and thread before you achieve success the first time. Always remember it is easier to create a line than to follow a pattern so give yourself the minimum of guide lines and build the design on the material. Machine embroidery is almost impossible to unpick—avoid doing so by covering up anything with which you are not pleased. Include your mistakes in the pattern adding more stitching and scraps of fabric to extend the design.

The two methods given here form the basis for all free-hand machine embroidery. Everything you do will be variations of straight stitch and zig-zag. The patterns and designs given in this chapter are designed to give you practice in as many variations as possible; but remember, they are only a starting point from which you can invent designs for yourself.

Diagram 3: Simple shapes and patterns worked in straight stitch without removing the fabric from the machine.

A machine embroidery frame with finished work. Courtesy Elna Australia.

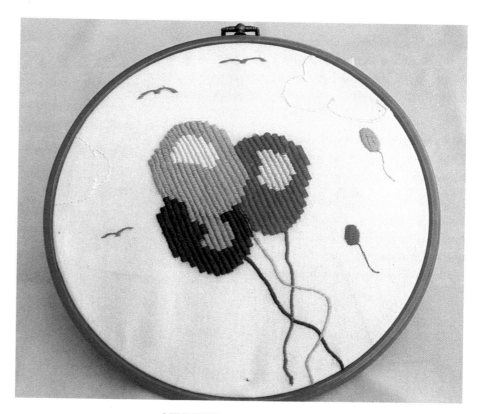

◆
Butterfly place mats

A set of place mats worked all in straight stitch for the beginner. This design (diagram 4, page 272) includes many of the textures and patterns that can be achieved with a simple straight stitching machine.

MATERIALS
Fabric
A closely woven fabric without too much texture, enough for four, six or eight mats measuring 16 x 12 ins (40 x 30 cm); allow 1 in (2.5 cm) all round for turnings or fringing.

Threads
Numbers 50 and 30 embroidery cottons, No. 8 perle cotton and either a soft cotton or 3-ply yarn. All the threads should be the same color, and a contrast to the background. The mats shown are on a bone background and stitched in black. A dark fabric with light stitching would look equally well. It is essential to use a good quality, colorfast thread.

Use a No. 80 needle in the machine and work in a frame throughout.

METHOD
After cutting out the mats [finished size, plus 1 in (2.5 cm) all round] zig-zag around the raw edges with a matching No. 50 embroidery thread; this is especially important with rayon "linen look" fabrics which fray a lot. Iron-on stiffening can be useful on flat pieces of work to hold the fabric in shape.

On the wrong side of the fabric mark out the design, working half at a time from a middle line. Dressmakers' carbon is useful for marking this type of design but only use it on the wrong side of the fabric as it is sometimes difficult to remove.

Work the cord lines on the design first. As cord is too thick to be used as a top thread on the machine it must be wound on the bobbin. Use the winder on the machine to do this if you can because winding by hand does not give an even tension. If your machine has a separate bobbin case it is useful to keep a spare case just for use with cords and metallic threads. The bobbin tension needs to be loosened to allow for the thickness of the cord. Thread the top with No. 30 embroidery thread and experiment a little to get the correct stitch. You will work from the WRONG side when using cord or metal threads.

Stitch in the main lines of the design with the foot on the machine, the feed up and a long stitch. You will find controlling the fabric easier if you work with a frame. Work the cord patterns next, this time free-hand (feed lowered, no foot) still from the wrong side.

Pull through all the ends and fasten off securely. This is very important on anything which has to withstand washing.

Replace the normal bobbin case or readjust the bobbin tension and thread with No. 30 embroidery cotton. As the main lines of the design are now marked it is easy to work the filling stitches from the right side in the spaces outlined by the cord.

Remember
Taut fabric whilst working with the embroidery frame.

A sharp needle.

A spare bobbin case or adjust the tension for cord and metal thread.

Fasten off all cord ends securely.

Note
This method of using heavy thread can be successfully used on any type of fabric once the correct tension for the thread is established.

Diagram 4: Place mat design

Opposite: Quilting has become one of the most popular home pursuits in recent years. A detail from an intricate quilt called "Magpies in the Garden" made by Fiona Gavens from furnishing fabrics. Courtesy Craft Australia.

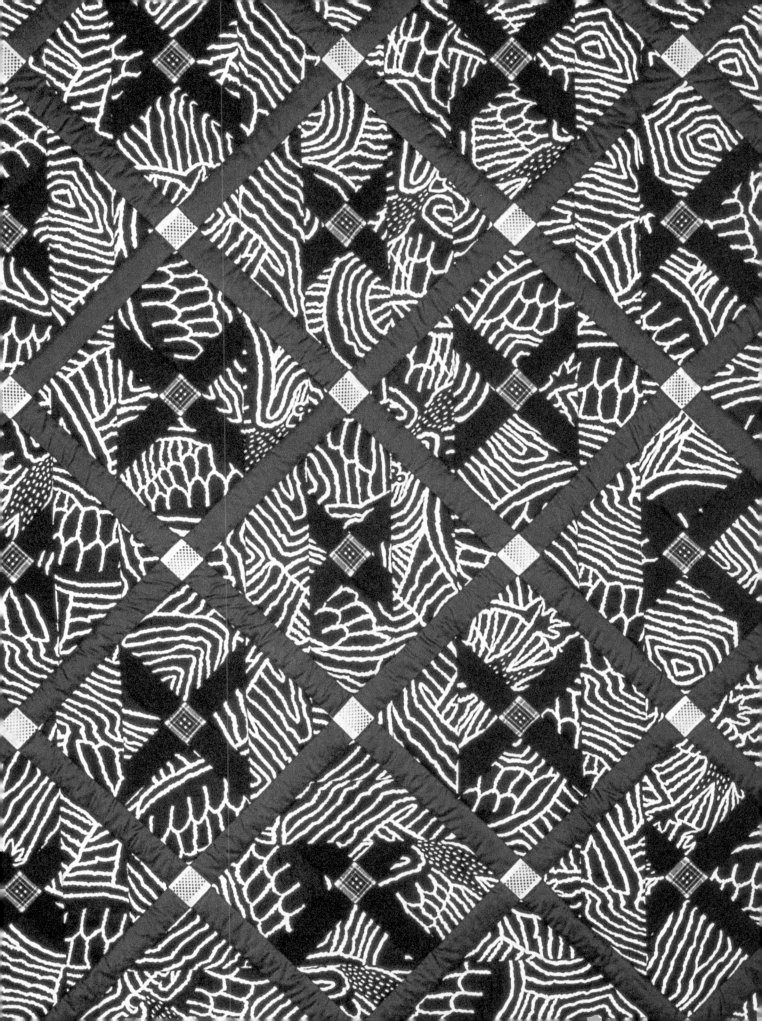

◆
Free-hand quilting

The method of quilting on the chair seat shown below could also be used for a bedcover, tea cosies or with a rich fabric for an evening handbag.

MATERIALS
Choose a patterned fabric with a bold design which will be easy to follow (diagram 5). In the cushion shown a curtain fabric has been used with one motif picked out to fit the chair seat. A soft fabric will quilt more easily than anything with a lot of dressing. Cut the fabric at least 3 ins (7.5 cm) bigger than the size of the finished article. For a thicker, softer look a stretch fabric will quilt very well.

For padding use four or more layers of Orlon, Terylene or nylon wadding. Foam rubber or plastic is not suitable as it is most difficult to sew through.

For lining use calico or a plain-colored cotton to match the top fabric.

To give the cushion a neat, finished-look cover a piping cord with matching bias binding or make a bias strip of the fabric used.

METHOD
Place the four layers of padding between the top fabric and a piece of calico. Stitch from the right side beginning from the middle—this is important, as working from the outside of the design often causes puckering in the top fabric.

Diagram 5: Suggested pattern for a chair seat

This quilt depicting leaves in fall (autumn) was made from assorted fabrics by Wendy Lugg. This detail courtesy Craft Australia.

As the fabrics are not stretched in a frame it is essential to keep them as flat as possible whilst sewing. You will need a darning foot on the machine (diagram 6). On this design, the middle of the flower was stitched first, three or four times around to accentuate the raised effect. Then the main radiating lines, followed by the petal outlines. Every line is sewn over twice so that there are no loose ends. Work from the middle out, and then back into the middle. When the main motif is complete the finished size should be marked with a tack thread. The space between the motif and the edge of the circle has been filled free-hand circles. Don't try to be precise with the shapes as the freely drawn shapes are often more lively and attractive.

If you choose to put a piped edge around the cushion sew the piping around the tacked edge, the cord side facing inward (diagram 7a overleaf). With the piping in position pin the lining fabric on the cushion (diagram 7b overleaf), with the right sides together

diagram 6

and carefully following the previous line of stitching sew around the cushion leaving 6 ins (15 cm) open for turning through. Trim away excess fabric before turning through and slip stitch the opening. If tapes are required to hold the cushion on the chair they should be put in position before the lining is sewn in position so that one line of stitching will serve both purposes (diagram 7c overleaf).

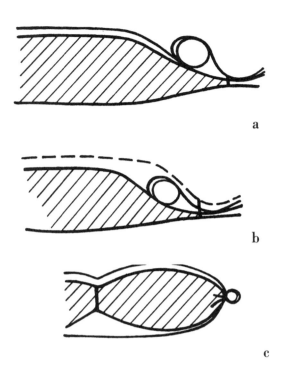

diagram 7

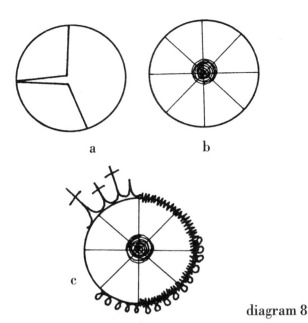

diagram 8

◆
Eyelet embroidery

There are two main types of openwork: eyelet embroidery on sheer fabrics, or drawn and pulled thread work on even weave and scrim.

This design could easily be adapted for sheer curtains or a simple caftan (see diagrams 10 and 11 overleaf).

MATERIAL
Use either cotton organdie, voile or a woven synthetic. Knitted fabrics are not suitable. You will need a fine cotton, a No. 50 or 60 embroidery thread and a No. 70 needle. Set your machine for freehand embroidery.

METHOD
When marking the design onto the fabric use as few lines as possible as they will show up through the fine cotton. Tacking threads can be used for the main lines and small dots rather than lines to mark the other details. Work the areas which are to be cut out first, stitching around each shape twice (diagram 8a). Cut out the middle close to the stitching line. When stitching across the center of the holes run the

machine slowly and smoothly—any jerkiness will cause the thread to break. The cobweb is sewn in the same way, stitching very slowly and letting the stitches form over the cross threads (diagram 8b). The raw edges are sewn last with a satin stitch (diagram 8c); work around the circle in small segments keeping all the stitches radiating from the middle.

To help achieve a good finish on this type of work it is a help to have the tension of the machine set as for buttonholes, that is with the bobbin thread slightly tight. Some machines have a special threading for this tightened bobbin tension (diagram 9).

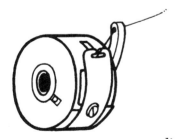

diagram 9

Opposite: A complete quilt that gives the appearance of having been "painted" in various fabrics. Called "Seventy-two Trail Street," it is the creation of Judy Turner. Courtesy Craft Australia.

When the holes marked in the design have been completed, the rest of the decoration is added. Use a very fine straight stitch for the details of the design and in choosing your thread remember that in this type of work the texture of the stitch and the pattern of holes is more important than the color, therefore it is most effective worked in the same color as the background fabric (diagrams 10 and 11).

diagram 10

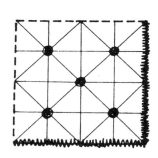

Ideas for openwork.   11a

11b

diagram 11

Simple appliqué on a woman's sweatshirt. Courtesy Avalon Craft Cottage.

◆

Pulled and drawn thread embroidery with the machine

Still using the tightened bobbin tension, fine thread and needle-drawn thread is easily worked on open weave linens and scrim. For all embroidery where the fabric is cut or any threads removed, the material must be stretched very tightly in a frame. As some of the threads are loose and the machine is often stitching over holes the remaining fabric must be kept taut otherwise the machine will miss stitches and you may have trouble with the thread breaking.

Using a very loosely woven fabric stretched tightly in a frame experiment with a zig-zag stitch over a varying number of threads. You will find that the zig-zag pulls the threads together.

Working with this idea and always keeping the threads vertical or horizontal, you will discover many interesting textures and patterns. Variations on this idea can be achieved by cutting some of the threads and drawing them out of the material; bind the remaining threads together with a satin stitch. Eyelet holes can be pulled into the fabric by working many lines of straight stitching into the same hole. If the fabric does not pull apart easily cut a few threads here and there and see what patterns you can make.

This style of embroidery can either be very formal with counted threads or completely free, combining extra threads to add thickness and depth.

◆

Embroidery on net

When using net as a background for embroidery great care should be taken when stretching the fabric onto the embroidery frame; to prevent the net from tearing it is better to use a double layer if this will not spoil the design. Many attractive effects can be gained by combining net and other transparent fabrics, adding extra fabric either on top or underneath the net. Open work looks very delicate when worked on a net background and with a little practice a really lacy pattern can be achieved. It is most effective to use straight stitching on net as a zig-zag can only be very uneven; experiment instead with the use of cords and heavy threads.

Because of its transparent quality net is most suitable for making a lampshade.

MATERIALS
Choose a plain tubular frame for the shade as anything shaped is far more difficult to make. To make construction easier bind the frame with white bias tape, keeping the tape as flat and neat as possible. A single layer of cotton organdie will make a good background to let the light through the layers of net. Use brightly colored nets cut into petals and arranged into large flower shapes.

METHOD
When you have an arrangement which is satisfying, pin the petals in place. Let the different colored nets overlap freely and make sure that the finished arrangement covers the whole area. A piece of net the same size as the background fabric is pinned over the whole design before any of the stitching is worked.

With the fabric in an embroidery frame work the middle of each flower separately; using a dark colored thread and keeping the stitch small, run a row of stitches up the center of each petal and draw the middle with a few tiny circles or a star shape. The top layer of net holds all the petals in position and stops the net from curling in the heat.

Opposite: Fabric and cord are appliquéd onto corduroy to create the design "Enchanted Forest". Instructions on page 290.

◆
Covering a lampshade

Diagram 12: Cylindrical lampshade frame.

Diagram 13: Bind frame with bias tape.

Diagram 14: Rectangle of background fabric.

Diagram 15: Arrangement of net flowers over the whole area, letting petals overlap freely.

Diagram 16: Net flower showing central stitching.

Diagram 17: Pin fabric along all ribs and top and bottom of frame. Smooth out any pleats or puckers and turn in overlap.

Diagram 18: Stitch with matching thread and small stitches along all the ribs and around top and bottom of frame. Fold the end under but don't leave too much excess fabric as this shows up when light shines through the shade.

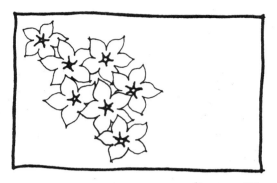

diagram 15

diagram 16

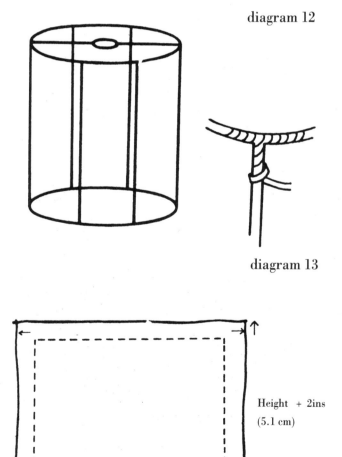

diagram 12

diagram 13

Height + 2ins
(5.1 cm)

diagram 14

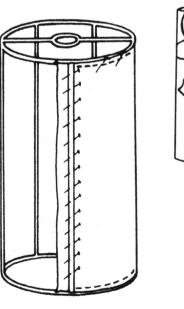

diagram 17

diagram 18

Above: Machine appliqué and embroidery on
children's clothing. © Courtesy Brother
Industries.

Right: Simple machined appliqué on guest towels.
Courtesy Avalon Craft Cottage.

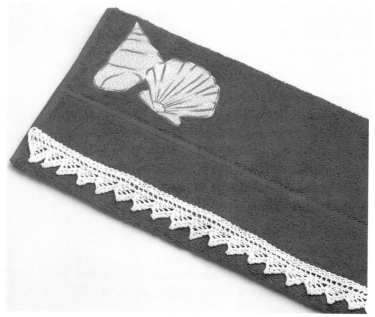

◆
Appliqué

In creative embroidery applied fabrics are often the quickest way of getting color and texture into a design before the stitching is commenced. The following method of appliqué is a sure way of placing each piece of fabric into its correct position. When you are more familiar with your machine and its capabilities you will find other ways of achieving a similar result. This is the easiest method for a beginner.

PHEASANT:
MATERIALS

A medium weight yarn or other textured fabric in a dark color is used for the background. This should be big enough to allow the frame to be used for each part of the design. A textured or flecked material will improve the picture or you could put a layer of a dark colored net over the whole background. The bird is built up from a collection of brightly colored scraps of fabric including velvet and satin which give a "feathery" effect.

METHOD

Trace the enlarged design onto tissue paper and tack in position on the background material. With the fabric in a frame, stitch along the outlines and the main lines inside the shape. Remove from the frame and tear away the tissue: the design is now marked on both sides of the fabric.

Working from the wrong side (again using the frame) stitch each part of the bird in position, trimming around each piece before fixing the next. Press from the wrong side before beginning the decorative stitching.

It is not necessary on a picture like this to satin stitch over all the raw edges, as a heavy line around all the shapes can spoil the finished effect; instead, use the pattern of the feathers to hold down the fabrics. Let the stitching overlap the edges of the applied fabrics in some places to add to the feathery effect.

The background can be finished by some line drawing in fine black cotton.

When the embroidery is complete, press from the wrong side through a damp cloth, pulling it all gently into shape.

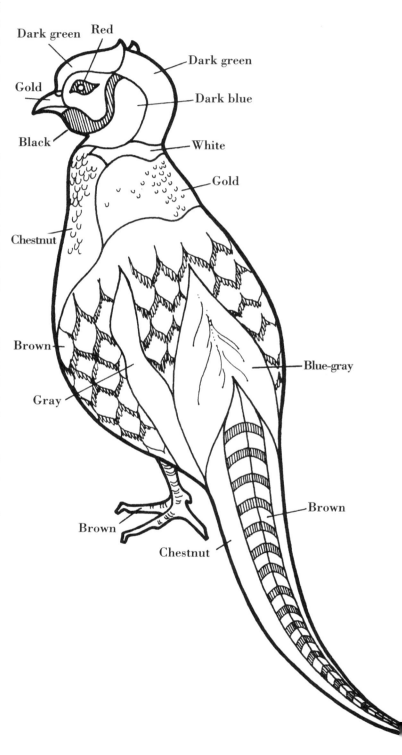

A floral wreath design attractively framed. Courtesy Coats Patons.

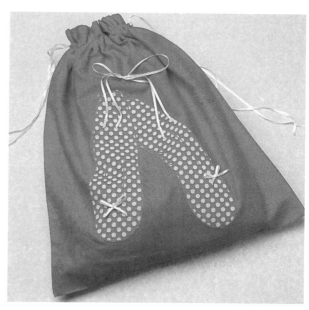

A bright appliqué design on a bag for carrying ballet shoes. Courtesy Avalon Craft Cottage.

◆

Automatic embroidery

Embroidery on a garment should be completed and well pressed before the garment is assembled. Make sure you use good quality colorfast threads and if applied fabrics are used they should be of the same type as the background. Firm, evenly woven fabrics are the easier and most successful for automatic embroidery.

Mark only the main lines of the design and work the automatic patterns first adding the free-hand embroidery afterward. Always press the fabric well before you begin and put a layer of thin typing paper under the work as you sew—this prevents the stitches pulling the fabric out of shape and puckering. Paper should be used under all automatic embroidery and satin stitch when a foot is used. An embroidery frame can help you to guide the work if the design includes lots of curves.

The addition of some free-hand stitching helps to enliven the work and soften the overall effect.

◆

Stretching and mounting

If you have worked with the material tightly stretched in an embroidery frame, your work should not be badly pulled out of shape. For most pieces of good work, a good press through a damp cloth should be sufficient to smooth and straighten. Always press embroidery from the wrong side and if you are going to include beads on the design, press well before sewing the beads in position.

A piece of work which has become badly misshapen or puckered can be dampened and stretched back into shape. You will need either a drawing-board or a sheet of fiberboard into which it is easy to push pins; plenty of drawing pins, newspaper and a ruler or straight edge. Make a pad of damp newspaper slightly larger than your embroidery and top with white paper or sheeting to prevent the print from coming through onto the material. With this pad on the board, place the embroidery face uppermost over the paper with a pin at the middle of each side. Pulling the embroidery taut as you go, work all around the material, putting pins about an inch apart along each side. Make sure the threads of the

fabric are straight and all warping and puckering is pulled flat. The paper pad should be sufficiently damp to allow the fabric to stretch easily, but do not put water on the surface of the embroidery. When the embroidery has been stretched as much as possible, leave it to dry naturally. This may take a day or two.

Care should be taken when mounting the finished embroidery to choose a frame or type of mount suitable to the individual work. Embroidery has a three-dimensional quality and is therefore best when mounted without glass. Never put glue under the embroidery, only use it on back of mount (diagrams 19 and 20).

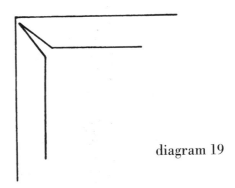

diagram 19

Take care sticking down the corners. Do not cut too close to the edges.

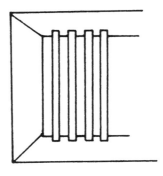

diagram 20

An alternative to gluing is cord stretched across the back. Sew corners flat.

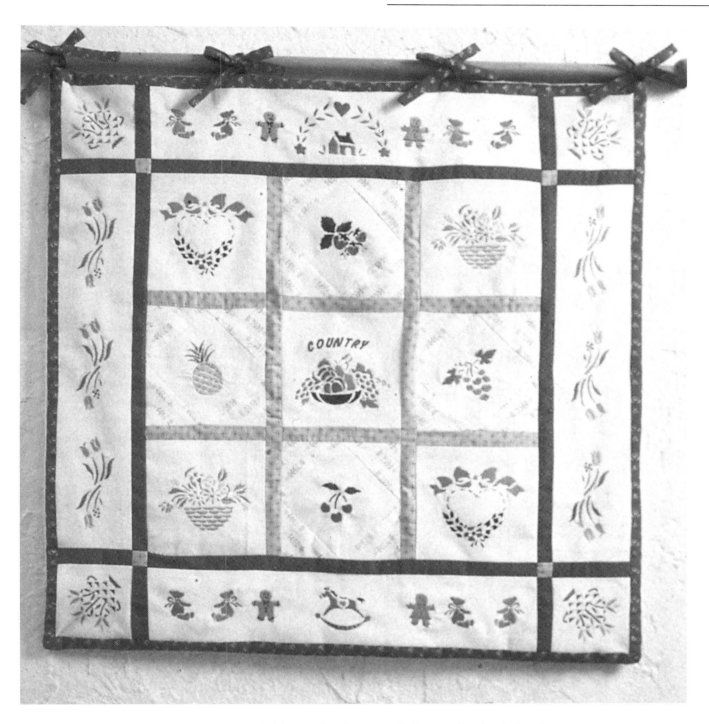

This machine-embroidered sampler is suspended from a dowel support. © Courtesy Brother Industries.

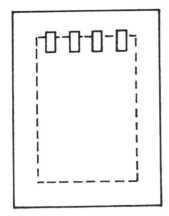

Tabs in position and stitching line marked.

diagram 21

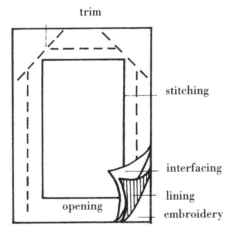

trim

stitching

interfacing

lining

embroidery

opening

diagram 22

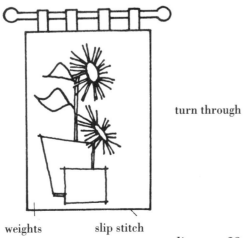

turn through

weights   slip stitch

diagram 23

The easiest way of mounting is to stretch the embroidery over a piece of hardboard cut to the correct size. This can be then either fitted into a frame or mounted against another board. The second board should be large enough to leave a border of 2 or 3 ins (5–7.5 cm) around the embroidery and can be covered with a plain fabric or painted. Choose a color for the background from the colors used in the design, or if you are using fabric, perhaps the same cloth as the embroidery in a different shade. This method of mounting is especially suitable for small, rich pieces of embroidery.

For large wall hangings, a soft mount is best. Press the embroidery or stretch, if that should be necessary. Make tabs of the chosen backing fabric and pin in place along the top of the embroidery (diagram 21). Stitch down along the edge of the picture and continue stitching around the edge of the embroidery (diagram 22). This marks the stitching line for the backing. Check that you have the corners square and the measurements of the rectangle accurate. Put the backing piece face down on the embroidery (right sides together) and the interfacing (stiffening) on top of that. Stitch around three sides, leaving the bottom open. Trim well, especially the corners; turn through and steam press the edges. Slip stitch the bottom edge. Include weights along the bottom, if necessary (diagram 23).

Note
Always leave a good margin around embroidery when marking out, to allow for mounting.

Mounted or sewn on everyday items, machine embroidery helps to make delightful gifts and decorations for the home. © Courtesy Brother Industries.

◆
Examples of machine embroidery designs

Machine embroidery provides you with an opportunity to be creative. Whether you prefer the automatic stitches of the latest computerized machines, or freehand machine stitching, you can create a truly individual work of art.

EMBROIDERED BOXES

See photograph opposite, top left.

Machine embroidery can be worked on boxes to create pretty articles. The backgrounds may be felt, corduroy and silk.

DRAWN-THREAD WORK

The design below is derived from the seed head of a waratah. It is worked in heavy threads on tapestry canvas. Some threads have been removed, and then hand stitching has been combined with machine stitching. Appliqué and padded appliqué (trapunto) have also been used to add texture.

DRAGON

See photograph opposite, below.

A panel of screen-printed fabric has been given added dimension with machine-embroidered detail.

BIRD OF PARADISE

See photograph opposite, top right.

This design has been worked on tapestry canvas, and includes appliqué of various fabrics, ranging from leather to net. Techniques used to work this design include couched threads, eyelets, and freehand machine embroidery.

ENCHANTED FOREST

See photograph on page 281.

This design has been worked on a corduroy fabric. Techniques used are straight stitching, appliqué, couched threads, satin stitch and freehand machine embroidery.

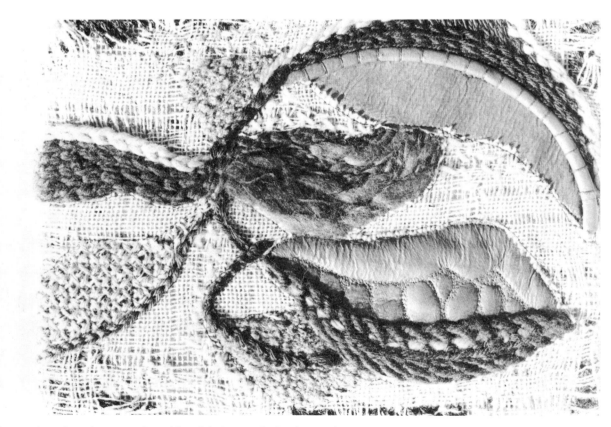

Drawn thread work: waratah seed head design worked in heavy threads on tapestry canvas.

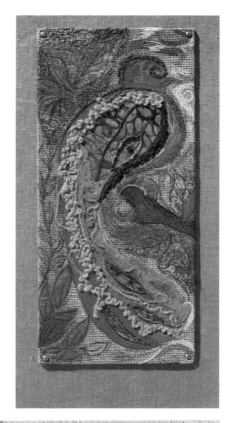

Above: Machine embroidery draws a dragon shape to enrich a piece of screen-printed fabric. Top left: A box covered with embroidered silk. Top right: A bird of paradise worked on tapestry canvas. For all these, see notes on the opposite page.

TAPESTRY

◆

Materials

Tapestry may be worked upon single or double mesh canvas. These canvases may range from fine, single thread petit point canvas through medium weight double thread to coarse double thread rug canvas. It is important to choose the thread most suited to the weight of the canvas and the canvas most suited to the particular article planned.

Ready-made tapestry designs printed, stencilled or tramméd on canvas are available in the needlework departments of larger stores. Plain canvas for charting your own designs is also available.

"Decorator" canvas with the design already worked is a boon for beginners in the art of tapestry as the background only remains to be stitched.

1. "DECORATOR" CANVAS
The design, usually floral, is already worked in tent stitch and the background only remains to be stitched. Available in fire screens, handbags, pictures, stool tops, etc.

2. TRAMMÉD CANVAS
The design is laid out in long horizontal stitches in the colours in which it is to be worked. It is then only a matter of stitching in half-cross or gros point over these laid threads. Available in fire screens, pictures, chair and stool tops, etc.

3. STENCILLED OR PAINTED CANVAS
The design is painted or stencilled in the appropriate colours to be embroidered. Available in children's and beginners' pictures, handbags, teenagers' tapestries, stool tops, petit point pictures, picture panels, fire screens, etc.

4. CHARTED DESIGNS
Following a chart, a design may be worked on any size canvas mesh desired to produce a large or small piece. Block in with color each square on the chart or graph. Each square represents a corresponding stitch to be taken in the canvas. You may create your own design on a sheet of graph paper.

5. ALL-OVER PATTERNS
This method consists of following a pattern from a started section of the design as in Florentine or Hungarian point tapestry. These geometrical patterns are made from repetition of counted threads.

◆

Thread

Either yarn or cotton is suitable, as recommended in the directions with each tapestry. Semco stranded cotton is ideal to work with, using the full six strands. It is available in an almost unlimited range of shades and is colorfast and long-wearing. One skein of Semco stranded cotton covers 5–6 in^2 (12–15 cm^2).

When purchasing thread for backgrounds, either cotton or yarn, it is advisable to buy the full amount at the same time, as it is impossible to prevent slight shade variation in different dye batches.

To estimate the amount of thread, select the type of thread best suited to the weight of the canvas, and stitch a 1 in (2.5 cm) square, noting the length of thread used. Calculate the number of square inches (sq cm) to be covered by each color in the design and multiply by the length used to stitch a 1 in (2.5 cm) square. This gives you the approximate yardage for each colour. For the number of skeins needed, divide this yardage by the number of yards (meters) in a skein.

◆

Needle

Tapestry needles have blunt points which will not split the thread or canvas, and are sold in packets of assorted sizes. Use one which will pass easily through the canvas with the thread. A thread about 18 in (46 cm) in length is sufficient.

◆

Frame

This is not necessary for small tapestries, but helpful for larger pieces. Tapestry frames are available from retailers or may be improvised from an old picture frame by fixing the canvas firmly to the back of the frame with drawing pins. When working on a frame the needle is put vertically through the canvas, using two hands, one above and one below.

An attractive tapestry piece. Courtesy Coats Patons.

◆

To enlarge or reduce a design

This may be done by using a larger or smaller mesh canvas (and suitable thread) than that for the original design.

Estimate the overall size of your design on the new background by counting the number of stitches, lengthwise and crosswise, on the original, then counting an equal number of meshes on the new background.

It will be necessary to re-estimate the amount of thread required.

◆

Starting your tapestry

Before beginning, bind all raw edges of canvas using adhesive tape or bias binding, or turn raw edges over and tack to prevent fraying. If the design is not distinctive, mark the top of the work with coloured thread to avoid mistakes in stitching.

Start near the top of the design so that the work is not soiled by the hand as it progresses. Leave the lighter shades until later, for the same reason. Remember, no tight stitches or gaps between rows. If the yarn becomes twisted, let the needle hang down and the yarn will straighten out.

Keep your tapestry clean by storing it in a plastic bag between work sessions. Should your piece need freshening, lightly brush over the surface with a clean cloth dipped in a drycleaning fluid.

TO START AND FINISH (see diagram 1)
Begin with a knot which is cut away later when the thread has been secured by the stitches. To finish off a thread, run it in and out of the canvas, or thread it through the back of the stitches. To start the next thread, run the needle behind a few adjacent stitches and bring it through to the front in the same holes used for the last stitch. Cut off all thread ends as you go, or they will spoil the finished appearance.

diagram 1

BACKGROUND (see diagram 2)
Work right across the canvas, with "staggered" joins rather than "blocked in" sections which would show up in the finished work.

Large areas—background or sky—may be worked diagonally, as this helps to keep the canvas in shape. Commence in the top right-hand corner. The needle passes under two vertical threads in the ascending lines, and under two horizontal threads in the descending lines, as shown in diagram 2.

diagram 2

◆

Tapestry stitches

HALF-CROSS STITCH (see diagram 3 overleaf)
Is suitable for framed pictures, wall hangings and articles which receive little wear. It uses a minimum of thread and works up quickly, but does not cover the back of the canvas. It may be worked either left to right or vice versa. All stitches are straight at the back of the canvas, and must all lie in the same direction. Work over a tramméd thread, except when using background yarn, as in decorator tapestries.

An attractive tapestry piece.
Courtesy Coats Patons.

Tapestry work fashioned into a cushion.
Courtesy Avalon Craft Cottage.

A tramméd thread is a thread stitched along the horizontal double thread of the canvas, the inclusion of which gives better wearing qualities and a richer appearance to the finished work.

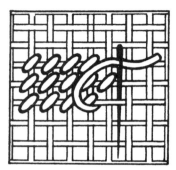

diagram 3

CROSS STITCH (see diagram 4)

Cross stitch appeals to many needleworkers, but take care that each stitch crosses in the same direction. Crosses may be made separately, but in large areas it is simpler and quicker to work half-cross stitches right along the row and then return crossing them.

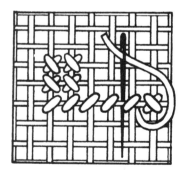

diagram 4

TENT STITCH

This is the general name for both gros point stitch and petit point stitch, but the former is worked on double canvas and the latter on single canvas. This stitch uses more thread, which covers the front and pads the back of the canvas, resulting in a more attractive piece of work with superior wearing qualities.

PETIT POINT (see diagram 5)

For fine work on single thread canvas or gauze. Work from right to left, back over one thread and forward behind two. Reverse canvas for each following stitch.

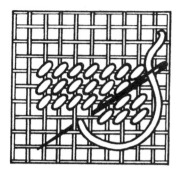

diagram 5

GROS POINT (see diagrams 6a and 6b)

The above stitch worked on double thread canvas. Petit point may be used in conjunction with gros point to show greater detail—faces and hands—for which the double thread is "split", that is, the threads are separated and worked singly. Diagram 6a shows the method of turning to commence the following row, and diagram 6b the longer stitch at the back of the canvas.

These are the four most commonly used tapestry stitches.

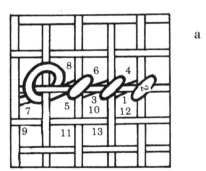

a

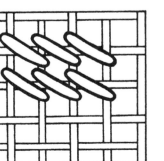

b

diagram 6

UPRIGHT GOBELIN STITCH (see diagram 7)

Cover a tramméd design with vertical stitches worked from right to left or left to right, one stitch in width.

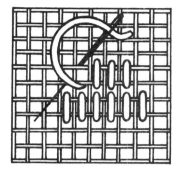

diagram 7

GOBELIN STITCH (see diagram 8)

Work as for upright gobelin, except that the needle is kept vertical, giving an oblique stitch on the right side. The stitch may be either two or three threads deep.

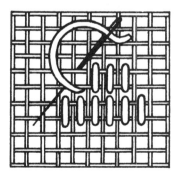

diagram 8

ENCROACHING GOBELIN STITCH
(see diagram 9)

Work as for gobelin stitch keeping needle vertical and stitches oblique. The stitches are four threads deep and each new line encroaches on the last two of the previous line.

diagram 9

DOUBLE CROSS STITCH (see diagram 10)

This is simple cross stitch worked on four threads both in height and width. A second cross stitch is worked over this.

diagram 10

FLORENTINE STITCH (see diagram 11)

Also known as Hungarian point, flame stitch or bargello, this canvas stitch has been used throughout Europe and England since the sixteenth century. The name originates from Florence in Italy where not only embroidery but woven fabrics are made in this distinctive pattern.

The apparently shimmering pattern of vibrant color makes cushions of this embroidery an effective accent for modern architecture.

The outstanding characteristics of Florentine work are its shading from light to dark and the upright stitch worked over two or four canvas meshes.

Double thread canvas is worked with a double thread of stranded cotton or tapestry yarn, and a tapestry needle.

As in all canvas work, the entire surface is covered with stitches. The wavy effect is obtained by working horizontally, using stitches of even length in vandykes of graduated color.

A chart is followed for the design. Working from right to left, insert the needle so that the stitch is vertical and four meshes deep. Each stitch is one thread to the left, and encroaches on the previous one by two meshes.

Note that on the upward journey, the needle points towards the worked part, and on the downward side it points away.

Subsequent rows follow the first, but lighter or deeper toned thread is used, thus after the initial counting, the work is straightforward.

There may be innumerable variations of size and shape in the vandykes, but these must be repeated regularly across the work.

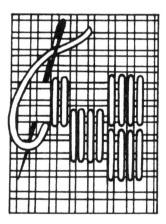

diagram 11

Blocking

If the finished work is out of shape it may be blocked squarely as follows:

1. Cover a drawing board with brown paper on which is drawn the original size of the canvas. Make sure the corners are square.

2. Slightly dampen back of work, place right side down and pin out to original shape with drawing pins placed ½ in (1.3 cm) apart, and away from stitches so that rust marks will be avoided. Make sure that warp and weft threads run at right angles to each other.

3. Leave to dry thoroughly and repeat if necessary.

Mounting and framing pictures

Frame mounted picture as desired, without glass. Pre-cut picture framing kits are now available at the big stores or you can have your work professionally mounted and framed.

Completion of handbags

Most leading retail stores in capital cities provide this service and offer a large selection of frames.

Opposite: Tapestry work in the frame, and in detail to show the stitches. Courtesy Avalon Craft Cottage.

Leathercraft

TRADITIONAL LEATHERWORK

Engraving, a craft from the Middle Ages, involves carving the leather with a special cutting tool to follow a pattern, and stamping the background, to provide relief, with steel stamping tools used to create light and shade on the design.

Embossing is done with only a modeling tool, using hand pressure on damp leather, hammering on the underside to bring up the design.

Outlining is the simplest form of tooling, using a combined tracer and modeler to compress the lines of the outline design. Flat modeling is similar to outline tooling, but parts of the design are depressed with a tool to make the work stand out from the background.

The best skins to choose for home leatherwork are calf (fine-grained, lightweight), cow and steer hide (tough, heavy), and morocco (made from goatskin, a fine and beautiful skin to work). But remember, if you buy your leather this way, the design on the leather must be completed before you start to assemble the final article.

For the beginner, the best bet is to go to a good handcraft store and ask advice. There, leather can be bought in a variety of weights and textures, ready for working. Or it can be purchased as "kits", already cut out for making belts, purses, wallets, key-rings, watchbands and pencil cases.

You do not need a large range of tools for your new hobby; a hard piece of board for cutting, ruler, square, sharp knife, scissors, special hammer, marker tool, awl, carving and modeling tools, eyelet punch, rotary leather punch for holes, thonging (usually kangaroo hide for durability), waxed threads, dye, and shoe polish. Beginners are advised to consult a good book on leatherwork techniques before embarking on too many ambitious projects.

◆
Engraving and embossing

When you have purchased a piece of leather suitable for the job and have decided on the pattern you want to work onto the leather, you are ready to go.

STEP 1:
Draw the design onto tracing paper.

STEP 2:
Dampen the leather all over on the underside to get a better impression with your tools (dampen it as necessary as the work proceeds) and pin it firmly to your cutting board.

STEP 3:
Pin the design over the leather and trace it through with a modeling tool.

STEP 4:
Take away the paper and impress the design again evenly and heavily.

STEP 5:
Now you take your carving tool (for engraving) or modeling tool (for embossing) and start to sink the background, pressing the tool onto the leather evenly in a sideways direction.

If you want to dye your design only, use a fine brush. If the whole article is to be dyed, use a pad of absorbent cotton, with even strokes, to obtain a regular finish.

All this will have taken a lot longer than you think, but the secret of success in leatherwork is patience and care.

As a general rule, when you are completing your design, use a fine stippled background for calf and hide, and a smooth background for morocco.

Opposite: Leathergoods simple enough for a beginner to make.

◆
How to thong (see diagrams 1 to 4)

Since olden times, one of the charms of handworked leather was that there was no stitching. All the joins were brought together with fine leather strips drawn tightly through holes at each edge of the article.

Leather thonging can be dyed with Raven oil or leather dye to match the hide on which you are working. An easy method is to saturate a piece of absorbent cotton with the dye and draw the thonging gently through it. Each application darkens the color, so continue until you have hide and thonging matched.

Punch holes from the right side of the leather along all edges to be thonged, about 3/16 in (0.5 cm) apart and 3/16 in (0.5 cm) from the edge (see diagram 1). Punches have a spacing attachment but, to keep holes straight, mark with ruler and awl. When rounding a corner, place holes slightly closer together. A small piece of card under the leather helps to make a cleaner hole with the punch. Tie articles together at intervals to make sure holes correspond and so prevent puckering when you start to thong.

diagram 1

OVERSEW THONGING is used for lacing garments, purses, hats, belts, book covers, and any number of articles. It may be used for joining or as a decorative stitch. The length of thonging needed is three times the distance to be covered. Bring thonging through first hole and secure firmly. Continue oversewing as shown (diagram 2).

diagram 2

CROSSED THONGING is worked in two rows, using alternate holes. The first goes left to right and the second from right to left, so making a cross. The length of thonging needed is about five times the distance to be covered (diagram 3).

diagram 3

TO START THONGING

Use a lacing needle or thonging needle or cut tip of thong to a point. Bring thonging through the first hole, leaving about 1 in (2.5 cm). Cover it by the thonging as you proceed. This prevents thonging unraveling.

Joins in thongs must not show. Pare ends of old and new thonging (diagram 4). Bring old thonging through last hole of finished end, catching in about 1 ½ ins (3.8 cm) of both old and new thongs and work them in together to show as little as possible.

TO FINISH THONGING

Leave the last six loops loose enough to tuck end through at back of work. Carefully tighten loops, bring end through firmly.

For that final finish to a dress or suit there is nothing like a beautiful belt made from suede or soft leather. Here are two suggestions for belts, but you might like to make up your own designs.

diagram 4

Opposite: Materials and equipment like these are readily available from leathergoods suppliers.

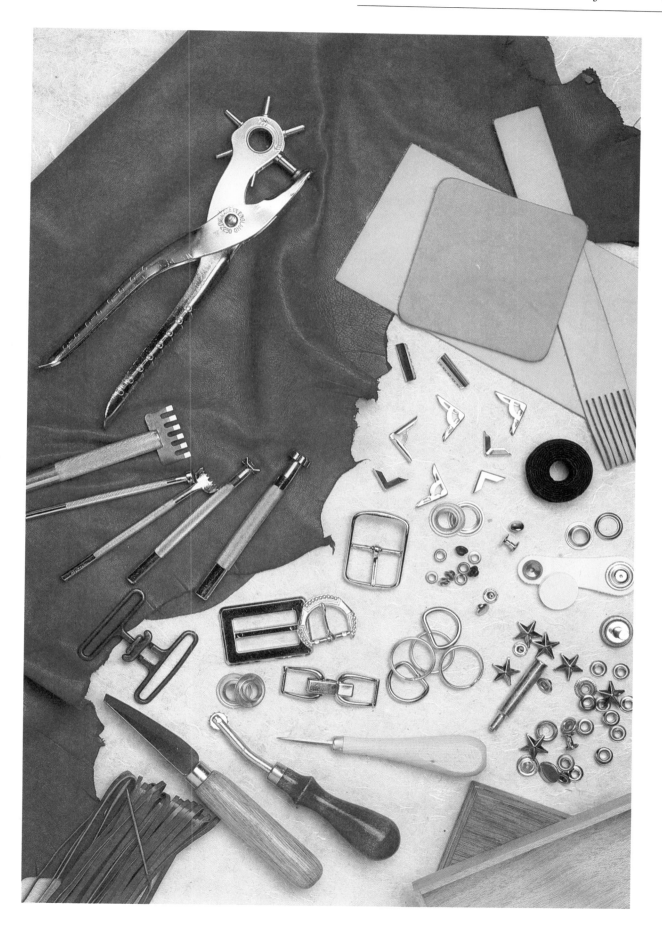

◆

Waist-cinching belt

You will need ¼ yd (23 cm) of suede and interlining.

Measure your waist, then cut suede to waist size in the shape you want. Cut interlining ½ in (1.3 cm) smaller than fabric. Turn fabric over lining and stitch the two together (see diagram 5). Cut another piece of suede to line belt. Use a punch and eyelets to make holes at each end of belt, ½ in (1.3 cm) apart (diagram 6). Lace with cord, leather or fabric strips.

diagram 5

diagram 6

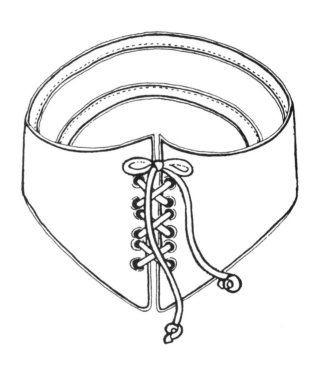

Opposite top: Wallets machine sewn in fine leather, by Steve Bate of Richmond, Adelaide.

Bottom: Bright pencil cases in glossy colored cowhide. For functional products like these, Steve Bate likes to use primary and secondary colors and leather with a full grain texture.

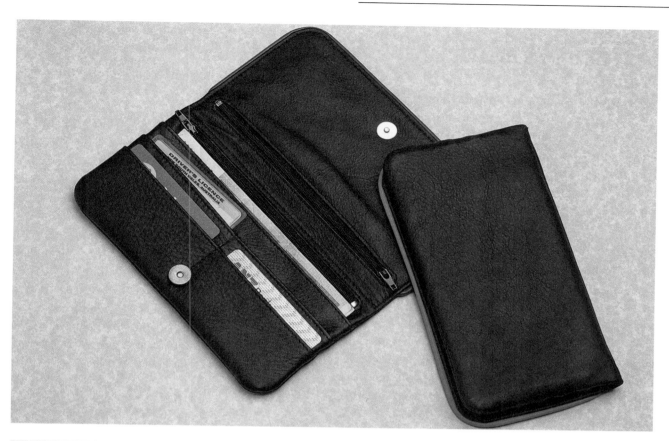

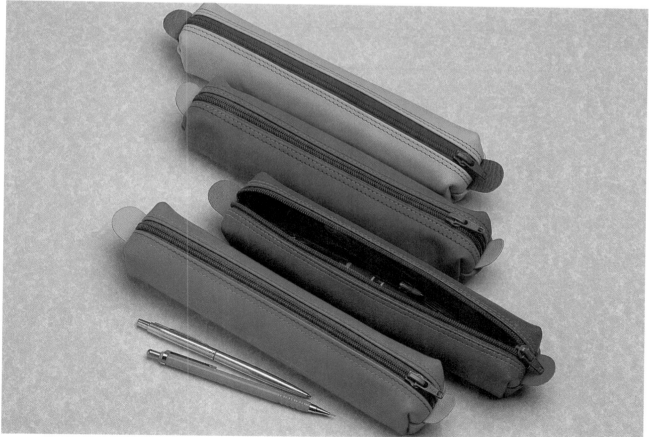

◆
Leather covered box

MATERIALS

Wooden box (available from craft shops) or an old cigar box; a piece of leather large enough to cover the box you have selected, and sufficiently thin and pliable to work with; leather stain or dye; a piece of felt for the lining; craft or PVA glue; Stanley knife and metal ruler; scissors; very fine sandpaper; pen for marking leather underside; graph paper for pattern.

METHOD

Place the box in the middle of the graph paper, and mark out a pattern. Allow extra all around, enough to cover the sides on the outside and the inside—do not forget to allow for the thickness of the sides as well. On the long sides, add ¼ in (1 cm) to the outside edge and thickness of side (see diagram). Check the pattern, by cutting around the lines marked, and fit it to the box. When you are satisfied that the pattern is correct, place it on the underside (skin) side of the leather, and trace around.

DO NOT PIN, as it will damage the leather. Cut out the leather with the scissors. Sand the box if necessary to remove any rough edges. Glue the underneath of the box to the marked base on the leather. Glue the sides, short ends first, gently stretching and working the leather for a firm fit. Fold the ¼ in (1 cm) flaps in as shown in diagram. Trim any excess carefully with a stanley knife.

For the lining, make a pattern or template of the box, and cut felt piece to the pattern. Cover the area to be lined with glue, and fit the felt. Remember that the felt may stretch, so work gently, but do not trim the felt until it is dry, as it may shrink again. If you have a box with a lid, follow the same procedure for both parts. If the box has a hinged lid, remove hinges until covering is complete, and glue is dry. Stain leather according to your choice of color.

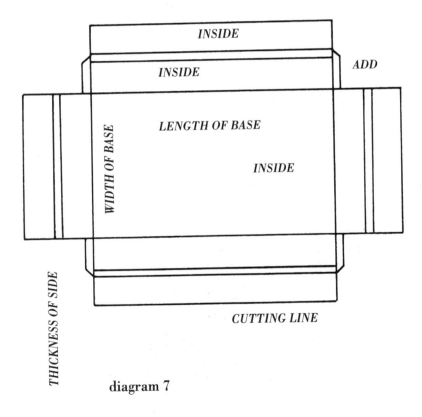

diagram 7

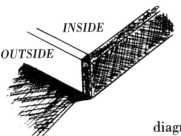

diagram 8

Left: Originality is one of the most satisfying qualities of leatherwork. This beautifully made handbag is the work of Steve Bate.
Below: A backpack/tote bag with a difference: exquisite work by Steve Bate in black cowhide, a full grain leather with a matt finish. The colored piping is also leather.

Gifts

◆
Gloves

MATERIALS
3 balls of Villawool 8 ply Machinewash; a pair of Nos. 8 and 9 needles.

MEASUREMENT
To fit 7½ ins (19 cm) hand, or as required.

TENSION
6 sts to 1 in (2.5 cm).

ABBREVIATIONS
See page 15.

RIGHT GLOVE
With No. 9 needles cast on 44 sts and work in rib of k1, p1 for 2¾ ins (7 cm), ending on right side of work.

Change to No. 8 needles and, beg with p row, work 5 rows in st st. **

Thumb gusset. Next row: K23, m1, k2, m1, k19.

Next row: P.

Rep above 2 rows 5 times, working 2 sts more at center after each inc to 56 sts. Work 6 rows straight.

Shape thumb. Next row: K38, turn, p14 and cast on 3 sts, turn.

Cont on these 17 sts for 2 ins (5.1 cm), ending on p row.

Shape top. Next row: K2, (k2 tog, k1) to end.

Next row: P.

Next row: (K2 tog) to end; break yarn and thread through rem sts; draw up and fasten off.

Join seam to base of thumb. Rsf, join in yarn at base of thumb, pick up and k 3 sts, k to end (45 sts). Work 7 rows.

Shape first finger. Next row: K29, turn, p13 and cast on 3 sts, turn.

Cont on these 16 sts for 2½ ins (6.3 cm), ending on p row.

Shape top. Next row: K1, (k2 tog, k1) to end.

Next row: P.

Next row: K1, (k2 tog) to end; break yarn and thread through rem sts; draw up and fasten off.

Join seam to base.

Shape second finger. Rsf, join in yarn at base of first finger, pick up and k 3 sts, k5, turn, p13 and cast on 3 sts, turn.

Cont on these 16 sts for 2¾ ins (7 cm), ending on p row, then finish as given for first finger.

Shape third finger. Work as given for second finger until 2½ ins (6.3 cm) have been worked, then finish as given for first finger.

Shape fourth finger. Rsf, join in yarn at base of third finger, pick up and k 3 sts, k to end. Cont on these 15 sts for 1¾ ins (4.4 cm), ending on p row.

Next row: (K2 tog, k1) to end.

Next row: P.

Next row: (K2 tog) to end.

Finish as given for first finger.

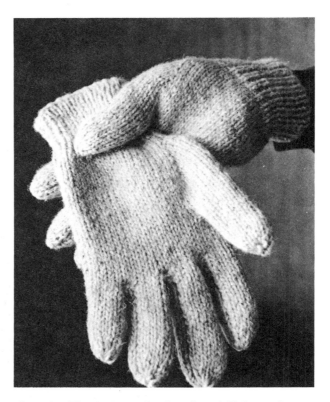

Opposite: The sewing and embroidery skills learnt from this book will enable you to make gifts that have your own personal touch. © Courtesy Brother Industries.

The sewing and embroidery skills learnt from this book will enable you to make gifts that have your own personal touch.
© *Courtesy Brother Industries.*

TO MAKE UP

Press work on the wrong side. Join seams.

LEFT GLOVE

Work as given for Right Glove to **.

Shape thumb. Next row: K19, m1, k2, m1, k23.

Next row: P.

Rep above 2 rows 5 times, working 2 sts more at center after each inc to 56 sts. Work 6 rows straight.

Next row: K32, cast on 3 sts, turn and p17, turn. Cont as given for Right Glove, having cast on 3 sts at opposite ends.

◆
Sox (socks)

MATERIALS

4 balls of Patons Patonyle 4 ply; a set of 4 double-pointed No. 11 needles.

MEASUREMENT

Length, 17 ins (43 cm) from beg to end. Size, adjustable.

TENSION

8 sts to 1 in (2.5 cm) over patt.

ABBREVIATIONS

See page 15.

METHOD

With set of No. 11 needles cast on 80 sts (26 x 26 x 28) and work in k1, p1 rib for 3½ ins (8.9 cm), then cont in patt:

1st round: (K3, p2) to end.

2nd, 3rd and 4th rounds: As 1st round.

5th round: P1, (k3, p2) to last 4 sts, k3, p1.

6th, 7th and 8th rounds: As 5th round.

9th round: (P2, k3) to end.

10th, 11th and 12th rounds: As 9th round.

13th round: K1, (p2, k3) to last 4 sts, p2, k2.

14th, 15th and 16th rounds: As 13th round.

17th round: K2, (p2, k3) to last 3 sts, p2, k1.

18th, 19th and 20th rounds: As 17th round.

Rep above 20 rounds until work measures 15 ins (38 cm) (or length required).

Shape toe. 1st round: (K3, k2 tog) to end (64 sts).

2nd round: K.

3rd round: K.

4th round: (K7, k2 tog) to last 10 sts, k7, k3 tog (56 sts).

5th and 6th rounds: As 2nd and 3rd rounds.

7th round: (K6, k2 tog) to end (49 sts).

8th and 9th rounds: As 2nd and 3rd rounds.

10th round: (K5, k2 tog) to end (42 sts).

11th and 12th rounds: As 2nd and 3rd rounds.

13th round: (K4, k2 tog) to end (35 sts).

14th and 15th rounds: As 2nd and 3rd rounds.

16th round: (K3, k2 tog) to end (28 sts).

17th and 18th rounds: As 2nd and 3rd rounds.

19th round: (K2, k2 tog) to end (21 sts).

20th and 21st rounds: As 2nd and 3rd rounds.

22nd round: (K1, k2 tog) to end (14 sts).

23rd and 24th rounds: As 2nd and 3rd rounds.

25th round: (K2 tog) to end (7 sts).

Break yarn; run thread through rem sts; draw up and fasten off.

◆
Clutch purse

MATERIALS

1 ball of Villawool Tasman 8 ply; a pair of No. 8 needles; 4½–5 ins (11.4–12.7 cm) mount; lining.

MEASUREMENTS

5 x 9 ins (12.7 x 23 cm).

Tension

6 sts to 1 in (2.5 cm).

ABBREVIATIONS

See page 15.

Note: Use yarn double throughout.

METHOD

With No. 8 needles cast on 32 sts and work in garter st, inc 1 st each end of next and every foll 2nd row to

Sewing skills alone are required to create these writing cases made from bought tapestry fabric. Courtesy Avalon Craft Cottage.

56 sts. Tie a marker at middle of last row, then cont until work measures 6 ins (15.2 cm) from marker. Dec 1 st each end of the next and every foll 2nd row until 32 sts rem. Work 1 row, then cast off.

TO MAKE UP
Cut lining larger than knitted piece and join seams to within 1½ ins (3.8 cm). Fold knitted piece in half and join side edges. Run a gathering stitch along top of purse and lining; draw up to the width of mount and neatly attach.

◆

Evening bag

MATERIALS
1 ball of Villawool Tasman 8 ply; a pair of No. 8 needles; 3½–4 ins (8.9–10.2 cm) mount; lining.

MEASUREMENT
5½ x 6 ins (14 x 15.2 cm).

TENSION
6 sts to 1 in (2.5 cm).

ABBREVIATIONS
See page 15.

Note: Use yarn double throughout.

METHOD
With No. 8 needles cast on 34 sts and work in part:

1st, 2nd and 3rd rows: (K1, p1) to end.

4th, 5th and 6th rows: (P1, k1) to end.

Rep above 6 rows, at the same time, inc 1 st each end of next 4 rows (42 sts). Cont straight until work measures 11 ins (28 cm), ending on 3rd or 6th row. Dec 1 st each end of next 4 rows, then work 6 rows straight. Cast off in patt.

TO MAKE UP
Cut lining larger than knitted piece and join seams to within 1½ ins (3.8 cm) of top. Fold knitted piece in half and join side edges. Neatly attach bag and lining to the mount.

◆
Bed sox (socks)

MATERIALS
3 balls of Villawool Machinewash 8 ply; a pair of No. 8 needles; ribbon.

MEASUREMENT
To fit average size foot.

TENSION
6 sts to 1 in (2.5 cm).

ABBREVIATIONS
See page 15.

METHOD
With No. 8 needles cast on 96 sts and work in g st, inc 1 st each end of every foll row to 110 sts. Cont straight until work measures 2½ ins (6.3 cm) from beg, then dec 1 st each end of every foll row until 96 sts rem. Cast off 23 sts at beg of next 2 rows (50 sts).

Next (ribbonhole) row: K3, * yfwd, k2 tog, k5; rep from * ending with k3 instead of k5. Cont in g st for 2 ¼ ins (5.2 cm) (or length required), then cast off.

TO MAKE UP
Fold work in half and join foot seam, the shaped toe edges and instep. Thread ribbon through ribbonholes and tie at front.

◆
Lady's hat

(See photograph page 314.)

MATERIALS
3 balls of Villawool Machinewash 12 ply; a pair of Nos. 5 and 9 needles.

MEASUREMENT
To fit an average size head.

TENSION
9 sts to 2 ins (5.1 cm) on No. 6 needles.

ABBREVIATIONS
See page 15.

METHOD
With No. 9 needles cast on 100 sts. Change to No. 5 needles and patt:

* 1st row: (P1, k2) to last st, p1.

2nd row: (K1, yfwd, k2, pass st formed by yfwd over the k2, k2) to end.

Rep above 2 rows 3 times more. *

Change to No. 9 needles and k 1 row, then p 1 row.

Change back to No. 5 needles. **

Rep from * to ** 3 times, then from * to * once.

Change to No. 9 needles.

Next row: K4, (k2 tog, sl1, k2 tog, psso, k10) 6 times, k2 tog, sl1, k2 tog, psso, k1.

Next row: P.

Change to No. 6 needles and work from * to * noting that 2nd row reps end on k1 not k2. Change to No. 9 needles.

Next row: K1, (k2 tog, k1) to end.

Next row: P.

Next row: (K2 tog) to last st, k1.

Next row: P.

Rep above 2 rows once.

Thread yarn through rem sts; draw up and fasten off.

TO MAKE UP
Join seam. Make a pom-pom and attach to top of hat.

An unusual gift: stuffed fillers to keep the toes of leather shoes smooth, intricately decorated with embroidery. Courtesy Avalon Craft Cottage.

This knitted pull-on hat features a large pom-pom as an accessory. Instructions page 312.

◆

Garter stitch coat hanger

MATERIALS

1 ball of Villawool Tasman 8 ply, a pair of No. 7 needles; coat hanger; foam rubber; ribbon.

ABBREVIATIONS

See page 15.

METHOD

With No. 7 needles cast on 19 sts and work in g st until knitting is long enough to cover coat hanger, then cast off.

TO MAKE UP

Cover coat hanger with foam rubber and secure.

Place knitted piece over the hanger and join edges tog. Cover hook with yarn or ribbon. Trim with a ribbon bow (optional).

◆

Loop stitch coat hanger

MATERIALS

1 ball of Villawool Tasman 8 ply, a pair of No. 8 needles; coat hanger; foam rubber; ribbon.

ABBREVIATIONS

See page 15.

METHOD

With No. 8 needles cast on 14 sts and k 1 row, then cont in loop patt:

1st row: K1, * insert needle into the next st as if to k, wind yarn over the right-hand needle and round the first finger of left hand twice, then over right-hand needle again, draw all 3 loops through st, put 3 loops onto left-hand needle and k tog with st (1 loop st made); rep from * to last st, k1.

2nd row: K.

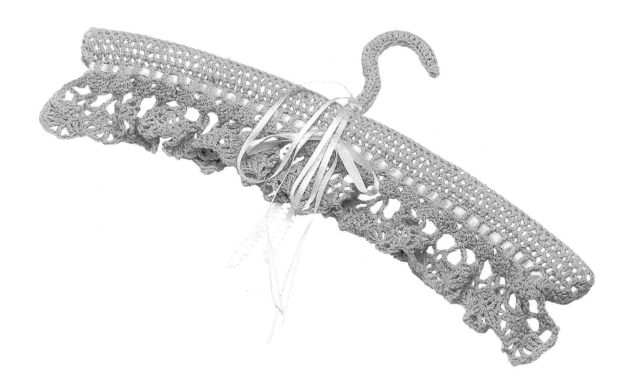

Besides the two knitted coathangers given, you may like to create one in crochet. Courtesy Avalon Craft Cottage.

Rep these 2 rows until work is long enough to cover coat hanger, ending on a loop st row, then cast off.

TO MAKE UP
Cover coat hanger with foam rubber and secure. Place knitted piece over the hanger and join edges tog. Cover hook with yarn or ribbon. Trim with a ribbon bow (optional).

◆

Octopus

MATERIALS
4 balls of Villawool Tasman 12 ply; a pair of No. 2 needles; stuffing; small quantity of red yarn.

MEASUREMENT
Approx 12 ins (30.5 cm) high.

TENSION
7 sts to 2 ins (5.1 cm).

ABBREVIATIONS
See page 15.

METHOD
Using two strands of yarn tog east on 5 sts for base.

1st row: (K and inc in next st, p1) to last st, k and inc (8 sts).

2nd row: P.

3rd row: (K and inc in next st) to end (16 sts).

Work 3 rows.

7th row: As 3rd row (32 sts).

Work 5 rows.

13th row: As 3rd row (64 sts).

Work 11 rows.

25th row: As 3rd row (128 sts).

Work 12 rows.

Next row: (K1, p1) to end.

Next row: (K2 tog) to end (64 sts).

Work 10 rows in st st.

Next row: (K1, p1) to end.

Next row: (K2 tog) to end (32 sts).

Work 4 rows in st st.

Next row: (K1, p1) to end.

Next row: (K2 tog) to end (16 sts).

Work 2 rows in st st, then break yarn, leaving a length. Thread needle to yarn and run through the sts; draw up and fasten off.

TO MAKE UP
Press work on the wrong side. Join seams tog, leaving an opening, then stuff firmly. Sew up opening.

LEGS
Cut 144 strands of yarn 66 ins (167.6 cm) long and divide into 4 groups of 36 strands. Tie end securely about 2 ins (5 cm) from the end, then divide these 36 strands evenly into 3 groups of 12 strands and plait. Tie firmly 2 ins (5 cm) from the end, leaving a tassel 2 ins (5 cm) long. Join each of the 4 legs in middle over each other and firmly attach to base (makes 8 legs). With red yarn embroider eyes, nose and mouth as illustrated. Make a pom-pom approx 5 ins (12.7 cm) in diameter and attach to top.

◆

Scrap-happy tortoise

PATTERN
Enlarge pattern pieces from graphs; one square equals 1½ (4 cm). [Note: ¼ in (1 cm) seams allowed.]

MATERIALS
1½ x 1 yd (150 x 90 cm) wide fabric for base, head, feet, tail and underneath frill. A piece of lining fabric 25 x 21¼ ins (64 x 54 cm) for top lining. Colored scraps of fabric 4 ins (11 cm) square for top cover and top frill. Two small pieces of fabric for eyes and eye centers. Foam filling from two standard size pillows.

TO CUT OUT
Cut one base piece; two heads and eight feet. Also cut three frill pieces 4 ins wide x 47 ins long (11 x 120 cm), and two tail pieces, 8⅜ x 8⅜ x 3½ ins (22 x 22 x 9 cm). Cut one top cover in patchwork and one in lining.

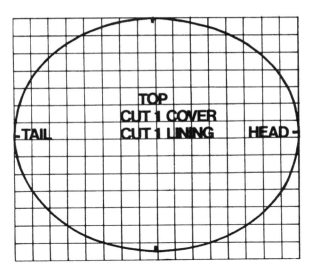

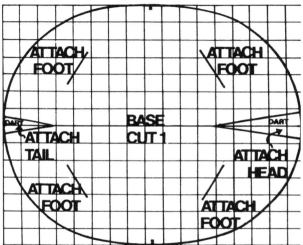

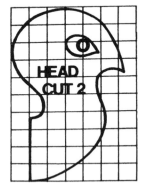

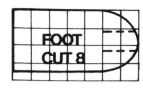

Scrap-happy tortise

Opposite: Stuffed toys may be knitted, crocheted or sewn. This rabbit is made from bought materials and decorated with a ribbon. Courtesy Avalon Craft Cottage.

To make the patchwork

Make a template from cardboard 4 ins (11 cm) square and use as pattern for patchwork squares. Cut out squares, making sure all edges are on straight grain. With right sides together, join patches either lengthways or crossways. Press all seams open.

With right sides together, match seams and stitch down the length or across the width, until you have joined up enough patches for the cover. Press firmly, then cut out. Join patches end on end for frill, to measure approx 4 yds (360 cm).

TO MAKE

Appliqué or stitch eye centers to eyes, then stitch eyes to head pieces where marked on pattern. With right sides together, stitch head pieces, leaving straight edge open. Clip around curves, turn to right side and fill firmly with filling.

Stitch straight edge together. Stitch straight edge of head to base where marked on pattern, then join the dart together. (It may be easier to use a zipper or cording foot.)

Join tail pieces, leaving straight edge open. Fill and stitch. Stitch to base where marked on pattern, then stitch dart together.

With right sides together, stitch around two foot pieces, leaving base open. Clip around curves, turn to right side. Run two rows of stitching down foot where marked by broken lines to form toes. Fill and stitch across base. Make the other three feet, stitch to base where marked.

Join underneath frill together end on end to make one long piece. With right sides together, stitch underneath frill and patchwork frill along one long edge, then join frill seam together. Fold frill in half and press.

Run a row of stitching around raw edge of frill to hold. Then, run two rows of gathering stitch around this edge and ease onto top edge of base piece.

Stitch patchwork to lining, then with right sides together stitch cover to base, leaving a space along one side. Fill firmly, slipstitch opening.

◆

Glove puppets

These puppets are made from face washers. They are delightful Christmas presents and bath time will no longer be an unpleasant chore.

MATERIALS

For one animal: two face washers, approximately 1 x 1 ft (30 x 30 cm); colored scraps of fabric; embroidery cotton and machine thread, plus a cake of soap.

METHOD

Consult the graph on page 320. Enlarge the animal pattern of your choice, remembering that each square equals ¾ in (2 cm). Cut out the main shape, pocket, ears, and the various small shapes in paper.

From the two face washers, cut out two main pieces; one pocket; four ears each for pig and cow; two ears each for dog and cat (the dog's and cat's ears are lined in fabric), leaving a small seam allowance around each piece. Also, cut out four horns for the cow from contrast fabric. Cut out the various small shapes from scraps, as they are, without adding a seam allowance.

Appliqué and embroider the various shapes to one side of the main shape, using the graph as a guide.

With right sides together, stitch around the outside edge of the ears (and horns if making a cow).

Clip around the curves, turn to the right side.

Pin ears (and horns on the cow) to face side of the main piece where marked on the graph. (Pin the ears so that the underside of the ears faces the right side of the main pieces.) Stitch.

Neaten along the top edge of the pocket. Pin the right side of the pocket base to the wrong side of the main piece base and stitch. Fold pocket back and pin in position.

Neaten along the base on the other main piece. With the right sides together, pin, then stitch around the main pieces. Clip around the curves, turn to the right side. Insert soap in pocket.

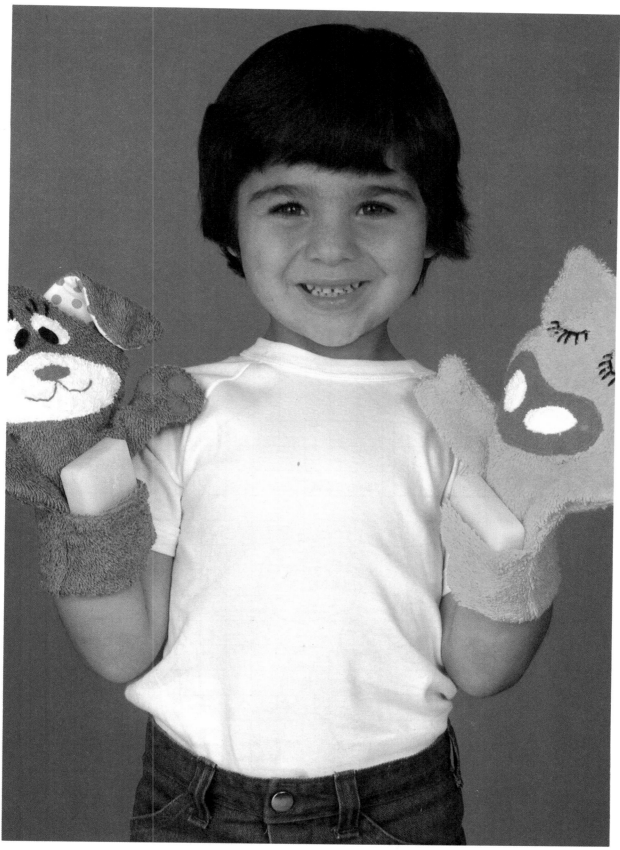

These glove puppets double as face washers and soap holders. Instructions opposite and on page 320.
Courtesy Woman's Day.

To make the pom-pom for the cat's nose.
Cut two small circles about the size of a dime or a 10-cent piece in cardboard. Make a large hole in the middle of each and place together. Wind embroidery thread around the circle until the middle is filled.

Cut carefully around the outside edge and pull the circles a little apart. Tie a thread around the middle between the circles and knot tightly. Remove the cardboard circles.

Glove puppets

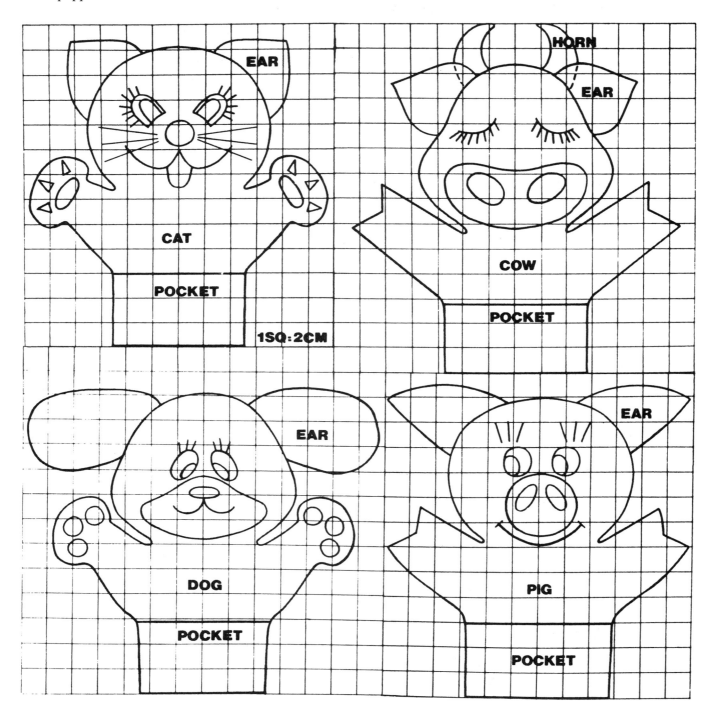

CAT

POCKET

1SQ:2CM

COW

POCKET

HORN

EAR

EAR

DOG

POCKET

EAR

PIG

EAR

POCKET

An idea for a clown. Instructions page 322-4. Courtesy Woman's Day.

◆
Clown

MATERIALS
You will need for the clown ¾ yd (68.5 cm) white sheeting; small pieces of black and pink felt for hands and feet; 1 ball yarn for hair (ours was purple); small quantity red yarn for nose and mouth; 3 buttons; 2 jewels for eyes; 2 yds (1.8 m) narrow ribbon; 1 yd (91.5 cm) wide ribbon; foam rubber crumbs for filling; black embroidery thread.

For jacket, pants and cap: small pieces of taffeta or silk.

See the graph on page 324. There is no pattern for legs and arms. For the legs, cut a piece of sheeting 15 x 4½ ins (38 x 11.4 cm). Mark a line across legs 6 ins (15.2 cm) from bottom (soxs are joined here). Arms are cut 12 x 4½ ins (30.5 x 10.8 cm).

MEASUREMENTS
Overall finished length is approximately 3 feet (91.5 cm).

LEGS
15 ins (38.1 cm) long, 4½ ins (11.4 cm) wide.

ARMS
12 ins (30.5 cm) long, 4½ ins (11.4 cm) wide.

METHOD
Sew shoulder and side seams of body, leaving lower edge and neck open. Turn to right side. Sew piece of taffeta across legs at marked line for socks.

Join legs across top and down side seam, joining in sock pieces, leaving bottom of legs open. Pull through to right side. Insert legs in body. Turn in seam and sew right across body. Fill body through opening at neck, legs from the bottom, with foam rubber filling.

Sew across top and down side seams of arms. Pull through to right side and fill with foam rubber filling. Join arms to body at shoulders. Cut hands (see diagram 1) from pink felt and stitch around, leaving open at wrist. Trim felt close to stitching and sew lines in to indicate fingers. Slightly pad hand and sew to arms.

Cut feet from black felt. Stitch around foot, leaving back of foot open, fill with foam filling and close back opening. Cut opening in top of foot where marked, insert leg and stitch firmly together.

HEAD
Mark on front piece crosses for eyes, and shape of mouth. Sew around head, leaving neck open. Turn to right side and fill head firmly with foam filling. Insert into neckline and sew head to body. For the eyes sew crosses in black stem stitch. Sew jewels to center of crosses.

To make pom-pom for nose, using pattern (see diagram 2), cut a 2 ins (5.1 cm) circle of cardboard. Cut smaller circle from middle. Wind red yarn through this circle until completely covered, then cut around outer edge. Tie a piece of yarn around the middle to make pom-pom and trim to shape.

For the mouth, place three strands of red yarn together and overstitch with red cotton around outline of mouth.

For the hair, unwind ball of yarn into hank about 12 ins (30.5 cm) in length. Use half for the fringe and back. Stitch across forehead (see diagram 3). Place rest of hank across the head and stitch down the middle to form a parting (see diagram 4).

JACKET
Cut back on fold. Join fronts to back at shoulder seams. Sew sleeve into armhole. Join side seams from sleeve to jacket edge in one operation. Turn under small hem on sleeves. Gather sleeve at wrist.

For frill cut piece of taffeta 15 x 6 ins (38 x 15.2 cm). Sew edges on long sides. Run a gathering thread down center and gather into double frill. Turn in small front facings and join frill to neckline.

PANTS
Join middle back and front seams. Join inside leg seam. Turn up small hem across leg edge. Join side seams and turn down small hem around top of pants. Thread elastic through top.

CAP
Join sides of cap from point to head edge. Turn a small hem around head edge. Sew ribbon trim to cap and place small bow on top. Tie ribbon around frill at neckline and tie narrow ribbon at wrists and around top of feet.

A second clown that can be constructed using the same principles as those used for the clown on page 322. Courtesy Avalon Craft Cottage.

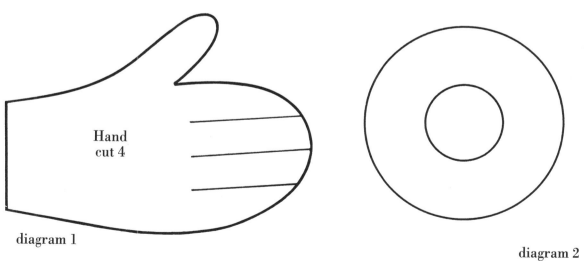

Hand
cut 4

diagram 1

diagram 2

circle for making pom-pom

diagram 3   diagram 4

diagram 5

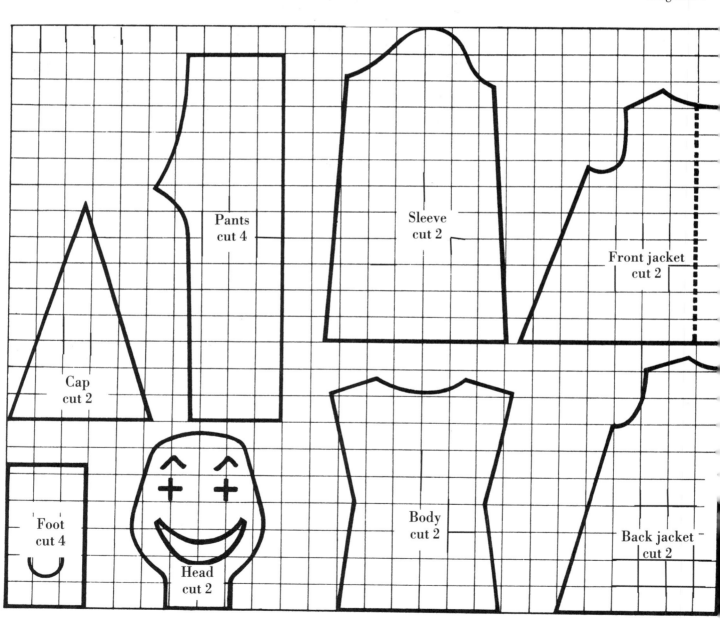

Heirloom dolls embroidered by machine, featuring lace entredeux.

◆

Poodle and rabbit

MATERIALS
1 ball of Villawool Tasman 12 ply; a pair of No. 5 needles; 2 buttons; stuffing; small quantity of black yarn.

MEASUREMENT
Approx 11½ ins (29.2 cm) high.

TENSION
9 sts to 2 ins (5.1 cm) over st st.

ABBREVIATIONS
See page 15.

BODY
Cast on 22 sts and work in st st for 10 rows. Cont in st st and dec 1 st each end of the foll 5th, 11th and 15th rows. Cont on these 16 sts without shaping until work measures 6 ins (15.2 cm), ending on k row. Cast off 6 sts at beg of next 2 rows, then cont on rein 4 sts for tail:

Next row: P to end and cast on 3 sts.

Next row: K7, cast on 3 sts.

Next row: P. Work 2 rows, then dec 1 st each end of next and foll 4th row.

Work 3 rows straight, then cast off.

LEGS
Cast on 7 sts and work in st st for 8 rows, ending p row.

Next row: Inc in each st (14 sts).

Next row: P to last st, inc (15 sts).

Cont in moss st.

Next row: K1, (p1, k1) to end.

Rep above row 23 times, then cast off. Make three more pieces in the same way.

NECK AND HEAD
Cast on 19 sts and work in moss st for 5 rows. Cont in moss st and cast on 4 sts at beg of next 4 rows (35 sts). Work 4 rows straight, then cast off 2 sts at beg of every row until 15 sts rem. Work 4 rows, then cast off.

EARS
Cast on 3 sts and work in moss st, inc 1 st each end of every 3rd row to 7 sts. Cont straight until work measures 2 ins (5.1 cm), then dec 1 st each end of next 2 rows. K3 tog and fasten off.

Make another piece in same way.

TO MAKE UP
Using a backstitch join long seam and wide end of body and stuff. Join tail seam and stuff. Join back seam of body and join tail at the same time. Sew head seams, leaving an opening at neck. Stuff and join to top of wide end of body piece. Join seams of legs, leaving opening at top. Stuff and close opening, then sew to sides of body as illustrated. Cut six lengths of yarn 2 ins (5.1 cm) long. Firmly tie yarn round lengths at middle to secure and join to ears. Make two small pom-poms and attach to head and tail as illustrated. Embroider nose with black yarn. Sew on buttons in position for eyes.

◆

Rabbit

MATERIALS
1 ball of Villawool Tasman 5 ply; a pair of No. 10 needles; stuffing; small quantities of black and blue yarn for features.

MEASUREMENT
Approx 11½ ins (29.2 cm) high.

TENSION
7 sts to 1 in (2.5 cm).

ABBREVIATIONS
See page 15.

METHOD
** *First back leg*
Cast on 14 sts, * k 7 rows.

Next row: K and inc 1 st each end (16 sts). K 7 rows.

Next row: K and inc 1 st each end (18 sts). K 10 rows *. Break yarn. With same needle holding 18 sts cast on 14 sts for second leg and work from * to * (18 sts). Do not break yarn.

Next row: K18 of one section, then k18 of other section (36 sts). Work as follows:

1st and 2nd rows: K.

3rd row: K2 tog, k to last 2 sts, k2 tog.

4th, 5th and 6th rows: K.

Poodle is knitted in a combination of stocking stitch and moss stitch. The ears are trimmed with tassels and the head and tail with pom-poms. Rabbit is knitted in garter stitch. Instructions opposite and on page 328.

7th to 14th rows: As 3rd to 6th rows.

Next row: (K2 tog, k2) to last 2 sts, k2 tog (22 sts).

Next row: As above (16 sts). K 16 rows. Cast off 3 sts at beg of next 2 rows, then cast off 2 sts at beg of next 2 rows. Cast off rem sts **. Make another piece working from ** to **. Join these two pieces tog, leaving neck open. Stuff body and legs.

HEAD
Cast on 12 sts.

1st row: K.

2nd row: Inc, k to end.

3rd and 4th rows: K.

5th row: As 2nd row.

6th row: K to last st, inc.

7th row: K and inc 1 st each end.

8th row: As 6th row.

9th row: As 2nd row.

10th and 11th rows: As 8th and 9th rows.

12th to 18th rows: K.

19th row: K2 tog, k to end.

20th row: K to last 2 sts, k2 tog.

21st to 30th rows: As 19th and 20th rows.

31st row: K2 tog, k to last 2 sts, k2 tog. Cast off. Work another piece in same way. Join seam, leaving neck open. Stuff head.

EARS
Cast on 3 sts and k 1 row.

1st row: K and inc 1 st each end.

2nd, 3rd and 4th rows: K.

Rep 1st to 4th rows to 17 sts, then k 17 rows straight.

Next row: K1, (k2 tog) to end (9 sts). Cast off.

Make three more pieces in same way. Join two pieces tog, leaving an opening at cast-on edges. Join other two pieces tog in the same way. Stitch ears to the head.

TAIL
Cast on 9 sts.

1st row: K.

2nd row: K and inc 1 st each end.

3rd and 4th rows: As 1st and 2nd rows. K 9 rows.

Next row: K2 tog, k to last 2 sts, k2 tog.

Next row: K.

Rep above 2 rows twice more, then cast off.

Make another piece in same way. Join seam, leaving a space for stuffing. Attach tail to body.

Feet

Cast on 11 sts.

1st row: K.

2nd row: K and inc 1 st each end.

3rd and 4th rows: As 1st and 2nd rows. K 12 rows.

Next row: K2 tog, k to last 2 sts, k2 tog.

Next row: K.

Rep above 2 rows once more.

Next row: K2 tog, k to last 2 sts, k2 tog. Cast off.

Make three more pieces in the same way. Join each pair tog, leaving an opening for stuffing. Attach feet to the legs. Mark feet with big sewing stitches in black yarn.

FRONT LEGS
Cast on 24 sts.

1st row: K.

2nd row: Inc, k10, inc in next 2 sts, k10, inc (28 sts). K 7 rows.

Next row: K2 tog, k10, (k2 tog) twice, k10, k2 tog.

Next row: K2 tog, k8, (k2 tog) twice, k8, k2 tog. K 15 rows.

Next row: K and inc 1 st each end. K 1 row.

Next row: K2 tog, k to last 2 sts, k2 tog.

Rep above row twice more. Cast off.

Make another piece in same way. Fold each piece in half lengthwise and join seams, leaving an opening at the top end for stuffing. Sew front legs to shoulders and mark feet with big sewing stitches in black yarn. Mark nose, eyes and mouth with black yarn, then fill the eyes with blue yarn.

Crochet is a very flexible technique to use when making inventive gifts for children. This crocheted bag opens out to reveal a teddy surrounded by a soft wool cocoon. Courtesy Avalon Craft Cottage.

◆
Frog family

MATERIALS
Colored scraps of fabric, buttons for eyes, coarse sand filling.

INSTRUCTIONS
Enlarge pattern from the graph, making the pattern as large or as small as you wish. To make several frogs of different sizes, use the following measurements: 1 square = 1⅛ in (3 cm) for small frogs, 1 square = 1½ in (4 cm) for medium-sized frogs, 1 square = 2 ins (5 cm) for large frogs.

TO SEW
Take two pieces of fabric and pin, so that right sides are together. Trace shape onto wrong side on one piece of fabric. Use a small stitch and stitch around shape, leaving a space between notches for turning through.

Stitch one or two stitches across the base of each finger, as this makes the fingers more noticeable when filled with sand. Trim around shape, leaving a small seam allowance. Clip around all curves. Turn frog to right side.

Fill with sand using a small cone made out of paper as a funnel. Do not fill to full, or the frog will not be pliable. Oversew the opening. Stitch buttons to eyes where marked on graph. (For a very small child use small pieces of felt instead of buttons.)

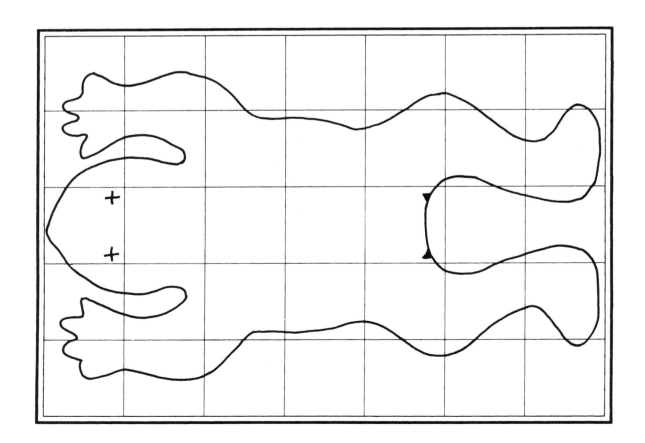

Besides the bee and flower mobile illustrated in the diagram, you may like to sew this easy butterfly mobile to stretch across a cot or pram. Courtesy Avalon Craft Cottage.

◆

Bee and flower mobile

MATERIALS

31 ins (80 cm) of 17½ in (45 cm) wide black felt, 24 ins (60 cm) of 17½ in (45 cm) wide yellow felt, 31 ins (80 cm) of 17½ in (45 cm) wide orange felt, 8 ins (20 cm) of 35½ in (90 cm) wide interfacing for wings, filling, black bias binding tape, eight 1 in (2.5 cm) diameter moveable eyes, four 12 in (30 cm) long yellow pipe cleaners, 7 in (18 cm) diameter styrofoam ball, eight 10 in (24 cm) length plastic tubing, eight 10 in (24 cm) lengths cane to be inserted in plastic tubing, 9 small wooden beads, 8 small nails, 1 metal ring ¾ in (2 cm) in diameter, strong thread (such as linen thread).

BEE (MAKE 4)

Make a paper pattern of all pieces in diagram to size.

For each bee, cut 2 bodies from black felt. Cut 2 of each appliqué stripe from yellow felt. Cut 4 wings from interfacing. Sew yellow stripes onto body pieces.

WINGS

Encase edge of wings in bias binding tape leaving wing edge that is attached to body free (indicated by dotted line).

Place 2 body pieces tog, right sides facing the outside. Fold one pipe cleaner in half and insert the fold between two body pieces at middle top of head.

Place 2 wings on either side of bee between 2 bodies; wing positions are indicated by dotted lines on diagram.

Stitch around outside edge leaving a small opening for filling. Stuff lightly with filling and stitch opening closed. Curl pipe cleaners and sew eyes onto face. Make 3 more bees the same as this one.

Top, bottom and middle strip of bee, plus flower middle = yellow appliqué felt.

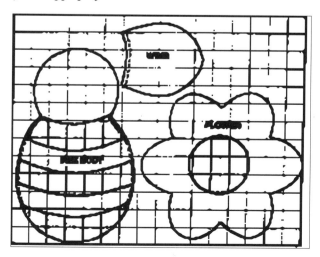

FLOWERS (MAKE 4)

For each flower, cut 2 flowers from orange felt. Cut 2 flower centers from yellow felt.

Sew flower centers onto flowers. Place two flower pieces together and stitch around edge.

ASSEMBLING THE MOBILE

Insert cane in plastic tubing. Insert one end of cane in stryofoam ball, repeat this with the other 7 spokes arranging them evenly around the ball.

Attach a bead onto each end of spokes with a nail. Thread the last bead onto a piece of cord, tie off one end around bead, insert the other end up through middle of bead as a hanging cord.

Attach a piece of thread to each mobile piece and then knot these cords onto ends of spokes arranging them alternatively one flower and one bee around spokes.

Make sure weights balance. Then continue the cords up as hanging threads. Place all hanging threads tog and tie off with an overhand knot above the middle of ball. Then knot these cords onto the metal ring and cut excess cord away.

◆
Pencil case

MATERIALS

Two pieces of fabric 12 ins long x 7 ins wide (30 x 18 cm); 10 in (25 cm) zip; colored pieces of felt and fabric glue.

METHOD

Enlarge diagram from graph, 1 square = ½ in (1.2 cm).

Carefully trace each shape on to paper, then cut out in felt. (Trace the whole of the shoe first, then the small shapes as they will be covering the shoe).

Using fabric glue, glue the various shapes to one piece of fabric. Turn under ½ in (1.2 cm) seam along top edge of both pieces and stitch in zip. Open zip, then turn case to wrong side. Stitch lower sides and along lower edge. Trim seams, turn to right side through zip opening.

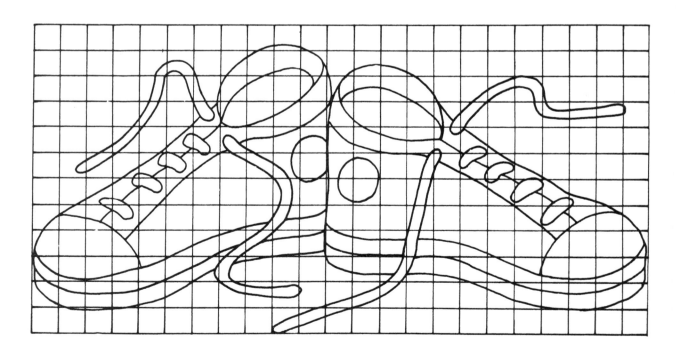

Pencil case design 1 square = ½ in (1.2 cm)

Machine embroidery put to decorative use in practical gifts. © Courtesy Brother Industries.

◆

Tea cosy in fabric and crochet

MATERIALS

12 ins (30 cm) of 35½ in (90 cm) wide fabric, wadding, lining and printed fabric; 1 ball Milford Strutts knitting cotton; No. 8 (2.00 mm) crochet hook.

SIZE

To fit a large teapot.

MOTIF SIZE

8 in (21 cm) diameter.

SEAM ALLOWANCE

A ½ in (1.2 cm) seam allowance has been included on pattern

CUTTING

Make a paper pattern of tea cosy from diagram on page 334 to size. From fabric cut 2 tea cosy pieces. From lining and wadding cut 2 tea cosy pieces omitting hem area (below dotted line). From printed fabric cut 2 frill pieces 29½ in long x 5 in wide (75 x 12 cm). Baste wadding pieces on to the wrong side of tea cosy pieces.

FRILL

Sew short ends of 2 frill pieces tog. Fold frill in half lengthwise, right sides tog and stitch ends tog. Turn through to the right side and press over in half. Gather raw edges up to size of outside edge of tea cosy leaving hem area free. Baste frill around curved edge of one tea cosy piece.

Place 2 tea cosy pieces tog, right sides tog and stitch around outside edge.

Turn through to the right side and press. Then press ¼ in (6 mm) to the wrong side on lower edge, and also press back seam allowance to the wrong side.

LINING

Sew 2 lining pieces tog, right sides tog, around curved edge. Insert lining in tea cosy, sew hem allowance of tea cosy over lining. Make crochet motif and stitch on to tea cosy.

CROCHET MOTIF

Using cotton yarn and No. 8 (2.00 mm) hook make 7 ch and join with a sl st to first ch to form a ring.

1st round: 2 ch (equivalent to 1 dc), 15 dc into ring, join with a sl st to 2nd ch at beg.

2nd round: 3 ch (equivalent to 1 tr), * 3 ch, miss 1 dc, 1 rt in next dc, rep from * 6 times, 3 ch, join with a sl st to 3rd ch at beg.

3rd round: 2 ch, * 1 dc, 1 htr, 5 tr, 1 htr, 1 dc in next 3 ch sp; rep from * around omitting last dc in last rep, join with a sl st to 2nd ch.

4th round: 1 ch, * 6 ch, 1 dc in sp between next 2 dc, rep from around, omitting dc in last rep, join with a sl st to 1st ch.

5th round: 2 ch (1 htr, 6 tr, 1 htr, 1 dc) in next 6 ch loop, * (1 dc, 1 htr, 6 tr, 1 htr, 1 dc) in next 6 ch loop, rep from * around, join with a sl st to 2nd ch.

6th round: Sl st across to 2nd tr of next group, 1 dc in 2nd tr, 5 ch, 1 dc in 5th tr of group, * 5 ch, 1 dc in 2nd tr of next group, 5 ch, 1 dc in 5th tr of same group, rep from * around ending with 2 ch, 1 dtr into first dc.

7th round: 3 ch, 2 tr over dtr, * 3 ch, miss next 5 ch loop, (3 tr, 2 ch, 3 tr) in next 5 ch loop; rep from * around ending with 3 ch, miss next 5 ch loop, (3 tr, 2 ch) in next loop, join with a sl st to 3rd ch at beg.

8th round: 8 ch, * (1 trip tr, 1 ch) 7 times, 1 trip tr in next 2 ch sp, 3 ch; rep from * around omitting last trip tr of last rep, join with a sl st to 5th ch at beg.

9th round: 5 ch, * (1 dc in next ch sp, 5 ch) 6 times, 1 dc in next ch sp, 4 ch; rep from * around omitting last 4 ch of last rep, join with a sl st to first ch.

10th round: Sl st across next 4 ch and up to the 3rd ch of next 5 ch group, 1 dc in same 5 ch loop, * (5 ch, 1 dc in next 5 ch loop) 5 times, 3 ch, 1 dc in next 5 ch loop, rep from * around omitting last dc, join with sl st to first dc.

11th round: Sl st across next 3 ch, 1 dc in same 5 ch loop, * (5 ch, 1 dc in next 5 ch loop) 4 times, 8 ch, 1 dc in next 5 ch loop, rep from * around omitting last dc join with a sl st to first dc.

12th round: Sl st across next 3 ch, 1 dc in same 5 ch loop, * (5 ch, 1 dc in next 5 ch loop) 3 times, 3 ch, (2 tr, 3 ch, 2 tr) in 3 ch loop, 3 ch, * 1 dc in next 5 ch loop, rep from around omitting last dc, join with a sl st to first dc.

13th round: Sl st across next 3 ch, 1 dc in same 5 ch loop, * (5 ch, 1 dc in next 5 ch loop) twice, 1 ch, miss 3 ch and 2 tr, (2 tr, 3 ch, 2 tr, 3 ch, 2 tr) in next 3 ch sp, 4 ch, 1 dc in next 5 ch loop, rep from * around omitting last dc, join with a sl st to first dc.

14th round: Sl st across next 3 ch, 1 dc in same 5 ch loop, * 5 ch, 1 dc, in next 5 ch loop, 6 ch, (2 tr, 3 ch, 2 tr) in next 3 ch sp, 3 ch, (2 tr, 3 ch, 2 tr) in next 3 ch sp, 6 ch, 1 dc in next 5 ch loop, rep from * around omitting last dc, join with a sl st to first dc.

15th round: Sl st across next 3 ch, 1 dc in same 5 ch loop, * 8 ch, (2 tr, 3 ch, 2 tr) in next 3 ch sp, (3 tr, 3 ch, 3 tr) in next 3 ch sp, (2 tr, 3 ch, 2 tr) in next 3 ch sp, 8 ch, 1 dc in next 5 ch loop, rep from * around omitting last dc of last rep, join with a sl st to first dc. End off yarn and darn back ends.

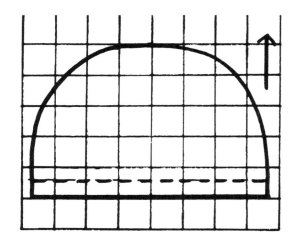

Pattern for fabric.

Opposite: These Christmas tree decorations are made from pieces of old American quilts.

◆
Two-color knitted tea cosy

MATERIALS
Three 50 g balls in one color (M) and one 50 g ball Patons Totem yarn in contrasting color; 1 pair 4.00 mm knitting needles.

TENSION
12 sts to 2 in (5 cm) in width measure over Fair Isle fabric.

SIZE
To fit an average size teapot.

METHOD
Fair Isle piece
Using M, cast on 58 sts.

1st row: K6 M, * k4 C1, k4 M, rep from * to last 2 sts k2 M.

2nd row: P6 M, * p4 C1, p 4 M, rep from * to last 2 sts p2 C1.

Rep above 2 rows once.

5th row: K6 C1, * k4 M, p4 C1, rep from * to last 2 sts k2 C1.

6th row: P6 C1, * p4 M, p4 C1, rep from * to last 2 sts p2 C1.

Rep above 2 rows once.

Repeat the above 8 rows until work measures 14½ ins (37 cm) from beg ending on either a 4th or 8th row of pattern.

Cast off in M.

LINING PIECE
Using M, cast on 52 sts. Knit in g st until piece measures the same length as Fair Isle piece. Cast off.

METHOD
Using a flat seam join lining to Fair Isle piece. Fold in half and sew up side seams for 1 in (2.5 cm). Fold back side edges to show g st lining and secure in place by stitching down.

Make a twisted cord from yarn left over 27½ in (70 cm) long. Thread through top and tie off in a bow.

◆
Three-color tea cosy

MATERIALS
Two 50 g balls Villawool Machinewash 12 ply in each of the following colors or whichever colors you desire; dark blue (M); light blue (C1); red (C2); and white (C3). One pair 4.50 mm knitting needles; 29½ (75 cm) of 1½ in (4 cm) wide gathered lace; two 29½ in (75 cm) lengths red cord; 12 in of 35½ in (30 cm of 90 cm) wide wadding and lining.

TENSION
10 sts to 2 ins (5 cm) in width measured over g st.

SIZE
To fit a large teapot.

COLOR ORDER
The striped color order used throughout is as follows:

* 8 rows M, 2 rows C3, 8 rows C1, 2 rows C3, 8 rows C2, 2 rows C3 and is rep from * throughout.

Using M cast on 30 sts.

1st row: K.

2nd row: Cast on 3 sts and k to end.

Rep 1st and 2nd rows once.

3rd row: K.

4th row: Cast on 2 sts and k to end.

Rep 3rd and 4th row 3 times.

Next row: K.

Next row: Cast on 1 st and knit to end. Rep last 2 rows 5 times.

Cont on these sts until work measures approx 11 ins (28 cm) from cast on sts and 2 rows have been completed of the 8 in a stripe.

Next row: K.

Next row: Cast off 1 st and knit to end. Rep last 2 rows 5 times.

Next row: K.

Opposite: This Christmas angel stands out against a richly embroidered background. You can dress angels like this in light fabric instead of paper.

Next row: Cast off 2 sts and k to end.

Rep the last 2 rows 3 times.

Next row: K.

Next row: Cast off 3 sts and k to end.

Rep last 2 rows once. Cast off.

Make another piece to correspond with the completed piece in following color order:

* 8 rows M, 2 rows C1, 8 rows C2, 2 rows C3, 8 rows C1, 2 rows C3, Rep from * throughout.

TO MAKE UP

Cut out 2 lining and 2 wadding pieces the same shape as knitted piece less 2 ins (5 cm) on the lower hem edge. Place lining pieces tog, right side tog with one wadding piece on either side of lining and stitch tog through all thicknesses around curved side and top edge.

Place 2 knitted pieces tog, right sides tog with lace between each around side and top edges [leaving 2 ins (5 cm) on lower side edges free from lace for hem]. Stitch tog.

Turn through to the right side. Insert lining piece in tea cosy.

Turn 2 ins (5 cm) of knitting to the wrong side on lower edge over lining as hem and stitch in place.

Sew cord around side and top edge of cosy.

◆

Trapunto cushion

Trapunto work, used to make raised designs on cushions, brings a new dimension in making decorative pieces for the home.

MATERIALS

You will need a length of satin fabric for the size of the cushion you wish to make, the one we made was 14 ins (35.5 cm) square; an equal length of silk organza; a small quantity of absorbent cotton or synthetic filling for the padding.

METHOD

Step 1: Cut the cover to the size required then cut the organza to fit.

Step 2: Trace the flower motif centerpiece on to the

middle of one layer of organza. You may choose a rose, a daisy or some other simple flower. Mark the petals round the middle and place this traced piece over the middle of one side of the cover.

Step 3: Using a straight machine stitch, sew round the outside of the middle of the flower, leaving a 2 ins (5 cm) opening at one side. Insert a thin layer of padding through the opening, evening it out as you do so. Stitch this opening. Fill in the middle with machine stitching to hold the padding.

Step 4: Next stitch along each side of the petals following the traced outline.

Step 5: Leave an opening at the top of each petal, pad the petals and stitch up the opening. Tack a piece of tissue paper or greaseproof paper to the back of the work to prevent stretching during stitching.

Step 6: Attach one of the fancy stitch discs to your machine and work round each petal over the original stitching. If you do not have a machine that does fancy stitches, work chain stitch or other embroidery stitches over the outer line of machining for a good finish.

Step 7: Tear the paper away from the back of the work and make up the cushion in the usual way.

◆

Library bag

MATERIALS
20 x 35½ in (50 x 90 cm) wide fabric; patterned fabric for appliqué; felt; iron-on Vilene and contrast thread.

Cut bag 14¼ x 35½ ins (36 x 90 cm). Cut ties 3 x 35½ ins (7 x 90 cm).

Important

½ in (1.5 cm) seams allowed on bag and ties. 1 in (2.5 cm) hem allowed on top edge. Enlarge diagram from graph. For the large elephant, 1 square = ½ in (1.5 cm). For the small elephant 1 square = ¼ in (1 cm). Carefully trace each body and ear shape onto paper.

METHOD
For the appliqué pieces reverse, then trace the shapes to the non-adhesive side of the Vilene. Cut out each piece carefully. Iron Vilene to wrong side of appliqué fabric, then trim fabric back to Vilene. Pin, then appliqué by machine, using a fine, wide zig-zag stitch, to one side of bag. Cut eyes from felt and glue in position. Make a machine buttonhole 1¼ in (3 cm) down from top edge on each side of bag. Fold bag in half so that right sides are together and stitch down each side. Turn to right side. Turn under and stitch hem around top edge. Join tie pieces together. Fold tie in half and stitch along length leaving an opening in the center. Trim seams, turn to right side and press, sew opening. Insert tie in top edge of bag, knot ends.

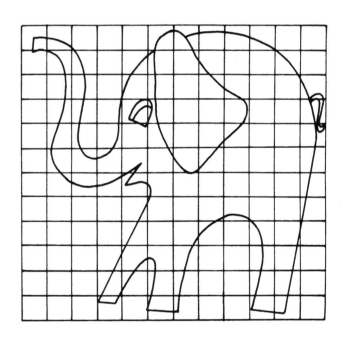

Pattern for library bag.

Opposite: Trapunto cushion

◆

Christmas stockings

MATERIALS (for two stockings)

Anchor Stranded Cotton: 1 skein each, scarlet (046); grass green (0245); parrot green (0256); gorse yellow (0304); oak brown (0355 and 0357); and black (0403). Use three strands throughout. A 16 x 8 in (40 x 20 cm) piece white blockweave fabric, 11 blocks to 1 in (2.5 cm); a 16 x 8 in (40 x 20 cm) piece of green felt, a 16 x 8 in (40 x 20 cm) piece of red felt; Coats bias binding to match green and red felt. Milward international range tapestry needle no. 24.

METHOD

Each stocking is worked and made up in the same way. Cut a piece from white fabric 8 x 5 ins (20 x 12 cm) and mark the middle block lengthwise and widthwise with a line of basting stitches. The diagram gives the complete design. The middle is indicated by arrows which should coincide with the basting stitches. Each background square on the diagram represents one block of fabric or one cross stitch.

The design is worked throughout in cross stitch and straight stitch, and it is important that the upper half of all crosses lie in the same direction throughout. With one long side of fabric facing, commence the design in the center and work embroidery following the diagram and the key to the diagram. On completion of the embroidery, press on the wrong side.

Trim fabric to within 4 blocks of embroidery on upper and side edges, and 6 blocks on lower edge. Cut a piece the same size from remaining white fabric for back. To make up stocking, make a paper pattern of shape using cutting layout. Fold felt in half, place pattern in the middle, and cut out shapes. Place lower edge of embroidered fabric to upper edge of one stocking shape, right sides together, raw edges even. Baste and stitch ¼ in (1 cm) from the edge. Press seam downwards. Bind upper edge of white fabric with contrast bias binding. Make up the back of stocking the same way. Place back and front wrong sides together, raw edges even, and bind outer edge of stocking.

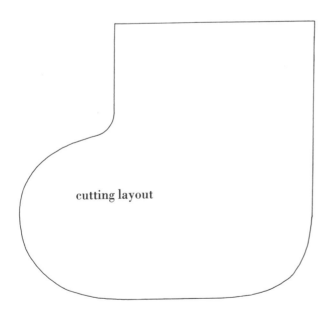

cutting layout

Key to diagram (opposite, top)

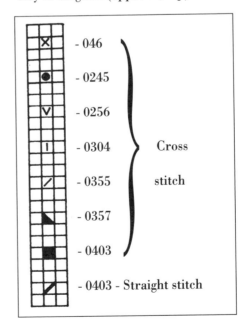

- 046
- 0245
- 0256
- 0304
- 0355
- 0357
- 0403

} Cross stitch

- 0403 - Straight stitch

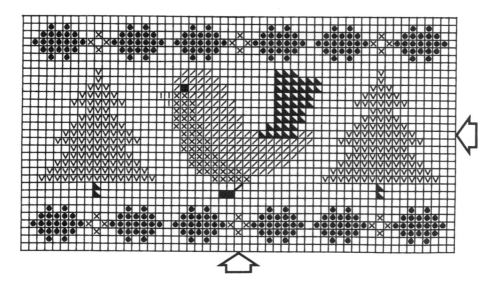

Cross-stitched Christmas stockings. Instructions on opposite page. Courtesy Coats Patons.

◆
Embroidered hot water bottle cover

MATERIALS

Anchor Stranded cotton: 1 skein each white (01), geranium (06), carnation (027), rose pink (050), nasturtium (0328), snuff brown (0374) and peat brown (0381). Use 4 strands for headboard and legs of bed, 3 strands for rest of embroidery. Cream fine weight embroidery fabric, sufficient to cover bottle. Sufficient Domette or other warm fabric for lining. Milward international range crewel needles nos. 7 and 6 for three and four strands, respectively.

METHOD

Cut a rectangle from embroidery fabric large enough to cover front of bottle, and allowing 1⅛ in (3 cm) extra on all sides. The combined full size drawing and diagram gives the complete design. With one short side of fabric facing, trace the outlines of the design (omitting arrows and numbers) in the desired position. Work embroidery following diagram and key to diagram. All parts similar to numbered parts are worked in the same color and stitch. To make up, make a paper pattern of hot water bottle, place to embroidery and cut out, allowing an extra ½ (1.5 cm) on all sides. Cut one piece from remaining embroidery fabric and 2 pieces the same shape from the lining fabric. Place wrong side of each piece of lining to wrong side of each piece of embroidery fabric, and baste in position. Bind round the edge of both pieces. Place back and front wrong sides together, and commencing 3 ins (7 cm) down from the shoulders, stitch the side seams and lower edge following the line of the binding. Make a tie from remaining bias binding, fold in half and attach to one side at neck of cover.

Key to diagram

No.	Cotton color	Stitch
1.	06	Satin stitch
2.	027	
3.	050	
4.	0328	
5.	0374	
6.	01	
7.	06	Stem stitch
8.	050	
9.	0374	French knots
10.	0381	
11.	0381	Backstitch

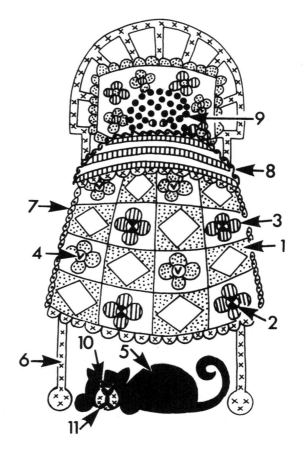

A pretty embroidered hot water bottle cover. Instructions opposite. Courtesy Coats Patons.

◆
Dog coat

MATERIALS
3 balls of Villawool Machinewash 8 ply, and 1 ball each of four contrasting colors for collar; a pair of Nos. 8 and 9 needles.

MEASUREMENT
Length, approx 14½ ins (37 cm).

TENSION
23 sts to 4 ins (10 cm).

ABBREVIATIONS
See page 15.

MAIN PART
With No. 8 needles cast on 55 sts and work in k1, p1 rib for 6 rows.

Next row: K.

Next row: K3, p to last 3 sts, k3.

Rep above 2 rows until work measures 2½ ins (6.4 cm), ending on p row. Cont in st st without the k3 border each end, cast on 7 sts at beg of next 2 rows (69 sts). Cont in st st for 10 rows.

Next row: K16, inc in next st, k34, inc in next st, k17. Work 13 rows.

Next row: K16, inc in next st, k36, inc in next st, k17. Work 13 rows.

Next row: K16, inc in next st, k38, inc in next st, k17. Work 13 rows.

Next row: Inc in first st, k15, inc in next st, k40, inc in next st, k15, inc in next st, k1 (79 sts). Work 7 rows.

Next row: K11, turn.

Work 20 rows on these 11 sts. Break yarn. Join yarn to sts on left-hand needle.

Next row: K57, turn.

Work 20 rows on these 57 sts. Break yarn. Join yarn to rem sts on left-hand needle and work 21 rows on these rem sts.

Next row: P across all sts. Work 5 rows.

Shape shoulders. 1st row: K21, sl1, k2 tog, psso, k to end.

2nd row: P21, sl1, p2 tog tbl, psso, p to end.

3rd row: K20, sl1, k2 tog, psso, k to end.

4th row: P20, sl1, p2 tog tbl, psso, p to end.

5th row: K19, sl1, k2 tog, psso, k to end.

6th row: P19, sl1, p2 tog tbl, psso, p to end.

7th row: K18, sl1, k2 tog, psso, k to end.

8th row: P18, sl1, p2 tog tbl, psso, p to end.

9th row: K17, sl1, k2 tog, psso, k to end.

10th row: P17, sl1, p2 tog tbl, psso, p to end.

Work 9 rows.

LOOPED COLLAR
Join in 3 contrasting colors and work a loop stitch row alternating the colors: k1, * insert needle into the next st as if to k, wind yarn over the right-hand needle and round the first finger of left hand twice, then over right-hand needle again, draw all 3 loops through st, put 3 loops on to lefthand needle and k tog with st (1 loop st made); rep from * to last st, k1.

K 1 row in main color.

With 4th contrasting color, work a loop stitch row.

K 1 row in main color.

With 3 contrasting colors, work a loop stitch row.

K 1 row in main color, then cast off.

UNDERBODY
With No. 9 needles cast on 30 sts and work in k1, p1 rib, dec 1 st each end of 10th row, then every foll 8th row until 10 sts rem. Cont straight until ribbing measures length of main part, excluding 2½ ins (6.4 cm) at beg. Cast off ribwise.

TO MAKE UP
Press main part on the wrong side. Attach underbody to main part, excluding the 2½ ins (6.4 cm) at beg.

This hot water bottle cover is embroidered with a delicate rose pattern. Courtesy Avalon Craft Cottage.

Soft Furnishings

FABRICS

One of the most exciting departments in any store for the homemaker is the fabric section. Here the wide variety of natural and man-made fibres, weaves, textures, special finishes, patterns, and colors is almost endless. There is something for every type of home, for every room in it and for every use.

These fabrics can be sewn on your sewing machine without any problems. Look for pre-shrunk fabrics with guaranteed color fastness so that your covers will look well all their working lives. Stretch covers are the newest fabrics on the market and are ideal for slipcovers where a close fit is needed. Vinyls may be used for covers, especially for outdoor furniture or for chunky cushions in children's rooms.

Fabrics used for decorating in homes with growing youngsters should be firm and sturdy to stand up to lots of hard wear and sometimes rough usage. Practically any washing fabric can be used for decorating rooms for children. Strong denims, cottons, sailcloths, ginghams, corduroy, mattress tickings, and burlaps are all effective when used in children's rooms. They will stand a lot of washing. Many of the drip-dry finishes need little or no ironing. Some of the newest fabrics have a permanent water and stain repellent finish that saves many a dry cleaning bill or permanent stain.

When decorating girls' rooms other materials can be added to the list: polished cottons, chintz, dress fabrics, such as crisp, fadeless cottons, and ginghams.

There are also crisp sheers, organdies and nylons—plain, flocked and embroidered. These fabrics are best washed by hand and hung out to dry almost dripping wet. Silks and other luxurious furnishing fabrics belong in homes where there are no small children.

When choosing fabrics with any kind of design, especially a large one, it may be necessary to buy extra yardage to make it possible to center the large design in slipcovers and curtains. How frequently the design is repeated and whether or not a design has a one-way direction are also matters to be considered when buying patterned fabrics. Plain fabrics and those with an all-over design are the easiest for beginners to use, as there is no problem of matching. Small designs can often be used with plain fabric in matching colors for an interesting striped effect.

While most of today's fabrics for home decorating can be washed or cleaned, not all are guaranteed against fading. So wherever possible, choose sunfast fabrics, especially in rooms that receive a lot of sun. Look among the dress fabrics for guaranteed fadeless fabrics for curtains, cloths and bedcovers. The 36 in (90 cm) width can be used very successfully for any of these. For furniture exposed to sun choose fabrics in pale tones, yellows, ivories, golds, sand tones, and whites—the fading of these colors will be barely noticeable.

EQUIPMENT

In sewing for your home do not forget that you are contributing your own time and effort. These are valuable and deserving of the best assistance in the way of equipment and supplies. The modern sewing machine is a boon to the home sewer with its variety of attachments that make the tedious jobs easier. Choose one that has a piping foot attachment—it will save hours of work. Embroidery attachments make it possible to give a professional look to tablecloths and place mats. Try to have clear working space to the left when working with your machine.

You will also need good sharp scissors, a handy size is 7–8 in (18–20 cm) from tip to handle, with handles large enough for the fingers to fit through comfortably. A tape measure, plastic coated and marked on both sides, preferably with one side metric, is a help. Tailor's chalk and a soft 2B pencil for marking fabrics. Steel dressmakers' pins will save marks on fabrics. Medium and heavy duty sewing needles will take care of different weight fabrics. Use a heavy needle with heavy duty thread. Use heavy duty mercerized thread for slipcovers and curtains, and the regular dressmaking weight for cotton sheer curtains. Sew synthetics with a fine needle and super sheen thread, and always cut the

Beautifully matched fabrics have been used to make these pinch pleated curtains and balloon blind.

selvages off before sewing, to prevent puckering. All sewing threads come in a wide range of colors, so matching thread to fabric presents no problem.

Keep an iron and ironing board beside you and press as you sew. Use a long table to cut fabrics; a card table close to your sewing machine will support the heavy weight of slipcovers and long draperies as you work on them.

When you shop for furnishing fabrics, take the exact measurements of the window, sofa, bed, or chair with you. Check with the salesperson that you have allowed enough for turnings, fullness in the case of sheers, pattern repeats if the fabric is printed. Buy only the type of fabric that is suitable for the job to be done. It pays to buy fabrics that are guaranteed washable, colorfast, and reasonably shrinkproof. A good brand name and a trained fabric salesperson are your best guides.

Whenever you can, buy the most economical width of fabric for your purpose. Some sheers are made in widths to 120 in (305 cm) which saves seaming if a large window is to be covered. Choose linings that are the same widths as the fabrics for more economical cutting. Do not be afraid to use new fabrics; learn how to handle them.

For nylon or Terylene nets use nylon or Terylene thread and stitch seams over tissue paper, pulling it away later.

For plastic curtains for bathrooms use talcum powder on the machine plate and use a fairly long stitch.

For vinyls use linen or Terylene thread and a large stitch. A mixture of equal parts of glycerine and water rubbed along the seams will prevent your machine sticking to the vinyl.

For fiberglass fabric use a mercerized thread, a long stitch, a loose tension on top-to-bottom threads and very light pressure on the pressure foot.

Pre-shrink all piping cord before making it up, unless guaranteed pre-shrunk.

Before cutting fabric find the true cross-grain of your fabric. Firm plain weaves can be torn. Heavy linens, textured and novelty weaves do not tear easily—pull a thread cross-wise and cut along this line.

Square up all fabrics by pulling from the corners on the bias, press straight with an iron.

HOW TO SEW FURNISHING FABRICS

Today furnishing fabrics vary in weight so it is important to use the right needle, the right sewing thread and the right length of stitch. They can be sewn successfully on a home sewing machine, so here is a general guide:

Fabric	Thread	Machine needle size	Stitches per inch (cm)
Net, lace, organdie, voile, fine cotton, gingham, lawn	No. 60 cotton or mercerized thread	11–14 depending on weight of fabric	16–14 according to fineness of fabric
Man-made fibres: nylon, Terylene, polyesters, sheers, etc.	Nylon or Terylene threads	11 (sew over tissue paper and pull away later)	12–15 according to fineness of fabric
Cotton, linen, rayon, chintz, fine cord, velvet, textured cottons, etc.	No. 40 cotton or mercerized thread	16	14
Heavy linen, burlap, tweed, brocade, velour, moquette, denim	No. 24 cotton or mercerized thread	18	12–14

An inventive mother fitted these homemade curtains so that they could be gathered in like the sail on a yacht, to complete the nautical character of her son's bedroom. Courtesy Colourwall Curtains.

◆

To adjust your machine

In your sewing machine manual you will find instructions for adjusting your machine to the right tension, the right pressure on the pressure foot and a balanced stitch. These adjustments vary with different fabrics, so test on scraps of the fabrics before you start. The wrong tension causes puckered seams and weak stitching. Light tension is needed on synthetics and blended fabrics. Too much pressure on pressure foot makes the top layer of fabric ripple as you stitch; too little makes such a loose seam that stitches will show when the seam is pressed open.

A well-balanced stitch will look the same on both sides. If you are using mercerized thread, test your stitching by folding a square of fabric in half diagonally, make a row of stitching ½ in (1.3 cm) in from and parallel to this fold. Grasp the stitching with your thumb and forefinger of each hand about 2 in (5 cm) apart and pull with a snap to make the threads break. If both threads break you have a balanced stitch and the right tension adjustment. If the top thread only breaks, loosen the upper tension; if only the bottom thread breaks, loosen the bobbin tension.

◆

For good stitching

Keep your machine clean and oiled. It is important to maintain a steady, even pace when stitching; if it is done in spurts your stitching will be uneven. Use a metal thimble for handsewing, find one that fits your middle finger comfortably, firmly and snugly. If it tends to slip off, moisten the end of your finger so suction will help to hold the thimble in place.

◆

Press hems and seams well

The best iron is a combination steam-and-dry. Those irons that give steam at low settings are useful for blends and synthetic fabrics. When working on curtains and other large articles a small table beside your ironing board will help to hold them.

AIDS FOR MAKING HOME FURNISHINGS

Tapes, cords, hooks, tie-backs, and decorative metal finishes for poles and rods are readily available from the home furnishing section of department stores.

There are pleater tapes with uniformly spaced pockets for use with four-pronged drapery hooks. The tape is sewn to the top of the curtains. This tape is firm enough to serve as a heading. Insert the hooks to form the pleats. The tape not only saves hours of measuring and stitching in making the curtains, but makes washing and ironing easy, since the hooks are simply pulled out and the curtains laundered as flat pieces of fabric. Tapes are usually 3 and 4 in (7.5 and 10 cm) wide.

Buckram, a type of stiff net, is used for headings on curtains and for making pelmets. It may be used instead of pleater tapes when you want to sew pleats down on silk curtains that will be dry-cleaned.

Piping cords for use on slipcovers, bedspreads, and cushions come in different weights. They need to be covered with a bias cut strip of the fabric being used. They are sewn into the seams to give a professional finish.

Tapes with cords already inserted and slots for curtain rings are also available for making shirred headings on sheer curtains. They are particularly useful in making Roman and Austrian shades. Cords for drawing up blinds are available by the yard.

Weights for curtains and draperies may be bought individually. They are meant to be covered with fabric and sewn to the bottoms of the side seams to make curtains hang well. For lighter fabrics, a chain type of weight, sold by the yard, is laid in the bottom hem of the curtain.

Decorative fringes and tapes for trims come in a wide variety of designs, styles, colors, and widths.

HOW TO MAKE CURTAINS

The basic shape of windows can be transformed by skilful curtain treatments. Curtains can make small rooms look larger, reduce a ceiling's height or unify a varied size collection of windows.

Choice of fabric will depend on the amount of shade and privacy needed; on whether the room's decoration scheme is to stem from the curtain pattern or to contrast with fabrics already in the room. Some fabrics are better for informal rooms, others lend themselves to tailored effects, still others make a room look bright and airy.

◆

Measuring up

(see diagram 1)

To calculate the basic amount of fabric needed, measure the width of the window (diagram 1, A). The measurement should cover the width of the glass, plus as much overlap at sides and middle as required.

The total curtain width, whether it is made up of two or more curtains, should be at least one and a half times the total measurement of the window width, plus overlaps.

A repeat design on a patterned fabric must hang at the same level right across the curtains. Before buying your fabric check the length of the repeat and

Opposite: Accessories and equipment for making soft furnishings.

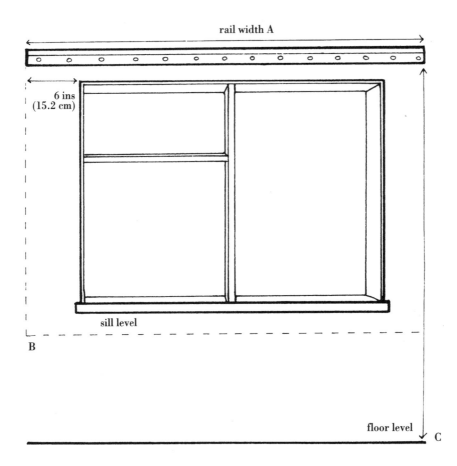

rail width A

6 ins
(15.2 cm)

sill level

B

floor level

C

diagram 1

calculate the extra length needed to allow for wastage in matching the pattern.

It is wise to add 1½ in (3.8 cm) a yard to allow for possible shrinkage in fabrics that are not guaranteed pre-shrunk.

Measure the length: see diagram 1, B, for a sill-length curtain or diagram 1, C, for a floor-length curtain.

Add to this length an allowance for the hem and heading tape (allow about double the width of the tape) plus an allowance for the bottom hem; 3 in (7.8cm) for short curtain, 5 in (13 cm) for long.

To calculate the yardage, divide the width of your fabric into the total curtain width to find the number of widths you need, then multiply this number by the overall length of the curtains.

◆

Preparing fabric

Carefully measure each length of fabric for the curtains with a tape measure, allowing for turnings and pattern matching before cutting.

Mark the top of every length to ensure that the fabric runs in the same direction on each curtain.

Be sure to cut the fabric absolutely straight. When joining widths of fabric match the pattern carefully at the join.

Cut selvages off altogether or clip at intervals right through them to prevent any drag.

Finish off raw edges neatly and press all seams.

Use French seams on fabrics tending to fray. On

This homemade curtain is tied back with a purchased cord and tassel. Courtesy Colourwall Curtains.

heavier fabrics flat seams with raw edges trimmed with pinking shears will suffice (see diagram 2a).

If using pullup tape be sure to leave ends of cord free.

Measure length of curtain, turn up hem and tack. Hang curtains at the windows for a few days before finally adjusting the length and stitching the hem.

PELMETS

These are used to hide the curtain rail when curtains are open. If you plan to have pleated or frilled pelmets at the top of the curtain measure the pelmet or valance rail including the two returns; these are the sections of rail which bend back at each end and join the wall.

For box pleating multiply 2½ times the length of the rail by 12 in (30.5 cm); this gives a pelmet or valance 8 in (20 cm) deep with allowance for turnings. Printed and patterned fabrics need an extra ½ yard (45.5 cm) to allow for pattern repeat. For frilling, allow half the width of the rail again and multiply by 12 in (30.5 cm).

LINING

Linings will prevent your curtains fading in strong sunlight. Having calculated your curtain fabric, you will need the same amount of lining fabric, but omit the allowance for pattern matching. Cotton sateen is one of the best fabrics for lining curtains. There is also an insulating material that may be used for lining, which prevents heat entering a room in summer and keeps a room warmer in winter by preventing heat escaping.

Choose lining colors carefully, especially if you plan to use the same color lining on all curtains, so that they look uniform from the outside of the house.

HEADINGS

Curtain tops which are left visible can be very elegant.

Special pleating tapes and hooks are available for making gathered or pleated headings. Stitch the tapes with pockets for hooks to the top of the curtain and use the pleater hooks to make the pinch pleats as desired.

More material must be allowed for the curtain width if it is to be pleated. The fabric allowance should be at least twice the width of the track across the window, and an allowance of 4–6 in (10–15 cm) should be made for each curtain length for the top hem.

VELVET CURTAINS

Be sure the pile runs in the same direction on each curtain length of fabric. For a silkier look and an easier-to-brush one that prevents dust collecting, hang the curtains with the pile down.

Line velvet curtains for preference. If unlined, all hems should be handsewn. Never press velvet flat. Steam all hems and turnings carefully by passing the iron lightly across the fabric without pressure.

NET AND SHEER

Sheer curtains never look attractive when skimped. Allow three times the width of the window when calculating fabric requirements. Make all seams as narrow as possible and turn narrow hems.

Use a fine needle and Terylene thread on man-made fibres.

Use lightweight tapes for the headings. It is more satisfactory to buy a ready-made frilling than to make it yourself.

◆
What you need to know to make curtains

CUTTING
Pin Terylene and other flimsy materials to paper when cutting. They are less slippery that way and easier to handle.

DRAW CORDS
These are threaded through heading tapes sewn to the tops of the curtains. Draw the cords to gather the curtains.

FACING
A piece of self or different fabric sewn on separately.

FITMENT
Pole, wire, rod or runner on which curtains are hung.

HEADING
The top hem of the curtain, or the top half of the top hem. Frills, pleats are used.

HEADING TAPE
This tape is sewn to the top of the curtains. It is slotted to take hooks or rings, but can also have draw cords to gather sheer and unlined curtains.

MATERIALS
Never buy curtain material until you know exactly what the material is made of. Velvet originally made from silk can now be nylon, cotton or rayon. It drapes well but needs special care and cleaning. Satin can be silk or rayon which will not wash and should be dry-cleaned, and cotton satin, which can be washed. Nylon mixed with other yarns helps to prevent shrinkage and creasing. Terylene is hard wearing, will wash well and pleat well. Always ask if material is pre-shrunk, washable and fast dye.

SEWING THREADS
Use cotton thread on cotton fabric, silk on silk, Terylene on Terylene, silk on rayon.

SHRINKAGE
Net curtains may shrink. It is a good idea to include an extra tuck in top or bottom hem to be picked out after the first washing.

SLOT CASE
This is the lower part of the top hem, divided from it

by a line of stitching. The ends are open for the wire or rod.

diagram 2a

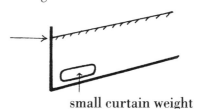

oversew edge of hem

small curtain weight

diagram 2b

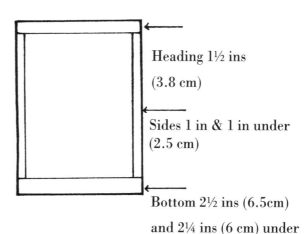

Heading 1½ ins (3.8 cm)

Sides 1 in & 1 in under (2.5 cm)

Bottom 2½ ins (6.5cm) and 2¼ ins (6 cm) under

diagram 2c

Top left: The pleats at the top of this curtain have been carefully made to suit the regular vertical pattern of the fabric. Courtesy Colourwall Curtains.

Top right: A gathered curtain from the right side. Courtesy Colourwall Curtains.

Right: When sewing the tape into the top of the curtain above right, the ends of the cords have been left free so that the curtain can be gathered to the desired width. Courtesy Colourwall Curtains.

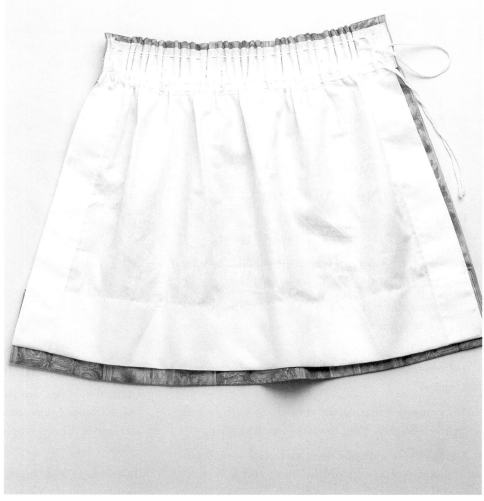

STITCHING
When machining, keep the bulk of your work on the left-hand side. Seam always in the same direction, if possible, so that the fabric is pushed the same way. Trim the selvages of Terylene before sewing seams to prevent drag.

TENSION
Test tension before starting curtain by stitching on a scrap of material, on the double bias, and pulling it. If thread snaps tension is too tight. Even a quarter turn of the adjustment screw has a marked effect.

VALANCE: A separate frill hung from side to side above the curtain.

VALANCE RAIL
The rod or runner standing out from the curtain rail to hold pleated or frilled valance.

WIRE OR ROD
Used where the curtains do not have to be drawn to and fro. It is excellent for curtains that remain in position all the time.

Use a French seam and match pattern when joining floral sheer fabric.

A small weight in lower hem improves the hang of the unlined curtains. Let loose weaves hang for a day before hemming in case the fabric stretches.

◆
Do's and don'ts for curtain making

1. Do be bold. Timidity leads to the use of so-called "safe colors" and this can mean dull decorating.

2. Do seek the advice of experts. At good furnishing stores experienced staff are always ready to help.

3. Do choose all fabrics in both daylight and artificial light, for it is only in this way can you gauge the color.

4. Do remember that lined curtains hang better and last longer.

5. Do remember that colors on a glossy surface will seem much brighter than those on a matt surface.

6. Don't choose curtains from materials spread out on a counter. They should be hung and looked at against the light.

7. Don't ruin the effect by skimping. Allow plenty of material for fullness; twice the width of your windows for heavy materials, and three times the width of the windows for sheer materials.

8. Don't wash curtains unless you're certain they are safe in water. It is better to have them dry-cleaned.

9. Don't choose a fabric unless you are sure it will suit your style of room.

10. Don't be sidetracked. Make your own choice or be guided by experts.

◆
How to miter a corner
(see diagram 3)

With right sides together fold corner of square diagonally in half. From raw edges measure depth of hem required and mark on fold with a pin. Fold point over in line with pin; with pencil, lightly mark sloped side of point onto fabric as shown in A. Stitch on this line. Fasten ends off securely. Trim away point leaving ¼ in (0.6 cm) turning. Turn corner to right side and press in place with seam through middle of corner (B). Continue to make hem in the usual way.

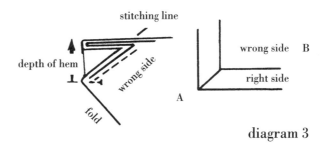

diagram 3

◆
Unlined curtains
Unlined curtains are the easiest of all to make, but like all sewing jobs, must be done correctly to look attractive. These simple instructions will make the job easy for you.

To estimate how much fabric you will need for a simple pair of draped curtains, first measure the

Two different methods of hanging curtains: both hooks and rings are threaded into this heading tape.
Courtesy Colourwall Curtains.

width of your window. This is the width of fabric you will need for one curtain. Where necessary sew two or more widths together for each curtain.

To work out the length of each unsewn curtain, measure the distance from curtain rail to the point you want the curtains to finish.

Add up to 12 in (30.5 cm) for hems and shrinkage (this is if the material has not been pre-shrunk). If the fabric has a large pattern repeat, add the length of one complete pattern to ensure accurate matching of each curtain pattern.

You may find you need to add a half-width of fabric to each curtain for fullness. If so, cut the length of 48 in-wide (122 cm) fabric down the middle and join the selvage edge of each 24 in-wide (61 cm) piece to the selvage edge of each curtain. Narrowly hem the cut edge of each curtain. You can, of course, join whole 48 in (122 cm) widths.

TO HEM

Make narrow side hems [about ½ in (1.3 cm)], make a 3 in (7.5 cm) hem along bottom. If you have allowed extra fabric for shrinkage, include this amount in the bottom hem, leaving the hem tacked until the curtains are first washed. Adjust then, if necessary. Pleating curtains without using tape is difficult. Buy ready-made pleating tape for an easy job. Lay the ready-made pleating tape on top of the lining and curtain heading (slot openings to the bottom), and stitch to curtain by machining along both long edges.

Insert the special pleating hooks in the slots at the required intervals and attach to the curtain rail runners.

The last step is to finish the top of the curtains. To do this, measure from bottom hem up each side edge and mark the required length of curtain with a pin on each side. From pin to pin fold top of curtains down on wrong side and trim this turning to depth of heading required—say 1½ in (3.8 cm). Cut a length of curtain tape 1 in (2.5 cm) longer than the width of curtains.

Turn under each cut end of tape for ½ in (1.3 cm) and tack.

If the tape is fitted with cords which are later drawn up to drape the curtain, pull these free before turning under the ends of tape.

Place the tape across the top of the curtain on the wrong side, with its top edge well below the top fold of curtain, and its lower edge covering raw edge of hem.

Sew top and bottom edges of tape to curtain. (Loosely knot cords at one end of the tape and leave them free at the other end.) (See Diagram 4.)

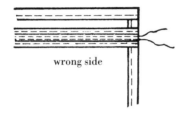

wrong side

top heading using curtain tape

diagram 4

◆

Lined curtains

Despite their elegant look, lined draperies are not difficult to make. The lining protects the more delicate drapery fabrics from soiling and fading and also gives a uniform outside appearance to windows. Before you buy your material, measure up accurately; this will save you a lot of time and money later.

To measure the length of material required, run your tape from the curtain rail or ring to within 1 in (2.5 cm) of the window ledge, or, for a longer curtain that will help to exclude the draught, 6 in (15 cm) below the window ledge, or within 1 in (2.5 cm) of the floor. Add 5 in (13 cm) if the heading is to be simply gathered; 9 in (23 cm) if it is to be deep or pleated.

If you choose a patterned material, you may need to allow extra yardage so that the pattern matches on each length. You can only calculate the amount when you have selected the pattern and know the length of each repeat. Lining should be 2 in (5 cm) shorter than the curtain length and 1 in (2.5cm) narrower than the width.

When calculating the width, allow one and a half times the length of the curtain rail; or twice the length of the rail if it is very long, when you will need to join the material. If you decide to have double or triple pleats along the heading, you will need to join the material.

Allow an extra 6 in (15 cm) wherever curtains are to overlap.

A good overlap helps to exclude draughts. Allow 1½ in (4 cm) for side turnings, or ½ in (1.5 cm) for any side that is to be joined to another. Almost the same yardage is needed for the lining, minus the amount allowed for matching pattern.

Here are simple, straightforward instructions for making lined curtains:

STEP 1:
If more than one width of material is used in a curtain, join by machining together with matching thread.

Turn in 1 ½ in (3.8 cm) side hems, pin and tack. Do not cut off selvage unless it is very tight. Sew both sides, working from left to right with a catch stitch.

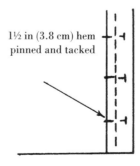

1½ in (3.8 cm) hem pinned and tacked

step 1

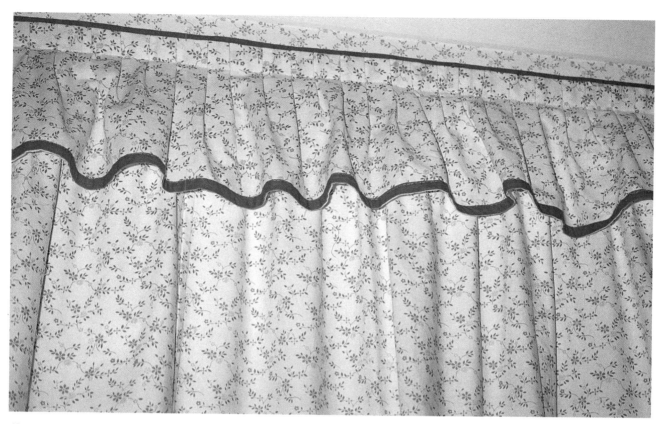

Above: A valance made with a pocket for the supporting rod. Courtesy Colourwall Curtains.
Below: Frilled curtains sewn in the same fabric. Courtesy Colourwall Curtains.

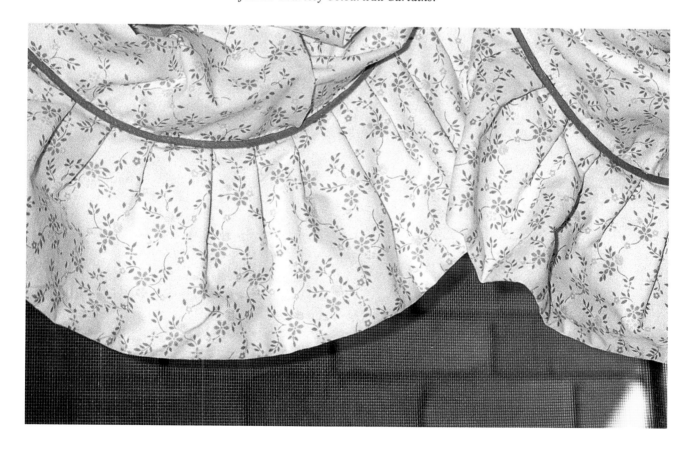

STEP 2:

Turn up hem 3 in (7.5 cm) and allow ½ in (1.3 cm) to turn under. Pin, tack. Mitre corners as shown in diagram; do not cut any fabric away if you are using velvet or other heavy material. (Note that each mitred corner starts a little way up the side.) Slipstitch hem and along mitred corners, being careful thread does not show on right side.

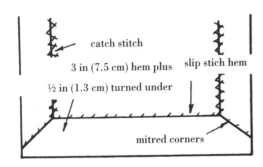

catch stitch

3 in (7.5 cm) hem plus

slip stich hem

½ in (1.3 cm) turned under

mitred corners

step 2

STEP 3:

Cut lining the same size as the curtain, plus 3½ in (9 cm) longer for hem. Turn hem of lining up 4½ in (11.5 cm)—that is, a 1½ in (3.8 cm) fold under a 3 in (7.5 cm) hem. Pin, tack, slipstitch hem. Turn side hems in 1 in (2.5 cm) and tack. Do not stitch yet.

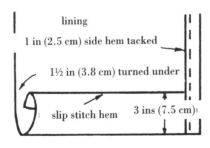

lining

1 in (2.5 cm) side hem tacked

1½ in (3.8 cm) turned under

slip stitch hem

3 ins (7.5 cm)

step 3

STEP 4:

Fold lining in half lengthwise, and place on half of curtain. Make certain it is even. Tack down center fold to hold lining in place. Catch lining to curtain with small buttonhole stitches along tacking line. Leave thread quite loose, as in diagram. Take out

tacking. Repeat every 12–15 in (30–38 cm), according to the width of the curtain.

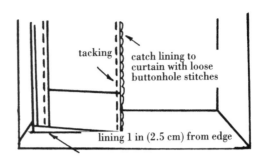

tacking

catch lining to curtain with loose buttonhole stitches

lining 1 in (2.5 cm) from edge

step 4

STEP 5:

Tack and slipstitch lining to curtain at sides. Slipstitch hem of lining to curtain, for 2 in (5.1 cm) only, along each side.

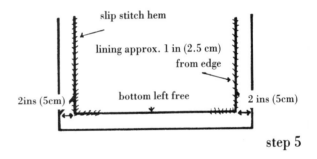

slip stitch hem

lining approx. 1 in (2.5 cm) from edge

2ins (5cm)

bottom left free

2 ins (5cm)

step 5

STEP 6:

Measure required length of curtain from bottom hem. If a pelmet is to be added, the allowance for the heading above the tape when finished is about 1 in (2.5 cm) therefore, allow 3 in (7.5 cm) for heading—1½ in (3.8 cm) when turned down.

If no pelmet is to be used, you will need a deeper heading. Allow 5 in (13 cm)—2½ in (6.5 cm) when turned down. Turn down heading, smoothing out lining underneath, tack and slipstitch. Gather curtain with two rows of gathers, using strong thread. If very large, gather in sections. Draw up to required size, usually about half curtain measurement.

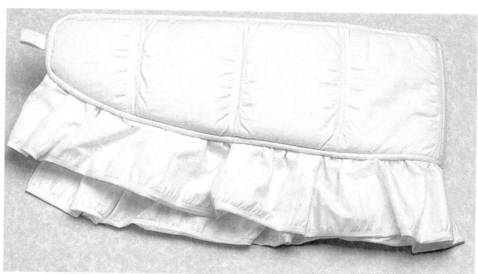

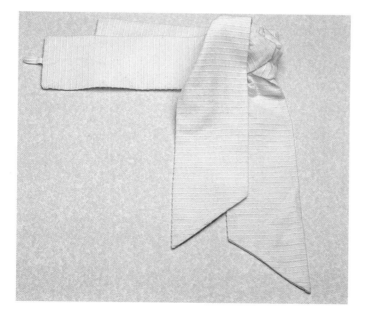

Different forms of tie-backs which lend character to lined or unlined curtains. Courtesy Colourwall Curtains.

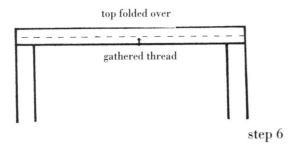

top folded over

gathered thread

step 6

STEP 7:

You will need heading tape, 1½ in (3.8 cm) wide, usually half curtain width, plus ½ in (1.3 cm) for each side for turnings. Sew each side, then pin tape into position. Equalize gathers on curtain, tack tape and sew top securely to curtain.

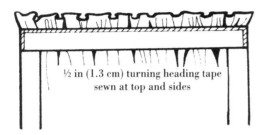

½ in (1.3 cm) turning heading tape
sewn at top and sides

step 7

STEP 8:

Cut a strip of lining the size of the heading tape, plus good turnings. Tack to underneath of tape (which has not yet been sewn down). Secure lining and heading tape to curtain at this edge. Sew hooks to tape, first one each end, then others every 2–2 ½ in (5–6 cm). Sew lining to tape.

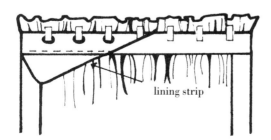

lining strip

step 8

diagram 5

◆
Pinch pleats

Special tapes and hooks are readily available to save all the hard work in making attractive pinch pleats; the hooks may be removed for laundering the curtains and are easier to handle as one long strip of fabric.

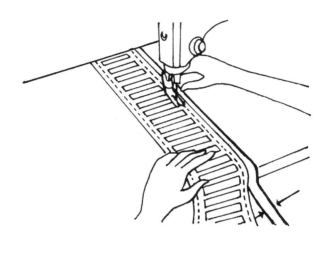

HOW TO MAKE THE PINCH PLEATS

Turn down fabric, and lining if you have used one, ¾ in (2 cm) on the wrong side. Place the pleater tape on this hem so that the pockets are equidistant from either end with ½ in (1.3 cm) extra tape at ends for turning under. Stitch pleater tape ¼ in (0.6 cm) from the top, then along the bottom of the tape and at the sides.

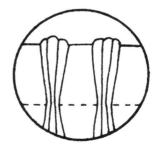

Insert end hooks in the end pockets. Skip one pocket and insert a pleater hook in the next four pockets of the tape. Insert it carefully so that the pockets remain straight and visible. By checking the front of the pleat you can see if all folds of the pleats are uniform. A little practice and the hooks will go in easily and quickly.

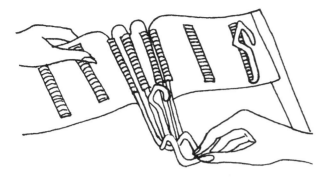

When the hook is in place, press the special lock attachment up and in to clip the pleat in position. The pleat will be held firmly from bottom to top. Skip a space and insert another hook in the following four pockets. Continue across the full width of the curtain, until the top is pleated, ending with an end hook.

How to arrange a simple hem and lining. Courtesy Colourwall Curtains.

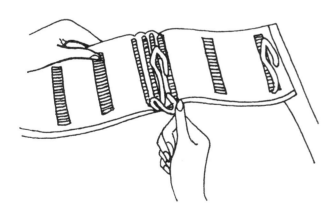

Hang curtains from the hooks on the pleater hooks by attaching them to the rings on the rollers on the curtain tracks.

To launder curtains, simply release the hooks and pull out of the pockets. The curtain is laundered as one long strip of fabric. After laundering and pressing, rehang curtains by inserting the hooks in the pockets as before.

◆

Draped cross-over curtains

Draped cross-over curtains are usually made up in pairs so that two curtains overlap at the top with a single heading and the same rod. The overlap may be a small one in the middle of the window or the complete width of the pane according to your sizes and how much of the glass you want to cover (see diagram 6).

Find the necessary length of material by measuring from the top left-hand corner of the window in a loose curve to the bottom right-hand corner (A–D). Add 12 in (30.5 cm) for the tail, plus 6–8 in (15–20 cm) for hems and shrinkage. This is your maximum length.

Multiply this total by two for a pair of curtains. In width you need two to 2 to 2½ times the window's width for cotton or nylon net and up to three times the width for fine sheers.

Cut the curtains to the maximum length, checking that the grain is straight.

As the tail must be cut on an angle measure the height of the window frame from C–D and add the allowance for tail and hems. This will be your minimum length and the curtains will end at the sill.

Mark this measurement on the outside (right) edge of the right-hand curtain, and on the left edge of the opposite curtain. Draw a line with chalk linking the maximum hem with the minimum hem and check carefully before you cut your fabric. There can be a difference from 9 in (23 cm) upwards. Turn over a small rolled hem along the slanting edge. This may be finished with frilling or a shell edge.

To hang the curtains in pairs, keep the slanting edge to the bottom. Lay one curtain over the other, right sides downwards. If the width of the double thickness of curtain is about twice the total width of the window frame you can have a complete cross-over with the necessary fullness. If it is the same width or less, move the top curtain sideways until the width measures from 2 to 2 ½ times the window size. This will reduce the actual overlap in the middle, but for a wide window it gives a very good effect.

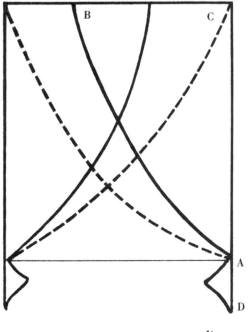

diagram 6

Pin the curtains together along the top, turn down a heading hem of about 1 ½ in (3.8 cm) and stitch on the curtain tape over the raw edge. Or if you are hanging the curtains on a light rod or plastic coated wire, use a plain tape to form a casing.

Gather up the curtain cord or thread the rod through the top until curtain width is the same as window frame size. Your curtains will hang in soft folds. Loop back the ends at the lower corners of the window with plain ties made from scraps of curtain fabric and fixed to a wall hook.

With a very wide window where a complete cross-over is not necessary, calculate your maximum length of curtain by measuring from B to D, but allow the same looping curve for the drapery.

ANOTHER WAY TO MAKE DRAPED CROSS-OVER CURTAINS
The width of each curtain should be about twice the width of the window. Measure the required length of curtain at side from top of window (C–D) add extra length for turnings and heading. It is usual to have frilling at the draped side and the bottom of the curtain.

Frilling by the yard can be bought ready to sew on the curtain. If you make your own, cut enough 6 in (15 cm) wide strips from the width of the material to equal twice the long side and the bottom of the curtain. Seam the strips together and hem all around the edges of the resulting long strip.

Use the gathering attachment on the sewing machine to gather the strip, reducing it to half its length. Place stitching 1 in (2.5 cm) in from long edge of the strip.

TO MAKE
Measure off one required length of curtain, plus turning allowance. Lay fabric flat on floor, mark off the window length on one side of the material and from this point cut off the bottom diagonally to the opposite corner. Trim off the selvages and make a small double hem along the sides and bottom of the curtain.

Machine the frill to the longer side and bottom edge of the curtain, placing the stitching on top of the gathering stitches. Lay the frill over the wrong side of the hem to do this, so that the side of the curtain that faces the window will have a finished appearance.

One kind of curtain pleat. A tube is created at the curtain top (left) and then folded into itself to create a butterfly pleat. Courtesy Colourwall Curtains.

Make up another curtain in the reverse way. Lay one curtain flat on the floor and place the other curtain two-thirds of the way over it so that the longer edges are overlapping. Pin the curtains together at the top, then tack. Turn down top hem and sew through both curtains to make a slot for the curtain rod or wire.

Curtain bands of the same material will hold the drapes in place. To make bands cut a 6 in (15 cm) wide strip of fabric by the required length. Fold in half widthwise and add frill on one side as you stitch together. Sew curtain rings to the ends of each strip. These can be slipped over a hook screwed into the windowframe.

◆
Pelmets

Most curtains need a pelmet to give them a finished appearance and, as a general rule, the pelmet should be roughly one-eighth the curtain depth.

HOW TO MAKE PELMETS
(see diagram 7)

The following materials will be needed: upholstery buckram for stiffening and making shape; fabric to match curtains; lining; braid or fringe for finishing.

STEP 1:
Measure front and sides of curtains. Make a paper pattern to the size and shape required. Try your pattern against the window.

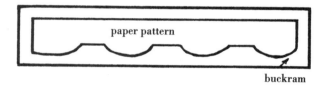

step 1

STEP 2:
Place paper pattern on buckram and mark around with tailor's chalk. Cut out on the chalk line.

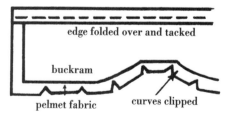

steps 2 & 3

STEP 3:
Place paper pattern on wrong side of material and pin. Allow 1½ in (3.8 cm) turning all round. If material is printed or figured, placement of pattern must be considered. Cut material to shape, including the turnings.

STEP 4:

Place material right side downwards on the table, making sure that there are no creases. Lay the buckram shape on this. Fold the edges of the material over the buckram, first pinning and then tacking with long, loose stitches. Press with a warm iron; the fabric should stick to the buckram.

step 4

STEP 5:

With the right side of the pelmet facing, place the braid or the fringe in place and tack with long, loose stitches. Sew through to the buckram.

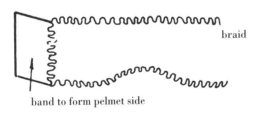

braid

band to form pelmet side

step 5

STEP 6:

To line the pelmet, cut lining 1 in (2.5 cm) larger all round than the buckram, to allow for turnings. Fold top edge of lining down 1 in (2.5 cm) and place on top of the pelmet. Pin, then tack. Fold all the lining in the same way. Slipstitch the lining to the material.

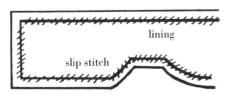

lining

slip stitch

step 6

STEP 7:

Take a piece of 1½ in (3.8 cm) wide heading tape the width of the pelmet plus ¾ in (2 cm) turnings at each end. Fold tape in half and tack to the upper edge of the pelmet.

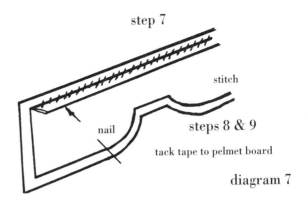

step 7

stitch

nail

steps 8 & 9

tack tape to pelmet board

diagram 7

STEP 8:

Pin the folded heading tape to the back of the pelmet. Stitch its top edge firmly through to the lining and buckram, lower edge free.

STEP 9:

Tack or nail the free edge of the tape to the cornice or pelmet board.

◆

Interesting curtain tops

DIAMOND CURTAIN HEADING

(see diagram 8)

Cut triangular shaped template from strong cardboard. Use this to cut out the top of your curtain in pointed shapes. Cut interlining to the same shape, and sew to the top of the curtain. Sew small brass rings to each point and hang curtain on a brass rod.

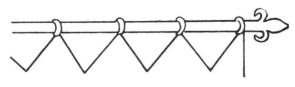

diagram 8

FRINGE ON TOP
(see diagram 9)

Put a fringe on top to give new interest to headings of pelmetless curtains. Use a saucer to shape the top of your curtain. Add stiffening. Sheer curtains could be trimmed with permanently pleated nylon—the kind used for lingerie. On plain curtains use a frill of permanently pleated matching cotton.

You can buy several yards of the newest bobble fringes and sew row upon row of them along the top of the curtains for a new and different look. If using long fringe, then one row should be enough, but if you are using narrow fringe, make an impression by sewing on several rows.

diagram 9

THREADED RIBBON
(see diagram 10)

For a window with an inner curtaining of sheer white nylon or Terylene, add color by suspending it on a brilliant threaded ribbon slotted through brass eyelet holes, and over a brass pole. Use this idea for stationary curtains only, as the ribbon cannot be drawn back.

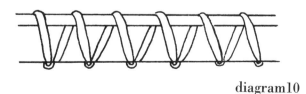

diagram10

TAB-TOP CURTAINS
(see diagram 11)

Sew tabs to the tops of your curtains and loop them over a brass rod. This is only suitable for curtains that are permanently in position—not for curtains that are drawn to and fro.

Another idea: sew huge rings to curtain tops and put on a fat pole. A white curtain with multi-colored painted wooden rings would be smart, or a wooden pole painted in a contrast color or covered with patterned fabric for plain curtains.

Let your imagination run riot. A whole host of exciting ideas can be put into play for interesting and individual curtain tops. There are lots of ways you can introduce color into your window decor cleverly and simply.

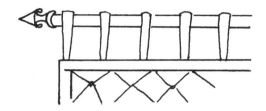

diagram 11

A tab top curtain. Courtesy Colourwall Curtains.

MEDIEVAL SCALLOPS
(see diagram 12)

Make pattern to the shape desired and place on material. Cut material and stiffening to shape. Sew curtain top. Sew rings to top of each scallop. Hang on rods.

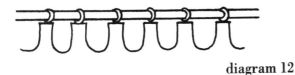

diagram 12

PINCH PLEATED
(see diagram 13)

A distinctive way to finish off a curtain heading and equally effective for plain or patterned fabrics. Add a glamour touch with fancy pins—say a huge gilt star with a pin at the back—pinned over the bunches of pleats. Slip them out for easy washing.

diagram 13

BUTTON-DOWN TABS
(see diagram 14)

Use a cup to shape the scallops between the tabs at the top of your curtain. Allow extra length in the tabs to turn over. Cut stiffening to same shape and sew to curtain top. Turn loops over and secure with a contrast button sewn through loop and curtain. Hang on a brass rail

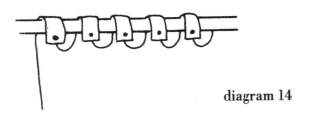

diagram 14

◆
Window blind

A roller blind is quite simple to make. Blind-making kits, containing wooden rollers and bonding fabric, are available in a variety of sizes to fit most windows; if none of these fits your window exactly, buy the nearest size above your window size and cut the roller to fit.

The roller has a rectangular pin and spring fitting at one end which goes at the left of the window. The other end of the roller is bare wood so that you can trim it to the required length if needed. A metal cap and round pin are supplied separately for fitting to the end of the roller.

Choose a fade-resistant, lightweight, closely woven fabric for the blind. Cotton and chintz are excellent, as they hold their shape. On standard fittings rollers turn inwards towards the room so that the wrong side of the rolled up blind will show. To hide the roller fit a pelmet of buckram and fabric to match above the blind.

Also included in the blind-making kit is a length of wood to weight the base of the blind and two metal brackets for hanging the blind. One is slotted to take the rectangular pin at the left of the window, the other has a hole to take the round pin at the right-hand edge.

Fix the roller brackets first, projecting forward from the window frame. Measure from the sill to make sure both brackets are parallel, then measure between them and cut the roller to size if necessary.

TO MAKE THE BLIND
(diagram 15)

Make the blind from fabric that is wider than the window; this means there will be no bulky seams. If you do use a narrower fabric then join the widths one on either side of the center strip, match the patterns carefully and seam them together. Press the seam open and stick the turnings to the wrong side of the fabric to make a smooth seam.

You will need enough fabric to cover the window, plus 5 ins (13 cm) at the top to cover the roller when the blind is down and 2 ins (5 cm) at the bottom to make a hem to take the lath. You need the same

A padded pelmet, with roman blind sewn in the same fabric, and contrasting curtains. Courtesy Colourwall Curtains.

amount of bonding interlining for stiffening, fabric adhesive for sticking the side hems, and fringe or braid for trimming if desired.

Cut your fabric to length and the exact width the roller. Turn in and press ½ in (1.3 cm) along each side edge. This is to ensure that fabric will clear the fittings if blind rolls up unevenly. Stick the turnings down to the wrong side to make non-bulky hems. Iron-on hemming tape is best. Iron the bonding to the back of the fabric using a hot, dry iron. Press thoroughly to prevent it becoming unstuck—this can take up to one hour of firm pressing. Turn in the side edges of the bonding to meet the fabric hems and slip stitch in place. For a simple straightedged hem, turn and press fabric to wrong side for ½ in (1.3 cm) then make hem about 1½ ins (3.8 cm) deep. Machine a second row of stitching close to hem edge. Insert lath in this slot. Hem may be trimmed with fringe, or braid; stab stitch it to the right side of the blind.

To attach fabric to roller, cut fabric straight across the top. Pass fabric behind the roller with right side in and lining on the outside. Lay the edge against the guideline already marked on the roller and fix to the

roller with the tacks provided, setting them about 1 in (2.5 cm) apart (B).

Note
Always iron the bonding fabric onto curtain fabric with a dry, hot iron. This releases the adhesive impregnated in the fabric.

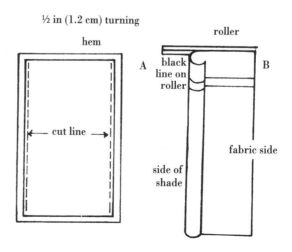

diagram 15

◆

Balloon blinds

MATERIALS FOR EACH BLIND

Fabric (see below); wooden batten to fit inside window frame; ring tape four times blind length plus 12 ins (30 cm); one cleat for fastening blind cords; dowelling for lower edge, ¼ in (1 cm) in diameter, and measuring 1 in (2.5 cm) less than the width of the window; eyelet screws—one for each length of ring tape; blind cord; 2 hooks to hold blind batten.

Optional: Eyelet tool and eyelets (diameter must allow blind cord to pass through freely).

To calculate fabric: measure the width and length of each window. You will need twice the width, and one length plus 12 ins (30 cm). Remember to allow for extra if it is necessary to join fabric for width. Join fabric with small flat seams.

METHOD

Join pieces if necessary to make required width. Turn under ¼ in (1 cm) on the sides and press. Turn over again 1 in (2.5 cm) and press. Turn the top of the fabric piece under ¼ in (1 cm), and press. Mark four positions on top hem—one at each side and two at evenly spaced intervals across blind. Either make a buttonhole at each position, or apply an eyelet. Turn over again, and sew top hem, allowing 2½ in (6 cm) for the batten pocket.

Fold the bottom hem under ¼ in (1 cm) and then another 1½ in (4 cm). Stitch hem.

Stitch the ring tape down the side hems (stitching hems in place at the same time), and at two equally spaced intervals across the blind, stitching from top to bottom. Make sure that the rings or loops are positioned at the same level on each tape, the first row of rings or loops placed just below the top hem, and ending just above the bottom hem line.

Thread a wooden batten through the top rod pocket. Fix four eyelet screws to the back of the rod (through the buttonholes or eyelets)—one at each end and two placed at equal intervals between. These will correspond with the tapes when blind top is gathered.

Decide whether you want to pull the blinds up from the left or the right. Starting on the OPPOSITE side

thread blind cord through the bottom loop and secure. Tie the bottom three loops or rings together. This will create a permanent pouf in the blind, even when it is completely lowered. Continue threading the cord towards the top, and through the corresponding eyelet in the batten. Thread cord through all eyelets, and down the side of the blind to the bottom. Repeat for the remaining rows of loops or rings. Braid all cords together.

Insert dowelling through lower edge of blind, and mount blind inside window frame. Position cleat on window frame, on the same side as the braided cord.

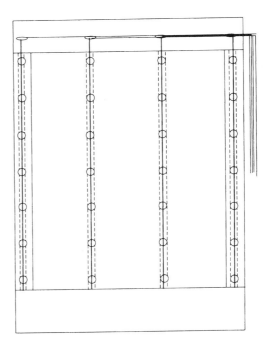

◆
Roman blinds

MATERIALS

Fabric for each window (see below); roman blind tape 4 times the length of the window plus 12 ins (30 cm); metal cleat; hook and loop tape the width of the window; timber mounting board ¾ in thick x 2 ¾ in deep (2 x 7 cm) to fit inside the window frame; one pair of metal L-shaped brackets with screws; nylon blind cord 8 times the length of the blind; 2 ¾ x 2 in (7 x 5 cm) wide timber battens—each one to fit across the width of the finished blind; a staple gun; 5 screw eyelets; dressmakers' chalk or vanishing marker pen.

To calculate fabric, measure the width and length of each window. You will need the width plus 2 ¾ in (7 cm) for hems multiplied by the length plus 32¼ ins (82 cm). (This is for top and bottom hem allowance, and 6 batten pockets.)

METHOD

Press fabric under ¼ in (1 cm) at each side and then press under a further 1 in (2.5 cm). Turn the top of the fabric under ⅛ in (0.5 cm) and press; turn over again a further 1 in (2.5 cm) and press. Attach loop side (soft side) of hook and loop tape to the top hem allowance and stitch on with two rows of stitching, thus hemming at the same time. Fold the bottom hem under ¼ in (1 cm) and then another 2¼ in (6 cm). Stitch hem. Measure the length of the hemmed blind to calculate batten positions.

Decide on the number of batten pockets you wish to have—6 is a good number for an average modern window. Multiply the number of pockets desired by 4 ¾ in (12 cm) [i.e. 6 pockets x 4 ¾ in (12 cm) = 28 ½ in (72 cm)]. Deduct this from the total length of your hemmed blind, and divide the balance by 6. This will show you where to begin your pockets.

On right side of fabric measure to where the first pocket will be, and mark with chalk. Measure up the blind a further 4 ¾ ins (12 cm), and mark a second line parallel to the first. Go to the next pocket position and repeat, until all positions are marked. On each pocket, bring the two parallel lines together; and machine across the width of the blind, thus creating a pocket on the front of the blind. Position ring tape on wrong side of fabric, taking care not to

pin closed the pockets. Remember to make sure that the rings or loops are positioned at the same level on each tape, the first row of rings or loops placed just below the top hem, and the last just above the bottom hem line.

Machine stitch the blind tape along the length of the blind, taking care to lift the machine foot over each pocket. This is to ensure that the pockets at sides of blind remain open for insertion of the battens.

On the ¼ in (1 cm) (top) side of the mounting board staple or glue the hook side of the hook and loop tape. Attach blind to mounting board using hook and loop tape, and screw the eyelet screws into the mounting board to align with the rows of blind tape.

Decide whether you wish to pull the blinds up from the right or the left. Starting on the OPPOSITE side, thread blind cord through the bottom loop and secure. Thread the cord to the top, and through the corresponding eyelet on the mounting board, thread cord through all the screw eyelets, and down the side of the blind to the bottom. Repeat with remaining rows of loops or rings. Braid all cords together. Insert battens into pockets and bottom hem, and mount board on angle brackets inside window frame. Position cleat on the window frame, on the same side as the braided cord.

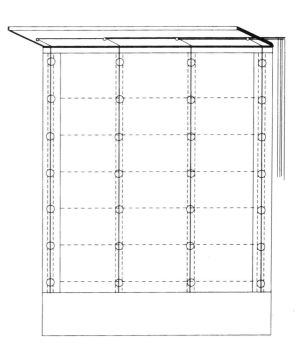

SLIPCOVERS

New slipcovers are a substantial economy in home decoration and bring fresh vigour into the color scheme of your room. Add pattern or texture for interest. Large patterns are more successful than small ones, as the bold design makes a natural centerpiece for the back of the chair. But the larger the pattern repeat, the higher the amount of wastage. Always measure the chair or settee in detail before buying the material.

It seems a big thing to make your own loose covers, but it is not as complicated as it appears, especially if you start by covering a very simple piece of furniture, progressing to a sofa only by degrees.

In making a slipcover for a particular piece of furniture, follow exactly the way the upholstery was done and you'll be all right. Cut the fabric for the arms according to the way the upholstery was cut and insert piping in the same places as it is on the upholstery.

Choose the material for slipcovers carefully. It must be tough, hard wearing, firm weave, colorfast and shrink-proof. Beware of material that is too heavy, bulky rayons and the like. They are difficult to clean and very heavy to handle when sewing them together. Choose a fabric that is suitable for your purpose; one is often tempted to use upholstery wool yarns, velvets and folk weaves that may shrink badly and be unusable after the first washing. If you yearn for a black-and-white striped chair cover, it is sensible to launder and shrink bed ticking before making into covers.

Measure up your chairs carefully; armchairs vary in design and no two sides are exactly alike. In the interests of economy, measure your particular chair, finding its basic width across the back and arms, to decide the width of material you can use most economically.

To estimate the yardage, add up the lengthwise measurements, including all seam allowances and tuck-ins. Add an extra yard (meter) for matching and placement of motifs. The total of these measurements and the width of the fabric will determine the yardage needed, Extra material is needed for gathered or pleated skirts.

◆

Cutting out

It is easier, quicker and just as accurate to pin the material right on the chair, a section at a time.

Before cutting them to shape, check that patterns match and make sure that any design on the material is the right way up. Cut out and complete each section as you go.

Individual pieces are much easier to handle than a big slipcover bristling with pins. As each completed section is pinned to the adjacent piece the slipcover can be fitted exactly and adjusted easily.

Do all pinning and cutting on the right side of the fabric. As the two sides of an upholstered piece often differ slightly, it is necessary to pin and cut each section separately. Pin the fabric along the straight of the goods (the straight grain) and do all fitting and adjusting at this stage. Have cushions in place when pinning fabric for the placement of large motifs, so that the design can be correctly centered on different parts of the furniture.

◆

How to measure an armchair

(see diagrams 16a, b, c)

MEASURING FOR YARDAGE
Measure a sofa or upholstered chair by the method shown in the diagrams.

STEP 1:
On the inside back, measure from A down the inside of the sofa or chair across the seat and to the lower edge of E, add 2 ins (5 cm) for seams and allow 6 ins (15 cm) for tuck-in. For width, measure from J to N and add 2 ins (5 cm) (diagram 16a).

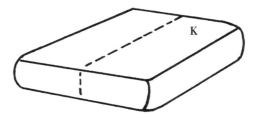

16a

A seat cushion with bows, made for a cottage-style wooden chair. Courtesy Colourwall Curtains.

STEP 2:
For outside back, measure from A to B, and add 2 ins (5 cm) for seam allowance and hem (diagram 16b).

STEP 3:
For outside arms, measure F, and add 2 ins (5 cm) for seam allowance and hem. Double this measurement for both arms.

STEP 4:
For inside arms, measure G, add 2 ins (5 cm) for seam allowance and 4 ins (10 cm) for tuck-in. Multiply by two for both arms.

STEP 5:
For facing on arms, measure J, add 2 ins (5 cm) for seam allowance. Double the measurement for two arms.

STEP 6:
Measure width of back at base L (diagram 16b) and width of sides outside.

STEP 7:
Measure sides H outside, add 2 ins (5 cm) for hem (diagram 16c).

STEP 8:
Allow ½ yd (45 cm) for flaps. These are attached to the sides, back and front of the sofa or chair to tie underneath to hide the shabby upholstery.

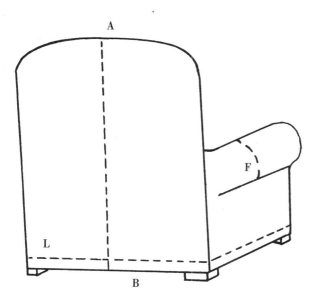

16b

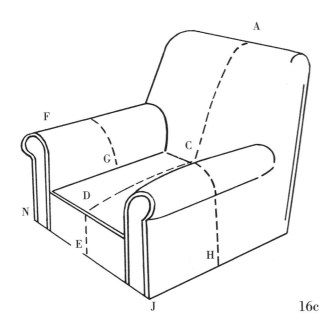

16c

diagram 16

STEP 9:
Allow 1 yd (91 cm) for piping the cover. This will give about 30 yds (27 m) of bias strips, ½ in (1.3 cm) wide.

STEP 10:
Measure cushion covers and box sides, allowing 1 in (2.5 cm) on all seams. For back of cushion, measure top of cushion K, and double for bottom, add 1 in (2.5 cm) seam allowance. Measure round the four sides for length of boxing strip. Measure depth of cushion, and allow 1 in (2.5 cm) seam allowance (diagram 16a).

◆

How to make piping

(see diagram 17)

Piping is used for decorative purposes on bedspreads and cushions, but on loose covers it serves two purposes: one is decorative, the other is to strengthen the seams of the cover at the weakest points.

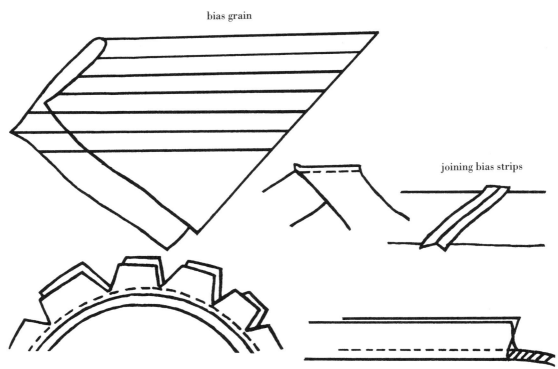

bias grain

joining bias strips

slashing the back of piping to go round curves

diagram 17

Material for piping is cut on the cross. Piping cord available from haberdashery counters and curtain departments of stores should be boiled and pre-shrunk before covering it with the material.

For an average size easy chair with loose cushions, 12–14 yds (11–12.8 m) of piping may be needed and a sofa with three cushions could take 25 yds (22.8 m).

Cut a yard of 36 ins (90 cm) material, on the bias, into 1 ½ ins (3.8 cm) wide strips; if using a heavier cord, the strips will need to be made wider. Join the strips together with stitching on the lengthwise grain and press the seams open. Join together to make one long strip, this is easier to work with and you can cut off the lengths as required.

Fold material down the middle, lay the cord in the fold and stitch close to the cord using the piping foot on your machine. Stretch the bias material slightly as you work. Roll the completed cord round a piece of cardboard for easy handling. When sewing piping to curved shapes, slash the back of the piping to go round the curves.

◆

To slipcover a large club chair

The simplest way to give new life to a large arm chair is to fit a new slipcover in one of the attractive designs now available in furnishing fabrics. Period designs are suitable and popular.

MATERIALS

Brown paper or large sheets of newspaper for patterns; transparent adhesive tape to join pattern pieces together where necessary; length of tape to go round base of chair; press studs or slide fasteners.

TO MEASURE THE EXACT AMOUNT OF FABRIC REQUIRED FOR CHAIR

First make pattern pieces using diagrams 18a and 18b as your guide. The pieces shown in diagram 18a are: A, inside back [allow 6 ins (15 cm) to tuck down into back of seat]; B, chair seat [allow 6 ins (15 cm) at the back and on either side to tuck away]; C, front of seat; D, arm roll (this piece goes right over the arm, starting just below the seat level inside, and ending on the outside at the point shown in diagram 18b); E, scroll.

Pattern pieces for the back of the chair (diagram

18b) are: F, outside arm; G, outside back; H, border strip. If there is a loose seat cushion, make two patterns, one for the top and one for the bottom of the cover and another pattern for the inset or boxing strip (the long strip round the sides connecting the top to the bottom cover).

For the skirt measure round the chair allowing an extra 16 ins (40 cm) for inverted pleats. Depth will be from bottom of chair to floor.

When you have cut all the pattern pieces, measure and mark the space on the floor 48 ins (122 cm) wide and 3 yds (2.75 m) long. Pretend this is a piece of fabric and on it place the pieces. Allow double the area for each piece, as they will either be cut twice or placed on the fold. Allow 1 in (2.5 cm) round the outside of each piece for seams and 1½ ins (3.8 cm) for lower hems on pieces C, F and G. Each time you fill the 48 ins (122 cm) by 3 yds (2.75 m) space you will need 3 yds (2.75 m) of fabric; add an extra yard of fabric for the facings.

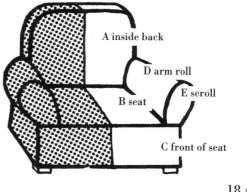

18 a

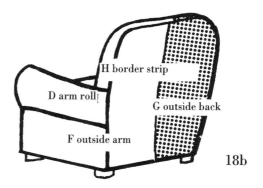

18b

diagram 18

TO MEASURE CUSHION COVERS

Allow 1 in (2.5 cm) seam allowance. Cut out cushion cover pieces and sew one long edge of inset to the top of cushion cover, the right sides facing and the raw edges level. Where they meet, join narrow edges of inset and trim off surplus fabric.

Sew the other long edge of inset round the bottom of the cover, starting on one side 2 ins (5 cm) from the end and finishing on the opposite side in the same position. This leaves an opening through which to insert the cushion.

Cut a piece of fabric for the facing (this is the flap attached to one edge of the cushion cover opening and it tucks between the cushion and the cover avoiding the need for a slide fastener). This facing will be the same width as the boxing strip and the length of the opening, plus 3 ins (7.5 cm) at either end.

Sew one long edge of the facing to the free edge of the bottom cover, right sides together and raw edges level, and leave the 3 ins (7.5 cm) overlap free on either side. Sew the lower edges of the 3 ins (7.5 cm) overlaps along the seam lines of bottom cover and inset. Neatly hemstitch raw edges of inset and facing.

TO MAKE CHAIR COVER

Cut out the pieces for the chair cover as follows: from single fabric, cut two pieces each for D, E, and F; cut remaining pieces A, B, C, G, H from double fabric, placing the straight edge of each piece (the mid-line of the chair) on the fold.

All shaping is done directly on the chair, by pinning each piece of cover on the appropriate part of the chair, right side of fabric outside.

Fit inside back (A) snugly at each top corner of chair by pinning darts. [Make a dart by pinching fabric to fit, then pin the fold into dart shape. Each dart will be about ¾ in (1.9 cm) to 1 in (2.5 cm) wide and only a few inches long.]

Shape outside back (G) to outline of chair, leave 1 in (2.5 cm) all round edge for turnings and trim off surplus fabric.

Where outside back curves over the back of the arm roll, carefully slash the fabric so it fits into the shallow hollow between back and arm, but leave about ½ in (1.3 cm) seam allowance unslashed.

Pin on seat piece (B) pushing the three tuck-away sides well down into the crevices of the chair, and shaping the piece to fit the chair seat. Pin on the rest of the pieces, shaping them to fit, and pin hem along lower edges of pieces C, F, and G. Mark seamlines with pins or tailor's chalk—arm roll (D), inside back (A) and seat piece (B) will be joined along their tuck-away edges. Remove cover pieces from the chair and stitch the darts.

Stitch all the seams (right sides facing, raw edges level) except side seams which join the outside back to outside arm, arm roll and part of border strip. Seam the tuck-away edges of arm roll, inside back and seat pieces with a double row of stitching, leaving ¼ in (0.6 cm) between each row—this strengthens the seams.

Stitch hems on pieces C, F, and G and through this continuous hem run a tape. When cover is placed on chair, the tape is drawn up and tied out of sight round one back leg.

To make plackets to fasten the cover, trim the seam allowance down each side opening to ½ in (1.3 cm), clipping in towards the stitching where the opening meets the top seam—this gives a smooth, non-wrinkle finish.

Cut four strips of fabric, two of them 4½ ins (11 cm) wide, the others 3 ins (7.6 cm) wide, each as long as the opening, plus 1 in (2.5 cm). Stitch narrow strips to the open edges of the outside back, wider strips to the other sides of the openings. In each case keep right sides of fabric facing and raw edges level and leave ½ in (1.3 cm) overlap at each narrow end of the strips. Turn each overlap to the wrong side and tack. Turn under ½ in (1.3 cm) raw edges of strips and tack. Cut the skirt to fit across the back, the other piece goes round three sides. Hem the skirt.

Attach back skirt separately to back piece, hem sides.

Slipstitch folded edges of strips to wrong side of cover along the seam lines. On the outside back, turn in plackets; slipstitch to wrong side; sew press studs on all plackets at 4 ins (10.2 cm) intervals—the narrow plackets tuck round the back of the chair under plackets on outside back.

Sew the rest of the skirt piece to the chair cover.

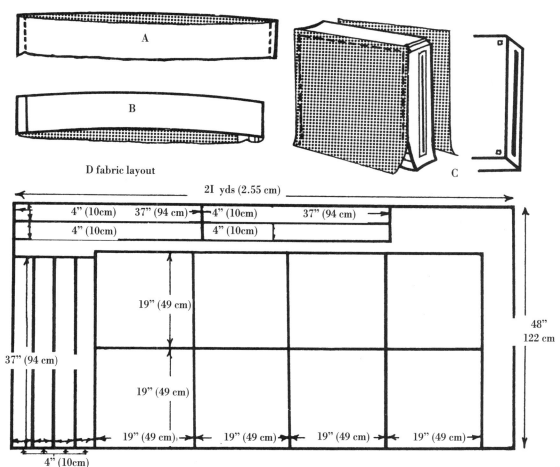

D fabric layout

diagram 19

Fit cover on chair. Push the tuck-away seams into the side and back crevices. To hold these in place push a roll of newspaper tightly into each crevice or use cardboard cylinders, such as used for calendars and pictures, deep into the crevices to hold the covers in place.

TO MAKE BOX CUSHION COVERS

To make (see diagrams 19a, b, c, d) the covers for a set of four box cushions, each 3 ins (7.6 cm) deep and 18 ins (45.7 cm) square, you will need 2 ¾ yds (2.5 m) of 48 ins (122 cm) strong furnishing fabric.

STEP 1:

Use the fabric layout (diagram 19D) and cut your fabric according to this diagram. There is ½ in (1.3 cm) allowance for turnings throughout.

STEP 2:

To form the box sides of the cushion covers, take two strips of fabric, each 37 ins (94 cm) by 4 ins (10 cm) wide. Make two seams by stitching the shorter edges together [allow ½ in (1.3 cm) turnings]. Press seams open.

STEP 3:

With the right side of the fabric outside measure 1 in (2.5 cm) from a seam and make a 16 ins (40 cm) cut lengthways, and then tack and stitch the slide fastener in place.

STEP 4:

Allowing ½ in (1.3 cm) turnings, tack the front and back of the cushion to the side panel, making sure that the two seams on the panel are placed at the corners for neatness. Stitch, then press open the seams. Turn the covers and insert the foam cushion.

CUSHIONS

A room without cushions looks quite bare, but good cushions are expensive, although fairly easy to make. Some new scatter cushions can make a lot of difference to a room where maybe you are not planning a big renovation of the furnishings.

Cushions add a note of bright color to a room and often give the finishing touch to the decor. Piled in colorful profusion they will dress up a feminine bedroom or add a touch of comfort to the living room.

If you are using cushions outdoors, cover them with a fabric that will stand up to the weather. The new plastics are the answer. All you need do is wipe them with a cloth after rain or dew. Use plastic foam, rubber or kapok for filling or the solid foam rubber or plastic cushion shape.

Always make an inner case of unbleached calico to take the filling. If this is made slightly larger than the outer cover you will have a firm cushion. Do not overstuff cushions, as this makes them too hard for comfort; too little filling gives a limp appearance.

◆

A bolster cushion

MATERIAL

You will need 1 yd (91 cm) x 36 ins (90 cm) chintz; 1½ yds (1.37 m) bobble fringe for trimming; 1 moulded foam rubber or plastic bolster shape. [Size used approx 25 x 9 ins (63 x 23 cm) diameter.]

TO MAKE

Cut one piece of fabric 25 ins (64 cm) long and 28 ins (71 cm) wide. Cut 2 circles each 9½ ins (24 cm) in diameter. Stitch the bobble fringe to the 28 ins (71 cm) edges on the right side. Turn to wrong side and sew the 25 ins (64 cm) sides together with a short seam at each end, leave a large opening to insert the bolster shape. Join the circular pieces one to each end of the tube. Turn to right side. Insert bolster pad. Slipstitch opening.

◆

Fringed triangle cushion

MATERIAL

You will need ¾ yd (0.68 m) x 42 ins (107 cm) furnishing satin; 3¼ yds (2.97 m) of cotton fringe; 1 triangular moulded shape in desired size.

TO MAKE

Make a pattern by placing the triangular shape on the paper and trace around it. Cut out the pattern allowing 1 in (2.5 cm) more on all sides. Place on the fabric and cut out.

Pattern will fit economically if you turn it upside down to cut second triangle.

TO MAKE UP

Place the two triangular pieces together right sides facing. Stitch together with ½ in (1.3 cm) seams leaving one side partly open to insert pad. Trim corners and seams. Turn to right side. Insert pad and slipstitch opening by hand. Sew fringe to outer edge by hand. Sew to middle of cushion in triangle design by hand.

◆

Square cushion with padded border

MATERIAL

You will need ½ yd (0.45 m) x 48 ins (1.22 m) fabric; 2 yds (1.82 m) piping cord; one 11 in (22.9 cm) square moulded foam rubber or plastic shape. Wadding to pad border.

TO MAKE

Cut two 16 ins (40 cm) squares from the fabric and enough 1½ ins (3.8 cm) bias strips to cover cord. Join the strips together into one length and cover the piping cord. Stitch the covered cord to the raw edges of one square. Join ends neatly. With right sides facing stitch the two squares together, leaving the two opposite sides unstitched for turning out and inserting the padding. Turn to right side and press well.

Mark a 10 in (25.5 cm) square in the middle of the square. Stitch along three sides of this square, leaving one side unstitched. Insert pad. Stitch up the fourth side of this inner square. Stuff the two stitched sides of the border with wadding, using a ruler to press it in. Fill the unstitched sides, pinning the turned edges as you fill each one up. Slipstitch these edges together invisibly by hand.

This bought cushion fabric has been quilted at home to give it texture and character. Courtesy Avalon Craft Cottage.

◆
Round boxed cushion with quilted top

MATERIAL

You will need an 18 ins (46 cm) square of chintz or other floral cotton with a pattern suitable for quilting; an 18 ins (46 cm) square of wadding and a piece of calico the same size; 20 ins (51 cm) of matching or contrasting fabric 36 ins (90 cm) wide; 3 yds (2.75 m) piping cord; 1 round boxed foam rubber or plastic shape 16 ins (41 cm) diameter.

TO MAKE

Quilt the patterned fabric. Place wadding on wrong side of fabric and place calico over it. Tack the three pieces together firmly. With the quilting attachment of your sewing machine follow the outline of printed design on right side of fabric. Remove tacking.

Cut a 16 in (41 cm) circle from your quilted fabric. Cut another 16 in (41 cm) circle from the plain fabric and a boxing strip 4 ins (10 cm) wide and 46 ins (117 cm) long (join if needed).

Cut bias strips 1½ ins (3.8 cm) wide, join these to make a strip long enough to cover piping cord.

TO MAKE UP

Join the short ends of the boxing strip together. Cover piping cord with bias strips by stitching close to cord with cording foot of your machine. Stitch piping to raw edges of boxing strip, both sides. Join quilted top to one piped edge of boxing strip. Join bottom circle of plain fabric to other edge of boxing strip, leaving an opening large enough to insert pad. Insert pad and slipstitch opening.

◆

Flat bordered cushion

MATERIAL

You will need ½ yd (0.45 m) x 36 ins (0.91 m) striped cotton; 1 ½ yds (1.37 m) black bobble fringe; one inset pad 12 ins (30.5 cm) diameter.

TO MAKE

Cut two 18 ins (46 cm) circles from the striped fabric. Stitch bobble fringe to the right side of one circle. With right sides facing stitch the two circles together leaving about 12 ins (30.5 cm) unsewn. Turn to right side and press well. Mark in middle of cover with pencil or chalk an 11 ½ ins (29 cm) circle. Stitch on this marked line leaving about one-third open to insert pad. Slip pad inside this circular piece, pin and sew round remainder of circle. Slipstitch opening.

◆

Frilled cushion

MATERIAL

You will need ¾ yd (0.68 m) x 36 ins (0.91 m) fabric; 2 buttons ⅝ in (1.6 cm) diameter; an inner pad 12 ins (30.5 cm) diameter.

TO MAKE

Cut two circles from the fabric 12 ½ ins (32 cm) diameter and three 4 ins (10 cm) wide strips across the width of fabric for frill.

Join the four-inch strips together across the short ends, form a tiny hem along one edge. Make circle. Run two rows of large, loose machine stitching along the other edge for gathering the frill.

Pull up gathering and pin to the outside edge of one circular piece. Distribute gathers evenly. Stitch frill around circle. Join the second circle leaving an opening to insert centerpad. Slipstitch opening. Cover button with fabric. Stitch through middle of cushion.

BEDSPREADS AND OTHER BEDROOM ACCESSORIES

Graceful bedroom furniture can be had quite inexpensively by providing frilled draperies on a dressing table or re-covering a bedroom stool in a brightly colored fabric. Decorative headboards can add a distinctive note to a plain bedhead.

Bedspreads are fun to make. You must start by following some basic rules, but then you can let your imagination run riot. We have included directions for basic types of spreads here, but you can add endless variations to produce exciting and unusual effects.

◆

Bedspreads

IMPORTANT MEASUREMENTS
(see diagrams 20a and 20b)

Begin by taking measurements when the bed is made up with blankets and sheets in place, since these will increase the size of the bed. Measure top length, top width, side overhang, foot overhang, head overhang, depth of top mattress, top of box spring to floor and "returns" at head overhang. Armed with these measurements it will be possible for you to make any type of spread.

"Return at head overhang" refers to beds with headboards. It is an extension of the side treatment at the head end, and rounds the corners to run 6–10 ins (15–26 cm) along the headboard, holding the side overhang in place. If a bed does not have headboards, but the head end is against the wall, the return is also used.

To the measurements add ½ in (1.3 cm) for each seam allowance and 2 ins (5 cm) for hems. If the pillow is to be covered by the spread add 30 ins (76 cm) to the top length measurement to allow for pillow covering and tuck-in. When planning your yardage requirements, always place the full width of the fabric down the middle of the bed. Then any necessary piecing can be done on either side.

Pretty machine-embroidered cushions. © Courtesy Brother Industries.

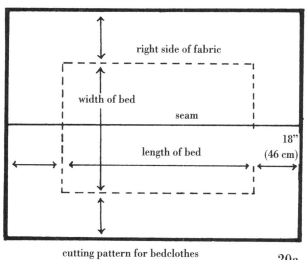

right side of fabric

width of bed

seam

18"
(46 cm)

length of bed

cutting pattern for bedclothes

20a

20b

diagram 20

◆
A throwover bedspread

(see diagram 21)

The throwover bedspread is the simplest and easiest of all to make. Choose your favourite plain color that will tone with the rest of the room or choose a patterned fabric to match a set of curtains.

For a single bed use 36 ins (0.91 m) fabric, for a double bed 48 ins (1.22 m) or 54 ins (1.4 m) fabric. If you use the wider fabric no seam down the middle will be needed. You will need 6 yds (5.5 m) of either width. Cut your fabric into two lengths of 3 yds (2.75 m) each. If using plain fabric, avoid a seam down the middle. Lay one piece down the middle of the bed. Cut the remaining piece in two lengthwise and join a length to each side of the middle strip. Round off the corners and hem or trim with fringe or braid.

If using a floral or printed fabric a center seam will be better since you can cut the fabric design to match when seamed together down the middle.

Measure the bed with the bedding in place. If using a sheer fabric be sure to line the spread so that the blanket will not show through.

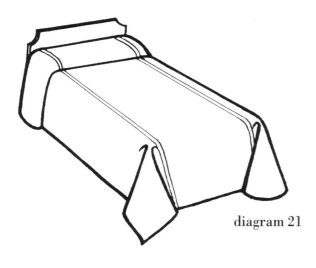

diagram 21

◆
A tailored bedspread

(see diagram 22)

The bedspread is the dominant decorating theme in the bedroom so it will provide the focal point in your color scheme. You can make it frilly and feminine or trim and tailored. Choose a fabric that will not wrinkle readily.

To work out the amount of material needed for the spread, make up the bed first. Measure the bed from head to foot and continue to the point where you plan to end the spread, then add a little extra for finishing the edges. This gives you the figure for one length.

For width, measure the bed across the top. Then measure from edge of the bed to the point where you plan to end the spread; double this figure and add it to the one you got across the top of the bed. This gives the width needed. Add all measurements together for yardage.

Allow ½ in (1.3 cm) for seams on middle and side panels and 2 ½ ins (6.5 cm) for bottom hem. For braid yardage measure round top of bed and along side panels where you plan to trim the bedspread. Add all measurements together for yardage.

Cut two pieces of fabric the length and width of the bed [54 ins (1.4 m) will not need joining]. Place one length as a panel directly down the middle of the bed. Split the other strip lengthwise for the two side panels. Cut another strip for foot of the bed, same depth as side panels and 16 ins (40.5 cm) wider than bed for box pleat allowance.

Stitch side panels to each end of bottom panel, forming inverted box pleats at corners, using 8 ins (20 cm) of bottom panel for each pleat. Attach side and bottom panels to center top panel. If using piping, insert between side and top panels as you sew. Turn up hem all around.

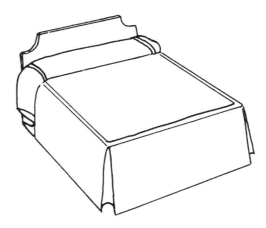

diagram 22

This lovely old stool newly covered with embroidered fabric would go well amongst antique furnishings in a bedroom.

◆
A stool cover with
full length frill

A very cheap way of adding a bright touch to a bedroom is to dress up a stool with a frill or "drapery". Some good materials are glazed chintz, small patterned cretonnes, sprigged dress cotton, and organdie flounces.

TO MAKE
(see diagrams 23a and 23b overleaf)

STEP 1:
Cut the material on the stool as if you were making a loose cover, make a rectangle or circle to fit the top allowing ½ in (1.3 cm) turnings. Make a border or boxing strip to go round the stool and the depth of the seat and enough piping to cover the fabric joins.

STEP 2:
Cut a strip of non-woven interlining the same size as the border to stiffen a lightweight fabric. Join border to top circle or rectangle.

STEP 3:
Measure the depth of frill from the bottom of the seat cushion to within ½ in (1.3 cm) of floor. Allow 1 in (2.5 cm) hem and ½ in (1.3 cm) turnings. Measure the circumference of stool and add half of this measurement for fullness.

STEP 4:

Cut fabric to these measurements of length and depth and turn up the skirt hem.

STEP 5:

Gather the top to fit the base of the border and join together inserting piping as you sew. Join side seam of skirt on the wrong side.

STEP 6:

Make four long ties from folded material and sew by hand to inside of the border at points near legs of stool.

STEP 7:

Slip cover over stool and tie the material tapes diagonally across the bottom of the underside of the stool or, if suitable, tie round the legs of the stool.

◆

Dressing table cover

A pretty dressing table cover will give a new lease of life to a chest of drawers or a dressing table that has seen better days. Any old shabby table can be turned into a graceful piece of bedroom furniture by providing it with frilled "petticoats".

If the top of the dressing table is narrow it will be necessary to fit a new and larger top so that it overhangs the underframe and drawers by at least 2 ins (5 cm). This will make for easier opening and closing of the drawers which will then not become tangled with the top valance each time they are in use. The valance is attached to the edge of the top while the skirt is hung either on curtain rails fixed to the overhang or fixed to two hinged arms which open out to expose the drawers. You will need to fix either of these attachments to your new top.

If the table is without drawers and there is no need to move the curtains, then a plastic coated spring wire is all that is needed. Attach this wire with a hook to one side of the dressing table and extend it right round to the other side where it is held firmly with another small hook.

For the curtains themselves any light sheer is suitable if you like a soft feminine look. Taffetas, chintz, spotted muslin and fine cottons are also suitable.

TO MAKE
(see diagram 24)

STEP 1:

Measure the depth from floor to table top allowing 3 ins (7.5 cm) for hems and turnings. For fullness measure round the dressing table and allow twice the width for cottons and the like and three times the width if using a sheer fabric. Make the curtains to overlap in the middle. The curtain hems should just clear the floor by about ½ in (1.3 cm).

STEP 2:

Make a paper pattern of the top of the dressing table, cut out fabric, and allow ½ in (1.3 cm) turnings all round.

STEP 3:

Make a pelmet either straight, curved or scalloped or trimmed with a bobble fringe, about 4 ins (10 cm) deep. Stitch this to a piece of non-woven interlining

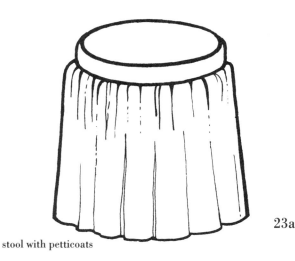

stool with petticoats

23a

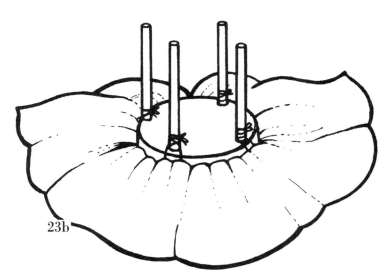

23b

underside of stool showing ties

diagram 23

cut to the same shape. Sew pelmet to top. Interlining will make your top cover washable.

STEP 4:

Make up the skirt as you would a pair of unlined simple curtains hemmed at top and bottom and along the sides.

If using a curtain wire, make a slot case at the top to take the wire.

If using a curtain rail, use either pleater tape and hooks or gathering tapes with hooks that fit into runners on the curtain rail.

If using hinged wooden arms, make the top for the dressing table separately and fix fabric down over the edge holding position with drawing pins.

STEP 5:

Make the valance or pelmet and skirt in four separate pieces. Fix the two front pieces to the hinged wooden arms and the other two pelmets and skirts at either end of the dressing table.

Made this way you will be able to swing the front curtains apart to use the drawers without becoming tangled in an overhanging valance or pelmet.

Your dressing table cover must be kept fresh and neat, so make it in such a way that it comes apart easily for laundering.

diagram 24

◆
Bag chair

MATERIALS

13 ¾ x 4 ft (4.2 x 1.22 m) wide washable fabric for outside cover [if using this striped fabric from Sekers Silk you will need 14 x 4 ft (4.4 x 1.22 m) wide fabric to match stripes], 13 ¾ x 4 ft (4.2 x 1.22 m) wide calico or similar fabric for lining, 13 ¾ ins (35 cm) zipper, No. 10 bag polystyrene pellets.

METHOD

To make the pattern pieces, enlarge pattern from graph [1 square = 4 ins (10 cm)]. Cut six side panels each 53½ ins (1.36 m) long, two pieces for base and one top piece from both outside fabric and lining.

Take ⅜ in (1 cm) seam allowance on all seams on outside fabric, ½ in (1.5 cm) seam allowance on all seams on lining.

The outside fabric and the lining are made in the same way. With right sides together, join all side panels together to form a tube. To strengthen the seams, fold both seam allowances over to one side and run a row of stitching ¼ in (0.6 cm) in front edge down each seam.

Run two rows of gathering stitch around top and lower edge of tube. Ease, then stitch the top piece into the tube. Join middle seam of base together, leaving an opening 13 ¾ ins (35 cm) long in the middle.

Pin, then stitch the zipper in base on outside fabric. With right sides together, ease, then stitch base into bag. Insert lining into bag and fill with pellets. Oversew opening, close zipper.

◆
Fitted bedspread with appliquéd motif

Before making the bedcover, check the length, width and height of the bed. This pattern is for a bed 75 ins x 36 ins wide x 18 ins high (1.88 x 0.9 x 0.46 m).

If making for a smaller size bed, the top part will be smaller across the width, but will still need the same amount of fabric if using this fabric design. If not, the top can be made from 36 ins (90 cm) wide fabric.

MATERIALS

6½ ft x 48 ins (2 x 1.12 m) wide fabric for the top piece; 14¾ ft x 48 ins (4.5 x 1.12 m) wide fabric for the flounce; iron-on vilene and scraps of colored fabric, lace, ribbon, beads and embroidery thread for the motif.

TO CUT OUT

Cut top piece 2 yds x 1 yds wide (1.92 x 0.94 m). This allows ¾ in (2 cm) seam allowance all round.

Cut eight pieces for the flounce 22 ins long x 48 ins wide (0.56 x 1.12 m) wide. This allows ¾ in (2 cm) seam allowance on top edge, 2¼ ins (6 cm) for frill, 18 ins (46 cm) for the drop and ¾ ins (2 cm) for hem on lower edge.

The diagram on page 388 gives the full motif. The lower edge on the motif is the lower edge on the top piece. The motif does not extend to the full length of the top piece.

Enlarge motif pieces from diagram and cut out in paper. One rectangle equals 3⅜ ins long x 4 ½ ins wide (8.5 x 11.5 cm). Cut out the various shapes in Lida or vilene and iron to the back of the colored fabric pieces.

Using the vilene side as a guide, trim around the pieces.

Bag Chair pattern

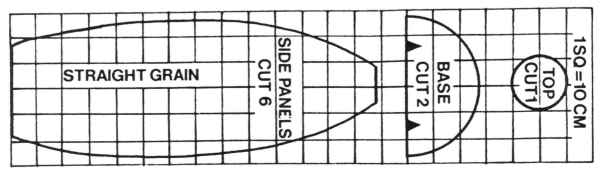

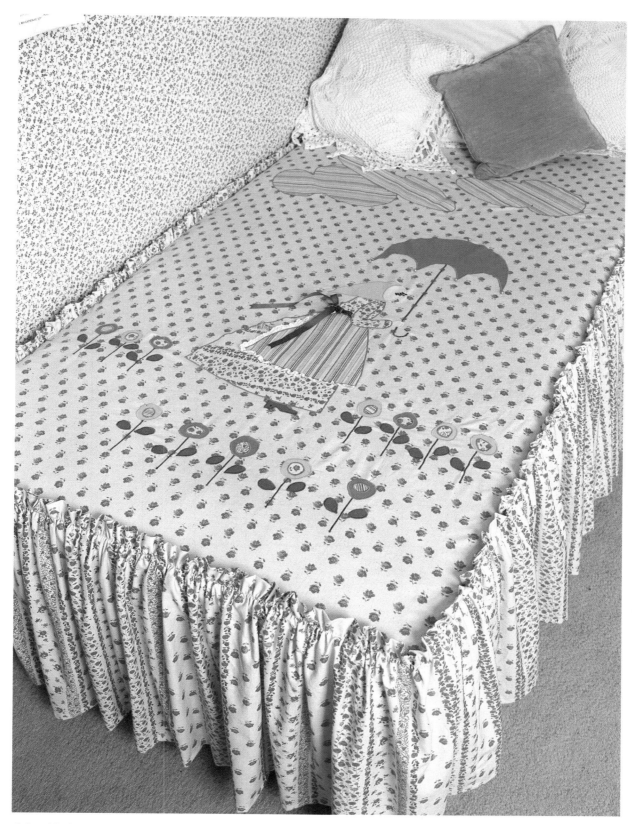

A fitted bedspread with appliquéd motif. Instructions on opposite page and page 388.

TO SEW

Appliqué the motif to the top piece. (Set the machine on satin stitch and practice on scraps first, so that the tension is correct.) Use the same satin stitch width to stitch the flower stems, set to full width to stitch the umbrella handle.

Place strips of vilene on the wrong side of cover top before stitching the stems and handle to prevent puckering. Tear away excess vilene after stitching.

With right sides together, join the flounce pieces along the short sides to make one long piece. Turn under a ¾ in (2 cm) hem on lower edge and stitch. Turn back 2 ins (5 cm) strip along top edge. Run two rows of gathering stitch 1⅜ ins (3 cm) down from folded edge along the length. Ease gathering stitch along flounce until it measures the same measurement as the sides and lower edge of top piece. Pin, then stitch flounce to top piece.

Turn under ¾ in (2 cm) hem along top edge on top piece and sides on flounce. Stitch a bead on points on umbrella, one on top. Embroider eyelashes.

one rectangle = 8.5 x 11.5 cm

◆
Bed set

Here's how to make a new cover for your continental quilt, a frill for the base of the bed, and pillow cases to match.

BED FRILL

You probably know the size of your mattress, but it's a good idea to take your own measurements as the actual bed may be a different measurement.

Remove the mattress and, with a tape, measure the length and width of the top of the bed. Then, measure from the top of the side edge down to the floor for the length of the frill (below).

As most furnishing fabrics measure 50–52 ins wide (120–122 cm), it will be necessary to join the fabric together for all sizes except a single bed size.

Cut and join fabric if necessary for the base, adding ⅜ in (1 cm) seams all round.

(If you want to save money, you could use an old sheet for the base.)

For the frill, measure along both sides and across the end. Double the measurement for a heavyweight cotton, triple the measurement for a lightweight fabric as you will need more fullness.

Cut the frill the length measurement, plus ¾ in (2 cm) seam allowance. Join frill pieces together, neaten

along lower edge, gather top edge and stitch to base along sides and across lower end.

Turn under ⅜ in (1 cm) seam on sides of frill and across top edge on base.

If your bed has a bed end, make a slit in the grill on each corner, so the frill will hang straight.

CONTINENTAL QUILT

For all except a single bed size, the fabric will have to be joined.

Measure the width of the quilt. Subtract the width of the fabric plus seam allowance from the width measurement. Divide this measurement in half and add seam allowances. When stitching, the two narrower widths are joined to each side of the large width. This avoids having a seam running down the middle of the quilt cover.

Measure the length and width of the quilt, add 2¼ ins (6 cm) to length [2 ins (5 cm) for hem and ⅜ in (1 cm) for seam allowance].

Calculate the widths you will need to make the top and bottom of the cover. Take ⅜ in (1 cm) seams and join widths together or both sides. Then, join the two pieces together around the outside edge, leaving lower edge open. Turn to right side. Turn under a 2 ins (5 cm) hem on lower edge and close with press stud fastening tape.

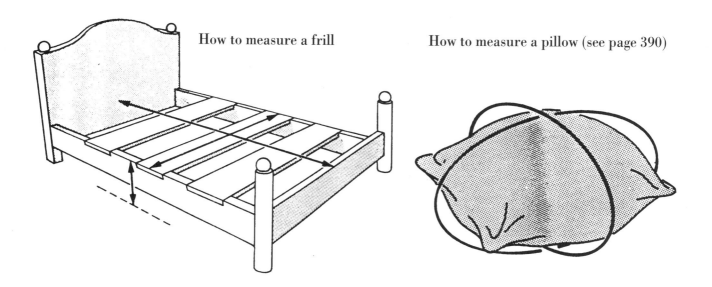

How to measure a frill   How to measure a pillow (see page 390)

PILLOWS

The easiest way to measure a pillow (see diagram page 389) is to put the tape right around the length and width of the pillow (see diagram), divide these measurements in half for one side of the pillowcase, and add seam allowances all round. Cut two pieces in fabric.

To make the frill, measure around the outside edge of one pillowcase piece, double the measurement for a firm fabric, triple the measurement for a soft fabric.

Cut the frill 4 ½ ins (12 cm) wide by the above measurement. Join pieces together, neaten along one edge and gather other edge. Take ⅜ in (1 cm) seams and stitch to one pillowcase piece. With right sides together, stitch the two pieces, leaving an opening along one end. Turn to right side and close with press stud fastening tape.

DECK CHAIR COVER

Replace your old deck chair cover with a brilliant new one without sewing a stitch. First, sand and paint or varnish the frame, tighten loose screws.

MATERIALS

1 piece canvas 42½ x 19¾ ins (1.08 x 0.5 m); 9 ¾ ft (3 m) fine plastic cord; 1 pkt of heavy duty tape; 1 pkt hemming tape; 1 pkt jumbo eyelets; hammer; scissors; tape measure.

For motif

1 pkt yellow Korbond jean patches for the sun shape; 3 pkts yellow Korbond iron-on mender for the sun's rays; 1 pkt red Korbond iron-on mender for the sails and boat; 1 pkt blue Korbond iron-on mender for the flag.

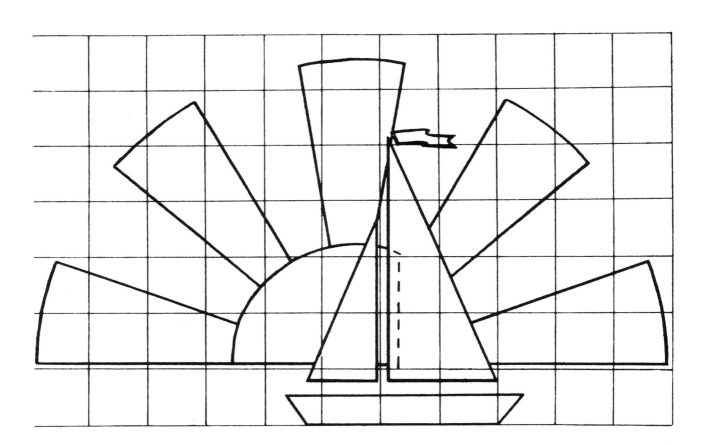

1sq = 4 cm

Opposite: To make this bright deck chair cover, see the instructions on this page and on page 392.

METHOD

1. Turn under a ¾ in (2 cm) hem down each side of the canvas and iron flat. Cover the raw edges with hemming tape and iron on.

2. Make 1¼ ins (3 cm) hem top and bottom. Iron flat. Cover raw edges with heavy duty tape. Iron with a hot, dry iron. Allow to cool. Check that adhesive has set.

3. Working right side up mark nine eyelet positions 2 ¼ ins (5.5 cm) apart, ⅜ in (1 cm) in from top, bottom edges. Place the flat side of the base of the setting punch (provided with the eyelets) under the fabric, put punch on top and tap with a hammer.

4. Turn to wrong side. Insert the eyelet into hole from underneath. Place positioned eyelet into the base of the setting punch which is curved to fit it. Insert top of the punch into the throat of the eyelet, tap with a hammer.

5. Enlarge the patterns for the motif. Each square equals 1½ ins (4 cm). Make patterns, cut out shapes. (Cut sun to broken line.) Using dry iron attach to canvas, sun first then the sun's rays, sails, boat, flag.

6. Place cover on deck chair frame. Cut cord in half. Thread it through the eyelets and wind it around the top of the frame to attach cover. Repeat for the bottom of the frame.

TABLECLOTHS

◆

Circular tablecloth

Circular tablecloths can be used for a dinner party or to cover an otherwise worn and shabby table permanently.

The round tablecloth may be short or floor length. If floor length it should clear the floor by an inch.

The cloth can be made from any width of fabric; a sheet is ideal for a floorlength cloth, since it does not need joining; 54 in (140 cm) fabric is suitable for the shorter length cloth. Narrower fabric means joins.

TO MEASURE

The amount of fabric needed depends on the size of the table and the width of fabric to be used. To find the amount needed for a floor length cloth, measure from the floor to the edge of the table, across the top diameter then to the floor again on the other side. If the measurement is wider than the fabric width you will need twice the amount of fabric.

The diameter of the cloth multiplied by 3 ½ times will give the amount of braid or fringe needed to trim the hem of the cloth. The same amount of bias binding will be needed for neatening the hem.

For a simple circular cloth you will need 1 ½ yds (1.4 m) square fabric and 8 yds (7.35 m) trimming.

TO MAKE

(see diagrams 25a and 25b)

Mark off a circle on the 54 ins (1.4 m) fabric, using your tape measure or a piece of string. Push a drawing pin into the 27 in (69 cm) mark of your tape measure.

STEP 1:

Fold the fabric into four and make a compass from a piece of string and a pencil or piece of chalk. Pin the string to the top corner and draw an arc with the pencil making the radius half that of the diameter of the floor length cloth. Cut along this marked line through four thicknesses. Cut one at a time so that they are accurate (diagram 25b) and secure the tape

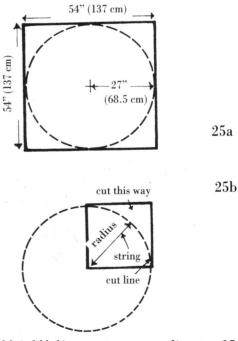

fabric folded into quarters   diagram 25

with the drawing pin at exact center of the fabric. Hold a tailor's chalk or pencil at end of the tape measure and carefully draw the circle with the tape held taut (diagram 25a). Cut out the circle, hem and trim as desired.

To make the cloth when fabric is not wide enough to avoid joins, cut the fabric in half across the width to give two pieces of equal length. Avoid a center seam by cutting the second length in half lengthways and joining one to each side of the main piece.

STEP 2:
Open out your large circle of fabric and neaten the hem by stitching the opened edge of the bias binding to the outside of the cloth ½ in (1.3 cm) from the edge. Trim and turn binding to the wrong side and machine the other turned edge of binding to the cloth.

STEP 3:
Pin and tack the fringe or braid to the outside hem.

CONTRASTING PRINT TABLECLOTHS
◆
Round cloth

MATERIALS
3¼ ft (1 m) of 4 ft (1.2 m) wide fabric in each of three fabrics with light background and three fabrics with dark background.

SEAM ALLOWANCE
A ⅜ in (1 cm) seam allowance has been included on pattern piece.

CUTTING
Make a paper pattern from the diagram illustrated. Cut out 2 pattern pieces from each piece of fabric. Make sure you keep pattern pieces on the straight grain of fabric as in the diagram.

TO MAKE
Sew 6 different pattern pieces together, alternating dark and light backgrounds and using French seams. Then repeat this pattern arrangement with the remaining 6 pattern pieces. Place the 2 halves together and stitch. Narrow hem the 6 side edges about ¼ in (0.6 cm) to the wrong side and then to the wrong side again and stitch in place.

◆
Napkins

MATERIALS
For each napkin use 1 piece of fabric 15¾ ins (40 cm) square, 1¾ yds (1.7 m) of ⅜ in (1 cm) wide edge lace.

TO MAKE
Press ¼ in (0.6 cm) to the wrong side on edges. Stitch down in place at the same time sewing lace around the edge.

◆
Oblong cloth

MATERIALS
3¼ ft (1 m) of 4 ft (1.2 m) wide fabric in each of 2 contrasting prints; 13⅜ ft (4.1 m) of 2½ ins (4 cm) wide lace, 19 ft (5.8 m) of 1 in (2.5 cm) wide edge lace.

SEAM ALLOWANCE
A ½ in (1.3 cm) seam allowance has been included on pattern measurements.

METHOD
Cutting

Cut each piece of fabric into 3 rectangles measuring 19¾ ins wide x 23½ ins long (50 x 60 cm).

TO MAKE
Narrow hem edges of all fabric pieces by turning ¼ in (0.6 cm) to the wrong side and stitch down in place.

Arrange the fabric pieces on a flat surface as in diagram 3, pinning the 2½ in (4 cm) wide lace inserts between each. Join fabric pieces together by top stitching lace in position close to the edges.

Stitch 1 in (2.5 cm) wide lace around the edge of the tablecloth.

LAMPSHADES

Making your own lampshades saves money. It also means that you can match them to your own soft furnishings, and it is one of the simplest ways of adding bright color notes to a room.

It is important that the lampshade be in proper proportion to the lamp base. The diameter of the shade can equal the height of the base from table top to the bottom of the shade. The depth of the shade should not be less than one-third and not more than two-thirds the height of the base.

Use pins with care when preparing your shade, as pin marks will show when the lamp is illuminated. Secure seams with two rows of stitching. For a good frame use cross stitch in sewing the hood and lining.

◆

A drum lampshade

The drum lampshade is quick and easy to make and is a suitable shape to use on almost any style of lamp.

MATERIALS

Two lampshade rings the same diameter, one plain, the other with a ring in the middle to take the lamp fitting; self-adhesive parchment (it has a sticky back) or buckram; covering fabric; clear adhesive, two clothes pegs for clamping, decorative braid for trimming top and/or bottom of shade.

Contact or self-adhesive parchment is available in sizes 12 ins (30.5 cm) high and 48 ins (122 cm) long, and 18 ins (45.5 cm) high and 48 ins (122 cm) long.

To make (see diagrams 26a, b, c)

STEP 1:

Measure the circumference of the ring with a tape measure, adding ½ in (1.3 cm) for overlap. Next decide the depth of the lampshade. Cut a rectangle of parchment and a rectangle of fabric to these two measurements.

STEP 2:

Place the wrong side of the fabric to the sticky side of the parchment and iron carefully with a moderately hot dry iron. Turn over and iron again on the back of the parchment. Do not have the iron too hot or the parchment may scorch.

STEP 3:

Shape into a drum with the fabric side out. Overlap the ends by about ½ in (1.3 cm) and stick with clear adhesive. Use the clothes pegs top and bottom to hold the shape while the adhesive dries. If you do not use adhesive, stitch the join by hand; the pegs will help you to keep the drum shape.

STEP 4:

Insert rings, top and bottom, with the ring fitting in correct position for use on the lamp. Secure rings to parchment with several oversew stitches.

STEP 5:

Stick white adhesive tape round the top and bottom, folding it over neatly to the wrong side to conceal rings and hold them in place. Snip at struts.

STEP 6:

Add decorative trims to top and bottom to conceal tape.

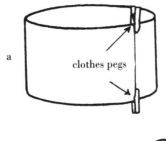

a clothes pegs

b

insert rings top and bottom

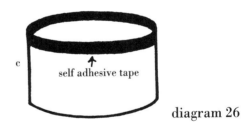

c self adhesive tape

diagram 26

◆

Making a shaped lampshade

TO MAKE

(see diagrams opposite)

STEP 1: Start binding top at a strut. Place one end of tape over and under the strut and back on top of the ring. Bind firmly with a slight overlap.

STEP 2:

Bind the frame tightly and smoothly in sections. Cut off tape and stitch firmly as you finish each section.

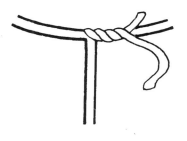

step 1

step 2

STEP 4:

Pin lining to inside of the bottom ring, drawing edges to the outside. Pull fabric up and over the top ring, stretch taut and pin any excess fabric into side seam. When lining is smooth, trim off excess fabric. Sew to the rings. Slipstitch side seams with small, neat stitches.

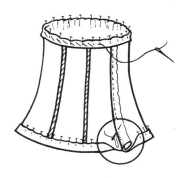

step 4

STEP 3:

Roll lampshade across a sheet of paper, marking the outline with a pencil. Cut out shape.

This gives you a pattern. Fold fabric on the bias. Cut out allowing 1 in (2.5 cm) all round for seams. Cut a matching piece for the lining using the same seam allowance.

STEP 5:

Pin outside cover part-way round bottom ring, stretch to the top and pin in position. Continue pinning cover to the bottom ring then to the top ring. Pin seam. Trim off excess fabric and sew with raw edges outside. Blind stitch the side seam. Cover the raw edges with a braid trim. Either handsew the braid in place or use a colorless adhesive specially made for fabrics.

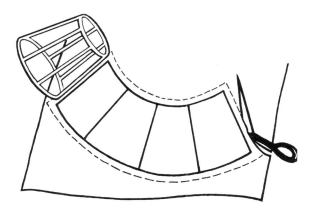

step 3

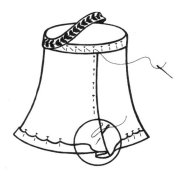

step 5

Index

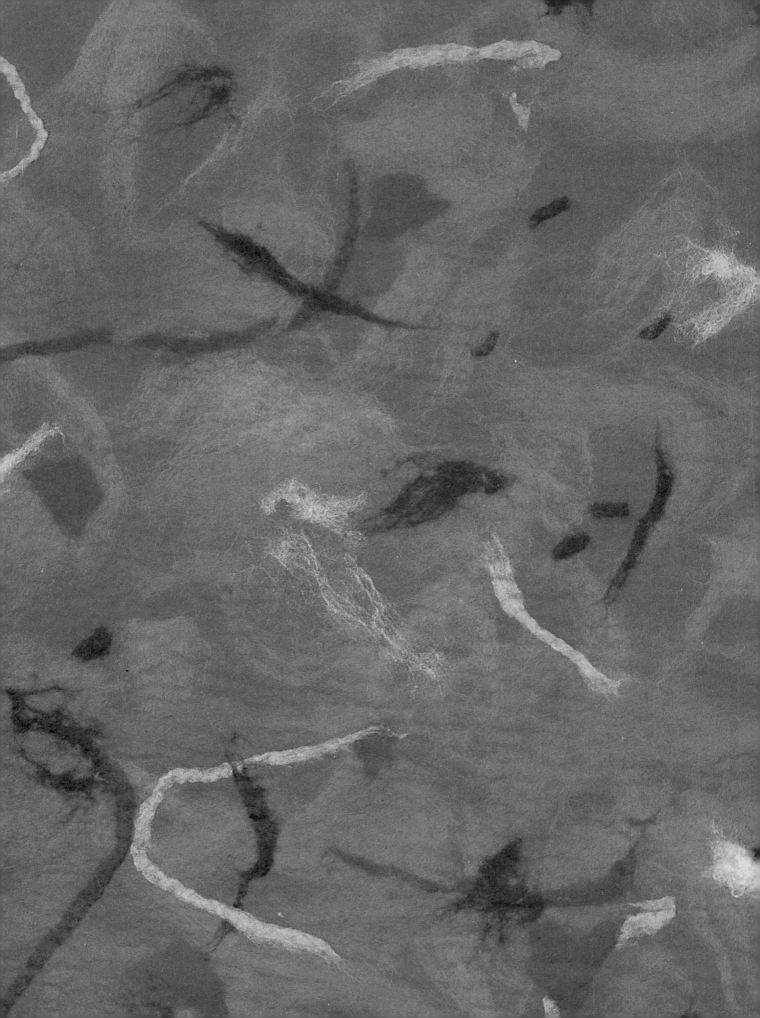